AF711870

Greening NAFTA

Greening NAFTA

The North American Commission for Environmental Cooperation

Edited by David L. Markell and John H. Knox

STANFORD LAW AND POLITICS
An imprint of Stanford University Press
Stanford, California
2003

Stanford University Press
Stanford, California
www.sup.org

© 2003 by the Board of Trustees of the Leland Stanford Junior University.
All rights reserved.

Library of Congress Cataloging-in-Publication Data

Greening NAFTA : the North American Commission for Environmental Cooperation / edited by David L. Markell and John H. Knox.
p. cm.
ISBN 0-8047-4604-4 (alk. paper)
1. Commission for Environmental Cooperation (Montréal, Québec)
2. Environmental law—North America. I. Markell, David L. II. Knox, John H.
KDZ670.G74 2003
344.7'046—dc21 2003010960

Printed in the United States of America on acid-free, archival-quality paper.

Original Printing 2003

Last figure below indicates year of this printing:
12 11 10 09 08 07 06 05 04 03

Designed and typeset at Stanford University Press in 10.5/12 Bembo

Special discounts for bulk quantities of Stanford Law and Politics books are available to corporations, professional associations, and other organizations. For details and discount information, contact the special sales department of Stanford University Press. Tel: (650) 736-1783, Fax: (650) 736-1784.

Contents

Illustrations and Tables

Figures

Map

Tables

Acknowledgments

It was a pleasure for the two of us to work on this project, in large part because we were able to work together with an unusually capable and responsive group of contributing authors. We were well aware from the outset that our contributors possess outstanding credentials and enormous expertise, but we were pleasantly surprised by their exceptional cooperation during the drafting and editing process. We want to thank them for that and for making the process an intellectually enriching experience for us. We particularly want to thank Dan Tarlock and the Chicago-Kent Law School Program in Environmental and Energy Law for hosting an informal meeting of the contributors in March 2002, which greatly facilitated exchanges of views among the contributors.

We are grateful to the administrations at Florida State University College of Law, Penn State–Dickinson School of Law, and Albany Law School for their encouragement and financial support for this project. The law library staff at all three institutions were exceptionally helpful. Anna Remet, Andy Cordo, John Sawyer, and Sean Shultz provided very useful research support. And we owe a great deal of thanks to Amanda Moran and the editors at Stanford University Press for their support for the project when it was more vision than reality and for their editing and other assistance.

More personally, we thank our families, Mona, Rebecca, Jenny, and Rachel Markell, and Julie Winterich and Rebecca, Emily, and Abigail Winterich-Knox for their encouragement and understanding. The aspirations and achievements (and expectations) of our spouses and children helped to influence our approach to this book, and the book is much the better for it.

Finally, we would like to say a word about John Wirth, who passed away on June 20, 2002, one day after participating in the annual meeting of the CEC Council. John was one of the original members of the CEC Joint Public Advisory Committee and contributed a chapter to this book on it. John provided invaluable advice to the CEC, but his interests and expertise ranged far beyond that. He was a scholar of Latin American history and, in more recent years, one of the strongest supporters of closer ties among the North American countries. To that end, he cofounded the North American Institute in Santa Fe, New Mexico. It would not be too much to say that he was one of the first citizens of North America. John will be sorely missed, and we dedicate this book to his memory.

Foreword

The 2002 World Summit on Sustainable Development in Johannesburg, South Africa, brought together more than one hundred world leaders and diverse parts of civil society to recommit to economic development that is socially and environmentally responsible and sustainable. As this book demonstrates, much can be done at the regional level to further these goals.

As early as the 1970s, countries began to see environmental protection and free trade as means to a common goal: sustainable development. When Canada, Mexico, and the United States negotiated the North American Free Trade Agreement (NAFTA) in the 1990s, environmental concerns were very much on the agenda. Members of the U.S. Congress and certain non-governmental organizations made it clear that an acceptable trade agreement must also provide for protecting the environment. Some were concerned that differences in environmental regulations and a failure to enforce them would distort a level playing field in trade. Others were concerned that by focusing on trade, countries would neglect environmental issues. In response to these concerns, the three countries negotiated the North American Agreement on Environmental Cooperation (NAAEC), which established the Commission for Environmental Cooperation (CEC).

Greening NAFTA: The North American Commission for Environmental Cooperation analyzes the near decade of experience with this agreement. It explores the Commission as a regional organization addressing regional environmental problems, as an institution for dealing with the trade and environment nexus, and as a forum in which civil society at the regional level can participate in policy deliberations and hold governments accountable for enforcing their environmental laws. The book is especially timely because of the initiative for a Free Trade Area of the Americas. Many of the authors are scholars who have been involved either directly or in peripheral capacities in implementing the NAAEC, and they bring seasoned insights into their analyses.

The book reflects the emerging international system in the twenty-first century. Since 1648 with the Peace of Westphalia, the international order has focused almost exclusively on sovereign, independent states as the central and indeed nearly the only relevant actors. But the international system at the beginning of the twenty-first century is very different. States are still central, but international organizations, nongovernmental organizations, the private sector, transnational groups and coalitions, and individuals are now important participants. The Yearbook of International Organizations reports, for example, that in the year 2000 there were 922 international intergovernmental organizations and 9,988 international nongovernmental organizations. If other kinds of international organizations are included, the total number of international organizations is nearly 30,000, with another 24,000 inactive or unconfirmed. As of April 2002, there were an estimated 6.2 billion individuals in the world. We need to consider the dynamic relationship today between states, international organizations, the private sector, and civil society generally. How does civil society participate in policy deliberations? How does it hold other actors accountable? How can it in turn be held accountable? This book tackles these difficult questions in the environment and trade field.

The North American Commission for Environmental Cooperation is an important regional model for incorporating civil society into the international system—in this case, at the regional level. The Joint Public Advisory Committee (JPAC) facilitates public input into policy decisions, while the Article 14–15 process provides procedures for individuals, nongovernmental organizations, and other actors (including corporations) to complain that a country is failing to enforce its environmental laws effectively. Many of the issues with JPAC and the Article 14–15 process concern transparency, participation, and accountability. These are critical issues in joining governments and civil society in environmental protection. They are also increasingly relevant to connecting civil society with trade deliberations and dispute resolution.

The NAAEC's Article 14–15 complaint procedure is being used more frequently. In other areas of international law, particularly human rights, the number of individual complaints before relevant courts or committees has grown exponentially, to the point where some analysts are considering whether the procedures for handling complaints need review. As the CEC's process for addressing complaints by individuals and groups in civil society matures, the CEC may well find that the number of complaints has increased to the point where the CEC may need to expand the resources devoted to it and/or refine the process further.

Greening NAFTA offers a road map for understanding how to foster responsible economic development and at the same time protect the robustness and integrity of the human environment. The authors astutely identify the successes and face the problems. The book is well informed and highly relevant for all those interested in reconciling environment and trade and in promoting environmentally responsible development not only in North America but throughout the Americas and the world.

EDITH BROWN WEISS

August 2002

Greening NAFTA

JOHN H. KNOX AND DAVID L. MARKELL

1

The Innovative North American Commission for Environmental Cooperation

IN JUNE 1990, when Presidents George H. W. Bush of the United States and Carlos Salinas de Gortari of Mexico announced that their governments would begin talks aimed at a free trade agreement, they could not have anticipated the degree to which environmental concerns would influence the eventual outcome. Environmental issues had not affected the most recent precedent, the 1989 Canada-U.S. Free Trade Agreement, and had rarely even been raised with respect to the many trade and investment agreements negotiated in the preceding decades.

But it quickly became clear that the negotiators of the North American Free Trade Agreement (NAFTA)—as it became known after Canada joined the talks—would face a different world, as environmental groups in all three countries mobilized popular opposition to NAFTA on the ground that liberalizing trade without adequate safeguards would harm the environment. The NAFTA debate thus began an argument over how trade agreements should reconcile environmental protection and economic integration that continues to this day. Indeed, it has become one of the flashpoints of international discourse, as the 1999 riots in Seattle over the unsuccessful attempt to begin a new round of World Trade Organization negotiations graphically showed.

The backdrop to the "trade and environment" debate has been an increasing awareness of the connections between environmental protection and economic development. In June 1992, during the NAFTA negotiations, the U.N. Conference on Environment and Development in Rio de Janeiro gave the imprimatur of the international community to development that is sustainable, that is, development that does not compromise the ability of future generations to meet their own needs, and said that "to achieve sustainable development, environmental protection shall constitute an integral part of the development process and cannot be considered in isolation from it."[1] In addition to warning against the pursuit of economic development in disregard of environmental protection, the Rio Conference also highlighted the need for more effective agreements and institutions to address worsening environmental problems. In this light, many saw NAFTA as an opportunity to improve international environmental cooperation among the North American nations.

Finally, the NAFTA debate included arguments over, and was itself an example of, the desire of citizens to participate directly in the development and implementation of international policies that affect them. With respect to economic integration and environmental protection, as well as many other areas of international cooperation, nations are struggling over how to respond to demands for greater public participation in realms that were once the exclusive province of government officials. Increasingly, international institutions are being reshaped to provide greater transparency and access to interested individuals and groups.

As a result of the NAFTA debate over these issues, the governments produced something significantly different than they had originally envisaged: a supplemental agreement to NAFTA called the North American Agreement on Environmental Cooperation (NAAEC), which established a new trilateral organization, the North American Commission for Environmental Cooperation (the NACEC, or CEC). The CEC is the first international organization created to address the environmental aspects of economic integration. It has innovative tools and almost unlimited jurisdiction to address regional environmental problems. And it provides unprecedented opportunities for participation by civil society at the international level.[2]

The lessons to be drawn from its experience should therefore be of great value to all those trying to reconcile environmental protection and economic integration, to promote more effective regional and global environmental organizations, and to find ways for civil society to participate in international policy. The NAAEC has already been used as a model for bilateral agreements between Canada and Chile and between the United States and Jordan.[3] Surprisingly, however, the CEC has received relatively little scholarly attention. Although political scientists and lawyers have described its relationship to NAFTA and have analyzed its submissions procedure, there are few comprehensive analyses of how it is fulfilling, or failing to fulfill, its mandates.[4]

We hope that this book helps to fill that gap. To that end, we invited experts on the CEC to evaluate its record and its potential on the basis of its first nine years of work. We acknowledge at the outset that both of us, as well as most of the other contributors, have had some connection to the

Commission. Two contributors are former officials of its Secretariat (Greg Block and David Markell), one was an original member of its Joint Public Advisory Committee (John Wirth), one participated in the negotiation of the agreement creating it (John Knox), three have chaired the U.S. National Advisory Committee on the CEC (Mary Kelly, Sanford Gaines, and John Knox), and others have provided advice to it as consultants or participated in its conferences and workshops. Of course, the vast majority of our professional experience has not involved the Commission, and we believe that our contributions show that none of us is an apologist for it. On the contrary, our connections with the CEC have given us insights into its shortcomings as well as its strengths.

In the remainder of this introduction, we review how the NAAEC emerged from the debate over NAFTA and describe the structure and functions of the CEC that it created. We then introduce the chapters that follow.

From NAFTA to the NAAEC

In November 1990, two months after President Salinas formally requested negotiation of a free trade agreement, the National Wildlife Federation and several environmental groups along the U.S.-Mexico border published a joint statement identifying two concerns that would resonate throughout the NAFTA debate: that a free trade agreement would further degrade the U.S.-Mexico border environment and that it would lead to environmentally harmful foreign investment throughout Mexico.[5]

They based these concerns on the problems caused by the Mexican *maquiladora* program, under which Mexico had encouraged foreign investment in factories built in a narrow strip along its northern border. The policy had been successful at attracting investment and creating jobs, but the *maquiladoras* had overwhelmed local facilities for providing clean water and treating waste. The environmental groups said that this experiment in increased international trade and investment had resulted in pollution of the Rio Grande and transboundary aquifers along the U.S.-Mexico border and had degraded environmental conditions throughout northern Mexico. They argued that a free trade agreement would exacerbate conditions along the border. They also argued that it would spread similar problems throughout Mexico, since under such an agreement "the Mexican government will further relax its rules on foreign investment, reducing the likelihood that foreign companies will be required to meet strict environmental requirements in order to invest in Mexico. At the same time, the certainty and predictability of an open investment climate will attract more foreign industries to Mexico, further taxing the country's ability to meet national and international environmental protection standards."[6]

Members of the U.S. Congress picked up on these concerns and demanded assurances that the Bush administration would address environmental as well as labor issues in the NAFTA negotiations. As part of a successful effort to persuade Congress to renew his "fast-track" authority to negotiate trade agreements, President Bush promised in May 1991 "to develop and implement an expanded program of environmental cooperation in parallel with the free trade talks."[7] The three governments formally began negotiating NAFTA the next month.

During the course of the negotiations, which concluded fifteen months later in August 1992, environmental groups in all three countries added to and elaborated upon these initial objections.[8] Their criticisms varied somewhat along national lines and according to the degree of their opposition to international trade generally, but on the whole their concerns were remarkably similar. In July 1992, fifty-one groups from all three countries signed a joint letter to the governments emphasizing that while the details of their specific proposals differed, they all were "seeking specific language in the NAFTA to ensure increased public participation and oversight, improved enforcement of environmental laws, increased funding for environmental programs, and protection of national, state and local standards intended to protect the environment and health."[9] Groups in the United States played a leading role in formulating and pressing these concerns, partly because of their greater resources and partly because the political situation in the United States (the 1992 presidential election and the closely divided views in Congress over whether to support NAFTA) made the U.S. government the most likely of the three to be responsive to environmental criticisms.[10]

The following sections describe the chief environmental objections to a free trade agreement and how the governments tried, or failed, to respond to them. At the risk of oversimplification, we group them into six categories.

1. *Border cleanup.* Environmentalists argued that the U.S. and Mexican governments should promise to clean up the U.S.-Mexico border, including through funding new wastewater treatment plants and solid waste facilities. In November 1990, Presidents Bush and Salinas announced that their administrations would prepare a "comprehensive plan" to improve cooperation in the area of environmental protection. The result was the Integrated Environmental Plan for the Mexican-U.S. Border Area.[11] Border groups criticized the plan as little more than a recitation of existing programs, with no new sources of funding. They urged the governments to commit new funds to the border and suggested that the money might come from the increased trade expected to result from NAFTA.[12]

2. *Environmental degradation in Mexico and "pollution havens."* One of the most often repeated concerns was that NAFTA would lead to increased foreign in-

vestment in Mexico, which would cause increased environmental degradation and loss of natural resources there.[13] A closely related concern, which perhaps had greater salience in the United States, was that Mexico would intentionally or inadvertently become a "pollution haven," leading U.S. and Canadian companies to shift their operations there to take advantage of lower environmental standards.[14] This might in turn put pressure on the U.S. and Canadian governments to lower their standards in order to keep the companies at home, resulting in a three-way race to the bottom. The Bush administration argued in vain that pollution havens were a myth without empirical support.[15] It may be that the intuitive appeal of the argument was too strong or that it dovetailed too neatly with similar fears that businesses would move to Mexico in search of lower wages, which Ross Perot characterized memorably as the "giant sucking sound."[16] Or perhaps the Bush response failed because it did not address an underlying criticism: that it was unfair to give access to the U.S. market to firms that did not have to comply with U.S. environmental standards.

Although the U.S. government was unable to deflate the pollution haven concern, it did reshape it. The Environmental Protection Agency sent a team of attorneys to Mexico in 1991 (and again in 1993, after the Clinton administration took office) to report on the status and implementation of Mexican environmental laws. The team concluded that, with some exceptions, Mexican laws on the books were "broadly comparable" to U.S. environmental laws.[17] Environmental groups accepted this conclusion to some extent, but they emphasized its corollary: there was an enormous gap between the laws on the books and the laws as enforced.[18] They therefore shifted their criticism from Mexico's laws to Mexico's failure to enforce them. To address this problem, they suggested that the governments create a new international institution, initially called the North American Commission on Trade and the Environment but later christened the North American Commission on the Environment. Composed of governmental and nongovernmental experts, the Commission should have a mandate, in the words of one U.S. environmental group, "to hear complaints from governments, non-governmental organizations, and citizens regarding the failure of any signatory to enforce its own environmental standards," to "enjoin polluting activities that violate applicable standards," and to "make recommendations on needed improvements in national policies in order to prevent any country from gaining competitive trade advantages through comparatively weak standards or enforcement."[19]

The only provision in NAFTA designed to address the pollution haven concern falls far short of this proposal. Article 1114 says: "The Parties recognize that it is inappropriate to encourage investment by relaxing domestic health, safety or environmental measures. Accordingly, a Party should not waive or otherwise derogate from, or offer to waive or otherwise derogate from, such measures as an encouragement for the establishment, acquisition, expansion or retention in its territory of an investment of an investor."[20] This nonbinding language ("should not") did little to placate critics. Nor did

NAFTA satisfactorily speak to more general concerns about the effect of increased trade and investment on the Mexican environment.

As political pressure to address the environmental objections to NAFTA increased during the 1992 presidential campaign, the Bush administration overcame its initial reluctance to accept a new international commission and proposed the idea to the other governments. As a result, the three North American environment ministers announced in September 1992 that they had "agreed in principle to the creation of a North American Commission on Environmental Cooperation."[21] They gave little detail as to what the Commission would do, however, and they failed to flesh out the proposal before the Bush administration left office.

3. *Threats to domestic environmental laws.* Before the NAFTA negotiations began, Mexico had brought a claim against the United States under the General Agreement on Tariffs and Trade (GATT), arguing that a U.S. law restricting imports of tuna caught in a manner that harmed dolphins violated U.S. obligations under GATT. In September 1991, the GATT arbitral panel published its decision, which largely agreed with Mexico.[22] Although the panel had no power to order the United States to amend its law, and under GATT rules at the time the United States could block adoption of the panel report, the decision nevertheless sent a shock wave through the environmental community. Environmentalists quickly recognized that according to the reasoning of the panel, other U.S. laws restricting imports for environmental reasons could be in violation of GATT. Moreover, they noted that even laws setting facially neutral but latently discriminatory health and safety standards might be subject to challenge. They believed, correctly, that NAFTA would incorporate much of the language relevant to these conflicts directly from GATT and the World Trade Organization agreements that were under negotiation at the same time. As a result, they pressed the North American governments to include language in NAFTA specifically protecting domestic environmental laws from trade-related challenges.[23] They were not successful. Although the Bush administration argued that NAFTA provided more protections to domestic environmental laws than GATT, its protections are not as strong as those the environmental groups had sought.[24]

4. *Threats to international environmental agreements.* Many multilateral environmental agreements, such as the Convention on International Trade in Endangered Species (CITES) and the Montreal Protocol on Ozone Depletion, restrict trade in particular types of goods.[25] The reasoning of the *Tuna-Dolphin* decision could allow challenges to these restrictions as inconsistent with GATT obligations. Environmentalists argued that NAFTA should make clear that it could not override the obligations set out in those agreements. Here, they were more successful. NAFTA provides that in the event of any inconsistency between it and a list of environmental agreements, which include CITES and the Montreal Protocol, the agreements shall prevail, provided that the least NAFTA-inconsistent way of complying with their obligations is taken.[26]

5. *Public participation.* Traditionally, negotiation of trade issues and resolution of trade disputes have been largely confidential. As a result, claims that environmental laws violated trade agreements could be resolved by tribunals meeting in secret. Moreover, the tribunals would be composed of trade officials with no environmental expertise. Environmental groups and others argued that NAFTA presented an opportunity to correct this "anachronism" in international trade policy by opening dispute resolution procedures and other NAFTA institutions to public input.[27] The negotiators of NAFTA did not agree and made no significant changes to NAFTA in this respect.

6. *Environmental assessment.* Environmental groups argued that NAFTA should be subject to the National Environmental Policy Act of 1969 (NEPA), the U.S. statute that requires environmental impact assessment of major federal actions significantly affecting the environment.[28] The Bush administration announced that it would conduct an environmental review of NAFTA, but it rejected the idea that it should be pursuant to the strict requirements of NEPA or subject to judicial oversight. Three groups sued the U.S. Trade Representative, seeking an injunction ordering it to carry out a full environmental review under NEPA. The Bush administration vigorously defended against the suit.

When the NAFTA negotiations concluded in August 1992, the environmental community was, on the whole, dissatisfied with the result. Their objections spilled into the broader debate over whether to approve NAFTA, which became one of the chief points of contention among the candidates in the 1992 U.S. presidential campaign. President Bush naturally defended NAFTA, arguing that his negotiators had successfully addressed its critics' environmental concerns. Indeed, his trade and environmental officials touted it as the "greenest" trade agreement ever signed. Ross Perot made his opposition to NAFTA the centerpiece of his campaign. Under pressure to choose one side or the other, Bill Clinton found middle ground. In October 1992, he announced that if elected he would support NAFTA but that before sending it to Congress he would negotiate strong supplemental agreements to protect labor and the environment.[29] The 1992 presidential election was in part a referendum on which approach to take, and Clinton's victory ensured that the United States would pursue his vision of "NAFTA plus."

When President Clinton took office in January 1993, however, he had little time to fulfill his campaign pledge. By its terms, NAFTA was due to enter into force on January 1, 1994, and to obtain congressional approval under fast-track rules, Clinton had to send it to Congress by the fall of 1993. Environmental groups hurried to give their recommendations as to what the supplemental agreement on environment should include. In May 1993, seven large U.S. groups pledged that they would support NAFTA if the environmental side agreement included specific elements, including: a powerful North American Commission on the Environment, staffed by a permanent

Secretariat with independent power to conduct investigations and prepare reports and advised by a nongovernmental board of citizens; the possibility of trade sanctions against parties that failed to comply with the Commission's recommendations; increased funding for border cleanup; added protections for domestic environmental laws against trade challenges; and increased public participation in dispute settlement.[30]

The groups' promise to endorse NAFTA if their requirements were met was a powerful inducement, since their endorsement might induce wavering members of Congress to support NAFTA. But there were also pressures in the opposite direction. While a weak agreement might not attract sufficient support from environmental groups or members of Congress, a strong agreement might cause staunch advocates of unencumbered free trade to withdraw their support. Even more important, anything that appeared to reopen the hard-fought compromises embodied in NAFTA itself would be sure to alienate Canada and Mexico.

As a result, the Clinton administration did not try to address environmental objections when doing so would entail reopening NAFTA. Specifically, it made little or no effort to pursue agreement with Canada and Mexico on new protections against challenges to domestic laws or on providing more public input into the procedures for resolving disputes under NAFTA. And it continued to defend against, and eventually won, the lawsuit seeking a full environmental impact assessment of NAFTA.[31]

Instead, the Clinton administration focused on two of the original objectives of the environmental groups: cleaning up the U.S.-Mexico border and strengthening domestic environmental standards and compliance. In both respects, it adopted in large part their proposed solutions: additional funding for border cleanup and a trilateral institution with a mandate to promote effective domestic standards and enforcement, backed by the possibility of trade sanctions. To address the first objective, it negotiated a bilateral agreement with Mexico creating a Border Environment Cooperation Commission (BECC) and a North American Development Bank (NADBank), which would certify and seek financing for water treatment, wastewater plants, and municipal waste disposal in communities along the U.S.-Mexico border.[32]

To address the second, in the spring of 1993 the Clinton administration proposed to Canada and Mexico a trilateral agreement that would have the characteristics the environmental groups sought: a requirement that the parties effectively enforce their domestic environmental laws, a new international commission to oversee and encourage that enforcement, and the possibility of trade sanctions against parties that persistently failed to enforce their laws. The Canadian and Mexican governments initially found the idea of trade sanctions particularly difficult to accept, but the negotiators eventually arrived at an agreement: the NAAEC, which representatives of the three nations signed in September 1993.[33] The NAAEC largely incorporates the U.S. proposals. But as the next section explains, it does much more than that.

The NAAEC and the CEC

The NAAEC has a simple structure. In order, its seven parts: (1) list its objectives; (2) give the parties specific obligations; (3) create an international organization, the CEC, composed of a Council of the Parties' environmental ministers, a permanent Secretariat, and an independent advisory committee; (4) provide for provision of information by the Parties to one another and to the Secretariat; (5) establish a system for resolving disputes; (6) include general provisions, such as an article on definitions; and (7) set out typical final clauses on, among other things, amendment, accession, and withdrawal.

Because of the way that the NAAEC emerged from the NAFTA debate, the most obvious way to see it is as a lengthy, detailed attempt to prevent pollution havens (and, more generally, to protect against degradation of the Mexican environment resulting from increased trade and investment). While Article 1114 of NAFTA discourages Parties from lowering their environmental standards to attract foreign investment, the NAAEC *requires* each Party to "ensure that its laws and regulations provide for high levels of environmental protection and [to] strive to continue to improve those laws and regulations" and to "effectively enforce its environmental laws and regulations through appropriate government action."[34] It also requires the Parties to publish their environmental laws, allow persons "appropriate access" to legal proceedings for the enforcement of the laws, and ensure that the parties' legal proceedings are fair and open.[35] Moreover, it creates two mechanisms to oversee and promote effective enforcement: a process under which a complaint by a citizen that a government is failing to effectively enforce its environmental law can lead to a public report describing the Party's record of enforcement, and a procedure through which complaints by one Party that another Party has persistently failed to enforce its environmental laws can result in sanctions against the Party in default.[36]

Although these elements largely track the environmental groups' proposed responses to their concerns about environmental degradation and pollution havens, the NAAEC has little to say about their other objections to NAFTA. In particular, it does not protect domestic environmental laws from all challenges under NAFTA, and it does not open NAFTA dispute resolution to public participation. Moreover, U.S. environmental groups that had pushed for strong sanctions for failure to enforce domestic environmental laws argued that the procedure the Parties would have to follow under Part Five of the NAAEC in order to trigger the sanctions was hedged with so many obstacles that it was virtually impossible to imagine sanctions ever being imposed. (Events have validated this view; none of the Parties has ever brought a claim under Part Five.) While some U.S. environmental groups, such as the National Wildlife Federation and the World Wildlife Fund, endorsed NAFTA on the basis of the NAAEC, the Sierra Club and other groups, including many groups in Mexico and Canada, dismissed the NAAEC as "greenwash" and continued to oppose NAFTA.[37]

Even viewed through the trade / environment prism, and despite the issues it does not address, the range and creativity of the tools the NAAEC brings to bear on the pollution haven problem are remarkable. But the NAAEC is not only, or even primarily, an agreement on "trade and the environment." Its greater importance may be that it is the first regional environmental organization in North America, with broad mandates to address almost any environmental issue arising anywhere on the continent.

Historically, international environmental law and policy have focused on transboundary issues and threats to areas beyond national jurisdiction—for example, cross-border pollution, ozone depletion, climate change, and marine pollution. A nation's treatment of the environment within its borders has traditionally been considered its affair and not the concern of its neighbors, much less the international community. This view is outdated in light of the innumerable ways that ecosystems connect with one another in disregard of national boundaries, and in principle states now recognize that sustainable development requires international attention to environmental issues previously considered to be solely of domestic concern.[38]

But nations are still reluctant to allow an international institution to examine, or even discuss, their domestic environmental policies. Even the three North American countries, which have a long tradition of establishing bilateral institutions to address environmental issues, have usually limited the scope of these institutions to specific issues arising along or across their borders. The oldest, and perhaps the most important, of these institutions are the International Joint Commission and the International Boundary and Water Commission, whose mandates are limited to the Canada-U.S. and the U.S.-Mexico border, respectively, and which address only a limited range of issues even within the border regions.

Whether or not pollution havens in Mexico were ever a realistic possibility, the attention the NAFTA debate brought to preventing them provided support for examining domestic environmental policies with no obvious transboundary environmental effect. And with the focus on maintaining and improving environmental standards and compliance, the need to connect the policies under discussion to some direct effect on trade and investment disappeared as well. As a result, it became easy—almost inevitable—for the negotiators of the NAAEC to draft an agreement with an extremely broad scope, providing the CEC the authority to address almost any environmental issue that might arise in the continent.[39]

The result can be seen most clearly in the extremely wide array of mandates Article 10 of the NAAEC gives to the Council, the governing body of the Commission.[40] A few of the mandates relate directly to environmental concerns raised during the NAFTA debate. Article 10(4) addresses the pollution haven concern by requiring the Council to encourage effective enforcement by each Party of its environmental laws. Echoes of other trade and environment issues appear in Article 10(6), which requires the Council to cooperate with the NAFTA Free Trade Commission, composed of the Parties' trade ministers, by acting as a point of inquiry and receipt for comments concerning NAFTA's environmental goals and objectives (a nod to the environmental groups' desire to open up the NAFTA institutions to public participation); to contribute to the prevention or resolution of environment-related trade disputes under NAFTA by making recommendations to the Free Trade Commission and identifying environmental experts to NAFTA bodies (a response to the concern that decisions under NAFTA would be slanted against the environment); and to consider on an ongoing basis the environmental effects of NAFTA (a mandate that may result from the failed attempt to obtain a full environmental assessment of NAFTA before it entered into force).

But most of the Council's mandates do not directly concern issues of economic integration. For example, the NAAEC requires the Council to promote and, as appropriate, develop recommendations on public access to environmental information, appropriate limits for specific pollutants, transboundary environmental impact assessment, and reciprocal access to domestic legal remedies for transboundary environmental harm.[41] The NAAEC also gives the Council a long list of topics with respect to which it may make recommendations, including pollution prevention, environmental reporting, scientific research and technology development, long-range transport of air and marine pollutants, wildlife protection, endangered species, and eco-labeling. The list concludes with a catch-all, allowing the Council to consider "other matters as it may decide."[42] The effect of these mandates is to authorize the Council to consider virtually any environmental issue of interest to the Parties.

The mandates of the Secretariat are similarly broad. The NAAEC instructs the Secretariat to provide technical, administrative, and operational support to the Council, and the Council appoints its Executive Director, but the Secretariat also has an important degree of independence from the Parties. The Executive Director appoints the other officials of the Secretariat, and the NAAEC provides that the Secretariat may receive instructions only from the Council, rather than from any individual government or external authority.[43] Moreover, the NAAEC requires the Secretariat to carry out two important types of reporting with limited Council oversight. Article 13 authorizes the Secretariat to prepare a report on any matter within the scope of the annual program without Council authorization and a report on any other environmental matter related to the cooperative functions of the NAAEC unless the Council objects by a two-thirds vote. Since the scope of the annual program has proved to be quite wide, and any environmental matter except a failure to enforce the law can be considered to be related to the cooperative functions of the NAAEC, the effect of Article 13 is to empower the Secretariat to report on almost any aspect of the North American environment that it considers worth exploring. Articles 14 and 15 instruct the Secretariat to administer the citizen submissions procedure—specifically, to decide which submissions meet the threshold requirements of the agreement, which merit a response from the Party at which they are directed, and which warrant preparation of a factual record. The Council decides whether to authorize a factual record, but, once authorized, it is prepared by the Secretariat.

Whether seen as a trade and environment organization or as a regional environmental organization, the CEC provides new avenues of participation to civil society. Three of these avenues are particularly important. First, the NAAEC creates, as one of the constitutive elements of the Commission, a Joint Public Advisory Committee composed of fifteen citizens, five from each Party, and authorizes it to advise the Council on any matter within the scope of the agreement and to provide relevant technical, scientific, or other information to the Secretariat.[44] (The NAAEC also authorizes, but does not require, each Party to convene a national advisory committee composed of members of its public and a governmental committee composed of representatives of federal and subfederal governments to advise it on the implementation and further elaboration of the agreement.) Second, the NAAEC authorizes the Secretariat to draw upon information submitted by individuals or nongovernmental organizations in its development of a report under Article 13. Third, the Article 14–15 submissions procedure allows any person or nongovernmental organization in any of the three countries to file a complaint alleging that a Party is failing to effectively enforce its environmental law. The NAAEC thus offers two ways that private persons may trigger independent reports on virtually any environmental issue, including sensitive allegations of failure to enforce domestic laws.

Evaluating the NAAEC and the CEC

In at least one respect, the NAAEC was undoubtedly successful. Together with the agreement creating the BECC and NADBank and another trilateral agreement on labor issues, it helped to attract support for NAFTA in the U.S. Congress, which approved NAFTA and its accompanying agreements in November 1993. All of the agreements entered into force together on January 1, 1994.

But the NAAEC and the CEC are much more than window dressing for NAFTA. The NAAEC establishes the first regional environmental organization in North America and gives it interesting, innovative mandates; it addresses environmental issues related to economic integration in more detail than any other agreement outside the European Union; and it provides new opportunities for direct public participation in its implementation. In all of these respects, the NAAEC offers lessons for other countries seeking to address shared environmental problems against a backdrop of increasing economic integration—which is to say, all countries.

What are these lessons? How well is the CEC fulfilling the mandates of the NAAEC? We believe that the record of the CEC over the past nine years provides a basis for analysis of its past performance and its potential for the future. To that end, we asked experts on various aspects of the Commission to analyze specific issues relevant to its work. We have organized their contributions into three sections, according to the three roles of the Commission we have described: as a regional environmental organization; as an institutional way to address trade and environment concerns; and as a means of facilitating public participation in international environmental policymaking. Obviously, this division is somewhat artificial. The roles overlap, and not all CEC functions and programs fall neatly into one category or another. Still, we think that the division helps to organize description and analysis.

The issues to be examined in evaluating the CEC vary depending on the particular role or mandate the CEC may be trying to fulfill. For example, an effective regional environmental organization might be expected to identify regional or transboundary problems and facilitate coordinated responses to them. It might also be expected to facilitate upward harmonization of domestic standards, including through convening networks of interested governmental and nongovernmental actors. As a trade and environment institution, the CEC would be expected to address the various concerns and criticisms regarding NAFTA, particularly those for which it has specific mandates, such as assessing NAFTA's effects, providing a voice for environmental concerns within the NAFTA institutions, and trying to prevent pollution havens. And, finally, assessments of the CEC as a public forum should examine the specific mechanisms through which the public may trigger or participate in CEC decisions.

THE CEC AS A REGIONAL ENVIRONMENTAL ORGANIZATION

One of the first tasks facing the CEC after its creation was to prioritize the open-ended mandates of the NAAEC. In the next chapter, Greg Block, the first Legal Director of the CEC in 1994–95 and its Director of Programs from 1996 to 2002, explains how the Secretariat and the Council organized the CEC cooperative programs into four general areas: Environment, Economy and Trade; Conservation of Biodiversity; Pollutants and Health; and Law and Policy. He also gives an overview of the Commission's work in each of these areas, highlighting some of its programs, such as its Sound Management of Chemicals program through which the Parties coordinated their treatment of certain persistent pollutants.

The next three chapters each analyze one area of cooperation in more detail. Mark Winfield describes the development of pollutant release and transfer registry (PRTR) programs—databases to which facilities report their releases of certain chemicals to the environment and their transfers of the chemicals to other sites. As he explains, PRTRs are a relatively recent addition to the range of instruments available for environmental regulation. The United States created the first such program, the Toxics Release Inventory, only in 1986. Canada began to develop a similar program in the early 1990s, and Mexico began considering its own PRTR program shortly thereafter. Winfield describes the role of the CEC in encouraging Mexico to institute mandatory PRTR and in building its capacity to do so. He also examines the Commission's *Taking Stock* reports, which incorporate information from the U.S. and Canadian PRTR systems, and their effect on PRTR in Canada.

Robert Glicksman analyzes the role of the CEC in protecting biological diversity in North America—an area in which, as he says, the Commission "has its work cut out for it." After reviewing the ecological and legal context, he describes eight CEC programs, which range from the general (developing a long-term agenda for continental biodiversity conservation) to the specific (supporting cooperative efforts by the three countries' wildlife services to conserve seventeen migratory and transboundary species). He then assesses them according to how well they fulfill four steps identified by Edward O. Wilson as necessary to protect biodiversity.

John Knox analyzes the CEC's record with respect to transboundary pollution, which has caused many of the continent's most controversial environmental problems. The challenge for the Commission here is to find a way to complement the many bilateral institutions the North American nations have created to address particular types of transboundary environmental harm. Knox examines the degree to which the CEC has implemented specific mandates given it by the NAAEC to promote transboundary environmental impact assessment and reciprocal access to domestic legal remedies for transboundary harm.

THE CEC AS A TRADE AND ENVIRONMENT ORGANIZATION

Mary Kelly and Cyrus Reed describe the CEC's Environment, Economy and Trade program, focusing on its efforts to assess the environmental effects of NAFTA. The CEC has developed an analytical framework for that assessment that differs in important ways from the standard models used by governments. Kelly and Reed analyze the framework, comparing it to the prevalent approaches. They also evaluate the extent to which the Commission's work on trade effects will affect domestic and regional policies on trade and development. Finally, they describe the relative lack of attention the CEC has given to investment disputes under NAFTA, many of which have involved environmental regulations.

The next chapters address specific aspects of the trade / investment / environment nexus. Kevin Gallagher evaluates the Commission's role in assisting abatement of environmental degradation in Mexico, the original motivation for the NAAEC. He examines Mexico's efforts to increase levels of enforcement, funding for modernizing equipment and less environmentally harmful technologies and systems, and public scrutiny of environmental practices, as well as the role of the CEC in promoting better compliance with environmental standards in Mexico.

Claudia Schatan analyzes data relevant to whether Mexico has acted as a pollution haven since NAFTA entered into force. She examines changes in exports of manufactured goods from Mexico to see whether exports from relatively high-polluting industries grew relative to other exports. Schatan also examines changes in pollution from twenty-eight manufacturing sectors from one year before to four years after NAFTA took effect, distinguishing between scale and composition effects. She compares the relative competitiveness in the U.S. market of highly polluting manufacturing sectors in Mexico and Canada. Finally, she looks at the destinations of foreign direct investment in Mexico since NAFTA.

Alejandro Nadal analyzes the effect of NAFTA on one particularly important area of Mexican life: corn production. He explains that one of the intended effects of NAFTA was to lower prices for corn as a result of imports from the United States and that several benefits were expected to follow: the reallocation of resources would allow Mexico to pursue its comparative advantage in other agricultural products, especially in fruit and horticultural production; subsidies for corn producers would become unnecessary; displaced workers would find jobs in areas of the economy with higher productivity; and consumers would reap the benefits of lower prices for tortillas and other corn products. But the effect on the genetic resources contained in Mexican corn production was ignored. Nadal examines that effect, including the effect of transgenic corn on Mexican genetic resources.

Sanford Gaines examines Chapter 11 of NAFTA, which protects foreign investors from discrimination and expropriation by host governments and allows investors to bring claims to independent arbitral tribunals if they believe the governments have violated their obligations. Because several Chapter 11 challenges have involved environmental laws, concerns have been raised that investors may be using Chapter 11 to undermine legitimate environmental regulation. Critics of Chapter 11 have called for the CEC to take a more active role in addressing these issues. Gaines assesses whether the decided cases threaten environmental protection, as well as democratic choice and autonomy of governments. He also examines whether, and how, the CEC should address Chapter 11 disputes and the issues they raise.

THE CEC AS A FORUM FOR INTERNATIONAL CIVIL SOCIETY

John Wirth, one of the original and longest-serving members of the Joint Public Advisory Committee (JPAC), describes its creation, history, and highlights. He explains that JPAC members saw themselves from the beginning not as representatives of particular governments or organizations but rather as North Americans, which greatly facilitated their ability to work together. He describes the way that JPAC has advised the Council, with varying degrees of success, on issues ranging across the entire spectrum of the CEC's work. He reviews in particular detail JPAC's contribution to the ongoing debate over the respective roles of the Council and Secretariat in the citizen submissions procedure.

Dan Tarlock and John Thorson examine Article 13 of the NAAEC, which allows the Secretariat to prepare reports on its own initiative or at the request of public or private entities. They see Article 13 as an example of postmodern "soft" or "reflexive" international law because it seeks to influence behavior without the threat of enforcement, instead relying on sunshine and information dissemination. They describe the Secretariat's 1999 report on the San Pedro River, which concluded that groundwater depletion in Arizona threatens to destroy a broadleaf riparian forest and recommended an altered pumping regime, and analyze it as an example of information disclosure used as an instrument of environmental policy.

Donald McRae compares the role of transparency through public participation in the fields of trade and investment law with its role in the field of international environmental regulation. In particular, he examines dispute resolution under the World Trade Organization and NAFTA and the citizen submissions procedure created by Articles 14 and 15 of the NAAEC, all of which can deal with allegations of violations of legal obligations involving environmental issues. He assesses the degree to which each institution provides transparency with respect to: initiating the process; access to information about the process; providing information to the process; access to oral proceedings; and participation in decision-making.

Kal Raustiala situates the citizen submissions procedure in the context of other "treaty review institutions"—that is, mechanisms that focus on the implementation of treaty obligations. He identifies two models of review: "police patrols," which are efforts by centralized authorities to look actively and systematically for problems or violations, and "fire alarms," which are procedures that may be triggered by citizens, organizations, or other groups to signal that a violation or problem has occurred. He explains that the citizen submissions procedure is an example of a fire alarm and analyzes its potential benefits, organizing them into three categories: effectiveness, efficiency, and participatory governance.

David Markell, the former head of the CEC Submissions Unit, describes the recent history of the submissions procedure, which has continued the long-running dispute over how much control the Council can and should exercise over the preparation of factual records. Markell reviews resolutions adopted by the Council in November 2001 that authorize the Secretariat to prepare five new factual records—two more than the Council had approved in the previous seven years—but which restrict the Secretariat's scope of review of the issues raised by the submissions. He evaluates whether these decisions help or hurt the long-term prospects of the procedure.

Our final chapter sums up the lessons to be drawn from the preceding fourteen. While the record of the CEC is not unblemished, we believe that it provides a basis on which to build. Economically and ecologically, all of us live on one planet. We believe that the CEC is an important step toward learning to live here more successfully.

Notes

1. Rio Declaration on Environment and Development, June 14, 1992, principle 4, 31 I.L.M. 874.

2. Of course, the institutions of the European Union are more powerful in many ways than the CEC. But as John Kirton and Virginia Maclaren note, "The European Union remains a very special supranational case, and thus one of limited utility for a world not wanting to proceed to Europe's prospective unified end state." John J. Kirton and Virginia W. Maclaren, "Forging the Trade-Environment-Social Cohesion Link: Global Challenges, North American Experiences," in *Linking Trade, Environment, and Social Cohesion* 21 n.1 (John J. Kirton and Virginia W. Maclaren eds., 2002).

3. Canada-Chile Agreement on Environmental Cooperation, Feb. 6, 1997, 36 I.L.M. 1193; Agreement between the United States of America and the Hashemite

Kingdom of Jordan on the Establishment of a Free Trade Area, Oct. 24, 2000, 41 I.L.M. 63.

4. Important works that do take a more comprehensive approach include Pierre Marc Johnson and André Beaulieu, *The Environment and NAFTA: Understanding and Implementing the New Continental Law* (1996) (a study of the environmental provisions of NAFTA and the NAAEC, written before the CEC had much of a record to review); Four-Year Review of the North American Agreement on Environmental Cooperation: Report of the Independent Review Committee (1998), available at *http://www.cec.org* (a report by independent experts on the work of the CEC over its first four years); Joseph DiMento and Pamela M. Doughman, "Soft Teeth in the Back of the Mouth: The NAFTA Environmental Side Agreement Implemented," 10 *Georgetown International Environmental Law Review* 651 (1998) (evaluating the CEC in large part on the basis of a survey of stakeholders in and observers of it); Kirton and Maclaren, supra (analyzing elements in the NAFTA agreements and institutions that connect trade to environmental and social concerns).

5. Their November 1990 paper was not the first time these concerns had been raised, particularly with respect to the border. "Since the 1980s border scholars and activists had voiced their concerns over the rapidly deteriorating conditions caused by massive regional industrialization," and border organizations like the Border Ecology Project and the Texas Center for Policy Studies "had long argued for greater attention to environmental issues related to trade, but [had been] unable to focus national attention on the problems." John J. Audley, *Green Politics and Global Trade: NAFTA and the Future of Environmental Politics* 50 (1997). The National Wildlife Federation's entry into the debate was significant in part because as "[o]ne of the oldest and largest national environmental organizations, NWF enjoyed considerable political influence with both Congress and the administration." Id., 51.

6. "Environmental Concerns Related to a United States-Mexico-Canada Free Trade Agreement," in *NAFTA and the Environment* 631, 634 (Daniel Magraw ed., 1995) (a very useful compilation of documents relevant to the negotiation and the agreement).

7. President George Bush to Lloyd Bentsen, chairman of the Senate Finance Committee; Richard A. Gephardt, House majority leader; and Dan Rostenkowski, chairman of the House Ways and Means Committee, 27 *Weekly Compilation of Presidential Documents* 536 (May 1, 1991).

8. For general descriptions of the way that the environmental concerns with NAFTA led to the NAAEC, see Johnson and Beaulieu, supra; DiMento and Doughman, supra; Gilbert R. Winham, "Enforcement of Environmental Measures: Negotiating the NAFTA Environmental Side Agreement," 3 *Journal of Environment and Development* 29 (1994). For analyses of the role of environmental groups in the NAFTA debate, see Audley, supra; Barbara Hogenboom, *Mexico and the NAFTA Environment Debate: The Transnational Politics of Economic Integration* (1998); Betty Ferber, Janine Ferretti, and Lynn Fischer, "Building an Environmental Protection Framework for North America: The Role of the Non-Governmental Community," in *Green Globe Yearbook of International Co-operation on Environment and Development* 83 (1995).

9. "Letter from 51 Environmental NGOs," in Magraw, supra, 679, 680.

10. Hogenboom, supra, 239; Johnson and Beaulieu, supra, 29.

11. Integrated Environmental Plan for the Mexican-U.S. Border Area (First Stage) 1992–1994, published jointly by the U.S. Environmental Protection Agency and Secretaría de Desarrollo Urbano y Ecología.

12. "Environmental Safeguards for the North American Free Trade Agreement: Priority Recommendations to Negotiators and Congress," June 1992, in Magraw, supra, 672, 673 (statement on behalf of fourteen environmental groups); Natural Resources Defense Council Statement Regarding Environmental Protection in the North American Free Trade Agreement, Sept. 3, 1991, in id., 658, 663, 666–67.

13. See id., 661–62; Hogenboom, supra, 151 (Mexican organizations' "main concern was that free trade with the US would speed up industrial expansion, agricultural modernization and the exploitation of natural resources at considerable environmental cost.").

14. Ferber, Ferretti, and Fischer, supra, 83; "Environmental Safeguards," supra, 675.

15. See Report of the [Bush] Administration on the North American Free Trade Agreement and Actions Taken in Fulfillment of the May 1, 1991, Commitments, in Magraw, supra, 239, 244.

16. As Sanford Gaines has said, "Although numerous economic analyses show that the presumed competitiveness effect scarcely appears in the real world, the argument has an intuitive logic that is hard to resist." Sanford E. Gaines, "The Free Trade Area of the Americas: Lessons from North America," in *The Greening of Trade Law* 193 (Richard H. Steinberg ed., 2002).

17. "Evaluation of Mexico's Environmental Laws, Regulations, and Standards," in Magraw, supra, 583, 615.

18. Ferber, Ferretti, and Fischer, supra, 85.

19. Natural Resources Defense Council Statement, supra, 665; see also "Environmental Safeguards," supra, 676–78 (proposing treaty language to create the Commission); Ferber, Ferretti, and Fischer, supra, 86 (describing nongovernmental groups' support for a "permanent, independent, trilateral panel or commission").

20. North American Free Trade Agreement (NAFTA), Dec. 17, 1992, art. 1114(2), 32 I.L.M. 642.

21. "Joint Press Release from the Ministers Responsible for the Environment of Canada, Mexico, and the United States," Sept. 17, 1992, in Magraw, supra, 79.

22. GATT Dispute Settlement Panel Report on United States Restrictions on Imports of Tuna, 30 I.L.M. 1594.

23. For example, Natural Resources Defense Council Statement, supra, 669–70.

24. See Ferber, Ferretti, and Fischer, supra, 87; see generally Johnson and Beaulieu, supra, 69–110; Steve Charnovitz, "The North American Free Trade Agreement: Green Law or Green Spin?" 26 *Law and Policy in International Business* 1 (1994).

25. Convention on International Trade in Endangered Species of Wild Fauna and Flora, Mar. 3, 1973, 993 U.N.T.S. 243, 27 U.S.T. 1087; Montreal Protocol on Substances that Deplete the Ozone Layer, Sept. 16, 1987, 26 I.L.M. 1550.

26. NAFTA, supra, art. 104(1).

27. For example, Natural Resources Defense Council Statement, supra, 670.

28. Letter from Six Environmental NGOs to Charles Ries, Office of the United States Trade Representative, July 9, 1991, in Magraw, supra, 653.

29. Remarks by Governor Bill Clinton at North Carolina State University, Oct. 4, 1992, in id., 263.

30. Letter from Seven NGOs to Ambassador Michael Kantor Regarding NAFTA Supplemental Agreements, in id., 714. "INAINE (Mexico) and Pollution Probe (Canada) took similar positions," Hogenboom, supra, 209, but more critical environmental groups in all three countries refrained from agreeing to endorse NAFTA if these elements were included. Moreover, Mexican groups opposed trade sanctions, which they thought would be abused by the United States. Id. at 209, 211.

31. See *Public Citizen v. U.S. Trade Representative*, 5 F.3d 549 (D.C. Cir. 1993).

32. Agreement between the Government of the United States of America and the Government of the United Mexican States Concerning the Establishment of a Border Environment Cooperation Commission and a North American Development Bank, Nov. 16 and 18, 1993, 32 I.L.M. 1545.

33. North American Agreement on Environmental Cooperation (NAAEC), Sept. 14, 1993, 32 I.L.M. 1480.

34. Id., arts. 3, 5.

35. Id., arts. 4, 6, 7.

36. Id., arts. 14, 15, 23–36.

37. For descriptions of the division between the "moderate" groups that supported NAFTA as a result of the side agreement and the more critical groups that continued to oppose it, see Audley, supra, 72–106; DiMento and Doughman, supra, 675–81; Hogenboom, supra, 208–11. The most important Canadian environmental group not to oppose NAFTA and the NAAEC was Pollution Probe, headed by Janine Ferretti, who later became the second Executive Director of the CEC.

38. See, e.g., Rio Declaration, supra, Principles 10, 11, 13 (stating that nations shall provide appropriate access to information and judicial proceedings, shall enact effective environmental legislation, and shall develop national law on liability and compensation for victims of pollution and environmental damage, without making a distinction between domestic and international environmental protection).

39. See J. Owen Saunders, "NAFTA and the North American Agreement on Environmental Cooperation: A New Model for International Collaboration on Trade and the Environment," 5 *Colorado Journal of International Environmental Law and Policy* 273, 289 (1994) (The NAAEC "goes beyond general international environmental law in articulating an interest by all Parties not only in environmental policies that may affect them through transboundary impacts, but also in what would normally be considered the purely domestic environmental issues of another state").

40. It can also be seen in the objectives of the NAAEC set out in Article 1, most of which have no direct connection to NAFTA at all. The first three objectives, for example, are to foster protection and improvement of the environment in North America, to promote sustainable development, and to increase cooperation between the Parties to better conserve, protect, and enhance the environment. NAAEC, supra, art. 1.

41. Id., art. 10(5), (7), (8), (9).

42. Id., art. 10(2).

43. Id., art. 11. The Council may reject, by a two-thirds vote, any appointment that does not meet specified "general standards." Id., art. 11(3).

44. Id., art. 16.

PART I

Regional Solutions to Regional Problems?

GREG BLOCK **2**

The CEC Cooperative Program of Work

A North American Agenda for Action

LATE IN THE SPRING of 1994, recently appointed North American Commission for Environmental Cooperation (CEC) Executive Director Victor Lichtinger returned to Mexico after having met for the first time with the government representatives charged with overseeing the newly created institution. Lichtinger produced from his pocket a paper napkin upon which he had scrawled a list of possible project areas discussed informally at dinner. The "napkin memo," later formalized in a letter from the Parties outlining a series of "cooperative work program activities," represents the earliest attempt to chart a course for the CEC by establishing several priority areas.[1]

Nearly a decade later, the modest tabletop origins of the CEC cooperative work program are still readily discernible in the twenty-four programs and projects contained in the nearly 150-page, detailed 2002 CEC program and budget. Having survived two Council "visioning" exercises designed to set long-term agendas, CEC cooperative programs cluster around two central themes: enhanced stewardship of shared continental ecosystems and natural resources, and environmental sustainability in open markets. For years to come, the achievements and shortcomings of the institution are likely to be measured against this ambitious agenda for North American cooperation.

The Broad Mandates of the North American Agreement on Environmental Cooperation

Although the North American Agreement on Environmental Cooperation (NAAEC), the constitutive document of the CEC, does not set a specific agenda, it does state general goals and broad mandates. The NAAEC's preamble recognizes the interrelationship of the environments of the three countries; acknowledges the growing economic and social links between them; underscores the essential role of cooperation for the conservation, protection, and enhancement of the environment for present and future generations; and concludes by identifying the CEC as a framework for environmental cooperation in North America.

While the NAAEC commits the Parties to provide for high levels of environmental protection and effective enforcement of environmental laws and to ensure private access to remedies and specific procedural guarantees, many of its other provisions are permissive. The Agreement identifies numerous areas the Council can address but requires it to take concrete actions on very few of them. Examples of required Council activities include strengthening cooperation on the development and continuing improvement of environmental laws and regulations; encouraging effective enforcement, compliance, and technical cooperation; and promoting public access to information and limits for specific pollutants.[2]

Most of the NAAEC's provisions are discretionary, providing the Council with a great deal of flexibility to identify areas of work. The nonexhaustive laundry list of potential Council issue areas set forth in Article 10(2) provides a good example. Here, the Agreement lists eighteen areas for Council consideration, including issues as diverse as eco-labeling, pollution prevention, the protection of endangered and protected species, the long-range transport of air and marine pollutants, and human resource training and development. Moreover, it allows the Council to consider and develop recommendations on virtually any "other matter[] as it may decide."[3] The NAAEC's provisions thus set forth an extensive range of potential issue areas bounded only loosely by common notions of "environment" and the need to reach consensus on the annual program and budget. The Agreement's sweeping reach is in some measure tempered by the limited powers of the CEC, as well as by practical limitations on human and financial resources. Nonetheless, the NAAEC's comprehensive and holistic terms establish an important new forum for regional environmental concerns with the potential to stimulate action across political boundaries.

DEVELOPING THE COOPERATIVE PROGRAM OF WORK

The development of the cooperative program of work is initiated by the Executive Director, who submits for the approval of the Council the "annual program and budget of the Commission, including provision for proposed cooperative activities and for the Secretariat to respond to contingencies."[4] In developing the proposed program, the Secretariat considers a variety of relevant information, including Council directives or guidance, advice from the Joint Public Advisory Committee (JPAC) and from National and Governmental Advisory Committees, and public input. To enhance transparency and public participation in the process, the Secretariat now develops and makes public an outline of major lines of action prior to preparing the detailed proposed program. Both the outline and detailed plan are made public at the same time as they are provided to governments, enabling interested citizens to monitor and track changes as the program is discussed, revised, and approved.

PRIORITY SETTING IN THE FIRST FEW YEARS

The fact that Council can pursue cooperative activities in virtually any area it sees fit poses a special challenge of its own—priority setting. The first two years of the CEC cooperative work program featured many start-up issues of the type every new international organization is likely to face, but the CEC got staff on board quickly and set out immediately to establish a voice of its own. To focus the institution on key areas, the CEC held a series of thematic "brainstorming" workshops with a diverse group of North American participants.[5] While these sessions helped the participants to gain a common understanding of the issues and nurture the formation of the emerging North American environmental community, they did little to assist the CEC in setting priorities. It would take some time for everyone to understand the CEC's comparative advantages, fully appreciate its operational limitations and constraints, and formulate successful project ideas.

The potentially sweeping mandate of the CEC makes priority setting doubly important and trebly challenging. To begin with, there are competing views on how an untested, modestly funded new institution should get under way. Given the polemic beginnings of the CEC and the lack of a broad consensus on what the organization should do, a number of commentators suggested lying low and quietly producing high-quality information for what largely would amount to a government constituency. Avoiding controversy and doing a few things well, it was argued, would solidify the CEC's legitimacy without agitating its detractors within and outside government. Others, pointing to the high expectations for the CEC held by a relatively small but politically active and vigilant group of citizens, called for a more aggressive approach, citing an urgent need for greater balance in the economy-trade-environment debate.[6] This latter group emphasized the disparity between the influence and power of multilateral trade bodies and the comparative weakness of the CEC. They argued that the lack of "teeth" in the NAAEC could best be compensated, though not overcome, by establishing an independent voice in key areas, such as assessing the environmental impacts of trade, reporting on the state of the environment, and, of course, investigating allegations of nonenforcement of environmental law.

While no deliberate decision was taken in favor of one or another of these viewpoints, the early CEC program—much like the Agreement itself—seems to reflect the tension between harder-edged policy initiatives on the one hand and noncontroversial information gathering, discussion forums, and similar initiatives on the other. In an attempt to reconcile these competing views, the Secretariat initially proposed a blend of fairly noncontroversial, information-based projects, with a handful that addressed more delicate topics. On the softer end of the spectrum, for example, projects listed in the 1994 Annual Program and Budget allotted funds to assess "state-of-the-environment" reporting methodologies, to evaluate capacity-building needs, and to develop a comparative environmental legal database.[7] Examples of more politically sensitive initiatives initiated during the 1994–95 period included projects to limit use of specific pollutants, to track and publish regional data on industrial emissions, to assess the environmental effects of NAFTA, and to report on enforcement and compliance efforts in the region. The first three of these have persevered, developing into highly successful initiatives, while the growth of the fourth remains stunted.

Before long, the CEC faced a problem of a different order. The 1995 Annual Program and Budget was organized into seven program areas, which mainly tracked the areas identified in the spring 1994 "napkin memo" and memorialized in the May 1994 letter from the Parties. By 1995, the seven areas already contained some thirty projects. But funding for the CEC remained (and remains) constant, with an annual budget of US$9 million, of which roughly $4 million are available for program activities.

Obviously, the large number of projects offended those who advocated "doing a few things well." On the other hand, the CEC had entered a creative period of experimentation, feeling its way through the complexities of North American environmental geopolitics. Some doors seemed worth leaning against on the chance that one day they might open. By reducing the number of projects too much, the CEC risked missing out on emerging areas of interest.

Moreover, the give-and-take dynamics of trilateral negotiation make it especially difficult to eliminate projects, particularly those that enjoy a governmental constituency base. While over the succeeding years the CEC has managed to reduce the number of its cooperative projects to its current level of between twenty and twenty-five, organized into four program areas (Environment, Economy and Trade; Pollutants and Health; Conservation of Biodiversity; and Law and Policy), an astute observer might glimpse the "Russian box" effect, where projects are nested to conceal their bulk. Nevertheless, the CEC's limited resources have forced a zero-sum program allocation that ultimately will impose a discipline of its own.

Articulating a Shared Vision

THE GHOSTS OF MEECH LAKE

Despite several notable successes discussed below, the first three full years of cooperative programs spawned surprisingly little cooperation among the officials tasked with overseeing the CEC. With the negotiating history of the more contested articles of the NAAEC still lingering, in 1996 the Parties remained deeply divided over the CEC's core mission. During this period, the United States continued to champion the citizen submission process, enforcement cooperation, and trade and environment areas; Mexico favored focusing on conservation of biodiversity, capacity building, and technical assistance; and Canada expended most of its energy trying to keep the peace between the other two. During one veritable outpouring of cooperative zeal, the Mexican Trade Ministry (SECOFI) blocked publication of the methodology developed for assessing the environmental effects of trade, the United States scolded Mexico for failing to adopt a toxic release inventory, and Canada balked at efforts to participate in a North American by-catch reduction strategy.

Everyone needed a breath of fresh air. In an effort to lower tensions and seek common ground, Canada proposed a gathering of senior officials to participate in a facilitated discussion of the goals and objectives of the CEC at the storied Meech Lake cabin.[8] Despite the warm personal relationship between the individuals participating in the retreat, the results were modest. A two-hour morning discussion failed to produce an agreement on a new CEC mission statement, and the postlunch discussions, while courteous, basically restated long-held viewpoints.

Basic disagreements over the interpretation of the provisions dealing with citizen submissions under Articles 14 and 15 dominated the discussion, eclipsing consideration of the many ongoing cooperative programs. That pattern has often continued to this day: the periodic meetings of senior government officials to review and decide CEC business become increasingly occupied with the citizen submission procedure, which crowds out substantive discussions of most cooperative program work.

THE "SHARED AGENDA FOR ACTION"

An atmosphere of crisis pervaded the CEC following the departure of the first Executive Director in 1998 amid the continued lack of agreement over the central mission of the organization. The Parties again needed to seek out common ground and articulate a shared vision of the CEC's role in regional environmental governance. This time, government officials, along with representatives of JPAC, the National Advisory Committees, and the Secretariat, met in the scenic Laurentian mountain resort area north of

Montreal. The result was "A Shared Agenda for Action," a four-page statement that the Council issued at its annual session, in Mérida, Mexico, on June 26, 1998.[9]

The "Shared Agenda" was based in large part on a comprehensive, independent review of the operation and effectiveness of the NAAEC during its first four years.[10] Two problems identified by the review were that the CEC was trying to undertake too many initiatives without clear goals and that it did not carry out long-term planning. The "Shared Agenda" stated that, given the CEC's limited resources, it was time for it to "sharpen its focus" and concentrate on a limited number of projects. In particular, the "Shared Agenda" identified two priority areas—Pursuing Environmental Sustainability in Open Markets and Stewardship of the North American Environment—and identified specific lines of action to pursue within each of these areas. In the first area, the lines of action included promoting trade in environmentally friendly goods and services; assessing the effects of NAFTA on an ongoing basis; and developing "compliance indicators" to facilitate comparison of environmental performance among countries. In the second, they included identifying emerging threats to the shared environment, cooperating on North American air quality issues, continuing the Sound Management of Chemicals (SMOC) program and the work on pollutant releases and transfers, and cooperating on protection of biodiversity. The "Shared Agenda" also extended the horizon of the CEC programs by moving from a one-year to a rolling three-year plan, which would continue to be proposed and approved on an annual basis.

The "Shared Agenda" has had a lasting impact on the cooperative work program of the CEC. Its two major lines of action continue to represent the twin pillars of the cooperative work program. A completely new set of Council members met in Guadalajara in 2001 with an opportunity to leave their own imprimatur on the program. While they did set forth a new framework for cooperative action, virtually all of the major lines of action identified in the "Shared Agenda" remain intact.[11]

Regional Environmental Cooperation in Practice

The following sections briefly describe several CEC programs that have achieved early successes. Some of the programs are described in more detail in later chapters.

THE SOUND MANAGEMENT OF CHEMICALS

The SMOC initiative has been one of the most successful CEC programs. It began in October 1995, when the Council adopted a resolution that established a framework for working collaboratively in addressing the sound management of chemicals in the region.[12] The resolution created a working group, composed of two senior officials from each Party, to develop North American Regional Action Plans (NARAPs) for the management and control of certain "persistent and toxic substances." In particular, the working group was to recommend concerted efforts to reduce the risks posed by the substances, which might range from nonregulatory measures like promoting cleaner products to phasing out or banning the chemicals if their use could not be adequately controlled.

Addressing toxic chemicals was a natural priority for the CEC, because they can easily be transported across national boundaries through air and water pollution and through traded goods and because they pose a serious threat to human health and the environment. Many of these substances bioaccumulate to dangerous levels in living organisms, and they may damage the nervous system, cause cancer, and interfere with reproduction. The NAAEC calls on the Council to promote appropriate limits for specific pollutants and requires each Party to consider implementing in its law any such limit the Council recommends.[13]

The 1995 Council resolution instructed the working group to begin with polychlorinated biphenyls (PCBs) and to choose three more substances from a list of twelve persistent bioaccumulative organic chemicals (the so-called dirty dozen persistent organic pollutants) targeted for action by the U.N. Environment Programme (UNEP) along with certain heavy metals, such as cadmium, mercury, and lead. In 1996, the working group chose chlordane, DDT, and mercury, and in 1997 the NARAPs for each of the first four substances were approved.

The program quickly achieved impressive results, especially in Mexico. The Mexican office of toxic substances within the environmental ministry was created in large part to help implement the SMOC program. Chlordane, which was occasionally used to kill termites, is now no longer registered for use or manufactured in North America, and the PCB action plan is working toward the virtual elimination of PCBs in the North American environment. The DDT NARAP may be the most important of the successes to date. Canada and the United States had already banned DDT, but Mexico still used it to kill mosquitoes that can carry malaria. The action plan for DDT called on Mexico to institute alternative antimalaria actions—increased community participation in nonchemical control measures, use of predatory bacteria and insects, and improved malaria diagnosis and treatment—with the aim of reducing its use of DDT 80 percent by 2002. The approach was so successful that Mexico phased out DDT entirely by 2000. A several-million dollar project sponsored by the CEC, Global Environment Fund, Pan American Health Organization, and UNEP is currently transferring the Mexican experience with DDT to Central American countries and is demonstrating that DDT-free methods for controlling malaria are replicable, cost effective, and sustainable.[14]

SMOC initially addressed chemicals in use primarily or solely in Mexico. The CEC faces considerable challenges of a higher order in developing and implementing regional action plans for more pervasive and widely used substances, such as dioxins and mercury, which will require significant action from all three countries. In 1999, the Council instructed the working group to prepare a NARAP for dioxins, furans, and hexachlorobenzene (all of which are found on the UNEP "dirty dozen" list) as a cluster, and in 2000 the Council approved a second phase of the mercury action plan, with the aim of reducing mercury releases from human activities to naturally occurring levels. The Council emphasized the importance of developing more information about sites with high levels of mercury, reporting on transportation of wastes containing mercury, and informing the public of how to reduce risks of exposure to mercury.[15] In 2002, the Council instructed the working group to prepare a NARAP for lindane. The working group is also considering whether to propose an action plan for lead. More generally, because of the importance of obtaining adequate information on exposure to and regulation of all of these toxic substances, in 1999 the Council mandated development of a NARAP on environmental monitoring and assessment.

One measure of the success of the SMOC program is the degree to which it anticipated similar action on a global level. In May 2001, representatives of the three North American countries, together with most of the other countries of the world, signed the Stockholm Convention on Persistent Organic Pollutants, which requires its parties to ban several of the "dirty dozen" chemicals immediately and to restrict the use of the others. The SMOC program will be an important model for the Stockholm parties as they try to phase out toxic chemicals.

TAKING STOCK OF POLLUTANT RELEASE AND TRANSFER REGISTRIES

Supporting regional uses for national pollutant release and transfer registries (PRTR), commonly known as "toxic release inventories" in the United States, is another CEC program that has produced measurable achievements. Regarded initially as more of an effort to stimulate comparable reporting initiatives in the three countries, the PRTR initiative has become much more. The project helps to establish a common information base for identifying and assessing North American trends for specific pollutant emissions and loading, highlights key information for policy-makers and the public, and provides an extra incentive for reducing emissions.

The initiative first gained considerable public attention in 1996 with the release of the initial *Taking Stock* report, which compiled government-reported data on a matched set of pollutants and ranked U.S. and Canadian states, provinces, and industries, putting the largest emitters at the top of the lists. The report and its successors attracted a surprising following among Canadian print and television media. Consequently, a number of Canadian industry groups (and one province) mounted unsuccessful attacks on the reports' methodology and assumptions, which remain largely unchanged. In subsequent years, companies and sectors began highlighting their descent in the rankings, and the reports are now more or less institutionalized, even featuring a searchable on-line database.

More important, the CEC has played an active role in promoting the development of a similar emissions inventory in Mexico. A review of every program of work since 1995 shows how the CEC has consistently supported capacity building in this area with Mexican nongovernmental organizations and industry. In 2001, Mexico enacted legislation calling for a PRTR, and the CEC continues to assist Mexico to implement the law and ensure that its information is compatible with information from its partners to the north.[16]

ASSESSING THE ENVIRONMENTAL IMPACT OF FREE TRADE

The NAAEC requires the Council to consider "on an ongoing basis the environmental effects of the NAFTA."[17] This is no easy task, given the absence of an accepted methodology for such an undertaking. Causation is notoriously elusive in complex economy-trade-environment relationships, particularly where few common environmental indicators correlate closely to trade data compiled for an entirely different purpose. Also, one should not overlook the fact that the proposition that trade could be responsible for *any* adverse environmental impacts stimulated a passionate debate that carries on to this day. How can three governments openly committed to free trade objectively assess and report on its impact on the environment? An initial conclusion might be that the difficulty is not so much methodological as political.

Nevertheless, both Canada and the United States have now committed to assessing the environmental impacts of future trade agreements, and a framework for conducting such assessments, developed by the CEC, has been applied by the Secretariat and the public to several sectors. In fall 2000, over three hundred participants attended the Symposium on Understanding Trade and Environment Linkages, held in cooperation with the World Bank in Washington, D.C. At the event, thirteen independent papers employing the CEC assessment methodology were discussed and critiqued. While no consensus was sought on conclusions, a number of participants validated the utility of the elements of the methodology: assessing geographically limited site- or area-specific studies; examining the impact of increased trade and investment on deficient environmental infrastructure; correlating trade-sensitive areas with selected natural resources; and securing additional resources for monitoring and assessment. Additionally, many participants acknowledged that the assessment process itself had to be more open and inclusive than the traditional application of economic tools. The CEC held a second symposium in early 2003.

Critics argue, however, that these assessments have not yet demonstrated their policy relevance and have not appreciably influenced the process of negotiating language in trade texts. Moreover, a growing number of commentators are questioning the entire assessment framework by asserting that any trade or economy policy discussion should first consider the levels at which commerce or specific economic activities can be undertaken in an environmentally sustainable manner. The so-called environment first paradigm and current assessment methodologies are both hampered by the lack of a complete, harmonized set of environmental indicators.

Notwithstanding the CEC's inability to produce a comprehensive assessment of NAFTA's impact on the environment, the organization has created a vital forum where the issues can be studied and evaluated, and the region has produced some of the most detailed and robust analytical work in this field.[18] Whether, in the longer term, the CEC will maintain enough airspace to further develop this work is unknown.[19]

THE NORTH AMERICAN BIRD CONSERVATION INITIATIVE

Citing the need to address conservation of all bird species in North America through a holistic and cooperative trinational strategy, in June 1999 the Council established the North American Bird Conservation Initiative (NABCI).[20] NABCI builds a coalition of private and public organizations to achieve regionally based, biologically driven, landscape-oriented partnerships delivering the full spectrum of bird conservation across the continent.

More often than not, the degradation or destruction of critical bird habitat is driven by local land-use decisions without consideration for regional planning or ecosystem needs. NABCI can help address this problem by identifying critical migratory pathways and raising the profile of local important bird areas within those corridors. It also has the potential to strengthen the network of scientists engaged in monitoring and research within the region.

The CEC has provided critical administrative and institutional support to NABCI for several years, including funding the salary of national NABCI coordinators and supporting the development of strategic and communications plans. Its institutional development has been solidified, but the true test of NABCI will be the delivery of successful on-the-ground conservation. In 2002, the CEC is funding demonstration projects with a view toward confirming the viability of the NABCI approach, as well as assessing NABCI's ability to operate independently in a self-sustaining fashion.[21]

BUILDING CONTINENT-WIDE PARTNERSHIPS

Few of the objectives identified in the CEC cooperative work program can be reached by government actions alone. Moreover, the Parties, the JPAC, the National and Governmental Advisory Committees, and members of the public all seem to agree that the CEC would squander a great deal of potential if it merely acted as a coordinating body for North American governments. It is no accident, then, that many CEC initiatives try to create and sustain networks, alliances, and partnerships that extend beyond the federal governments. Advanced communication technologies enable the CEC to establish electronic databases and "virtual" networks for issues as diverse as marine protected areas, shade agriculture, and renewable energy portfolio criteria. Building partnerships by linking issues with people across borders remains a key to gaining support for many CEC initiatives.

Future Challenges

An honest examination of sustainable development in North America will at times pose serious and controversial challenges to reigning paradigms. Early on, the CEC had to come to terms with the fact that avoiding difficult and polemic issues might isolate the institution from the most important regional environmental issues of the day. Put another way, if the CEC were to become more than a mere forum for discussion and coordination—if it sought to do something more than identify some of the driving forces of environmental pressures in the region—then it would have to buckle up for a turbulent ride. That ride has begun. There is no guarantee, however, that its three drivers won't shunt the institution off onto a smoother and quieter track by using the CEC primarily as a tool to gather and exchange information.

That would be a mistake. Despite its relatively modest achievements, the CEC has found a voice on a number of issues that cry out for a regional approach. Whether issuing recommendations on the environmental dimensions of the evolving North American electricity markets or comparing laws and standards for confined agricultural feedlots, there is a growing need to apply a regional lens to improve environmental policies and practices.

International institutions typically influence public policy by wielding substantial resources, by exercising their adjudicative mechanisms, or by establishing an authoritative voice on a number of important issues within their mandates. Of these, only the last tool is available to the CEC, but it is an exceptionally important one. The CEC is one of the few international institutions with the authority to call for environmental improvements in North America and the only one whose jurisdiction extends throughout the continent. For it to be successful, the Parties and the public must continue to nurture the CEC's ability to examine problems, question policies, facilitate agreements, and highlight solutions.

Notes

1. "Cooperative work program activities" typically include the programmatic activities approved in the CEC's annual program and budget. They exclude the Secretariat reports prepared under Article 13 and the citizen submission procedure established by Articles 14 and 15. See NAAEC, Sept. 14, 1993, arts. 13–15, 32 I.L.M. 1480.

2. NAAEC, supra, art. 10(3), (4), (5). Even these apparently mandatory requirements, which use the term "shall" in describing the Council's action, are softened by the succeeding verb ("strengthen cooperation," "encourage," "promote").

3. Id., art. 10(2)(s). This language is not limited by the cramped Article 45(2)(a) definition of "environmental law" that applies to Article 14 and Part Five of the Agreement.

4. Id., art. 11(6). As with its other functions, in preparing the draft program the Secretariat is expected to act in an independent manner. Article 11(4) reads: "In the performance of their duties, the Executive Director and the staff shall not seek or receive instructions from any government or any other authority external to the Council. Each Party shall respect the international character of the responsibilities of the Executive Director and the staff and shall not seek to influence them in the discharge of their responsibilities."

5. Workshop topics included conservation and ecosystem protection, economic instruments, and capacity building and technical cooperation.

6. For a thorough compilation of claims and arguments during the NAFTA debate, see CEC, "NAFTA Effects: Claims and Arguments 1991–1994" (1996). It and other CEC documents are available at the CEC website, *http://www.cec.org*.

7. Today this database, available at *http://www.cec.org/pubs_info_resources/*, receives more visitors than any other CEC web-based publication. Not all information-based initiatives fared so well. In 1995, efforts to examine cultural and ethnic aspects of ecosystem protection and conservation, regional ecosystem planning, and sustainable development policy mechanisms sputtered and were quietly abandoned.

8. The cabin was the site of the historic attempt to negotiate a grand constitutional reform package known as the Meech Lake Accord. The accord failed, though the dramatic process has been mythologized and represents an important milestone in Canadian history. Evidently, the CEC meeting left a considerably smaller historic residue.

9. "A Shared Agenda for Action" is reprinted as an annex to the CEC 1999–2001 Annual Program and Budget.

10. "Four-Year Review of the North American Agreement on Environmental Cooperation: Report of the Independent Review Committee" (1998), available at *http://www.cec.org*. Article 10(1)(b) of the NAAEC required the four-year review.

11. The framework can be found in Annex C of the 2002–4 Annual Program and Budget. It lists six elements: (1) gathering, compiling, and sharing high-quality information; (2) promoting the use of market-based approaches; (3) cooperating regionally in the implementation of global commitments; (4) building capacity for stronger environmental partnerships; (5) strengthening strategic linkages to improve sustainability; and (6) promoting public participation in the CEC's work.

12. CEC Council Resolution 9-5, Oct. 13, 1995.

13. NAAEC, supra, arts. 10(5)(b), 2(2).

14. See CEC, Overview and Update of the Sound Management of Chemicals (SMOC) Initiative, Sept. 2001.

15. CEC Council Resolution 00-06, June 13, 2000.

16. For additional discussion of the PRTR program, see ch. 3, infra.

17. NAAEC, supra, art. 10(6)(d).

18. See, e.g., CEC, *The Environmental Effects of Free Trade* (2002) (presenting the fall 2000 symposium papers).

19. For additional discussion of the CEC's work in this area, see ch. 6, infra.

20. CEC Council Resolution 99-03, June 28, 1999.

21. For additional discussion of the CEC's biodiversity programs, see ch. 4, infra.

MARK S. WINFIELD 3

North American Pollutant Release and Transfer Registries

A Case Study in Environmental Policy Convergence

THE CONCEPTS of the range of policy instruments governments can employ to protect the environment have undergone enormous expansion since the enactment of the first national environmental protection laws in North America over thirty years ago. Although we live in what is often referred to as the "information age," the full potential of the gathering and dissemination of information as a tool for environmental protection has only begun to be fully recognized in the past five years. Perhaps the strongest expression of this potential has been the emergence of pollutant release and transfer registry (PRTR) programs around the world. A PRTR is a database to which facilities must report, usually annually, their releases of specified chemicals to the environment and transfers of these chemicals off-site. The reported data is then made available to the public.

North America has been at the center of these developments, and the North American Commission for Environmental Cooperation (CEC) has played an increasingly important role in this process since its creation, particularly in Canada and Mexico. Indeed, the North American PRTR story is emerging as one of the best examples of upward environmental policy convergence in the post-NAFTA period. Central to this process has been the emergence of a strong trinational policy network around PRTRs, facilitated by the CEC, with members from the governmental, industry, nongovernmental, and academic sectors. Indeed, the CEC PRTR experience demonstrates the importance of such networks in cross-national learning and policy transfer.[1]

This chapter provides an overview of the development and promotion of the PRTR concept and the key uses and audiences for PRTR information that have emerged. It also outlines the development of the PRTR systems in all three North American countries and the impact of the CEC's activities on these processes.

PRTRs: Definitions, Uses, and Audiences

The importance of and potential for PRTRs was recognized in Chapter 19 (on environmentally sound management of toxic chemicals) of Agenda 21, adopted at the June 1992 U.N. Conference on Environment and Development. Agenda 21 encouraged governments to establish emission inventories of toxic chemicals and, in the absence of such requirements, industry to report voluntarily to the public on its emissions.[2] In 1996, the Council of the Organization for Economic Cooperation and Development (OECD), of which Canada, the United States, and Mexico are members, adopted a resolution recommending that member countries take steps to establish, implement, and make publicly available PRTR systems.[3] The OECD has defined a PRTR as follows: "A PRTR is a database or register of chemicals released to air, water and land, and transfers of chemicals off-site. Based on a list of priority chemicals, facilities that release one or more of the listed chemicals report periodically—usually annually—on the amount released and/or transferred, and to which environmental media. Reported data are then made available to the public."[4] The CEC Council further refined this definition in its June 2000 resolution on PRTRs, emphasizing the importance of standardized database structures to facilitate electronic reporting; data collection, analysis, and dissemination; limited data confidentiality; and public disclosure of data on a facility and chemical-specific basis.[5]

Although a tool with obvious potential in environmental management, PRTR systems were a relatively late addition to the range of environmental policy instruments employed by governments. Their full potential has only come to be recognized in the past five years, in large part due to the emergence of the technical capacity in personal computers and the World Wide Web to support the collection, provision of access to, and analysis of PRTR data sets. The data and information generated through PRTR programs can be used for many purposes by governments, nongovernmental organizations, industry, financial institutions, and academe. These include:

(a) the identification of priorities for pollution prevention and control initiatives, such as the major sources of key pollutants;

(b) the evaluation of the impact of existing programs on pollutant generation, releases, and transfers;

(c) the identification of opportunities to prevent pollution and increase efficiencies within industrial facilities;

(d) the identification and characterization of facilities that are major sources of pollution in their host communities and to support community interactions with such facilities to reduce their emissions and waste transfers; and

(e) the evaluation of the efficiency and environmental risks associated with particular facilities to assess investment risks.[6]

The direct impact of the release of PRTR data on facility environmental behavior remains a matter of debate. Claims have been made that PRTRs have outperformed regulatory initiatives in driving reductions in pollutant releases.[7] While there is anecdotal evidence of changes in individual facility performance in response to rankings as large sources of pollutant releases and transfers in PRTR reports,[8] the impact of public PRTR data releases per se, versus other factors such as regulatory initiatives, at the aggregate level is much less certain. On the other hand, the value of PRTR data in the identification of leading sources of priority pollutants, evaluation of program and policy instrument effectiveness, and raising community and facility awareness of emissions that otherwise would not be identified is more firmly established.[9]

International interest in the development and implementation of PRTR continues to grow. A PRTR protocol to the 1998 U.N. Economic Commission for Europe Convention on Access to Information, Public Participation in Decision-Making and Access to Justice in Environmental Matters is under negotiation.[10]

The Evolution of PRTRs in North America

THE U.S. TOXICS RELEASE INVENTORY

The United States was the first country to establish what would come to be called a PRTR. The Toxics Release Inventory (TRI) has served as the model for point-source PRTRs in other countries, such as Canada, Australia, and Mexico.

The TRI was created through Title III of the 1986 Superfund Amendment and Reauthorization Act, known as the Emergency Planning and Community Right to Know Act (EPCRA). The establishment of the TRI was driven by a number of factors. The most immediate considerations were the 1984 Union Carbide methyl isocyanate accident in Bhopal, India, which killed several thousand people, and a serious chemical release at a Union Carbide plant in West Virginia shortly thereafter. At the same time, under pressure from community groups and workers, many state and local governments had begun to adopt community right-to-know measures requiring the release of information on pollutant emissions and the on-site storage of hazardous chemicals.[11]

Section 313 of EPCRA required that certain manufacturing facilities with the equivalent of ten or more full-time employees, that annually manufacture or process more than 25,000 pounds, or otherwise use more than 10,000 pounds, of 340 designated substances report annually to the U.S. Environmental Protection Agency (EPA) and to state governments on their releases to the air, water, or land and on their transfers off-site of waste for treatment or disposal.[12] Data began to be collected from industry from the 1987 calendar year onward. The data is made available to the public through annual summary reports issued by the EPA and state governments, and, more recently, through websites operated by the EPA and a number of nongovernmental organizations.[13]

The immediate impact of the release of the TRI data was substantial. The simple scale and scope of the pollutant releases and transfers captured were themselves the subject of significant attention. Facilities identified as leading sources of pollutant releases and transfers at national, regional, and sectoral levels found themselves the focus of media attention and public concern. This, among other things, drew senior management attention to the issue of facility environmental performance.[14] The availability of TRI data also began to shift the power balance over environmental issues between industrial facilities and host communities by providing detailed, chemical-specific information that permitted comparisons between the performance of local plants and that of facilities in the same sector in other parts of the country.[15]

The 1990 Pollution Prevention Act significantly expanded reporting requirements under the TRI. Beginning with the 1991 reporting year, facilities were required to indicate the amounts of chemicals that they recycled, used for energy recovery, or treated on-site. In addition, facilities were required to indicate what source reduction activities they were implementing.[16]

The further expansion of the TRI was a major commitment for the administration of President Bill Clinton, who came to office in 1993. In 1994, the Clinton administration announced its intention to proceed with a three-stage expansion of the TRI, including the addition of new substances, the expansion of the range of sectors required to report, and the addition of information on substance use by facilities. Implementation of these changes began in the 1995 reporting year, with the introduction of requirements for reporting by all federal facilities and the addition of 286 new substances, including 150 pesticides.[17]

In 1997, seven additional industrial sectors were required to report pollutant releases and transfers, beginning in the 1998 reporting year. These included metal and coal mining, electrical utilities burning coal or oil, hazardous waste treatment and disposal facilities, wholesale distributors of chemicals and allied products, petroleum bulk plants and terminals, and solvent recovery services.[18] The addition of these sectors had a major impact on the profile of pollutant releases reported to the TRI, accounting for 70 percent of releases in the 1998 reporting year.[19] The expansion of the TRI continued with the adoption in October 1999 of a new rule for substances meeting criteria for being persistent, bioaccumulative, and toxic (PBT) chemicals and reducing the reporting thresholds for manufacturing, processing, or otherwise using such substances. In addition, seventeen dioxin and dioxin-like compounds were added, along with seven other PBT chemicals, for the 2000 reporting year.[20] The third phase of the Clinton administration's proposals, to collect data on chemical use, failed to be implemented before the end of the administration's term in 2001.

The TRI program provided the template for PRTR programs subsequently adopted in other countries, including Canada's National Pollutant Release Inventory (NPRI) and Australia's National Pollutant Inventory (NPI). The establishment of the TRI has also made the United States the key center for innovation in terms of public access and use of PRTR data. A number of U.S. environmental nongovernmental organizations have undertaken ambitious projects using the TRI data, most notably the Right-to-Know Network's website, which provides for user-designed TRI data searches, and Environmental Defense's Chemical Scorecard website, which combines pollutant release data with toxicity weightings and geographic information systems.[21] Extensive experience has also been gained with the use of TRI data in addressing industrial pollution issues at the community level.[22]

CANADA'S NATIONAL POLLUTANT RELEASE INVENTORY

Canada has often followed the lead of the United States on environmental policy innovations, and this was very much the case with respect to the NPRI.[23] Interest in the establishment of a PRTR in Canada emerged shortly after the creation of the TRI in the United States in 1986. The Canadian federal government's 1990 national environmental Green Plan committed to the development of a national database of hazardous pollutants being released from industrial and transportation sources. Reporting requirements for industry were to be established by 1992, with the first reports scheduled for public release no later than 1994.[24]

In 1991, the Minister of the Environment established a multistakeholder advisory committee on the development of the inventory, consisting of representatives of industry, environmental and labor organizations, and federal departments and provincial governments. In December 1992, the committee delivered a report recommending an inventory similar in structure to the TRI.[25] An initial list of 178 substances was proposed on the basis of a review of the substances on the TRI and the Canadian Chemical Producers' National Emissions Reduction Master Plan program, retaining those known to be in Canadian commerce.[26]

A Ministerial Order was issued under the Canadian Environmental Protection Act (CEPA 1988) in 1992, which required reporting for the 1993 calendar year. As with the TRI, on-site releases of substances to the air, surface water, or land or for underground injection were required to be reported annually, along with transfers off-site for disposal, treatment, or storage. Reporting of transfers for recovery, reuse, or recycling was mandatory for the first reporting year but became voluntary from 1994 until 1998.[27] Reporting requirements only applied to facilities with the equivalent of ten or more full-time employees and which manufactured, processed, or otherwise used ten tons or more of an NPRI substance per year. Unlike the TRI, reporting requirements applied to all facilities, unless they fell under one of a number of specific exemptions.[28] As the EPA does with the TRI, Environment Canada publishes an annual summary report of the NPRI data and makes the data available to the public through its website.[29]

The next major phase in the development of the NPRI began in 1998 with the creation of a new multistakeholder Work Group on Substances consisting of representatives of industry, environmental nongovernmental organizations, and several provinces. The Work Group's efforts led to the addition of seventy-three new substances to the NPRI for the 1999 reporting year. Among other things, these additions responded to concerns on the part of the federal Commissioner for Environment and Sustainable Development regarding the lack of linkages between the substances listed on NPRI and those identified as policy priorities by the federal government.[30]

The adoption of a revised CEPA by the Canadian Parliament in 1999 (CEPA 1999) provided a clearer statutory basis for the NPRI and established a statutory requirement that the inventory be published on an annual basis.[31] Further expansions of the NPRI occurred in the 2000 reporting year, with the inclusion of new substances including dioxins, furans, hexachlorobenzene, and seventeen polycyclic aromatic hydrocarbons. In addition, the reporting threshold for mercury was lowered to 5 kg and the employee threshold eliminated for certain sources.[32]

Criteria air pollutants—nitrogen oxides, sulfur dioxide, carbon monoxide, total volatile organic compounds (VOCs), total particulate matter (TPM), particulate matter less than 10 microns (PM10), and particulate matter less than 2.5 microns (PM2.5)—were added to the inventory for the 2002 reporting year in December 2001. The Minister of the Environment has stated his intention to add greenhouse gases (carbon dioxide, methane, nitrous oxide, hydrofluorocarbons, and perfluorocarbons) to the NPRI in the near future.[33] These proposals flowed from the October 2000 Ozone Annex to the 1991 Canada-U.S. Air Quality Agreement and the Kyoto Protocol on Climate Change.

Progress on the development of the NPRI has accelerated rapidly since the reestablishment of the multistakeholder Work Group on Substances. This progress has reflected a growing recognition within Environment Canada at the political and official levels of the potential value of the NPRI, particularly in terms of identifying and tracking sources of priority pollutants. In addition, following the lead of their U.S. counterparts, Canadian environmental nongovernmental organizations have begun to make creative use of NPRI data, most notably through the creation of a Canadian version of Environmental Defense's Chemical Scorecard, called pollutionwatch.[34]

MEXICO'S REGISTRO DE EMISIONES Y TRANSFERENCIA DE CONTAMINANTES

As in the United States, the concept of developing a PRTR for Mexico flowed from a number of sources. Drawing on U.S. experience with the TRI, in the late 1980s nongovernmental organizations on the U.S.-Mexico border began to express the need for a publicly accessible pollutant inventory in Mexico as a result of concerns over the environmental impacts of increased economic activity resulting from reduced barriers to trade.[35] These pressures were reinforced by the provisions of Agenda 21 encouraging the establishment of national PRTR programs. In early 1994, the United Nations Institute for Training and Research, in cooperation with other U.N. agencies and the OECD, initiated pilot projects in Mexico, Egypt, and the Czech Republic to facilitate the establishment of national PRTR systems. The Mexican initiative took the name Registro de Emisiones y Transferencia de Contaminantes (RETC), with the National Institute of Ecology (Instituto Nacional de Ecología [INE]) acting as the focal point.[36]

INE established the National Coordinating Group (Grupo Nacional Coordinador), a consultative forum of thirty-eight governmental, industrial, academic, and nongovernmental organizations, which met over two years to design the technical, administrative, and legal infrastructure for the RETC.[37] As part of the project, in 1995–96 an RETC pilot trial was conducted in the State of Querétaro. Eighty facilities were invited to participate in the project, and fifty-one completed the reporting forms. The information received varied widely in quality, however, largely due to lack of experience in estimating and reporting releases.[38] In addition, in 1996 amendments were made to Mexico's Ley General del Equilibrio Ecológico y la Protección al Ambiente (LGEEPA) establishing the public's right to access to environmental information held by the government.[39]

The National Coordinating Group completed a National Executive Proposal for the RETC in March 1997. Under this proposal, the RETC would require reporting from facilities under federal jurisdiction with thirty or more full-time employees that manufactured, processed, or otherwise used any of 178 chemicals on the RETC list.[40] However, a number of important issues remained unresolved, particularly how the public would access information gathered through RETC reporting and whether facility-specific information was to be made publicly available.[41]

In April 1997, the Mexican environment department (Secretaría de Medio Ambiente, Recursos Naturales y Pesca—SEMARNAP) announced a new integrated system for the environmental regulation of industrial facilities under federal jurisdiction. One of the key elements of this system, which was adopted in April 1998, was a requirement that facilities obtain an annual certificate of operation (Cédula de Operación Anual—COA). Under the COA, facilities are required to report annually on their air emissions of sulfur dioxide, nitrogen dioxide, hydrocarbons from combustion, carbon monoxide, carbon dioxide, particulates, and VOCs. However, reporting of releases and transfers of the 178 RETC pollutants under the COA was voluntary. SEMARNAP identified the lack of a legal list of chemicals to be reported under the RETC as a key barrier to the implementation of mandatory reporting,[42] although resistance from key economic agencies of the government may also have been an important factor.

The first RETC report, issued in December 1999, did not contain data reported under the RETC but rather presented a summary of information from a number of different programs on criteria air pollutants and greenhouse gases, wastewater discharge volumes, and hazardous waste generation. The voluntary status of the RETC emerged as a significant weakness. In the first year of reporting (1997), fewer than 5 percent of facilities under federal jurisdiction completed the RETC component of their COA reports. Similar results were seen in the 1998 reporting year. Interviews conducted by consultants working in cooperation with INE with a number of Mexican facilities in 2000 indicated that the lack of a mandatory reporting requirement was the major reason for not reporting pollutant releases and transfers.[43]

In September 2000, INE issued a draft voluntary standard for the RETC, establishing the applicability of RETC reporting to facilities and setting out a list of 104 substances for which releases and transfers would be reported, reporting thresholds based on annual use, the reporting format (via the COA), and the rationale for the listed substances. INE, together with the Comité Nacional de Normalización para la Protección Ambiental, finalized and approved the standard in December 2000. Under the standard, information provided by facilities was to be used for statistical purposes only and not considered evidence before any administrative or fiscal agency or administrative tribunal. The information made publicly available would not be facility-specific. Rather, it would be released on a sectoral, geographic, or chemical-specific basis.[44]

The change in government in Mexico following the election of President Vicente Fox opened a new chapter in the RETC story. Victor Lichtinger, the former Executive Director of the CEC, was appointed Secretary for Environment and Natural Resources in December 2000. On June 5, 2001, Secretary Lichtinger publicly stated his support for a public and mandatory RETC.[45] The Mexican government's commitment to seek legislation to establish a mandatory reporting system for pollutant releases and transfers was reiterated at the eighth regular session of the CEC Council in Guadalajara, Mexico, later that month.[46]

On October 4, 2001, an executive proposal was made to the Chamber of Deputies of the Mexican Congress for amendments to LGEEPA. The proposal required the Secretaría de Medio Ambiente y Recursos Naturales (SEMARNAT) (the successor to SEMARNAP), as well as states, municipalities, and the federal district, to compile a registry of emissions and transfers of contaminants to the air, water, and land and transfers of wastes under their jurisdiction. The inclusion of other levels of government was intended to ensure coverage of facilities outside federal jurisdiction. The amendment also required public access to the information gathered through the registry.[47] However, the proposed amendments did not require mandatory reporting by facilities.

Following a November meeting between Secretary Lichtinger and a number of Mexican environmental organizations, the proposed legislation was amended to include provisions requiring mandatory reporting.[48] The amended proposals were approved by the Mexican legislature and came into force on January 1, 2002. Although implementation of the RETC has yet to be completed, these events have now set the stage for the establishment of the third mandatory PRTR system in North America.

The Role of the CEC

The impact of the CEC on the evolution of PRTRs and use of information generated through these systems in North America has been significant. Article 10(2)(a) of the North American Agreement on Environmental Cooperation (NAAEC) states that the CEC Council may consider, and develop recommendations regarding, the comparability of techniques and methodologies for data gathering and analysis, data management, and electronic data communications on matters covered by the NAAEC. PRTRs were an early focus of the Commission's attention in this regard.

The CEC Council committed to the creation of a North American Pollutant Release Inventory at its second annual regular session in 1995. This commitment was reiterated in 1996, with the intention of helping to improve the quality of the environment by providing the public with information to assess North American pollutant sources and risks.[49] In June 1997, the Council adopted a resolution committing the three governments to work toward more comparable PRTRs and to continue to cooperate with the CEC in the preparation of an annual North American PRTR report. The resolution recognized the goal of a higher degree of comparability among PRTRs, but, perhaps reflecting the uncertain status of Mexico's RETC, the resolution also noted that each national PRTR program had developed unique processes for the collection and management of data.[50]

Two major CEC activities have flowed from these commitments and resolutions: ongoing PRTR capacity building to government agencies, industry, and nongovernmental organizations in Mexico to support the development and implementation of the RETC; and the publication of the annual *Taking Stock* report on North American pollutant releases and transfers. In fact, the *Taking Stock* report has emerged as a flagship publication of the Commission.

PRTR CAPACITY BUILDING IN MEXICO

The development of the RETC in Mexico has been a major focus of the CEC's PRTR program. Indeed, encouraging the completion of the RETC was a major purpose of the original 1997 CEC Council resolution on PRTRs. Subsequently, the CEC Council was a consistent source of pressure on Mexico to implement a mandatory PRTR system. The communiqué from the Council's sixth meeting in June 1999 emphasized the goal of mandatory reporting for all nations, and a June 2000 Council resolution stressed the need for both mandatory reporting and public disclosure of reported data on a facility- and chemical-specific basis.[51]

In addition to these efforts at the political level, the CEC has provided support to INE for such purposes as outreach and training, including the development of technical guidance for industry. Assistance has also been provided for seminars in major cities in Mexico, organized in cooperation with INE, to promote industrial reporting of RETC data by industry and to identify and overcome barriers to reporting.[52] The CEC's North American Fund for Environmental Cooperation has provided support to Mexican nongovernmental organizations in order to develop their capacity to access and use PRTR data.

These activities facilitated the emergence of a very strong trinational nongovernmental organization network around PRTR issues in North America. This was an important factor in providing ongoing practical and political support to Mexican nongovernmental organizations working to advance the RETC. Activities associated with the CEC PRTR program, such as workshops and the trinational annual consultative meetings on the program, also provided opportunities for nongovernmental constituencies to reinforce the Mexican government's commitments regarding the development and implementation of a PRTR system. Program stakeholder meetings have brought Canadian and U.S. government and industry experience with the NPRI and TRI to the table in Mexico and were important mechanisms for addressing industry concerns regarding potential community responses to the release of PRTR data. In effect, the CEC processes provided an alternative venue for policy actors blocked domestically in Mexico on the establishment of a mandatory PRTR.[53]

TAKING STOCK AND ITS IMPACT ON PRTRS IN NORTH AMERICA

The CEC published its first *Taking Stock* report in July 1997, using 1994 TRI and NPRI Data.[54] At the report's core was a series of analyses, developed using a matched data set of substances and sectors from the Canadian and U.S. inventories, ranking provinces, states, and facilities in terms of their pollutant releases and transfers. A description of developments regarding the RETC in Mexico was also provided, although no Mexican data was available to be included in the report.

The report's release had little impact in the United States, as it reflected the EPA's standard practices with the annual public release of TRI data, which included ranking states and facilities on the basis of their pollutant releases and transfers. The story in Canada was very different. The report attracted a very high level of media and public attention, and it was the subject of significant criticism by certain provincial governments and industries.[55]

There were a number of reasons for this response in Canada. *Taking Stock* provided analyses of the NPRI data that had not been undertaken by Environment Canada and were at that point beyond the capacity of Canadian environmental nongovernmental organizations to conduct themselves. The annual summary reports issued by Environment Canada to accompany each year's NPRI data release had been limited to aggregate provincial-level data, and indications of facility performance were on an individual substance release basis only. Comparative analyses of facility and jurisdictional performance had not been provided. As a result, these elements of the *Taking Stock* report proved to be a major focus of media and public attention in Canada, as they placed the environmental performance of provincial governments and local facilities in a wider comparative context.

Taking Stock also provided the first truly comprehensive analysis of the environmental performance of Canadian provinces and facilities relative to their U.S. counterparts.[56] The consistent ranking of the province of Ontario as among the top four largest sources of total pollutant releases and transfers in Canada and the United States drew particular attention.[57] The media and public focus on Ontario was in part a function of the aggressive and controversial program of environmental deregulation and dramatic reductions in the funding of environmental agencies being undertaken by the provincial government at the time.[58] The apparent poor performance of Canadian facilities relative to U.S. counterparts, with Canadian facilities consistently reporting approximately 1.4 times the total releases and transfers of pollutants of U.S. facilities, also drew considerable attention.[59] This difference in performance was widely interpreted as a reflection of a weaker regulatory regime in Canada, particularly at the federal level, relative to the United States.[60]

Given these impacts, the report prompted very strong adverse reactions from some Canadian industry sectors and provincial governments, especially Ontario.[61] The practice of ranking jurisdictional and facility performance, especially on the basis of aggregate releases and total releases and transfers, was the major target of these attacks.[62] Changes were made to subsequent *Taking Stock* reports, particularly through the addition of disaggregated analyses of specific classes of pollutants, such as recognized or suspected carcinogens, in response to these concerns. However, the basic structure of the *Taking Stock* report remained unchanged. The strong support from the EPA for the Commission's approach to the report was an important factor in this outcome, and the CEC Council's June 2000 resolution on PRTR reaffirmed political commitment to the report in all three countries.[63]

Despite the controversies surrounding their publication in Canada, the *Taking Stock* reports had a very strong positive impact on the profile, development, and use of the NPRI. Prior to the publication of the first *Taking Stock* report in 1997, the NPRI had drawn little public or media attention, and knowledge about its existence and potential uses was limited to a few highly specialized constituencies. The *Taking Stock* reports demonstrated to a wide variety of audiences the availability through NPRI of community- and facility-specific information and the potential range of analyses that could be performed with the data generated through the program.[64]

Analyses within the *Taking Stock* reports highlighted, for example, the positive impact on pollutant releases of the adoption of new discharge regulations on the pulp and paper sector by the federal and provincial governments in the early 1990s. These accounted in large measure for a 65 percent reduction in reported surface water discharges by Canadian facilities between 1995 and 1998.[65] The report also highlighted the very limited effects of the federal government's high-profile voluntary Accelerated Reduction and Elimination of Toxics (ARET) program, initiated in 1994.[66] In addition, prompted in part by the impact of the CEC reports, the government of

Ontario decided in 1998 to establish its own emission inventory. The Ontario program is limited to air releases, but it covers a wider range of substances than does the NPRI, including criteria air pollutants, greenhouse gases, and seventy-nine toxic substances over and above the NPRI list.[67]

As has been the case in the United States with the TRI, Canadian industry has generally come to accept the *Taking Stock* report, particularly in the context of the June 2000 CEC Council resolution reaffirming the parties' commitment to the undertaking. The emergence of nongovernmental organization projects that involve ranking industrial facilities on the basis of NPRI data, such as the pollutionwatch website, has also had the effect of reducing the focus on the CEC's work. And the addition of data for the electric power generation sector in the 1998 report, released in July 2001, shifted some of the media attention toward U.S. rather than Canadian sources.[68]

Although the CEC Council's original 1995 vision of a North American Pollutant Release Inventory remains incomplete pending implementation of the RETC in Mexico, the Commission has recently completed its own PRTR website, which permits user-designed searches of the TRI and NPRI databases.[69] In addition to their impact on the development and use of PRTR data in Canada and Mexico, the *Taking Stock* reports also identified a number of important trends in the NPRI and TRI data. The most pronounced of these have been a 12 percent reduction between 1995 and 1998 in direct on-site releases of pollutants to the air, water, and land but a 35 percent increase in transfers of pollutants off-site to disposal and an 11 percent increase in transfers off-site for further treatment. The trend toward reduced direct releases and dramatic increases in transfers off-site for disposal and treatment is evident in both Canada and the United States. The net result has only been a 2 percent reduction in total releases and transfers (and, by implication, generation) of reported pollutants within the matched data set used for the report, suggesting that Canadian and U.S. facilities continue to focus on the installation of end-of-process pollution control technologies rather than the adoption of pollution prevention measures.[70]

Conclusions

The North American PRTR story has emerged as one of positive policy convergence and upward harmonization in environmental policies. The CEC has played no small role in this outcome. It has facilitated the emergence of a continental policy network around PRTRs, consisting of governmental, industrial, nongovernmental, and academic sectors from Canada, Mexico, and the United States. It has also acted as a catalyst for strong networking among PRTR officials in all three countries.

In Canada, the Commission's work, particularly the *Taking Stock* report series, has drawn public attention to the existence of the NPRI and the kinds of information available through it, particularly at the local level. The CEC has also demonstrated the types of analyses possible using the data generated through the inventory, including identification of leading sources of priority pollutants and assessment of the effectiveness of governmental policy initiatives, such as the introduction of new regulations or voluntary initiatives.

It is doubtful whether the RETC would have reached its current status, with the amendments to the LGEEPA adopted in December 2001, without the interventions of the Commission. The CEC provided a forum in which the concept of a mandatory PRTR providing publicly accessible chemical and facility-specific information was kept alive, reinforced this direction through Council resolutions, and worked to build capacity to implement and use the RETC in the governmental, industry, and nongovernmental sectors in Mexico. Although the final chapter in the RETC story remains to be written, the Commission has played a central role in its development.

The CEC PRTR experience demonstrates the importance of international policy commitments to domestic environmental policy, as well as the impact of innovations by governments and nongovernmental organizations in one jurisdiction on others. The development of strong networks of contacts among key actors in each jurisdiction has been an important factor in the latter process, and the CEC has played a central role in their development in the North American PRTR case.

In addition, the placement of jurisdictions in an explicitly comparative context, as occurred through both the *Taking Stock* reports and the annual consultative meetings around the CEC PRTR program, has promoted domestic policy debates in lagging jurisdictions about the reasons for these outcomes and encouraged the upward movement of policies and requirements. This has been particularly true in Canada and Mexico.

The PRTR case demonstrates the CEC's success as a regional environmental organization. It has functioned as a provider of environmental analyses and information at the continental and local levels that were not otherwise available, either within governments or to the public; as the convener and focal point for an international policy network involving governments, industry, and nongovernmental organizations; and as a source of political and practical support for the development of Mexico's RETC. In carrying out these roles, the CEC has been a central catalyst in the evolution and convergence of PRTR systems in North America.

Notes

The author would like to thank a number of individuals for their assistance in the development of this chapter, particularly Marisa Jacott with El Programa Laneta in Mexico City and Paul Orum with the Working Group on Community Right to Know in Washington, D.C.

1. On the importance of transnational policy networks to policy learning and convergence, see M. Howlett, "Complex Network Management and Governance of the Environment," in *Governing the Environment: Persistent Challenges, Uncertain Innovations* (E. Parsons ed., 2001).

2. Agenda 21, ch. 19 ("Environmentally Sound Management of Toxic Chemicals Including Prevention of Illegal International Traffic in Toxic and Dangerous Products"), ¶¶ 19.49(b), 19.50(c), Report of the United Nations Conference on Environment and Development, June 14, 1992, reprinted in *Agenda 21: The United Nations Programme of Action from Rio*, UN Sales No. E.93.I.11.

3. OECD Council, Recommendation on Implementing Pollutant Release and Transfer Registries, C(96)41/Final (Feb. 20, 1996).

4. OECD Environment Directorate, "Why Pollutant Release and Transfer Registers (PRTRs) Differ: A Review of National Programmes," ENV/JM/MOMO (2001) 16 (Dec. 6, 2001), at 12.

5. CEC Council Resolution 00-07, June 13, 2000.

6. OECD Environment Directorate, "Presentation and Dissemination of PRTR Data: Practices and Experiences/Getting the Words and Numbers Out," ENV/JM/MONO (2000)17 (Jan. 30, 2001), at 17.

7. See, e.g., Archon Fung and Dara O'Rourke, "Reinventing Environmental Regulation from the Grassroots up: Explaining and Expanding the Success of the Toxics Release Inventory," 25 *Environmental Management* 115–27 (2000).

8. See, e.g., "CO-STEEL LASCO, and Changes in the CEC's Taking Stock 1999 Report" (Nov. 2001) (briefing note prepared by CO-STEEL LASCO, a steel mill in Whitby, Ontario, which was identified as the leading source of pollutant releases and transfers in the early *Taking Stock* reports).

9. See, e.g., Kathryn Harrison and Werner Antweiler, "Environmental Regulation vs. Environmental Information: A View from Canada's National Pollutant Release Inventory," working paper, University of British Columbia (Jan. 2001); Wilma Subra, "Evaluating the Role of a Pollutant Release Transfer Registry at the Community Level," Proceedings of the OECD International Conference on Pollutant Release and Transfer Programs, PRTRs: Global and National Responsibility, Tokyo, Japan (Sept. 1998), OECD Environment Directorate Doc. ENV/JM/MONO (1999) 16/PART1 (hereafter OECD PRTR Conference).

10. Although Canada and the United States are members of the U.N. Economic Commission for Europe, they have not signed the convention. They are participating in discussions regarding the PRTR protocol, however.

11. See, e.g., Caron Chess, *Winning the Right-to-Know: A Handbook for Toxics Activists* (1984), regarding the adoption of right-to-know legislation by the Philadelphia City Council in 1981. By 1986, it is estimated that approximately half of U.S. states

had a worker or community right-to-know law. Paul Orum, "Right-to-Know in the United States: Some Successful Aspects" (presentation to the CEC Workshop on Forging Alliances to Prevent Industrial Pollution, Tijuana, Baja California, Nov. 6, 2000).

12. EPA, "What Is the Toxics Release Inventory?" available at *http://www.epa.gov/tri/general.htm*.

13. See, e.g., EPA, "The 1999 Public Data Release Report," available at *http://www.epa.gov/tri/tri99/pdr/index.htm*. See also *http://www.epa.gov/triexplorer/* and *http://d1.rtknet.org/tri/*.

14. Some examples of industry comments: the 1987 TRI data "shocked a lot of industry folks, the magnitude of these releases. It really hit home. People from boardrooms all the way down to plants recognized they had to get aggressive and try to find ways to reduce these emissions," Dan Borne, Louisiana Chemical Association, quoted in *New Orleans Times-Picayune*, Feb. 17, 1991; "It genuinely bothered me . . . we said, 'if there's going to be a list, we don't want to be on it.' Right there, I made a decision: we were either going to improve or get out of this business," Cyrus Jaffari, Caspian Inc., quoted in Amy Wallace, "Air-Polluter Rankings Prompts Firm to Clean Up Environment: Some Find that Reducing Toxics Can Even Be Good for Business," *Los Angeles Times*, Dec. 9, 1991.

15. See, e.g., Subra, supra.

16. EPA, "Pollution Prevention and the TRI," available at *http://www.epa.gov/tri/general.htm*.

17. CEC, *Taking Stock 1995*, 7 (1998). The *Taking Stock* series and other CEC publications are available at *http://www.cec.org*.

18. See EPA, "Standard Industrial Classification (SIC) Codes in TRI Reporting," available at *http://www.epa.gov/tri/report/siccode.htm*.

19. EPA, *1999 Toxics Release Inventory* (April 2001), available at *http://www.epa.gov/tri/tridata/tri99/pdr/1999pdr.pdf*.

20. CEC, *Taking Stock 1998*, 7 (2001).

21. The address of the Right-to-Know Network's website is *http://d1.rtknet.org/tri*, and the Chemical Scorecard website is at *http://www.scorecard.org*.

22. See, e.g., Subra, supra.

23. See, e.g., George Hoberg, "Governing the Environment: Comparing Policy in Canada and the United States," in *Degrees of Freedom: Canada and the United States in a Changing World* (Keith Banting, George Hoberg, and Richard Simeon eds., 1997).

24. Government of Canada, *Canada's Green Plan* (1990), 49.

25. "A National Pollutant Release Inventory for Canada: Final Report of the Multi-Stakeholder Advisory Committee" (1992).

26. Environment Canada, 1994 Summary Report: National Pollutant Release Inventory, at 2.

27. Id., 9.

28. These include facilities engaged in education; training, research, or testing; vehicle maintenance and repair; the distribution, storage, or sale of fuels; the retail or wholesale sale of listed substances or products containing listed substances; the grow-

ing, harvesting, or management of renewable resources; mining; and the drilling and operation of oil and gas wells. Id., 1.

29. See "On-line Search of the NPRI Database," available at *http://www.ec.gc.ca/pdb/npri/npri_dat_rep_e.cfm#search.*

30. Commissioner for Environment and Sustainable Development, "Managing the Risks of Toxic Substances: Obstacles to Progress," ch. 4, in *1999 Report to the House of Commons,* ¶¶ 4.129–34. The Commissioner is attached to the Office of the Auditor General of Canada and is mandated to report to Parliament on the performance of the federal government with respect to the environment and sustainable development.

31. Canadian Environmental Protection Act, R.S.C., § 48 1 (1999).

32. *Taking Stock 1998,* supra, 8. These included biomedical and nonhazardous waste incinerators burning over 100 tons of waste per year, hazardous waste and sewage sludge incinerators, and wood preservation facilities.

33. See Environment Canada, *Providing Cleaner Air to Canadians* (Feb. 2001).

34. See *http://www.scorecard.org/pollutionwatch.*

35. Laura Durazo, "Challenges and Opportunities of Meeting Public Needs through NGO Involvement in the PRTR System in Mexico" (paper presented at OECD PRTR Conference, supra).

36. L. Sanchez-Catano, Rina Aguirre, and Hilda Martinez, "Design and Implementation of the Mexican Pollutant Release and Transfer Register (PRTR)" (paper presented at OECD PRTR Conference, supra).

37. CEC, *Taking Stock 1997,* 10 (1999).

38. For a detailed summary of the Querétaro project, see CEC, *Taking Stock 1994,* ch. 8 (1997).

39. Ley General del Equilibrio Ecológico y la Protección al Ambiente, art. 159 bis, *Diario Oficial de la Federación* (Jan. 28, 1988; amended Dec. 13, 1996). See also Durazo, supra.

40. This covers eleven sectors, including petroleum, chemical and petrochemical, paints and dyes, metallurgy (including iron and steel), automobile manufacture, cellulose and paper, cement and limestone, asbestos, glass, electric power generation, and hazardous waste management.

41. CEC, Background Paper for Roundtable Discussion of PRTR Reporting in Mexico, 4 (Mar. 2001).

42. CEC, *Taking Stock 1996,* 7–9 (1999).

43. CEC, Background Paper, supra.

44. Id., 3.

45. Anuncia Víctor Lichtinger Nueva Política de la SEMARNAT en Materia de Transparencia y Acceso a la Información (June 2001), available at *http://www.semarnat.gob.mx/comunicacionsocial/boletines_2002_105.shtml.*

46. See CEC Council Communiqué, June 29, 2001.

47. "Indiciativa de Decreto," LGEEPA art. 109 bis, *Gaceta Cámara de Deputados* (Oct. 4, 2001).

48. Marisa Jacott, "Cronología Sobre el Desarrollo de RETC," Jan. 27, 2002 (unpublished research note, prepared for El Programa Laneta, Mexico City). The legis-

lation was amended through the Ecology Commission (Committee) of the Chamber of Deputies.

49. CEC, *Taking Stock 1994* (1997), 9.

50. CEC Council Resolution 97-04, June 12, 1997.

51. *Taking Stock 1997*, supra, 5; CEC Council Resolution 00-07, supra.

52. CEC, Background Paper, supra, 8.

53. On the role of international institutions in this sense, see Miles Kahler, *International Institutions and the Political Economy of Integration* (1995). See also Steven Bernstein and Benjamin Cashore, "Globalization, Four Paths of Internationalization, and Domestic Policy Change: The Case of Eco-Forestry in British Columbia," 33 *Canadian Journal of Political Science* 67–100 (2000).

54. *Taking Stock 1994*, supra.

55. See, e.g., "Ontario among Top Polluters," *Globe and Mail* (Toronto), July 29, 1997; "Canada 'Outspews' the US," *Ottawa Citizen*, July 29, 1997.

56. The Canada-U.S. International Joint Commission attempted to undertake comparisons of facility performance in the Great Lakes basin in the context of differing regulatory regimes in the 1980s but found that the data sources then available could not support such an analysis.

57. See, e.g., Barrie McKenna, "Ontario Third-Worst Industrial Polluter," *Globe and Mail* (Toronto), May 31, 2000.

58. See Mark Winfield and Greg Jenish, *Ontario's Environment and the "Common Sense Revolution"* (1999).

59. See *Taking Stock 1996*, supra, table 5-49; *Taking Stock 1997*, supra, table 5-28, *Taking Stock 1998*, supra, table 6-44. See also *Taking Stock 1996*, supra, 180, for a discussion of the potential reasons for these differences in performance. Analysis by the CEC indicates that the ratio is due to differences in facility performance rather than reporting formats or average facility size.

60. See, e.g., Sue Bailey, "Ontario Continues to Make Its Toxic Mark Because of Weak Green Laws, Environmental Activists Charge," *C.P. Wire*, Aug. 10, 1999.

61. "Pollution Report Slams Steel Giants," *Hamilton (Ontario) Spectator*, Aug. 11, 1999. The province's attacks also targeted the NPRI. See Ontario Ministry of the Environment, "National Pollutant Release Inventory: A Seriously Flawed Document," press release, July 28, 1998.

62. CEC, "Response to Comments on Draft North American Report on Pollutant Release and Transfers (1994 data)," 7 (1997); CEC, "Response to Comments Received on the Development of the 1998 Taking Stock Report," May 31, 2000.

63. CEC Council Resolution 00-07, supra.

64. Editorial, "Now We Know Who Pollutes," *Toronto Star*, Aug. 11, 1999.

65. See *Taking Stock 1995*, supra, ch. 8; *Taking Stock 1998*, supra, table 6-1.

66. See *Taking Stock 1996*, supra, table 7-5.

67. For more information, see the website on the program maintained by the Ontario Ministry of Environment and Energy: *http://www.ene.gov.on.ca/envision/monitoring/monitoring.htm*.

68. Associated Press, "Report: Electricity Plants Top List of Industrial Polluters," *East Valley (Arizona) Tribune*, July 22, 2001.

69. The address is *http://www.cec.org/takingstock/querybuilder/index.cfm?varlan=english.*

70. *Taking Stock 1998*, supra, table 6-42. Under the NPRI there is some potential for double counting of transfers as releases at receiving facilities. However, release data from hazardous waste receivers was not included in the matched data set used by the CEC for these analyses over time, as hazardous waste facilities did not begin to report releases and transfers to the TRI until 1998.

ROBERT L. GLICKSMAN **4**

The CEC's Biodiversity Conservation Agenda

IN ADDRESSING threats to continental biodiversity, the North American Commission for Environmental Cooperation (CEC), established by the North American Agreement on Environmental Cooperation (NAAEC),[1] has its work cut out for it. A draft report prepared for the CEC in 1999 describes the problem as a series of "downward spirals affecting the continent's biological wealth" that have "led to a crisis that is unprecedented and not confined to any one country or region."[2] Land development and habitat fragmentation have adversely affected both large predators and the species on which they depend. Overfishing, marine pollution, and dam building have taken a severe toll on marine and freshwater habitats.[3] The resulting biodiversity crisis has produced a "cascading" or "ripple" effect, affecting individual species, the ecosystems in which they live, and the economies of the three North American nations experiencing these problems.[4] According to another recent CEC report, the continent "has experienced some of the most dramatic landscape transformations and reductions in species abundance of any part of the world."[5] Yet, the 1999 draft report continues, in each of the three countries the science of managing and restoring large-scale ecosystems is extremely inadequate. Institutional mechanisms for achieving such management and restoration are similarly deficient. The growing realization that the practice of setting aside isolated protected areas will not yield effective biodiversity conservation has not yet produced sufficient substantive action to protect North America's biological heritage.

This chapter surveys the role of the CEC in protecting continental biodiversity. After defining the concept of biodiversity and describing the threats to biodiversity and their consequences, the chapter focuses on the powers of the CEC as they relate to the task of biodiversity protection as well as the manner in which the agency has exercised those powers. The chapter concludes with an assessment of the CEC's biodiversity protection initiatives, past and future. It suggests that the CEC may play a useful role in surveying the natural resources at risk in Canada, the United States, and Mexico, characterizing what action is needed to protect biodiversity, developing plans to meet those needs, and assisting in the implementation of those plans by existing domestic and international institutions. The CEC's objectives should include prompting a strengthening of domestic environmental enforcement mechanisms, the adoption of more protective substantive domestic environmental laws, and the development of new or more effective international cooperative mechanisms. The cross-boundary nature of many threats to biodiversity, coupled with the CEC's lack of independent lawmaking and enforcement authority, makes many of these changes problematic, particularly those that relate to changes in substantive domestic environmental protection laws. The CEC can nevertheless play a useful role developing standards for national or local implementation and assisting in the establishment of transboundary partnerships for biodiversity protection.

The Nature and Importance of Biodiversity Protection

The Convention on Biological Diversity (CBD) defines biological diversity as "the variability among living organisms from all sources including, *inter alia*, terrestrial, marine and other aquatic ecosystems and the ecological complexes of which they are a part; this includes diversity within species, between species and of ecosystems."[6] Five years before the execution of the CBD, the U.S. Office of Technology Assessment produced a similar definition:

> Biological diversity refers to the variety and variability among living organisms and the ecological complexes in which they occur. Diversity can be defined as the number of different items and their relative frequency. For biological diversity, these items are organized at many levels, ranging from complete ecosystems to the chemical structures that are the molecular basis of heredity. Thus, the term encompasses different ecosystems, species, genes, and their relative abundance.[7]

Genetic diversity deals with genetic variation among members of the same species. Species diversity refers to the variety of species within an ecosystem. Ecological diversity relates to the variety of biological communities found on the planet.[8]

According to Dan Tarlock, scientists are developing a set of measures for biodiversity on various scales to generate information about the status of ecological trends and about progress in meeting biodiversity protection objectives.[9] These measures have shown that global biological diversity is declining at an ever-increasing rate.[10] Conditions and activities such as conversion of land to economically productive uses, habitat loss and fragmentation, pollution, global climate change, overharvesting, resource management efforts, and the introduction of nonnative species have contributed to the estimated extinction of thousands of species each year.[11]

Efforts to prevent such losses can be justified on utilitarian, aesthetic, and moral grounds.[12] Individual species can provide a source of food, medicine, and specialty chemicals. Natural ecosystems provide an array of services, which include watershed protection, local climate regulation, pollution absorption, soil maintenance, flood control, energy production, nutrient recycling, and water purification.[13] Because of our ignorance of the relationships among various components of the environment, the protection of biodiversity can be viewed as "an insurance policy against future catastrophes" or against "declines in beneficial services and interactions."[14] Aesthetic value is derived at the genetic, species, and ecosystem levels.[15] To some, ethical and religious arguments in favor of biodiversity protection transcend both the utilitarian and aesthetic justifications.[16] In this view, humans have an ethical obligation not to destroy nonhuman living organisms that have, if not rights, then at least intrinsic value.

International Biodiversity Protection Measures

The efforts of the CEC to protect continental biodiversity have not occurred in a vacuum. The international community has adopted a variety of measures whose purpose or effect was the preservation of biodiversity. These include regional wildlife protection agreements and measures to protect habitat types that extended beyond national or even regional boundaries.[17] Two events at the U.N. Conference on Environment and Development (the Earth Summit) in Rio de Janeiro in June 1992 focused international attention even more directly on the need to protect biological diversity. The first was the execution of Agenda 21, which includes a specific chapter on biodiversity protection as well as separate sets of provisions that relate to protection of specific ecosystems such as oceans, mountain systems, deserts, and forests.[18] "[A]ll the chapters in Agenda 21 hold promise, directly or indirectly, as avenues through which to promote the conservation, sustainable use, and benefit sharing of biodiversity."[19]

The second was the adoption of the CBD, a framework agreement that established "an international legal structure for a coordinated response to the loss of biological diversity."[20] The CBD characterizes the conservation of biological diversity as "a common concern of humankind" and makes states party to it responsible for conserving their biological diversity and using biological resources in a sustainable manner. The agreement imposes environmental assessment responsibilities, seeks to facilitate information exchanges, and encourages the execution of bilateral, regional, or multilateral arrangements to mitigate activities within one country with adverse effects on the biological diversity of another.

In some respects, the CBD creates a framework for protecting global biodiversity that is akin to that put in place by the NAAEC for the conservation of North American biodiversity. By defining objectives, the CBD may encourage the execution of legal instruments that contain binding obligations. If so, it may provide a starting point for meaningful action to conserve biodiversity by establishing "a conceptual framework for national and international implementation and management actions."[21] The remainder of this chapter analyzes whether the NAAEC effectively creates similar mechanisms for biodiversity protection on a continental level. The fact that the United States is not a party to the CBD (although Canada and Mexico are) makes the NAAEC particularly important as a device for achieving effective conservation of North American biological diversity.

The Role of the CEC in Protecting Biodiversity

Even though the NAAEC never specifically mentions biodiversity, there is no doubt that its objectives are sufficiently broad to support biodiversity protection efforts. President Clinton recognized as much when, in a 1994 executive order, he mandated that the NAAEC be implemented "to advance . . . ecosystem protection . . . and biodiversity preservation."[22] Further, the NAAEC's delegations of authority to the CEC provide a clear basis upon which the CEC may premise activities whose goal is the conservation of biological diversity. Article 10(2) authorizes the CEC to sponsor efforts to facilitate joint collection, assessment, and dissemination of databases on matters such as the existing state of continental biological diversity. Article 10(2) also authorizes CEC recommendations on transboundary and border issues and potentially harmful exotic species.[23] Exotic species can threaten biodiversity by killing native species, and a host of activities (such as pollution) that occur in the territory of one Party may result in threats to biodiversity in another Party. Finally, the NAAEC enables the CEC to make recommendations on the conservation and protection of wild flora and fauna and their habitat and on specially protected areas, as well as on the protection of endangered and threatened species.

Article 13 authorizes the CEC Secretariat to prepare a report for the CEC Council on any matter within the scope of the annual program, one of whose principal topics is always conservation of biodiversity.[24] The Secretariat may prepare a report on "any other environmental matter related to the cooperative functions" of the NAAEC (other than issues related to whether a Party has failed to enforce its environmental laws) upon notification to the CEC and absent the Council's objection.[25] The Secretariat has taken advantage of this authority to commission and issue reports on topics directly relevant to biodiversity protection. In 1995, the Secretariat submitted to the Council a report on the mass mortality of migratory waterbirds experienced the previous winter in the Silva Reservoir, located in Mexico's Guanajuato State.[26] The Secretariat included a series of recommendations for monitoring the reservoir for waterbird mortality and developing a response plan in the event mortality is observed. Four years later, the Secretariat issued a report related to the preservation of wildlife habitat along the upper San Pedro River.[27] The report proposed actions that purported to balance human requirements for water and the need to protect the viability of important riparian migratory bird habitat. As the report indicated, "[b]ird populations are key indicators for the overall health of biodiversity because birds respond so quickly to changes and stresses in the ecosystems they inhabit."[28]

Another mechanism that may serve as a means of protecting continental biodiversity is the unique citizen submission process created by Articles 14 and 15 of the NAAEC.[29] Article 14 empowers the CEC Secretariat to consider submissions from nongovernmental organizations (NGOs) or other persons asserting that a Party is failing to effectively enforce its environmental law, provided certain conditions are met. If the Secretariat finds that the submission meets the minimum criteria set forth in the agreement, it may determine that the submission merits requesting a response from the Party. If in the Secretariat's view the submission, in light of the Party's response, warrants the development of a factual record, the Secretariat, pursuant to Article 15, must inform the CEC Council. The Secretariat must prepare a factual record if the Council, by a two-thirds vote, instructs it to do so. The Council may, by another two-thirds vote, make the final factual record developed by the Secretariat publicly available.[30]

Although the CEC lacks the power to mandate changes in the enforcement practices of any Party, a Party may be induced by the publicity generated through the submissions process to redress any enforcement failures documented by the Secretariat.[31] The submissions process "rel[ies] on the effect of 'sunshine' to induce compliance" and has the "potential to enhance domestic government institutions' performance of their enforcement responsibilities," although the process has not existed long enough to provide the basis for a definitive assessment as to its ability to realize that potential.[32] The NAAEC's citizen submission process can play a meaningful role in the protection of continental biodiversity if it succeeds in inducing enhanced environmental enforcement by the three Parties.[33] As indicated in the section below that assesses the value of the CEC's biodiversity protection initiatives, various submissions for which factual records have already been ordered and developed illustrate the potential for the submission process to benefit biodiversity protection efforts in this way.

Thus, although the NAAEC, unlike the CBD, does not address biodiversity protection by name, many of its provisions provide avenues through which the CEC can take steps to promote biodiversity conservation. The next part of this chapter details the many ways in which the CEC has advanced biodiversity protection to a prominent place on its agenda.

The CEC's Biodiversity Protection Measures

The importance of biodiversity protection to the CEC's work is reflected in the annual designation of conservation of biodiversity as one of its four core substantive program areas. A June 2001 Council resolution establishing a Biodiversity Conservation Working Group, composed of governmental and nongovernmental representatives, provides further evidence of the organization's commitment to the protection of biodiversity.[34] The resolution acknowledges "the need to develop a long-term, comprehensive strategy to conserve and sustainably use biodiversity in North America" and reaffirms the NAAEC objectives relevant to the conservation of biodiversity. These include increased cooperation among the Parties to better conserve, protect, and enhance the environment and strengthened cooperation on the development and improvement of environmental laws, policies, and practices. Among other things, the Working Group will identify areas of emerging interest or opportunities for biodiversity conservation, promote the integration of the CEC's biodiversity-related activities, and support finalization and effective implementation of the strategic plan for biodiversity conservation, discussed below.

The Council commits itself in the 2001 resolution to direct support of the Working Group's initiatives. The 2001 resolution, however, is short on specifics. To develop a better understanding of what those initiatives are likely to entail, it is useful to survey the existing CEC projects that relate to biodiversity protection. The remainder of this section provides a nutshell description of these projects. Later sections of the chapter elaborate upon and assess the value of these projects.

STRATEGIC AND COOPERATIVE ACTION FOR THE CONSERVATION OF BIODIVERSITY IN NORTH AMERICA

The CEC has pursued at least eight significant projects aimed at the conservation of biological diversity.[35] Perhaps the broadest of these is the Strategic and Cooperative Action for the Conservation of Biodiversity in North America. This project, which is intended to guide the CEC's long-term agenda for continental biodiversity conservation, will provide both the public and private sectors with environmental targets and performance indicators. The CEC will seek to ensure that key issues affecting the conservation and sustainable use of marine, coastal, and terrestrial biodiversity are benefiting from concerted action on a continental scale and that conservation challenges of priority geographical regions are being addressed through the development and implementation of regional action plans. In short, the project may "provide [the CEC] with a clear sense of direction and priorities to effectively influence biodiversity in North America."[36] Rather than constituting a North American biodiversity strategy, the project is conceived of as guidance to the CEC on "how best to catalyze conservation action that will be effective at the continental level," including the development of "common responses by the Parties to shared problems."[37]

One significant step in the development of the Strategic and Cooperative Action for the Conservation of Biodiversity occurred in early 2001, when the CEC issued a draft *Strategy for the Conservation of Biodiversity in North America*.[38] The *Strategy* aims to "foster a continental, integrated perspective to the management, conservation and sustainable use of biodiversity; contribute to the maintenance of the ecological integrity of North American ecoregions; and, contribute to the mitigation, reduction and eventual elimination of current and future threats to North American shared species and ecosystems."[39] The draft discusses at length objectives that include safeguarding the ecological integrity of key North American ecosystems by promoting collaborative networks, fostering the collaboration required to ensure conservation and recovery of North American migratory and transboundary species, taking stock of the continental resource base and improving understanding of the state of continental biodiversity, and assisting in responding to common threats to biodiversity. For each objective, the draft proposes action that, if approved, would become the basis for the development of individual projects that support the *Strategy*'s objectives. Once the CEC adopts the final *Strategy*, it will develop a series of five-year action plans that identify the work needed to achieve the identified biodiversity protection objectives. That work will then be elaborated upon in individual projects undertaken by the Secretariat.

NORTH AMERICAN BIRD CONSERVATION INITIATIVE

A second biodiversity conservation project, the North American Bird Conservation Initiative (NABCI), obviously seeks to protect the North American bird populations. It began with the identification of 150 Important Bird Areas. The ultimate goal is to prompt cooperative efforts by the Parties to establish protection for these areas and the birds that inhabit them.[40]

SPECIES OF COMMON CONSERVATION CONCERN

The Species of Common Conservation Concern (SCCC) is designed to support the conservation of a selected group of seventeen migratory and transboundary species (beginning with terrestrial avian and mammalian species) and their habitats through collaboration among the three North American wildlife services and the promotion of joint conservation initiatives, including recovery plans. To promote program objectives, the SCCC would be used as one of the criteria for funding by the North American Fund for Environmental Cooperation (NAFEC). As an example, NAFEC chose to fund a project that provides economic incentives for hunting outfitters in Arizona to support Mexican wolf reintroduction efforts. In addition, the CEC seeks to assist in the development of investment opportunities related to biodiversity conservation, such as strategies for private landowner development/mitigation trade-offs. Eventually, the program, if successful, will result in delisting of SCCC species as endangered or threatened and improvement of these species' habitats.

MAPPING MARINE AND ESTUARINE ECOSYSTEMS OF NORTH AMERICA

The Mapping Marine and Estuarine Ecosystems of North America project entails the development of a mapping system and a habitat and ecosystem classification system for the conservation and sustainable use of continental marine and coastal ecosystems. One end product will be a geographical information system map of major marine and coastal ecosystems in North America. A marine gap analysis program will provide managers with information needed to set priorities for the conservation of marine and coastal resources. Gap analysis helps to identify the degree to which native animal species and natural communities are represented in areas targeted for conservation. Species, communities, and ecosystems that are not represented constitute conservation "gaps." Following development of the map and assessment of the gap analysis, the CEC will develop an action plan to identify priorities and specific actions for the conservation of North American coastal and marine ecosystems not adequately incorporated in currently protected areas.

NORTH AMERICAN MARINE PROTECTED AREA NETWORKS

The goal of the North American Marine Protected Area Networks project is to enhance conservation of marine biodiversity in critical marine habitats throughout North America. One component will be the establishment of a network of North American marine protected areas (MPAs) linked electronically through the Internet. The CEC also will seek to develop and implement conservation initiatives involving MPA sites with shared ecological links, such as critical migratory habitat, across Canada, the United States, and Mexico. Existing MPA sites and programs tend to operate independently, without much sharing of information, strategies, or feedback. Better coordination of MPAs might produce more effective protection. In 1999, the CEC-MPA Steering Committee issued the comprehensive MPA Action Plan Framework, which addressed topics such as an evaluation of the economic benefits of MPAs, the development of integrated management planning, and the development of protective standards. The Committee then selected the Baja California to Bering Sea (B2B) region, a priority region for the CEC, for initiation of a pilot study.

GLOBAL PROGRAMME OF ACTION FOR THE PROTECTION OF THE MARINE ENVIRONMENT FROM LAND-BASED ACTIVITIES IN NORTH AMERICA

Another related project, the Global Programme of Action for the Protection of the Marine Environment from Land-Based Activities in North America, is designed to protect marine and aquatic ecosystems from the effects of land-based human activity, including physical alterations of the environment and pollution. The CEC developed binational pilot projects to protect these resources in two transboundary coastal areas, the Bight of the Californias and the Gulf of Maine. The former project has spawned water-quality monitoring and the development of a Geographic Information System–based point and nonpoint source inventory of coastal contamination. With respect to the Gulf of Maine, the pilot project resulted in 1997 in the creation of a Global Programme of Action Coalition (GPAC), which developed consensus on fifteen priority environmental issues common throughout the Gulf region and targeted strategies to address those issues. Individual projects have focused on reducing emissions of specific pollutants in the Gulf region and protecting marine and coastal habitats through improved land development practices.

CLOSING THE PATHWAYS OF AQUATIC INVASIVE SPECIES ACROSS NORTH AMERICA

The Closing the Pathways of Aquatic Invasive Species Across North America project seeks to protect marine and aquatic ecosystems from the effects of plants and animals (including predators and pathogens) that invade new habitat and outcompete native species. Examples of particularly disruptive invasive animal species in the United States include brown tree snakes, flathead catfish, zebra mussels, and green crabs.[41] The CEC is committed to developing a coordinated, multinational prevention and control campaign to eliminate pathways for the introduction of invasive species among the coastal and fresh waters of the Parties. Invasive species can displace and even cause the extinction of important native species, destroy commercial and recreational fisheries, impede traditional cultural uses of coastal resources, and compromise the ecological integrity of marine protected areas. To date, few management efforts to prevent the spread of alien species have reached across political borders. The CEC has taken the position that invasive species require sustained international collaboration, which this project is designed to facilitate.

NORTH AMERICAN BIODIVERSITY INFORMATION NETWORK

The North American Biodiversity Information Network (NABIN) seeks to create an integrated North American database of biodiversity information on the assumption that accurate scientific information is essential for effective conservation.[42] The project will assist institutions that collect, manage, or use biodiversity data in being able to access information of that sort across the continent. It will link NABIN with national information generation initiatives to create a biodiversity information network that is publicly accessible and free and encourage the exchange of biodiversity data among private and public users. The CEC hopes that the information generated through this project will serve as a predictive tool for biodiversity loss, which can then be used by wildlife managers.

Assessment of the CEC's Biodiversity Protection Initiatives

The CEC has embarked upon a seemingly ambitious agenda for enhancing continental biodiversity protection. How effectively has that agenda proceeded to date, and how likely is it to succeed in the future? Edward O. Wilson has suggested four steps that are necessary to protect biodiversity. An assessment of the degree to which the CEC biodiversity agenda has promoted each of these steps can provide one measure of the efficacy of that agenda. The four steps are surveying what we have, defining needs, developing plans to meet those needs, and adapting institutions so they can implement those plans.[43]

SURVEYING WHAT WE HAVE

According to Joseph Sax, the most essential aspect of surveying what we have is to identify "hot spots" that are richest in biodiversity and that should receive priority attention for protection. Creating a set of maps that indicate where protective work is needed would go a long way toward setting a biodiversity agenda: "It has focus and it tells people that there is a determinable priority job to be done."[44]

The CEC biodiversity agenda is perhaps strongest in its efforts to tackle this first step of the biodiversity protection process. The eight projects described above are loaded with information-gathering components. The draft status report that the CEC relied upon in developing its 2001 draft *Strategy for the Conservation of Biodiversity in North America* recommended investment in "applied research that gives better understanding of all the key factors contributing to the problem."[45] Indeed, one of the six principal objectives of the draft *Strategy* itself is "taking stock of our natural endowment" so as to improve understanding of the state of North American biodiversity. Proposed actions include fostering the development of a regular series of *Taking Stock* reports (including a list of species at risk) and development of a North American biodiversity clearinghouse mechanism for issues of common concern (including a biodiversity information network on transboundary ecosystems, migratory and transboundary species, common threats, and management techniques). The draft *Strategy* also stressed the need to complete NABIN to "facilitate access to the wealth of information stored in collections on the Continent's biodiversity and provide the basis for monitoring its status."[46] The fundamental premise behind NABIN is that enhanced access to "accurate scientific information is essential for effective conservation."[47]

The CEC has strongly supported the mapping efforts that Sax characterized as essential to setting biodiversity protection priorities. The CEC, in the course of developing its conservation strategy, identified fourteen priority regions in terms of ecological significance, conservation threat, and opportunities for conservation. The 2001 draft *Strategy* urges as a necessary step toward safeguarding the ecological integrity of key ecosystems the development of a common approach to ecological mapping. At least one project's raison d'être is the production of maps of areas targeted for protection. The Mapping Marine and Estuarine Ecosystems of North America project is geared toward development of a Geographic Information System–based map of major marine and coastal ecological regions in North America. Similarly, NABCI identified 150 Important Bird Areas that would provide the underpinning for an action plan for the conservation of North American birds.

Christopher Stone recently listed several hindrances to stimulating institutional reforms to practices that contribute to the loss of biodiversity.[48] He pointed first to the absence of an agreed-upon biodiversity indicator. According to Stone, the single term "biodiversity" tends to be applied "to many distinguishable environmental characteristics."[49] In addition, scientists and policy-makers often lack crucial data necessary to measure the scope of the problem being addressed and information on how to arrest declines in biodiversity. Stone claims, for example, that there is wide uncertainty about how much territory and what conditions are needed to effectively protect a targeted resource. Similarly, he identifies as an additional problem the lack of knowledge about the cost of a decline in biodiversity. It is difficult to ascertain how much the loss of a species or ecosystem will cost largely due to a lack of understanding of the effects of loss of particular ecosystem components on human well-being.

The CEC mapping and related information-gathering efforts are likely to address many of the sources of uncertainty that Stone has characterized as hindrances to effective biodiversity protection, including uncertainty over the location and scope of existing threats to biodiversity. Absent a definition of the scope and location of the problem as well as the objectives for resolving it, it will be difficult to promote an effective biodiversity protection agenda. The CEC has devoted considerable productive effort to these tasks already and promises to continue doing so in the future. It is important, however, that the "surveying" process be an ongoing one. Information gathering must not stop when the CEC begins to identify needs and to develop and implement plans to meet them. Rather, the CEC should continually adjust its definitions of biodiversity problems and the solutions it devises to address them as new information becomes available.[50]

DEFINING NEEDS

The second and third steps of the four-step process described by Edward O. Wilson appear to go hand in hand. The second involves identifying threats to biodiversity and the necessary conditions for mitigating those threats so that actions necessary to provide effective protection measures may be devised. The ensuing step involves devising a strategy or establishing a framework for implementing these actions. The CEC has engaged in considerable effort on both these fronts.

A prerequisite to defining what is needed to protect biodiversity is identification of the activities that are threatening it. The 2001 draft *Strategy* summarizes the CEC's findings as to the causes of biodiversity loss, including habitat fragmentation, overfishing, pollution, global climate change, filling of wetlands, destruction of mountain creeks, excessive sedimentation, and dam building, among others. The *Strategy* also describes the CEC's focus as concrete identification of opportunities for mitigating the adverse effects of these activities. As the preceding status report explained, the goal of the Strategic and Cooperative Action for the Conservation of Biodiversity in North America project is not only to diagnose the current state of continental biodiversity but also to develop lines of action to address identified conservation priorities. More specifically, the Global Programme of Action reached consensus on a set of fifteen priority environmental issues that needed addressing in order to meet the project's objective of reducing threats to marine species and habitats arising from land-based activities. By identifying the sources of aquatic invasive species, the CEC in effect concluded that action had to be taken to minimize the discharge of ballast water originating in other waters and to control activities such as the disposal of unused live bait or the release of unwanted aquarium animals. These examples indicate that the CEC has consistently sought to reduce uncertainty about the conditions necessary to protect effectively targeted resources such as migratory birds or important coastal or aquatic species or habitats.

DEVELOPING PLANS TO MEET IDENTIFIED NEEDS

Once the CEC has identified the necessary conditions for the protection of biological diversity, it must proceed to develop plans for the fulfillment of those conditions. The CEC's biodiversity protection initiatives are replete with a series of strategic, recovery, and action plans. The CEC will implement its Strategy for the Conservation of Biodiversity in North America through a series of five-year action plans that will "identify the fundamental work needed to realize each set of five-year goals. These actions will be fully elaborated into projects to be undertaken by CEC's Secretariat."[51] The agency will pursue its SCCC initiative through support or implementation of recovery plans for migratory or transboundary species that are at risk or that are of conservation concern to one or more of the member countries. Under the North American Marine Protected Area Networks project, the CEC-MPA Steering Committee has developed a comprehensive MPA Action Plan Framework that sets out seven areas for further action. As part of that project, the B2B Marine Conservation Initiative developed in 2001 a draft strategic plan to help conserve and restore biodiversity in the Baja to Bering region. Similarly, the CEC approved an action plan for the NABCI in 1999, and GPAC developed an action plan for the Gulf of Maine to help effectuate priority regional pollutant reduction and habitat protection objectives. Thus, the CEC has routinely sought to codify its biodiversity protection agenda through adoption of a series of plans whose purpose is to assist governments, private actors, and NGOs in the three Parties in creating the conditions deemed necessary to accomplish biodiversity conservation goals.

ADAPTING INSTITUTIONS TO IMPLEMENT BIODIVERSITY PROTECTION PLANS

The final step in Wilson's process is the adaptation of institutions in ways that enable relevant actors to implement the biodiversity protection plans that have been developed. The provision of information generated during the first step of the process would be helpful to others undertaking biodiversity protection initiatives, even if the CEC were itself to refrain from engaging in anything more than a data-generation function. The definition of needs also might be useful to others intent upon protecting biological diversity, even if the CEC, after specifying the necessary conditions for protection, chose not to proceed or was unable to proceed with actions to supply those conditions. Even the formulation of CEC plans might be of value to other environmental policy-makers devising their own biodiversity protection efforts. Assessments of the CEC's planning efforts are likely to turn, however, on the degree to which the agency is capable of successful plan implementation.

Reading the documents that describe the CEC's various plans for promoting biodiversity conservation can be an extremely frustrating exercise. Many of the documents contain impenetrable bureaucratese; they discuss plan development and implementation, for example, in the passive voice. It is therefore impossible to tell in many instances which entities the CEC envisions that will be responsible for implementing the action plans and what the CEC's role will be in taking its own steps or assisting in the steps taken by others. The 2001–3 Agenda for Action, in describing NABCI, slates as a planned action for 2002 under the heading of law and policy: "stimulate the development of legal initiatives and other instruments to benefit bird populations." Development by whom? The same document lists as one of the components of the MPA network process the formulation of an Area Action Plan, including "developing protection standards." Developed by whom? Similarly, the 2002–4 Agenda for Action indicates that one of the expected results of the biodiversity conservation strategy is "Action Plans developed and implemented in CEC priority regions." Developed and implemented by whom? Because of these and a host of other inscrutable project descriptions, one can only guess at what role the CEC has staked out for itself, the governments of the Parties, NGOs, private landowners, and other interested entities in carrying out CEC-sponsored plans.

Reading between the lines of the official documents, there appear to be at least three contexts in which the CEC may seek to prompt existing institutions to take steps to facilitate implementation of its myriad biodiversity protection plans and initiatives. The CEC may seek to induce the Parties to strengthen domestic environmental enforcement mechanisms, to adopt more effective domestic substantive environmental protection laws, and to create international environmental cooperation and compulsion mechanisms. Each presents difficulties for the CEC in light of the limited degree to which it is capable of intruding into the domestic affairs of the three Parties or of adopting binding international standards of conduct for either the Parties or the various private actors functioning within the Parties. These limitations on the scope of the CEC's authority can be expected to make the final step of Wilson's four-step process the most resistant to successful CEC inroads. Despite these difficulties, however, the CEC has a useful role to play in facilitating change in each of these three contexts.

Strengthening Domestic Environmental Enforcement Mechanisms

The CEC has already begun to play a useful role in the strengthening of domestic environmental enforcement mechanisms through the NAAEC's unique citizen submission process. The *Cozumel Pier* submission, one of the submissions for which a factual record was prepared, alleged that the Mexican authorities failed to comply with a series of environmental laws in connection with the construction of a cruise ship pier project for tourist cruises on the island of Cozumel.[52] Among other things, the submitters charged that the project was located within a natural area for marine flora and fauna protected under a special legal regime intended to ensure the rational use of ecosystems and that construction of the tunnel posed serious and immediate dangers for the survival and development of barrier reefs off the island. In another submission for which a factual record was developed, *BC Hydro*, the submitters alleged that the Canadian government was failing to enforce relevant provisions of the Fisheries Act and to use its powers to ensure the protection of fish and fish habitat in British Columbia's rivers from ongoing and repeated environmental damage caused by hydroelectric dams.[53] Assuming that the factual record supported the conclusion in either of these proceedings that the Parties were not adequately enforcing their environmental laws and that the inadequacy had resulted in harm to the ecosystems involved, the submissions process might, by publicizing the deficiencies, prompt more effective enforcement with resulting enhanced protections for the affected ecosystems.

Enhancing Substantive Domestic Law

The CEC may be a useful contributor not only to the strengthening of the processes of enforcing domestic environmental laws but also to the adoption of more effective substantive environmental laws themselves. The CEC lacks the authority in response to a citizen submission to order the governments of the three Parties to alter their environmental law enforcement practices. Similarly, the CEC has no power to require that the Parties adopt more effective laws whose goal is protection of biological diversity. The CEC may nevertheless provide guidance to the governments of the Parties on desirable changes, and it has already begun doing so. Unfortunately, the recommendations often relate to an area of domestic law—land-use control—in which domestic law (at least in the United States) is least equipped to provide effective protection of biodiversity and in which governments are typically reluctant to act. Widespread adoption of these CEC recommendations is therefore probably unlikely in the foreseeable future.

Because land-use conversion is generally acknowledged to be the principal cause of biodiversity loss, land-use policy can be expected to play a central role in biodiversity conservation policy.[54] Effective biodiversity protection will entail dedication of land to habitat reserves, management of public lands dedicated to commodity production such as timber harvesting and livestock grazing, and changes in prevailing private land-use development practices.[55] Legal changes affecting private land-use practices need not be confined to traditional tools, such as zoning laws, or to more recently adopted constraints such as prohibitions on development in the habitat of protected species. Many observers agree that the elimination of counterproductive subsidies is of paramount importance. Stone, for example, has argued that "the first legal measure and the clear starting point for conservation reform is to eliminate subsidies that aggravate the demand for virgin forest by artificially fostering conflicting uses, such as agriculture and logging."[56] The status report that preceded the CEC's 2001 draft *Strategy* agreed that "subsidies are at the root of much habitat destruction." The report preliminarily recommended the development of "more appropriate incentives for biodiversity conservation" and sought to commit the CEC to working with governments to identify and eliminate "perverse incentives such as subsidies and tax measures that work against environmental and biodiversity protection."[57]

Elimination of perverse incentives can be supplemented by the enhanced availability of incentives to engage in land-use practices that promote conservation.[58] The status report insists that "adequate protection demands payment in lieu of other economically productive activities" and that "the nature of these incentives and who should pay are matters of international interest."[59] Similarly, the 2001 draft *Strategy* endorses increased reliance on positive economic incentives as part of its objective of tapping into opportunities arising from the expansion of regional trade. The proposed actions designed to promote this objective include working with the governments of the Parties to identify the role of incentives in the conservation and sustainable use of biodiversity. Because conservation efforts must address the "root causes" of ecological stress, "economic, financial, and legal mechanisms need to be analyzed and effective mechanisms and instruments need to be promoted to bolster conservation and sustainable use efforts."[60]

Such sentiments are certainly laudable, but they are not yet supported by detailed strategies for implementation. Tarlock has asserted that "biodiversity protection is difficult because the very idea of biodiversity protection is antithetical to the Western idea of human economic progress through science, technology and the encouragement of individual initiative."[61] Whether or not one accepts the premise that biodiversity protection is necessarily inconsistent with Western conceptions of economic progress, it is hard to dispute that effective biodiversity protection hinges in large part on land-use regulation. That kind of regulation infringes upon development expectations that have long been reinforced by existing laws and institutions.[62] Given that domestically sponsored legal changes such as reductions in historically available subsidies to environmentally damaging activities on both public and private land have often provoked stiff resistance, there is little reason to expect that CEC initiatives in this direction will proceed smoothly toward domestic adoption and implementation.

To a limited extent, the CEC can make a direct contribution to the development of appropriate incentives through its own funding mechanisms. The CEC has supported biodiversity conservation efforts through the NAFEC, which has made grants of more than $4.8 million to community-based environmental projects.[63] As indicated above, NAFEC funded a project that provides economic incentives for hunting outfitters in Arizona to support Mexican wolf reintroduction efforts. Additional efforts of this sort can affect at the margin domestic incentives to engage in land-use practices that protect biological diversity and to avoid destructive practices. A greater infusion of grant money obviously would increase the value of these efforts. The United States has had some success in inducing the coastal states to engage in land-use planning by providing grants under the Coastal Zone Management Act (CZMA) to states that develop management programs that meet minimum federally specified standards.[64] The CEC might consider seeking to procure from the Parties the funds necessary to supply a similar set of biodiversity planning incentives. It is not clear how useful a model the CZMA would provide in this context, if only because the funding made available by the CEC to Parties taking the required steps to protect biodiversity would ultimately come at least in part from the Parties themselves.

Beyond the provision of direct financial support, the CEC should continue to engage in research into the role of economic incentives (both positive and negative) in the protection of biodiversity and refine its suggestions and models for alterations in land-use practices. The national governments can then take advantage of the information provided by the CEC and consider the adoption of suggested controls and standards. Because of its extremely limited role in the internal lawmaking processes of the Parties and the barriers to change in this area generally, however, the CEC may find more fertile ground for its efforts to effectuate changes in land-use and other damaging practices through sponsorship of international cooperation mechanisms, particularly in regard to cross-boundary threats to biodiversity.[65]

Creating International Cooperation Mechanisms

The adverse effects of practices damaging to biodiversity do not stop at political borders. The external origin of the damage makes it difficult for any one nation to provide an effective set of solutions for loss of biodiversity within its borders. The CEC may be able to play an effective role as an "honest broker and facilitator" in the development of binational or trinational approaches to the resolution of these problems.[66] One of the six principal objectives of the 2001 draft *Strategy* is responding to common threats to North American biodiversity. The CEC has proposed as part of its efforts in this direction to foster the development of transboundary partnerships to address regional threats to biodiversity. The *Strategy* even envisions the possibility of joint management in special cases of shared resources or transboundary habitats.[67] The 1995 report on the death of migratory birds at the Silva Reservoir in Mexico provides some examples of what kinds of joint efforts the CEC may sponsor. The Secretariat endorsed the suggestion that the governments of Canada and the United States work with Mexico to enhance the Turbio Basin Initiative and similar initiatives for other watersheds through technology transfers; joint government, academic, industry, and foundation endeavors; and professional exchanges involving experts in hydrology and engineering, watershed research, and water-quality monitoring and modeling.[68] Specific steps might include preventing pollution that contributes to contamination of watersheds through enhancement of sewage treatment capacity, relocation of industry, and the creation of wildlife health surveillance and wildlife disease outbreak investigation programs.[69]

But the CEC need not and should not confine its efforts to induce cooperative action to problems with transboundary aspects. As Sanford Gaines has argued, some of the CEC's most significant contributions have come and should come in the form of the development of common approaches to the resolution of problems, such as limits on emissions of persistent organic pollutants that, while they may have transboundary aspects, are not necessarily limited to that context.[70] Although the CEC has no authority to establish binding legal obligations on the governments of the three Parties or on private entities operating within them, it may be able, through efforts to procure the Parties' agreement on common objectives, to establish conceptual frameworks or starting points for the negotiation by the Parties of more detailed treaties and other commitments that elaborate on the CEC's earlier work. Some observers have praised the CBD, which is also largely incapable of establishing binding international legal obligations, for functioning in this role.[71] The CEC has committed itself to the promotion of compatible laws and policies at a continental level and to the development of complementary regulatory approaches.[72] The status report that preceded the 2001 draft *Strategy* recognized that "the trend is toward taking on more international obligations and harmonizing domestic law."[73] The CEC's plan to establish a periodic North American Round Table among stakeholders to promote a continuing dialogue on biodiversity issues of common concern to the three Parties seems well suited to fostering this process of securing agreement on common goals and approaches.

Conclusion

The CEC has been very active in pursuing its biodiversity conservation agenda through at least eight projects, headed by the process of adopting a Strategic Plan for the Conservation of Biodiversity in North America. Because most of these projects are at the initial stages of implementation, it is premature to assess their effects on protection of continental biodiversity. The early indications, however, are that the CEC has probably been most successful to date in accumulating information that is vital to narrowing the information gaps that present obstacles to effective biodiversity protection. An international organization such as the CEC is well placed to sponsor research and draw upon the existing resources of government agencies, academia, industry, and NGOs to buttress the biodiversity information base. The CEC's mapping efforts provide an example of the kind of work that the agency ought to continue actively pursuing. The more the CEC accumulates information about the nature and scope of threats to biological diversity, the easier it will be to define the necessary preconditions to minimizing those threats.

Based on its assessment of the changes in law and policy that are essential to achieving biodiversity protection objectives, the CEC has begun to develop plans (some more specific than others) for effectuating these changes. The toughest challenge facing the CEC in its pursuit of biodiversity conservation is playing a useful role in facilitating implementation of the identified changes by existing domestic and international institutions. The relative weakness of international environmental law in general and the CEC's lack of authority to compel substantive legal action by Canada, the United States, and Mexico are likely to create significant obstacles to that kind of impact. Still, the CEC has begun to play a useful role in strengthening domestic enforcement practices through its citizen submissions process. It may be able to provide incentives for the pursuit of environmentally friendly land-use practices through its own funding initiatives. It will likely be harder to persuade the Parties to provide such incentives under the domestic laws of the three countries. Finally, the CEC may serve as an initiator of cooperative efforts to tackle problems such as transboundary threats to the maintenance of biological diversity and of efforts to harmonize protective standards under new binational or trinational regimes.

The CEC appears to be asking the right questions about the state of continental biodiversity and what is needed to avert threats to it. It is also engaged in concerted efforts to supply answers to those questions or at least to point the Parties in the direction of the answers. The CEC is an organization of limited authority, but it seems to be taking advantage of the authority it has in facilitating efforts to protect North American biodiversity.

Notes

1. 32 I.L.M. 1480 (1993).

2. "Securing the Continent's Biological Wealth: Towards Effective Biodiversity Conservation in North America," working draft of a Status Report for Stakeholder Input (provisional abbreviated version, prepared as the Integrated Baseline Summary Report for the Strategic Directions for the Conservation of Biodiversity Project 99.02.01, Mar. 7, 2000), at 4.

3. "The precipitous decline in the stocks of a number of fish species has led to serious reductions or even collapses in a number of fisheries." CEC, *The North American Mosaic: A State of the Environment Report* x (2001).

4. "Securing the Continent's Biological Wealth," supra, 6.

5. CEC, *The North American Mosaic*, supra, 36.

6. United Nations, Convention on Biological Diversity, June 2, 1992, 31 I.L.M. 818. The CEC has put matters more simply: biodiversity "refers to all life on earth." CEC, *The North American Mosaic*, supra, 36.

7. U.S. Congress, Office of Technology Assessment, *Technologies to Maintain Biological Diversity* 3 (1987).

8. Boyce Thorne-Miller, *The Living Ocean: Understanding and Protecting Marine Biodiversity* 7 (2d ed. 1999).

9. A. Dan Tarlock, "Biodiversity Federalism," 54 *Maryland Law Review* 1315, 1324–25 (1995).

10. Edith Brown Weiss, *In Fairness to Future Generations* 193 (1989).

11. For example, Neil Gunningham and Mike D. Young, "Toward Optimal Environmental Policy: The Case of Biodiversity Conservation," 24 *Ecology Law Quarterly* 243, 248 (1997); J. B. Ruhl, "Biodiversity Conservation and the Ever-Expanding Web of Federal Laws Regulating Nonfederal Lands: Time for Something Completely Different?" 66 *University of Colorado Law Review* 555, 571 (1995).

12. See Holly Doremus, "Patching the Ark: Improving Legal Protection of Biological Diversity," 18 *Ecology Law Quarterly* 265, 269–70 (1991).

13. Id., 271; Bradley C. Karkkainen, "Biodiversity and Land," 83 *Cornell Law Review* 1, 2 n.5 (1997). See also "Biological Extinction: Its Scope and Meaning for Us," in *Protection of Global Biodiversity: Converging Strategies* 26 (Lakshman D. Guruswamy and Jeffrey A. MacNeely eds., 1998).

14. A. Dan Tarlock, "Local Government Protection of Biodiversity: What Is Its Niche?" 60 *University of Chicago Law Review* 555, 557 (1993); Christopher D. Stone, "Land Use and Biodiversity," 27 *Ecology Law Quarterly* 967, 977 (2001). See also Daniel M. Bodansky, "International Law and the Protection of Biological Diversity," 28 *Vanderbilt Journal of Transnational Law* 623, 625–26 (1995).

15. Doremus, supra, 272.

16. Mark Sagoff, "On the Uses of Biodiversity," in Guruswamy and MacNeely, supra, 265.

17. *Biodiversity and the Law* 84–85 (William J. Snape II ed., 1996); Bodansky, supra, 629.

18. *Agenda 21: The United Nations Programme of Action from Rio*, UN Sales No. E.93.I.11.

19. Scott Hajost and Curtis Fish, "Biodiversity Conservation and International Instruments," in Snape, supra, 132.

20. Walter V. Reid, "Halting the Loss of Biodiversity: International Institutional Measures," in Guruswamy and MacNeely, supra, 172.

21. Lee A. Kimball, "The Biodiversity Convention: How to Make It Work," 28 *Vanderbilt Journal of Transnational Law* 763, 765 (1995).

22. Executive Order 12,915, § 1(a), 59 Fed. Reg. 25,775 (1994).

23. Under Article 10(7), the CEC must consider and develop recommendations on the assessment of environmental impacts of proposed projects likely to cause significant adverse transboundary effects, on the notification of and consultation between parties with respect to those projects, and on the mitigation of potential adverse effects.

24. See John H. Knox, "A New Approach to Compliance with International Environmental Law: The Submissions Procedure of the NAFTA Environmental Commission," 28 *Ecology Law Quarterly* 1, 57 (2001).

25. The Council, which is comprised of cabinet-level or equivalent representatives of the parties, is the governing body of the CEC.

26. CEC, *Report on the Death of Migratory Birds at the Silva Reservoir* (Oct. 1995).

27. CEC, *Ribbon of Life: An Agenda for Preserving Transboundary Migratory Bird Habitat on the Upper San Pedro River* (1999). For a discussion of the report, see ch. 12, infra.

28. Id., 1.

29. See generally ch. 15, infra; Knox, supra; David L. Markell, "The Commission for Environmental Cooperation's Citizen Submission Process," 12 *Georgetown International Environmental Law Review* 545 (2000). See also chs. 13, 14, infra.

30. Knox points out that "public outcry would result from a Council attempt to suppress a final report relevant to compliance by one of the state parties with its obligation to effectively enforce. . . . As a result, it seems unlikely that the Council would ever decline to make a factual record public." Knox, supra, 67.

31. "[I]nternational law often operates far more by information generation and production than by mandate." Zygmunt J. B. Plater et al., *Environmental Law and Policy: Nature, Law, and Society* 612 (2d ed. 1998).

32. See Markell, supra, 571 (stating that the NAAEC citizen submission process "offers the prospect of a 'spotlight' on domestic enforcement practices"); David L. Markell, "The Citizen Spotlight Process," 18 *Environmental Forum* 32 (Mar./Apr. 2001). As a former director of the CEC's Submissions on Enforcement Matters Unit has commented, "It is still too early to say with any degree of certainty how effective this spotlight will be." Id., 43.

33. As Markell has indicated, "enhancement of domestic enforcement is a means to an end, and the end is to promote compliance and thereby enhance environmental protection." Markell, "Submission Process," supra, 569.

34. CEC Council Resolution 01-03, June 29, 2001.

35. Much of the information in this section was derived from the CEC's three-year program plans for 2000–2002, 2001–3, and 2002–4, called "North American Agenda for Action," as well as the CEC's website, *http://www.cec.org*.

36. "Securing the Continent's Biological Wealth," supra, 3.

37. Id., 2.

38. CEC, *Strategy for the Conservation of Biodiversity in North America* (first draft for review, Mar. 22, 2001).

39. Id., iii.

40. Karen L. Smith, "Habitat Protection for the New Millennium: An Analysis of Domestic and International Regimes in North America," 13 *Georgetown International Environmental Law Review* 509, 556 (2001).

41. The zebra mussel, which has been called the "'poster-child' for alien species," was introduced into the Great Lakes system in the ballast water of tankers from the Caspian or Black Sea in Russia. Brown tree snakes threaten to devastate native bird species in Hawaii. David Hunter et al., *International Environmental Law and Policy* 1005–6 (1998).

42. See Smith, supra, 557.

43. See Joseph L. Sax, "Comment on John Harte's Paper, 'Land Use, Biodiversity, and Ecosystem Integrity: The Challenge of Preserving Earth's Life Support System,'" 27 *Ecology Law Quarterly* 1003, 1009 (2001) (citing Edward O. Wilson, *The Diversity of Life* 311–42 [1992]).

44. Id., 1009.

45. "Securing the Continent's Biological Wealth," supra, 14.

46. CEC, *Strategy for the Conservation of Biodiversity*, supra, 9.

47. Smith, supra, 557.

48. Stone, supra, 967.

49. Id., 969–70.

50. See Ruhl, supra, 555, 572 (arguing that "information gaps and the inherent complexity and uncertainty of biological systems requires [*sic*] a continual research and monitoring program and an acknowledgment that uncertainty remains more the norm than the exception at this time").

51. CEC, *Strategy for the Conservation of Biodiversity*, supra, iv, 17.

52. SEM-96-001, summarized at *http://www.cec.org*, under Citizen Submissions on Enforcement Matters, Status.

53. SEM-97-001, summarized at *http://www.cec.org*, under Citizen Submissions on Enforcement Matters, Status. Similarly, the submitters in *BC Logging*, SEM-00-004, alleged harmful effects on fish habitat as a result of the Canadian government's failure to enforce the Fisheries Act against private loggers in British Columbia, and the submitters in *BC Mining* made related allegations concerning mining activities in that province. The *Migratory Birds* submission, SEM-99-002, involved allegations that the United States was failing to enforce the Migratory Bird Treaty Act, 16 U.S.C. §§ 703–12, as it applies to logging activities. All of these submissions, for which the Secretariat has recommended development of a factual record, involve alleged enforcement failures concerning laws that are designed to protect wildlife resources and their habitats and that therefore contribute to the protection of biodiversity.

54. See Karkkainen, supra, 7.

55. See Tarlock, "Biodiversity Federalism," supra, 1332–33.

56. "Subsidization need not take the form of overt payments to converters, but

can include favorable tax incentives and insufficient charges for use of public lands, such as inadequate grazing and stumpage fees." Stone, supra, 983.

57. "Securing the Continent's Biological Wealth," supra, 18.

58. John Harte, "Land Use, Biodiversity, and Ecosystem Integrity: The Challenge of Preserving Earth's Life Support System," 27 *Ecology Law Quarterly* 929, 961 (2001) (supporting provision of property tax breaks and other financial incentives for landowners who preserve habitat as a desirable solution to biodiversity loss).

59. "Securing the Continent's Biological Wealth," supra, 18.

60. CEC, *Strategy for the Conservation of Biodiversity*, supra, 16.

61. Tarlock, "Biodiversity Federalism," supra, 1316.

62. Id., 1337.

63. "Securing the Continent's Biological Wealth," supra, 10.

64. 16 U.S.C. §§ 1451–65.

65. See, e.g., Sax, supra, 1011 (the U.S. "Congress will undoubtedly not provide more ecologically attractive redefinitions of private property rights").

66. CEC, *Strategy for the Conservation of Biodiversity*, supra, 8–9.

67. Id., 16.

68. CEC, *Report on the Death of Migratory Birds*, supra, 5.

69. See, e.g., Christopher N. Bolinger, Note, "Assessing the CEC on Its Record to Date," 28 *Law and Policy in International Business* 1107, 1117 (1997).

70. Sanford E. Gaines, "CEC Is Working, but Don't Bring Other Countries In," 14 *Environmental Forum* 41 (Sept./Oct. 1997).

71. See, e.g., Kimball, supra, 765.

72. CEC, *Strategy for the Conservation of Biodiversity*, supra, 15–16.

73. "Securing the Continent's Biological Wealth," supra, 18.

JOHN H. KNOX 5

The CEC and Transboundary Pollution

TRANSBOUNDARY POLLUTION in North America has received international attention for over ninety years.[1] Famous, or infamous, examples from the past include the sulfur dioxide emitted by a smelter near Trail, British Columbia, in the 1920s; the salinization of the Colorado River in the 1960s; and the contribution of U.S. power plants to Canadian acid rain in the 1980s. Despite a series of bilateral agreements and institutions addressing particular concerns and some notable successes, transboundary pollution continues. Indeed, every section of both borders seems to have its own notorious problem. San Diegans complain that sewage from Tijuana befouls their beaches; Texans accuse power plants in Coahuila of clouding the skies over Big Bend National Park; Mexicans protest against proposals to site waste disposal facilities in South Texas; Ontario argues that U.S. power plants cause most of its air pollution; and Alaskans worry about the downstream effects of mining in British Columbia. Moreover, thousands of sources, on both sides of the border, pollute shared bodies of water such as the Great Lakes and the Rio Grande and shared airsheds such as that over El Paso and Ciudad Juárez.[2]

What, if anything, should the Commission for Environmental Cooperation (CEC) do about transboundary pollution? In particular, should it coordinate the work of the bilateral institutions and fill gaps in their coverage? After evaluating how the CEC has handled issues of transboundary environmental harm, this chapter concludes that the answer to this question is a qualified No. The CEC should not try to oversee the work of the bilateral institutions, and it should address only one important type of transboundary pollution outside their jurisdiction: pollution that directly affects all three countries.

North American Responses to Transboundary Pollution

Responses by the federal governments (and, increasingly, subfederal governments) to transboundary pollution have been similar in several ways.[3] First, the governments have nearly always pursued cooperative rather than confrontational solutions. Second, their solutions have relied on international institutions, which the governments have authorized to study problems, facilitate discussion, and implement agreements. Third, these institutions and agreements were always bilateral until 1993, when the governments signed the North American Agreement on Environmental Cooperation (NAAEC) creating the CEC.

The oldest of the bilateral institutions are the International Joint Commission (IJC) and the International Boundary and Water Commission (IBWC), created, respectively, by the 1909 Boundary Waters Treaty between the United Kingdom (on behalf of Canada) and the United States and the 1944 Water Treaty between Mexico and the United States.[4] Neither of these treaties was primarily concerned with transboundary pollution, although both included provisions addressing it. The chief aims of the Boundary Waters Treaty were to establish freedom of navigation in the boundary waters along the Canada-U.S. border (in particular, the Great Lakes and the limitrophe portion of the St. Lawrence River) and to prohibit unilateral obstruction of or diversion from the boundary waters without the approval of the IJC. The treaty prohibits pollution of the boundary waters and waters flowing across the border, but it does not give the IJC power to enforce that prohibition. It does, however, allow the parties to ask the IJC to prepare reports on questions involving the rights, obligations, or interests of either party in relation to the other or its inhabitants along the border, and from the inception of the agreement the governments have used this "reference" authority to ask the IJC to examine cases of transboundary pollution.[5]

The primary purposes of the 1944 Water Treaty were to allocate the water of the Colorado River and the Rio Grande between Mexico and the United States and to create dams and reservoirs in order to maximize the amount of water available. The treaty established the IBWC to develop the necessary public works and to ensure that withdrawals by each country are within the limits set by the treaty. Unlike the 1909 treaty, the 1944 treaty neither prohibits transboundary water pollution nor includes a general "reference" authority, but it does say that the governments "agree to give preferential attention to the solution of all border sanitation problems." On the basis of this provision, in the late 1940s and early 1950s the IBWC developed a wastewater treatment plant to serve the twin cities of Nogales on the Arizona/Sonora border.[6]

In the 1970s, the governments moved environmental considerations from the periphery to the center of the work of the two commissions. In 1972, Canada and the United States signed a Great Lakes Water Quality Agreement setting specific objectives for water quality in the Great Lakes and mandating detailed programs to meet those objectives. The Agreement authorized the IJC to assist the parties in implementing the Agreement and to report and make recommendations on the water quality of the Great Lakes and the goals of the Agreement.[7] The next year, under the auspices of the IBWC, Mexico and the United States resolved Mexican complaints about the salinity of the Colorado River.[8] In 1979, they approved a decision of the IBWC to treat all cases of transboundary water pollution that endanger the health of the inhabitants of either side of the border or impair the uses of the border waters as "border sanitation problems" for which the IBWC would recommend specific responses, effectively enhancing its authority to plan and build wastewater treatment plants along the border.[9]

In 1983, Mexico and the United States signed the La Paz Agreement, which for the first time established a framework for addressing all border environmental issues.[10] Rather than creating another bilateral institution with quasi-independent commissioners, like the IJC and IBWC, the La Paz Agreement provides for an ongoing dialogue between the federal governments, led by two "national coordinators" who oversee permanent working groups composed of government experts, with mandates to exchange information and coordinate policies on particular issues, including air pollution, water pollution, and hazardous waste. In the 1980s, the parties added five annexes to the La Paz Agreement, through which they agreed to specific obligations on, among other things, air pollution and transboundary shipment of hazardous substances.

In the early 1990s, the North American governments reached two more bilateral agreements. Spurred by Canadian complaints over the contribution by U.S. industrial sources to acid rain in Canada, the United States and Canada signed an Air Quality Agreement in 1991. Like the Great Lakes Water Quality Agreement, it includes specific restrictions on emissions of pollutants and gives the IJC a role (albeit a minor one) in overseeing its implementation.[11] Shortly thereafter, during the North American Free Trade Agreement (NAFTA) debate, it became obvious that the growth in population and industry in northern Mexico resulting from the *maquiladora* program had overwhelmed facilities for water, wastewater treatment, and municipal waste disposal and that on the U.S. side of the border, unscrupulous developers had built hundreds of *colonias*—groups of houses with little or no access to drinking water or waste disposal. As a result, in 1993 Mexico and the United States signed an agreement creating two new organizations, the Border Environment Cooperation Commission (BECC) and the North

American Development Bank, and charged them with certifying and helping to fund water, wastewater, and solid waste facilities along the border.[12]

The Authority of the CEC to Address Transboundary Pollution

As the brief history in the preceding section shows, the North American nations have never developed an overall plan to address transboundary environmental harm. Instead, for nearly a century the governments have responded to particular problems one by one, usually by establishing or referring problems to a bilateral organization. The resulting patchwork of institutions, each with its own mandate and jurisdiction, has been criticized for not addressing transboundary environmental problems comprehensively. It is tempting to see the CEC, a trilateral organization with broad mandates to address almost any type of environmental problem in the continent, as the answer to this criticism.

Could the CEC play this role? Article 10(2)(g) of the NAAEC authorizes the CEC Council to consider, and make recommendations regarding, "transboundary and border environmental issues." Articles 10(7), 10(8), and 10(9) specifically instruct the Council to consider two cross-cutting procedural issues: transboundary environmental impact assessment and reciprocal access to domestic legal remedies for transboundary harm. Moreover, the general powers of the CEC to promote environmental protection throughout the continent do not exclude the border regions or transboundary issues. The Council and Secretariat could use the ability of the CEC to investigate, issue reports, make recommendations, and facilitate agreements to address almost any issue of transboundary harm, including those that might also fall within the jurisdiction of bilateral institutions. Although the commissioners of the IJC, the IBWC, and the BECC might object, there is little doubt that the governments could, if they chose, use the CEC to coordinate their responses to transboundary pollution in North America. In particular, the CEC could oversee the work of the bilateral institutions and fill gaps in their coverage.

In practice, the governments have not asked the CEC to oversee the bilateral institutions, and the CEC has showed little interest in addressing many issues of transboundary pollution, even those not within the jurisdiction of the bilateral organizations. Is this a mistake? Should the CEC play a more active role with respect to transboundary pollution? One way to answer these questions is to examine the record of the CEC with respect to its specific mandates to address transboundary environmental impact assessment and access to domestic legal remedies for transboundary harm. These mandates are relatively narrow and do not fall within the jurisdiction of any of the bilateral institutions. They therefore provide the CEC a relatively uncomplicated opportunity to demonstrate whether it can address issues of transboundary pollution effectively. The following sections describe each mandate and the record of the CEC in fulfilling it.

TRANSBOUNDARY ENVIRONMENTAL IMPACT ASSESSMENT

The domestic law of each of the North American nations requires potential environmental impacts of certain actions to be assessed before the actions are undertaken.[13] The laws are similar in important respects. Each law provides opportunities for public participation in the environmental impact assessment (EIA) procedure. Each country uses EIA to force government decision-makers to take environmental considerations into account in deciding whether to carry out or authorize a project; the laws do not prevent the decision-makers from deciding that other factors outweigh the environmental costs and allowing a potentially harmful project to proceed. An important difference, however, is that Canadian and U.S. federal laws normally require EIA only for actions involving the federal government, while Mexico requires EIA for both public and private projects that fall within specified categories.

Another point on which the North American laws are not in harmony is whether to require EIA of the extraterritorial effects of projects within each country's jurisdiction—that is, transboundary EIA. Canadian law requires EIA of federal projects to include transboundary effects, and it also provides that the federal government may assess the transboundary impacts of nonfederal projects.[14] The law in the United States and Mexico is less clear. U.S. law does not specifically address transboundary EIA. Although some judicial decisions have assumed that the federal government should take into account extraterritorial effects of actions within the United States, courts have not held that federal law requires that result.[15] Similarly, the Mexican statute requiring EIA does not say whether it must include the extraterritorial effects of actions within Mexico. A 1988 regulation implementing the statute seemed to require EIA for projects with extraterritorial effects, but it was replaced in 2000 by a regulation that does not mention transboundary EIA.[16]

An international agreement requiring transboundary EIA could ensure that all three countries fully consider the extraterritorial effects of projects within their jurisdiction.[17] Canada, the country with the clearest domestic authority to conduct transboundary EIA, proposed including a reference to it in the NAAEC. The proposal eventually became Article 10(7), which requires the Council to "consider and develop recommendations" regarding transboundary EIA, "with a view to agreement between the Parties pursuant to this Article within three years [that is, by January 1, 1997] on obligations." The Council and Secretariat moved fairly quickly to prepare the groundwork for meeting this goal. In October 1995, in one of its first resolutions, the Council adopted overarching principles to guide the implementation of Article 10(7). The Secretariat prepared background papers comparing the domestic EIA laws of the Parties and describing international precedents for transboundary EIA.[18]

The Parties began their talks by convening an expert group composed of federal officials, which released a draft agreement on transboundary EIA in 1997. The draft agreement would require the "Party of origin"—that is, any Party within whose territory a proposed project would be undertaken—to take several actions: (1) notify "potentially affected Parties" of proposed projects if the projects are either located within 100 kilometers of a border and of a type listed in an annex to the agreement or determined by the Party of origin to have the potential to cause adverse transboundary environmental impacts; (2) assess the transboundary environmental impacts of proposed projects; and (3) allow the potentially affected Party and its public to participate in the assessment process.[19]

In June 1997, the Council issued a resolution stating that the Parties "agree to complete a legally-binding agreement consistent with their obligations under Article 10(7) . . . by April 15, 1998." But more than five years past that deadline, the negotiations are still not complete. The Parties are deadlocked over the scope of the agreement—specifically, which actions should be considered "proposed projects" and therefore subject to notification and assessment. Article 10(7) contemplates that the agreement will apply only to proposed projects that are "subject to decisions by a competent government authority," but this language does not clearly cover decisions by subfederal governments. As I have argued elsewhere, the general approach of the agreement is to extend the Parties' domestic EIA laws to transboundary effects rather than require substantive changes to the laws.[20] That approach might suggest that Canada and the United States would only require transboundary EIA for projects with federal involvement, since those are the projects normally subject to EIA under their federal laws. But Mexico has argued that since its law requires EIA for certain private projects with no federal involvement, Canada and the United States must ensure that projects with state and provincial government involvement are included in order to make the obligations of the Parties more closely equivalent.

Of course, the Agreement could also make the obligations equivalent by requiring transboundary EIA only for projects with federal involvement and providing that Mexico need only undertake transboundary EIA for projects of a type for which EIA would be required under U.S. or Canadian law. But Mexico finds that alternative unpalatable. Its position results in large part from recent proposals to build facilities for the disposal of hazardous waste near the Mexican border.[21] Mexicans have strongly opposed these projects, especially a proposal to site a low-level radioactive waste facility near Sierra Blanca, Texas. These facilities are not typically federal projects for the purpose of U.S. federal EIA law and would not be covered by a transboundary EIA agreement whose scope was limited to projects with federal involvement. Although Texas eventually denied a permit to the Sierra Blanca facility, Mexican officials have made clear that they cannot accept a transboundary EIA agreement that would not apply to similar proposals in the future.[22] Legally, the United States could almost certainly extend EIA to nonfederal projects with extraterritorial effects on the basis of an international agreement requiring it to do so. It is doubtful, however, that such an effort by the U.S. government would receive the necessary political support. Canada appears to face similar constraints.[23] As a result of these conflicting pressures, the negotiations for an agreement on transboundary EIA are at an impasse.

RECIPROCAL ACCESS TO DOMESTIC LEGAL REMEDIES FOR TRANSBOUNDARY POLLUTION

Legal obstacles often restrict the ability of foreign residents to bring claims for transboundary pollution in domestic courts. A famous example is the Trail Smelter dispute. If the farms affected by the pollution from the smelter had been in British Columbia, their owners could have brought a nuisance claim there. But Canadian courts had adopted the local action rule, under which a court may hear claims for damage to land only if the land is located within the jurisdiction of the court. The Washington farmers were therefore without an effective legal remedy.[24] The Trail Smelter case was eventually resolved through international arbitration of a claim brought on the farmers' behalf by the U.S. government.[25] But international arbitration is expensive, controversial, and slow, and governments have rarely been willing to pursue it on behalf of citizens alleging transboundary harm.

In the 1970s, the Organization for Economic Cooperation and Development (OECD) encouraged its member countries to adopt the principle of equal access.[26] Equal access would allow a resident of a country who is or may be harmed by transboundary pollution to seek relief through legal proceedings in the country in which the pollution originates. It would not require the creation of new substantive standards for transboundary pollution; it would only allow foreign residents to pursue whatever remedies the country of origin would provide to its own residents if the harm occurred there. The concept is also limited to allowing the victims of transboundary harm to sue the polluter in the country where the pollution originates; it does not speak to whether victims may sue the polluter in their own country. The appeal of equal access is that opening domestic courts to claims of transboundary pollution would allow international disputes to be resolved through existing courts, on the basis of existing law, without the involvement of the federal governments.

Some domestic laws in North America provide for equal access on a reciprocal basis with respect to particular types of harm. For example, U.S. laws allow foreign residents to recover response costs and damages resulting from discharges of oil or hazardous waste in their territorial sea or navigable waters from vessels or facilities under U.S. jurisdiction, as long as the claimants' country provides a comparable remedy for U.S. claimants.[27] But these laws obviously do not apply to most instances of transboundary pollution. More generally, the U.S. and Canadian governments have adopted laws giving foreign governments limited rights to participate in administrative hearings designed to address whether domestic air and water pollution standards should be tightened to regulate transboundary pollution.[28] In practice, however, these provisions seem to have been of little or no value. The country of origin has been unwilling to invoke the provisions, and the country affected by the transboundary pollution has been unable to force it to do so.[29]

In 1979, a joint working group of the American and Canadian Bar Associations incorporated the OECD proposal into a draft treaty, which would require each country in which transboundary pollution originates to ensure that any victim of the pollution residing in the other country would receive treatment at least equivalent to that afforded in the country of origin.[30] Despite the endorsement of the bar associations, the governments did not pursue adoption of the draft treaty. The bar associations next proposed reciprocal legislation. At their suggestion, a liaison committee of the U.S. National Conference of Commissioners on Uniform State Laws and the Canadian Uniform Law Conference drafted a Uniform Transboundary Pollution Reciprocal Access Act in 1982. Its key provision states:

> A person who suffers, or is threatened with, injury to his person or property in a reciprocating jurisdiction caused by pollution originating, or that may originate, in this jurisdiction has the same rights to relief with respect to the injury or threatened injury, and may enforce those rights in this jurisdiction as if the injury or threatened injury occurred in this jurisdiction.[31]

If adopted by federal and subfederal governments, this language would provide equal access on a reciprocal basis throughout North America. It has not been widely adopted, however, for several reasons. First, it excludes Mexico. It defines "reciprocating jurisdiction" as a U.S. state or a Canadian province or territory that has either enacted the Act or that "provides substantially equivalent access to its courts and administrative agencies," and its commentary makes clear that it "does not apply to U.S./Mexico transboundary pollution or to pollution from any other nation."[32] Second, the U.S. and Canadian governments have shown no interest in adopting the

Uniform Act at the federal level. Third, the initial interest in the Act by U.S. states and Canadian provinces has waned. In the first ten years after its adoption by the uniform law conferences, seven states and four provinces enacted it, but none has done so since 1992.[33]

Against this backdrop, the inclusion of two provisions in the NAAEC on reciprocal access appeared to indicate that the Parties would renew efforts to obtain reciprocal access throughout North America. Article 10(8) of the NAAEC calls on the Council to "encourage the establishment by each Party of appropriate administrative procedures pursuant to its environmental laws to permit another Party to seek the reduction, elimination or mitigation of transboundary pollution on a reciprocal basis," and Article 10(9) requires the Council to "consider and, as appropriate, develop recommendations on the provision by a Party, on a reciprocal basis, of access to and rights and remedies before its courts and administrative agencies for persons in another Party's territory who have suffered or are likely to suffer damage or injury caused by pollution originating in its territory as if the damage or injury were suffered in its territory."

The implementation of Articles 10(8) and 10(9) has been disappointing, however. The Council has made no effort to encourage reciprocal access either by governments to administrative relief or by citizens to legal remedies. The only step toward implementation of either of the provisions is a Secretariat report, published in 1999, that describes potential legal barriers in each country to equal access and concludes that serious obstacles still exist.[34] For example, most Canadian provinces continue to apply a strict version of the local action rule, which would prevent transboundary suits based in nuisance.[35] In the United States, the local action rule appears unlikely to be a barrier in many cases, but some courts have denied standing to Canadian plaintiffs under U.S. statutes on the basis of a presumption that the statutes are not concerned with the environment beyond the U.S. borders.[36] More generally, while few statutes in the United States and Canada explicitly bar foreign residents from bringing suit, few statutes explicitly provide that they may have standing. As a result, their right to participate in domestic legal proceedings is often uncertain. As for Mexico, the report concludes that the problem is not that domestic remedies for environmental harm bar access to those complaining of transboundary harm but rather that Mexican legal remedies for environmental harm "do not have the same scope as the remedies available in Canada and the United States."[37]

The joint working group of the bar associations, which has included representatives from the Mexican bar since the early 1990s, reviewed the Secretariat draft report on reciprocal access in 1997. The group noted that the North American countries could provide for equal access through a treaty but that a treaty would face political and legal difficulties, and the Canadian and U.S. governments had shown no interest in a treaty in the past. It recommended that the NAAEC Parties instead build on the Uniform Act by amending it to apply to Mexico and by pursuing wider adoption of it by federal and subfederal governments throughout North America.[38] The Council has not taken any action in response to these recommendations or the Secretariat report.

When Should the CEC Address Transboundary Pollution?

Why has the CEC failed to fulfill its specific mandates on transboundary environmental harm? And what lessons does its failure have with respect to its ability to address transboundary pollution in other ways?

Although many factors may have contributed to the failure of the CEC to facilitate agreement on transboundary EIA and to promote reciprocal access to domestic legal remedies, one obvious problem is that the CEC is a trilateral organization, and these issues are essentially bilateral. A commonplace among theorists and diplomats is that international agreement becomes more difficult as more countries are added to the mix. Richard Williamson, a former U.S. diplomat, says, "The preponderant fraction of environmental issues with international implications is bilateral and should be handled as such. With few exceptions, bilateral negotiations are far more efficient than multilateral diplomacy." He says that this point "should seem so obvious as not to merit mention yet . . . [t]here are strong pressures to regionalize or globalize problems which are inherently national or bilateral in scope, in the mistaken belief that doing so will accelerate progress."[39]

Seeking a uniform trilateral agreement on transboundary EIA has prevented the Parties from seeking more attainable bilateral agreements. If Canada and the United States were not enmeshed in the stalled trilateral negotiation, they could reach a bilateral agreement tomorrow. But that potential agreement is blocked by the deadlock between the United States and Mexico over how to address EIA along their border. Similarly, the Council's lack of interest in reciprocal access may be due in part to the fact that the obstacles to access are quite different along the two borders. For example, Canada is still grappling with the local action rule, while in Mexico, according to the Secretariat report, the problem is inadequate remedies for environmental claims generally. Moreover, some state and provincial laws already provide for reciprocal access along the Canada-U.S. border. Pushing that legislation further or extending it to the federal government raises different issues than introducing equivalent legislation for the first time along the U.S.-Mexico border. Attempting to find continent-wide solutions for the lack of reciprocal access thus may obscure the problems rather than shed light on them.[40]

A bilateral agreement may be easier to obtain, but it may also be less comprehensive than a trilateral agreement. As Kenneth Oye has said, "reductions in the number of actors can usually only be purchased at the expense of the magnitude of gains from cooperation."[41] The attainable U.S.-Canada agreement on transboundary EIA would be limited to federal projects and to effects across the Canada-U.S. border. These limitations are undesirable from an environmental point of view, since they would exclude many North American projects that might have significant transboundary effects.[42] But a limited agreement would be far better than nothing. In particular, it would clearly establish for the first time that the United States must require EIA for federal projects within its territory that have effects in Canada. Moreover, it would not foreclose an agreement between the United States and Mexico, which those governments could continue to pursue. Indeed, the fear of being left behind might spur those interested in transboundary EIA along the U.S.-Mexico border to greater efforts to reach an agreement.

Of course, if an agreement must be uniform among all three Parties for reasons of effectiveness or fairness, then any delay necessary to obtain the consent of all three countries would be unavoidable. But most cases of transboundary pollution do not directly concern all three North American countries. Article 10(7) of the NAAEC recognizes "the significant bilateral nature of many transboundary environmental issues." Issues arising along one border may well be similar, or parallel, to those arising on the other, but a uniform approach to parallel bilateral issues is not necessary. There is no reason why Canada and the United States must have the same type of arrangement regarding transboundary EIA or reciprocal access as Mexico and the United States do, any more than it is necessary for the IJC and the IBWC to have identical powers. The border regions are different in many ways, as are the bilateral relations between the countries. The countries can reasonably seek to reach different solutions to parallel problems.

What role does this leave for the CEC with respect to transboundary pollution? In theory, the CEC might try to oversee the negotiation of separate bilateral agreements. The CEC could, for example, host simultaneous negotiations aimed at two transboundary EIA agreements or serve as a conduit for public participation with respect to particular cases of bilateral transboundary pollution. But it is hard to see how a trilateral institution would be better than a bilateral institution at hosting bilateral negotiations or facilitating public participation concerning bilateral issues. Representatives of the third Party would be superfluous to any serious bilateral negotiations. And it seems self-evident that a bilateral institution like the BECC, with a binational secretariat based in Ciudad Juárez, would be better at organizing a public meeting on an issue of U.S.-Mexico pollution than would the trinational, Montreal-based CEC Secretariat.

For all of these reasons, the CEC is ill-suited to addressing issues of transboundary harm that are primarily bilateral. The Parties should continue to use bilateral institutions such as the IJC, the La Paz mechanisms, the IBWC, and the BECC to address these issues and refrain from using the CEC to supervise them.

What about gaps in the coverage of the bilateral institutions? One argument for referring issues of transboundary harm to the CEC is that there may not be a bilateral institution capable of addressing the issues. Along the Canada-U.S. border, the IJC has the power under the 1909 Boundary Waters Treaty to receive references and produce objective reports on almost any issue of transboundary harm, but in recent years the governments have only rarely referred such issues to it. Moreover, the IJC may not initiate studies on its own or at the request of anyone other than the federal governments. Along the U.S.-Mexico border, neither the IBWC nor the BECC has a mandate to address transboundary pollution generally. The La Paz consultative mechanism can address almost any border issue, but it has no independent commissioners or secretariat able to produce objective, professional reports like those of the CEC or IJC.

The response to these gaps in the jurisdiction of the bilateral institutions should not be to give the CEC mandates for which it is poorly suited but rather to add the necessary functions at the bilateral level. For example, the governments could establish a professional, binational secretariat able to support the work of the La Paz national coordinators and working groups and give it the power to investigate, report on, and facilitate agreement between the concerned parties with respect to border and transboundary issues.[43] With respect to Canada-U.S. issues, the obvious solution is to take greater advantage of the IJC's reference authority. One possibility would be to allow the IJC, subfederal governments, and private parties to initiate references, although the federal governments would presumably resist this diminution in their control.[44] To address government concerns, Stephen Toope and Jutta Brunnee have suggested that the IJC look to Article 13 of the NAAEC, which authorizes the CEC Secretariat to report on issues on its own initiative or based on requests from any source but also gives the Council the power to block the Secretariat from preparing or publishing reports under certain conditions. They suggest that "efforts should be made to adapt this balancing of legitimate interests in independence and control so as to suit the role of the IJC as it has evolved over the decades."[45]

Despite the importance of the bilateral institutions in addressing transboundary pollution, the CEC has at least two important roles to play. First, it can facilitate the exchange of information. There is no reason why the countries must reach uniform trilateral solutions to similar bilateral problems, but understanding how parallel issues have been addressed along the other border might often help the Parties reach an effective bilateral agreement. The CEC reports on reciprocal access and transboundary EIA show that the Secretariat is capable of providing a high-quality comparative study on a trilateral basis.

Second, the CEC can play an indispensable role in addressing transboundary pollution that is trilateral in nature. Some issues of transboundary harm do concern all three countries directly. When the ecosystem affected by transboundary pollution is continental in scope, then the CEC is perfectly situated to address the problem, and no bilateral institution can address it as well.

The CEC has begun to address air pollution on such a continental basis. In 1997, the Secretariat prepared a report under Article 13 on "continental pollutant pathways," which examined long-range transport of air pollution throughout North America.[46] The report focused on five types of pollutants—acid deposition, mercury, ground-level ozone, particulate matter, and persistent organic pollutants—and concluded that such "continental pollutants" are "affecting human health and the environment throughout North America." It identified major sources of the pollutants and techniques to reduce emissions, and it emphasized the necessity for trilateral collaboration to address the problem on the basis of an integrated ecosystem approach. The report made several specific recommendations to the Council, including that it assume a lead responsibility for promoting and coordinating trinational action to reduce the exposure of humans and the environment to continental pollutants and that it establish a high-level working group composed of experts responsible for regulating air pollution to advise the Council on priorities for action, air-quality objectives, cooperative measures, and so forth.[47] At its June 2002 annual meeting, the Council established such a working group, to be called the North American Air Working Group, and gave it a mandate to provide advice to the Council on the development and implementation of CEC activities involving air issues.[48]

Of course, the line between transboundary harm that is primarily bilateral and harm that is primarily trilateral will often be difficult to draw. Many instances of transboundary harm may have continental implications, even if they appear to be primarily bilateral or even national. Indeed, the NAAEC is founded upon the idea that, after NAFTA, the residents of North America all have an interest in ensuring that the three countries improve and effectively enforce their environmental laws, even concerning matters that appear purely domestic. Even though in a sense everything is connected, however, some connections are stronger than others. Using bilateral institutions to address transboundary harm that is primarily bilateral and the CEC to address transboundary harm that is primarily trilateral is the best way to use the available institutional resources most effectively.

In sum, the lesson of the failed implementation of Articles 10(7), 10(8), and 10(9) is that the CEC should focus on areas in which it has a comparative advantage. Environmental harm that affects the continental ecosystem, such as long-range air pollution, certainly qualifies. With respect to issues that are primarily bilateral, the CEC should do no more than prepare a comparative report. If more specific solutions are sought, the CEC should refer the issue to the appropriate bilateral institution.[49] Moreover, it should encourage the governments to strengthen the capability of the bilateral institutions to receive such references, from private parties as well as governments, so that they can produce objective, professional reports and facilitate agreement on transboundary issues. The best way the CEC can help to solve issues of bilateral transboundary harm is to encourage and facilitate their bilateral resolution.

Notes

1. By "transboundary pollution" I mean pollution arising on one side of an international border that causes harm on the other side. Although this chapter focuses on transboundary pollution, transboundary environmental harm can be considered more broadly, to include harm to migratory species, for example.

2. See *Environmental Management on North America's Borders* (Richard Kiy and John D. Wirth eds., 1998) (describing several current transboundary problems).

3. See Roberto A. Sánchez-Rodriguez, Konrad von Moltke, Steven Mumme, John Kirton, and Don Munton, "The Dynamics of Transboundary Environmental Agreements in North America," in id., 32, which describes a database of transboundary environmental agreements, including subfederal agreements, prepared for the CEC. Like other CEC documents, the database is available at *http://www.cec.org*.

4. Treaty Relating to the Boundary Waters and Questions Arising Along the Boundary Between the United States and Canada, Jan. 11, 1909, 36 Stat. 2448, 12 Bevans 319; Treaty Relating to the Utilization of Waters of the Colorado and Tijuana Rivers and of the Rio Grande, Feb. 3, 1944, 59 Stat. 1219, 9 Bevans 1166. For a comprehensive evaluation of the IJC and the IBWC, see the papers published at 33 *Natural Resources Journal* 1–200, 233–459 (1993).

5. In only their second reference to the IJC, in 1912, the governments asked it to investigate pollution of boundary waters on one side of the border that affected the boundary waters on the other side. The IJC recommended that the governments authorize it to regulate transboundary pollution, but the governments did not accept a convention drafted by the IJC in 1920 that would have given it broad powers to do so. Before the 1970s, the governments made nine more references asking the IJC to

report on particular instances of transboundary pollution. See Richard B. Bilder, "Controlling Great Lakes Pollution: A Study in United States–Canadian Environmental Cooperation," 70 *Michigan Law Review* 469, 489–501 (1972).

6. See Helen Ingram and David R. White, "International Boundary and Water Commission: An Institutional Mismatch for Resolving Transboundary Water Problems," 33 *Natural Resources Journal* 154 (1993).

7. U.S.-Canada Agreement on Great Lakes Water Quality, Apr. 15, 1972, 23 U.S.T. 301. The 1972 agreement was superseded by the Great Lakes Water Quality Agreement of 1978, Nov. 22, 1978, 30 U.S.T. 1383, which incorporated an ecosystem approach to Great Lakes environmental protection. The 1978 agreement continued the IJC's mandate to assist and monitor implementation by the parties. The 1978 Agreement was amended in 1983 and 1987.

8. Agreement Approving IBWC Minute 242 Setting Forth a Permanent and Definitive Solution to the International Problem of the Salinity of the Colorado River, Aug. 30, 1973, 24 U.S.T. 1968. Essentially, the United States agreed to ensure that the water of the Colorado would not exceed a specified salinity when it crossed the border into Mexico.

9. IBWC Minute 261 Concerning Recommendations for the Solution to the Border Sanitation Problems, Sept. 24, 1979, 31 U.S.T. 5099.

10. La Paz Agreement for the Protection and Improvement of the Environment in the Border Area, Aug. 14, 1983, 1352 U.N.T.S. 67.

11. U.S.-Canada Air Quality Agreement, Mar. 13, 1991, 30 I.L.M. 676.

12. Agreement Concerning the Establishment of a Border Environment Cooperation Commission and a North American Development Bank, Nov. 16, 1993, 32 I.L.M. 1545.

13. See National Environmental Policy Act of 1969 (NEPA), 42 U.S.C. § 4332; Canadian Environmental Assessment Act (CEAA), S.C. ch. 37 (1992); Ley General del Equilibrio Ecológico y la Protección al Ambiente (LGEEPA), arts. 28–35, *Diario Oficial de la Federación* (Jan. 28, 1988; amended Dec. 13, 1996). For a comparative description of the laws, see CEC Secretariat, "Environmental Impact Assessment: Law and Practice in North America," 3 *North American Environmental Law and Policy* 3 (1999).

14. CEAA, supra, § 2(1) (defining "environmental effect" that is to be assessed to include transboundary effects); § 47 (authorizing ministers of environment and foreign affairs to refer projects for assessment of their transboundary effects where they are not otherwise subject to EIA under the CEAA and where they may cause significant adverse environmental effects outside Canada).

15. See *Swinomish Tribal Community v. Federal Energy Regulatory Commission*, 627 F.2d 499 (D.C. Cir. 1980) (assuming that NEPA applies to effects in Canada of raising dam on Skagit River); *Wilderness Society v. Morton*, 463 F.2d 1261 (D.C. Cir. 1972) (assuming that NEPA applies to Alaskan oil pipeline's impacts in Canada). In *Environmental Defense Fund v. Massey*, 986 F.2d 528 (D.C. Cir. 1993), the court held that NEPA required EIA for federal decisions taken in the United States whose effects would occur in Antarctica. If extended to effects in sovereign countries, the holding would seem to require transboundary EIA. No court has so extended it, however.

See *NEPA Coalition of Japan v. Aspin*, 837 F. Supp. 466 (D.D.C. 1993) (declining to require EIA for U.S. military bases in Japan).

16. See Reglamento de la Ley General del Equilibrio Ecológico y la Protección al Ambiente en Materia del Impacto Ambiental, art. 5, § XIII, *Diario Oficial de la Federación* (June 7, 1988); Reglamento de la Ley General del Equilibrio Ecológico y la Protección al Ambiente en Materia de Evaluación del Impacto Ambiental, *Diaro Oficial de la Federacion* (May 30, 2000).

17. Some North American agreements might already seem to require transboundary EIA. See La Paz Agreement, supra, art. 7 ("The Parties shall assess, as appropriate, in accordance with their respective national laws, regulations and policies, projects that may have significant impacts on the environment of the border area, so that appropriate measures may be considered to avoid or mitigate adverse environmental effects."); Air Quality Agreement, supra, art. V(1) ("Each Party shall, as appropriate and as required by its laws, regulations and policies, assess those proposed actions, activities and projects within the area under its jurisdiction that, if carried out, would be likely to cause significant transboundary air pollution, including consideration of appropriate mitigation measures."). Despite the apparent meaning of these provisions, however, they seem to have been interpreted to avoid requiring the parties to do more to assess transboundary effects than their domestic law already requires them to do.

In 1991, Canada and the United States, together with many European countries, signed the Espoo Convention on Environmental Impact in a Transboundary Context, Feb. 25, 1991, 30 I.L.M. 800, which would clearly require transboundary EIA. Canada ratified the convention in 1998, but the United States has yet to ratify it.

18. See "Environmental Impact Assessment," supra, 13; "Transboundary Environmental Impact Assessment," 4 *North American Environmental Law and Policy* 3 (2000).

19. See Draft North American Agreement on Transboundary Environmental Impact Assessment, available at *http://www.cec.org/pubs_info_resources/law_treat_agree/*.

20. See John H. Knox, "The Myth and Reality of Transboundary Environmental Impact Assessment," 96 *American Journal of International Law* 291 (2002).

21. For a description of several of the proposals and the local opposition to them, written by one of the opponents, see Alfredo Gutiérrez Jr., "Milagro Beanfield War Revisited: Low-Level Hazardous Waste Sites in Del Rio, Dryden, and Spofford, Texas," in Kiy and Wirth, supra, 221.

22. See Dora Delgado, "NAFTA: U.S., Mexico Still Need to Resolve Reciprocity Issues on Assessments," *BNA Daily Environmental Report* (July 2, 1998); "NAFTA: Mexico Denounces U.S. Position on NAFTA Impact Assessment Guidelines," *BNA Daily Environmental Report* (May 21, 1998).

23. In ratifying the Espoo Convention, Canada attached a reservation "in respect of proposed activities (as defined in this Convention) that fall outside of federal legislative jurisdiction exercised in respect of environmental assessment." Although CEAA § 47 seems to give the federal government broad authority to require transboundary EIA for projects without federal involvement, it leaves the decision to the discretion of federal officials. It has been suggested that even though the Canadian

constitution provides a strong basis for the exercise of federal jurisdiction with respect to transboundary impacts, the federal government will be reluctant for political reasons to exercise that jurisdiction. Steven A. Kennett, "The *Canadian Environmental Assessment Act*'s Transboundary Provisions: Trojan Horse or Paper Tiger?" 5 *Journal of Environmental Law and Practice* 263 (1995).

24. See John E. Read, "The Trail Smelter Dispute," *Canadian Yearbook of International Law*, 213, 222 (1963). The farmers could have tried to sue the smelter in Washington, but jurisdiction over foreign polluters is not always clear, and enforcing judgments against them is usually problematic.

25. Trail Smelter Arbitration (U.S. v. Canada), 3 R.I.A.A. 1905 (1941). See John D. Wirth, *Smelter Smoke in North America: The Politics of Transborder Pollution* (2000) (describing the case and its historical context).

26. See OECD Council, "Implementation of a Regime of Equal Right of Access and Non-Discrimination in Relation to Transfrontier Pollution," res. C(77)28 (May 17, 1977), reprinted in OECD, *OECD and the Environment* 150 (1986); OECD Council, "Equal Right of Access in Relation to Transfrontier Pollution," res. C(76)55 (May 11, 1976), reprinted in id., 148. Canada and the United States are longstanding members of the OECD; Mexico joined in 1994.

27. See Oil Pollution Act of 1990, § 1007, 33 U.S.C. § 2707; Comprehensive Environmental Response, Compensation and Liability Act of 1980, § 111(*l*), 42 U.S.C. § 9611(*l*).

28. U.S. Clean Water Act, § 310, 33 U.S.C. § 1320; U.S. Clean Air Act, § 115, 42 U.S.C. § 7415; Canadian Environmental Protection Act, S.C. 1999, ch. 33, §§ 166, 176.

29. See *Her Majesty the Queen in Right of Ontario v. U.S. Environmental Protection Agency*, 912 F. 2d 1525 (D.C. Cir. 1990) (refusing to overturn EPA's rejection of a petition by Ontario seeking to trigger § 115 of the Clean Air Act). See also Thomas W. Merrill, "Golden Rules for Transboundary Pollution," 46 *Duke Law Journal* 931, 959 (1997) (concluding that § 115 has "proven to be a dead letter").

30. See "Report of the Joint Working Group to the 1979 Annual Meeting of the Canadian Bar Association," in *Settlement of International Disputes between Canada and the USA: Resolutions Adopted by the American Bar Association and the Canadian Bar Association with Accompanying Reports and Recommendations* (1979).

31. Uniform Transboundary Reciprocal Access Act, § 3.

32. See id., § 1(1) and accompanying commentary.

33. The states are: Colorado, Col. Rev. Stat. §§ 13-1.5-101 to 13-1.5-109; Connecticut, Conn. Gen. Stat. § 51-351b; Michigan, Mich. Comp. Laws §§ 324.1801 to 324.1807; Montana, Mont. Code §§ 75-16-101 to 75-16-109; New Jersey, N.J. Stat. §§ 2A:58A-1 to 2A:58A-8; Oregon, Ore. Rev. Stat. §§ 468.076 to 468.089; and Wisconsin, Wisc. Stat. §144.995. The provinces are: Manitoba, R.S.M. 1985–86, c. 11; Nova Scotia, R.S.N.S. 1994–95, c. 1, part XVI; Ontario, R.S.O., c. T-18; and Prince Edward Island, R.S.P.E.I. 1988, c. T-5.

34. "Background Paper on Access to Courts and Administrative Agencies in Transboundary Pollution Matters," 4 *North American Environmental Law and Policy* 205 (2000).

35. Id., 229–30. The provinces that appear to have done away with the rule are

Manitoba, Nova Scotia, Ontario, and Prince Edward Island. Quebec never adopted the local action rule, an artifact of common law, but it did have a civil-law equivalent, which it has now repealed.

36. See id., 232–36. See also, e.g., *Corrosion Proof Fittings v. Environmental Protection Agency*, 947 F.2d 1201 (5th Cir. 1991) (holding that the governments of Canada and Quebec did not have standing to contest an EPA rule banning asbestos because the statute on which the rule was based did not require EPA to consider extraterritorial effects); *Detroit Audubon Society v. City of Detroit*, 696 F. Supp. 249 (E.D. Mich. 1988) (holding that Ontario lacked standing to bring suit under the Michigan Environmental Protection Act because the act was concerned with protecting Michigan's natural resources), *reversed on other grounds*, *Her Majesty the Queen in Right of the Province of Ontario v. City of Detroit*, 874 F.2d 332 (6th Cir. 1989).

37. "Background Paper on Access to Courts and Administrative Agencies," supra, 298.

38. See "Recommendations of the Joint Working Group of the American Bar Association, Barra Mexicana and Canadian Bar Association" (Dec. 1997) (on file with author). Members of the joint working group participated in drafting the CEC report on reciprocal access. I have been a member of the joint working group since 1994 and helped to draft and review the report.

39. Richard L. Williamson Jr., "Building the International Environmental Regime: A Status Report," 21 *Inter-American Law Review* 679, 747, 748 n.280 (1990). See Kenneth A. Oye, "Explaining Cooperation under Anarchy: Hypotheses and Strategies," in *Cooperation under Anarchy* 18–22 (Kenneth A. Oye ed., 1986) (using game theory to explain why the prospects for cooperation diminish as the number of players increases).

40. I do not mean to suggest that the difficulty of addressing reciprocal access on a trilateral basis is the main reason that the federal governments have not pursued the issue. Other reasons may include disinclination among the governments, especially in the United States and Canada, to take action on an issue that would require changes in state and provincial laws and a lack of pressure from environmental groups to clarify the rules concerning reciprocal access. This lack of pressure is somewhat puzzling, but it may result from a belief that, despite the legal obstacles, foreign residents do have some access to domestic courts for transboundary pollution claims. See, e.g., *United States v. Hooker*, 101 F.R.D. 444 (W.D.N.Y. 1984) (allowing Ontario to intervene in case involving transboundary pollution to protect its nuisance claim); *Michie v. Great Lakes Steel Division, National Steel Corp.*, 495 F.2d 213 (6th Cir. 1974) (allowing Ontario residents to bring nuisance action under Michigan law against corporations operating plants in the United States that emit air pollution); *Wilderness Society v. Morton*, 463 F.2d 1261 (D.C. Cir. 1972) (allowing Canadian citizens and environmental groups to intervene in a suit claiming failure to conduct an adequate EIA of the trans-Alaska pipeline). Or it may result from a belief that few such claims would be brought even if all legal obstacles were removed. The Secretariat report on reciprocal access found no reported cases under the Uniform Transboundary Pollution Reciprocal Access Act in any of the jurisdictions that have adopted it.

41. Oye, supra, 21.

42. See John H. Knox, "Federal, State and Provincial Interplay Regarding Cross-Border Environmental Pollution," 27 *Canada-U.S. Law Journal* 199, 202–3 (2001).

43. See Leonard B. Dworsky and Albert E. Utton, "Assessing North America's Management of Its Transboundary Waters," 33 *Natural Resources Journal* 413, 447 n.59 (1993).

44. The governments reacted unfavorably to efforts in the 1970s to expand the authority of the IJC. See David Lemarquand, "The International Joint Commission and Changing Canada-United States Boundary Relations," 33 *Natural Resources Journal* 59, 74–77 (1993); Don Munton, "Paradoxes and Prospects," *The International Joint Commission Seventy Years On* 60, 75–81 (Robert Spencer et al. eds., 1981).

45. Stephen J. Toope and Jutta Brunnee, "Freshwater Regimes: The Mandate of the International Joint Commission," 15 *Arizona Journal of International and Comparative Law* 273, 282–83 (1998). See also Environmental Law Institute, *An Evaluation of the Effectiveness of the International Joint Commission* 58 (1995) (suggesting that the IJC should incorporate a public petition procedure like that created by NAAEC Articles 14 and 15).

46. CEC, *Continental Pollutant Pathways: An Agenda for Cooperation to Address Long-Range Transport of Air Pollution in North America* (1997).

47. Id., 36–38. The CEC Secretariat has since followed up that report with a more detailed study of the pollutant pathways of dioxin, which indicates that dioxin from specific sources in the United States and Mexico is traveling thousands of kilometers to Nunavit in the Canadian Arctic. CEC, *Long-range Air Transport of Dioxin from North American Sources to Ecologically Vulnerable Receptors in Nunavit, Arctic Canada* (Sept. 2000).

48. CEC Council Resolution 02-04, June 19, 2002. Current CEC activities concerning air quality include programs to improve coordination between the Parties' air-quality management agencies and support the development of an association of Mexican air-quality professionals, to develop comparable information about air pollution emissions in the three countries in order to facilitate effective cooperative efforts to reduce those emissions, and to study air pollution caused by freight transport along highways used as "trade corridors" throughout the continent. See CEC, *North American Agenda for Action: 2002–2004*, at 55–67.

49. A CEC Council reference to the IJC would provide a legal basis for the IJC to prepare a comprehensive report on the referred issue. Under Article IX of the Boundary Waters Treaty, supra, either the U.S. or the Canadian government may refer an issue to the IJC unilaterally, but in practice the referrals have always been joint. A unanimous request by the ministers sitting in Council would meet either standard.

PART 2

Trade and Environment in North America

MARY E. KELLY AND CYRUS REED 6

The CEC's Trade and Environment Program

Cutting-Edge Analysis but Untapped Potential

A CENTRAL ELEMENT of the work of the Commission for Environmental Cooperation (CEC) is its Environment, Economy and Trade program.[1] Included within this program are projects designed to assess the environmental effects of the North American Free Trade Agreement (NAFTA), in accordance with Article 10(6)(d) of the North American Agreement on Environmental Cooperation (NAAEC). More recently, the CEC has undertaken projects to examine the environmental effects of an integrated North American electricity market, including expanded cross-border trade in electricity, and the effects of agricultural market integration on biodiversity, forestry, and freshwater resources.

Despite a slow and controversial start, the CEC's trade and environment work has succeeded in producing a cutting-edge analysis methodology.[2] It has applied that methodology to explore and illuminate North American trade and environment linkages in the important areas of agriculture (corn, in particular), transportation, energy, forestry, hazardous wastes, industrial pollution, and electricity production. The CEC's work has shown that careful sector- or case-specific studies conducted in an open and transparent manner can provide a better understanding of the links between trade and environment than most of the limited-scope macroeconomic models in which effects are masked by modeling assumptions, data aggregation, and data unavailability.[3] And in some instances the CEC's trade effects work has led to increased North American cooperation on environmental issues.

Yet it is still unclear how the CEC's work can or will be used to influence the outcome of ongoing and future trade negotiations, such as the current discussions surrounding the proposed Free Trade Area of the Americas (FTAA). Even more troubling to some, the North American governments have yet to call on the CEC's significant trade and environment experience to inform either the deliberations of NAFTA's Free Trade Commission or the environmentally related disputes being played out under NAFTA Chapter 11 provisions.[4]

This chapter examines the CEC's trade and environment work, with a focus on its work on assessing the effects of NAFTA. It also discusses some of the lessons learned from this work, both from the CEC's perspective and from the perspective of outside observers. The chapter concludes with a discussion of how the CEC's Trade and Environment program is or is not influencing ongoing trade discussions, both within and beyond the NAFTA framework.

Overview of the CEC's Trade and Environment Program

The CEC's Trade and Environment program currently has four major elements:[5]

(1) assessing the environment in the context of North American market integration;[6]

(2) supporting environmental protection and conservation through green goods and services;

(3) financing in support of environmental protection and conservation; and

(4) exploring market-based mechanisms for carbon sequestration, energy efficiency, and renewable energy in North America.

Though each of these elements is important in its own regard, this chapter focuses on the CEC's work in assessing environment and trade relationships.[7] This work arises from the directive of Article 10(6)(d) of the NAAEC, which provides that the CEC Council shall "cooperate with the NAFTA Free Trade Commission to achieve the environmental goals and objectives of NAFTA by . . . considering on an ongoing basis the environmental effects of the NAFTA." Article 10(6) also charges the Council with a number of responsibilities to "cooperate with" the Free Trade Commission, including "contributing to the prevention or resolution of environment-related trade disputes."[8] As discussed later in this chapter, however, the dispute resolution aspect of the CEC's charge has yet to materialize in any significant way.

As expressed by the CEC, the goal of its assessment work is to "clarify the extent to which market integration—driven by trade and trade-related investment among the NAFTA partners—directly or indirectly affects environmental quality and environmental policies." The CEC predicts that this work will "provide a sound basis for identifying proactive policies—both in the environmental and economic policy arenas—intended to mitigate negative environmental effects of market integration, and maximize positive environmental outcomes."[9]

Briefly, the CEC's assessment work, which began in 1995, has taken place in five stages. The Commission first examined existing attempts to model the environmental effects of trade.[10] Then, in 1996, it convened an "experts" workshop of invited governmental, academic, and nongovernmental organization representatives to discuss the nature of trade and environment relationships in the North American context.[11] During this step, it also received advice on assessment methodology from the Joint Public Advisory Committee.

The CEC spent the next three years developing a peer-reviewed analytical framework and testing that framework on three specific sectors: maize production in Mexico; cattle feedlots in Canada and the United States; and electricity production in Canada, the United States, and Mexico.[12] After the release of the framework and the initial studies, the Commission issued a public call for proposals applying the framework to other issues and sectors. In October 2000, the results of these studies were presented in a high-profile symposium in Washington, D.C.[13] These studies analyzed trade and environment linkages in such specific areas as trade dispute resolution under NAFTA Chapter 11; forestry in Chihuahua; water exports from Canada; transboundary shipments of hazardous waste in North America; changes in the stone-washed garment industry in El Paso; and air quality in key NAFTA transportation corridors.

Following the symposium, CEC continued its assessment work by: looking more closely at environmental impacts of NAFTA transportation corridors and U.S.-Mexico corn trade;[14] initiating further study of the environmental effects of an integrated North American electricity market;[15] and convening experts on environmental assessments of trade agreements.[16]

To those who followed the early stages of the CEC's assessment program, these accomplishments are impressive, given that the NAFTA governments initially sought to block the Commission from doing anything to examine trade and environment linkages.[17] According to William Nitze, former U.S. Environmental Protection Agency Assistant Administrator for International Affairs, the trade ministries in all three countries were very sensitive to the CEC's initiating anything that might "throw sand in the gears of trade liberalization."[18] Facing the need to create almost one million new jobs per year, Mexico, in particular, was concerned about the impact of any such assessments on the level of future foreign direct investment in Mexico, according to Nitze and others involved in the process. In addition, in the period immediately following NAFTA's approval, the U.S. Trade Representative's office—and trade experts in general—still doubted the merits of dealing with environmental effects of free trade.[19]

In the end, however, the clear directive of Article 10(6)(d), as well as continued pressure from the environmental agencies and nongovernmental organizations in all three countries and the CEC staff's careful, objective, and transparent approach to constructing a peer-reviewed analytical framework, overcame the governments' resistance, and the assessment program was able to proceed.[20] The desire to put a positive spin on this work (no matter what the assessment results might show) is, nevertheless, still reflected in the posture that the work will be used to "*mitigate* negative environmental effects" (emphasis added). There is no acknowledgment of the possibility that the assessments might show that trade rules and regimes put in place by NAFTA should be adjusted to *prevent* negative effects on the North American environment. The emphasis remains, instead, on trying to lessen the severity of adverse impacts, in this case after the fact (that is, after NAFTA has been implemented).

Assessment Methodology and a Sampling of Results

THE ASSESSMENT METHODOLOGY

The analytical framework developed by the CEC to assess trade and environment linkages in the NAFTA context has four basic elements.[21] First, the framework requires that the issue or sector being studied be put in its appropriate environmental, economic, social, and geographic context. Second, the framework proposes analyzing connections to NAFTA in terms of NAFTA rule changes, NAFTA's institutions, trade flows, transborder investment flows, and other "economic conditioning" factors such as aggregate demand, income and population growth, and interest and exchange rates. Next, it contemplates an analysis of how NAFTA-induced changes in trade and investment relate to changes in production, management, technology, physical infrastructure, social organization, and government policy.[22] Finally, the framework provides fairly detailed guidance for evaluating environmental effects through the use of various indicators.[23] The CEC framework recognizes that data availability or suitability for this type of analysis might be a problem in some cases, and it encourages the identification of such data gaps.

The innovative aspects of this framework, as opposed, for example, to the more rigid, macroeconomic modeling approaches of the U.S. Trade Representative's environmental review process, are quite important.[24] The CEC framework does not ignore contextual issues such as domestic economic forces or social factors such as labor mobility or migration pressures. It also looks at more than just NAFTA-related tariff reductions—going deeper to examine the demonstrated or potential impacts of NAFTA-related rule changes, such as constraints on government procurement programs or restrictions on nontariff trade barriers. The framework recognizes that how "NAFTA-associated trade and investment affects the environment can best be assessed for current purposes, not at a broad macro level through quantitative modeling, but through an examination of the operations of individual plants and firms, the physical infrastructure that services them, the social organization that surrounds them, and the government policy that regulates their behavior and that of their stakeholders."[25]

The flexibility of the CEC's analytical framework allowed it to be used—both in the three initial case studies and in many of the papers prepared for the October 2000 symposium—to explore relevant and concrete examples of environmental effects linked to NAFTA-related changes. As illustrated in the next section, these studies do not necessarily produce sound-bite results (for example, trade is good or bad for the environment). Instead, the analyses often dramatically show the inherent complexity of trade/environment linkages, the strong influence of domestic economic and social conditions, and the ability (or inability, given NAFTA-related rule changes) of the governments to employ regulation or incentives to remedy adverse environmental effects.

SOME SAMPLE RESULTS OF EMPLOYING THE CEC ANALYTICAL FRAMEWORK

Corn Production in Mexico

The CEC's initial test of the analytical framework involved an examination of one of the most controversial and important issues in the NAFTA debate: the effects of tariff reductions on corn imported into Mexico.[26] The study provided a thorough examination of the economic, social, and other contexts for corn production in Mexico, and it reviewed some of the effects of the 1992 agricultural and land-tenure reforms Mexico enacted in anticipation of NAFTA.[27] It concluded that, depending on how fast the tariff reductions were actually phased in and depending on their size, location, and other factors, Mexican corn producers would likely have one of three principal responses to increasing imports of corn from the United States: (a) modernize to meet the challenges posed by imports, which could either increase or decrease the intensity of water and agricultural chemical use, depending on the methods employed by the growers; (b) substitute other crops or other land uses for corn, with a shift to higher-value horticultural crops generally implying increased water and agricultural chemical use; or (c) continue traditional subsistence corn farming, which may result in continued erosion problems on low-quality/marginal land. The study also identified the loss of genetic diversity in corn in Mexico as a grave concern, particularly if the small, subsistence producers who have been the guardians of that diversity were forced to abandon production in the face of competition from lower-priced imports.[28]

The CEC has expanded its work on agricultural trade and environmental effects. It has produced a background document on the status of agricultural negotiations at the World Trade Organization, focusing on the NAFTA parties, and a background paper on indicators that can be used to measure environmental effects of trade in the agricultural sector.[29] In addition, a preliminary report prepared for the CEC by authors from the Global Development and Environment Institute at Tufts University provides an updated look at changes in corn production in both the United States and Mexico.[30] This research found that after 1994, U.S. corn exports to Mexico amounted to about 2 percent of total U.S. corn production, compared to about 1 percent before NAFTA. This represents an increase from 14 percent to 24 percent of total Mexican corn consumption being supplied by U.S. imports. Though it did reinforce some of the concerns about the effect of increased U.S. corn imports on the genetic diversity of Mexican corn, the Tufts study found that corn production actually increased in states with a heavy concentration of traditional, subsistence producers.[31] In contrast, post-NAFTA production of traditional corn crops declined rapidly in northern Mexico, being replaced by export crops that require more water and agricultural chemicals.

Electricity Production

Another of the CEC's initial applications of its analytical framework involved an examination of the environmental effects of NAFTA's provisions for electricity production.[32] This study produced several interesting findings, among them:

a. NAFTA had significant and discernible effects on trade and investment flows in the electricity sector, even though other domestic economic and other forces were important.

b. Though trade liberalization was not the primary cause of the changes under way in the electricity sector, the NAFTA regime "contributed to the push for open access and restructuring in North American electricity markets."

c. In certain areas, NAFTA-related requirements (such as open cross-border distribution grids or removal of regulatory subsidies), combined with some incentives, could lead to an overall use of cleaner fuels, more renewable energy, and higher energy efficiency standards. The study did, however, also identify some NAFTA rules as potential barriers to measures or fees designed to promote use of renewable energy or condition access to markets.

The CEC's new Article 13 study on the electricity sector is exploring these and related issues in much more detail.[33] The CEC staff has produced an initial working paper, entitled "Environmental Challenges and Opportunities of the Evolving Continental Electricity Market." As of this writing, the Commission is taking public comment on this paper, and it held a public symposium on the issues in November 2001. In trademark CEC form, the project also has a diverse group of experts in the electricity and environmental fields to help advise the project and review the studies. Given the current attention to developing a hemispheric energy policy with a North American component, the CEC's work on this issue is timely and, given the right circumstances, could have significant influence on policy development.[34]

Trade Corridors

One of the studies prepared for the CEC's October 2000 Trade and Environment Symposium showed a "robust, direct link" between NAFTA trade and increased air pollution at key U.S./Mexico and U.S./Canada border freight crossings.[35] The study also showed that transportation and border-crossing infrastructure had not kept up with the increased movement of NAFTA trade via roads and rail, exacerbating the pollution problems at the crossings.

A follow-up report prepared for the CEC looked at five trade corridor segments in more detail and concluded that NAFTA trade contributes "significantly" to air pollution in the major north-south North American trade corridors.[36] This follow-up report also predicts that "expected reductions in emission rates for U.S. and Canadian trucks" by 2020 will cause emissions of nitrogen oxides (NO_x) and small particulate matter (PM10) to decrease or stay constant as compared to current levels.[37] Air pollution from rail transport is likely to increase in some corridors, however, and, under current regulations, the study predicts a large increase in carbon monoxide and carbon dioxide (a greenhouse gas) from this source.

The report recommends some "mitigation" strategies, including: reducing delays and increased use of truck preclearance at border crossings, using natural gas vehicles in the San Antonio–Monterrey corridor, use of low-sulfur diesel fuel in Mexican trucks, reducing the percentage of empty trucks, and increasing allowable truck weights.[38] Unfortunately, the CEC does not appear to have any follow-up activities planned to ensure these recommendations are adopted, nor are such recommendations binding on the governments under the NAAEC.

Hazardous Waste Disposal

Another study prepared for the October 2000 CEC symposium used the analytical framework to examine transboundary movements of hazardous waste in North America.[39] The study found, among other things, that less stringent hazardous waste disposal regulatory requirements in Ontario and Quebec were a key factor in a significant increase of waste exports from the United States to Canada since NAFTA's approval. It also concluded that Mexico's ban on importing hazardous waste for final disposal limited increases in exports of waste from the United States to Mexico that might otherwise have been expected to materialize, given differences in regulatory standards between the two countries. This study also identified the clear effect of NAFTA rules, specifically the potential limiting effect of NAFTA Chapter 11 investment provisions, on governments' ability to regulate siting of disposal facilities.[40]

Subsequent to the publication of this study and a Canadian government report with similar conclusions, the issue of Canadian standards for hazardous waste disposal received considerable attention in the press.[41] At its June 2001 meeting in Guadalajara, Mexico, the CEC Council adopted a resolution stating that the three ministers agreed to "initiate the development of a North American approach to the environmentally sound management of hazardous wastes, recognizing the serious environmental and human health consequences of improper tracking and disposal."[42] In December 2001, the Ontario government announced that it was undertaking an effort to make its hazardous waste land-disposal restrictions at least as stringent as those in the United States.[43]

This issue provides an example of how trade effects assessment can be made relevant to policy decisions if it is combined with an organized constituency and publicity to draw the attention of the relevant national or subnational government. Standing alone, however, effects studies are unlikely to create the political will required to generate appropriate governmental policy responses.

Lessons Learned

The NAFTA effects assessment work at CEC has, on the whole, helped illuminate many aspects of trade and environment linkages. There is also much to be learned from CEC's assessment methodology, especially as compared to many of the other previous and current attempts to apply macroscale economic modeling to environmental reviews of current or proposed trade agreements.[44]

The CEC's own evaluation of its NAFTA effects work identifies several important lessons, including:[45]

a. Specific environment-trade linkages do exist and should be examined, though other "nontrade driving forces," such as domestic political and economic conditions, global demand, and others, should also be factored into the analysis.

b. Macroscale analyses, with their highly aggregated data and broad sweep, can mask or miss significant effects and are only useful if supplemented by smaller-scale analyses of local, regional, or sector-specific effects.

c. "Scale effects" associated with increased cross-border trade and investment flows may outstrip the available physical infrastructure and/or the ability of governments to monitor and regulate or prevent adverse environmental effects.[46] In addition, the CEC concludes that to date there is "little evidence supporting the notion that, in the near term, greater revenues associated with increased trade correlate with increased resources for environmental authorities to address scale effects."[47] Given the nonrenewable nature of many critical environmental resources, the lack of additional resources necessary to mitigate adverse effects at the time those effects are occurring should not be ignored.[48]

d. The absence of available, high-quality environmental data, especially at the local, regional, and sectoral levels, hampers potentially useful smaller-scale analyses of trade/environment linkages.[49]

e. Open, transparent, and inclusive approaches to analyzing trade and environment linkages are very important to the credibility, usefulness, and acceptability of the analyses.[50]

The jury is still out on one aspect of the CEC's NAFTA effects work, however: how can or will the Commission's analyses have policy relevance? That is, can and will the studies be used to influence not only domestic environmental policies but also regional and even global trade policy and, maybe more important, regional development policy?

The available evidence on this question is still slim. It does appear that the North American hazardous waste study sponsored under the CEC's NAFTA effects program, combined with domestic developments, policy advocacy, and media attention, has resulted in a proposal for stronger hazardous waste disposal regulations in Ontario.[51] The CEC's NAFTA effects work is also contributing to trade and environment discussions at the World Trade Organization and the Organization for Economic Cooperation and Development.[52] Notably, however, the CEC's assessment methodology was not even mentioned in the U.S. Trade Representative's proposal for an environmental review of the FTAA.[53]

But the CEC's NAFTA effects work has implications that go well beyond just tinkering with trade or environment policy. It provides many indications that governments should be thinking in terms of "development policy," not just trade policy. If the goal of economic integration is indeed, as its backers claim, improving the economies, quality of life, and social conditions in participating countries, then the CEC's work indicates clearly that there are development policy conditions that must be in place if liberalized trade and investment are to make positive contributions to this goal on the environmental front.[54]

The most important of these conditions may be the ability to identify and adequately fund the necessary environmental monitoring, regulatory, and enforcement functions and environmental infrastructure improvements in the developing country trading partners. This requires more than just putting in place reactive "flanking" policies to mitigate identified adverse environmental effects of increased trade and investment.[55] Instead, it implies a more comprehensive, and maybe even a more phased, approach to trade and investment liberalization, and it involves identifying clear and sufficient funding mechanisms for these development needs.[56]

The Missing Link: CEC and NAFTA Chapter 11

For all the progress CEC has made in its Trade and Environment program, in one critical area it has been virtually shut out by the NAFTA governments. Despite the fact that Article 10(6) of the NAAEC provides that the CEC shall cooperate with the NAFTA Free Trade Commission in helping to avoid environment-related disputes between the governments, identifying experts and otherwise assisting the Free Trade Commission in environment-related matters, the CEC has not been consulted or involved in the resolution or prevention of the many environmentally related NAFTA investor-initiated arbitrations under NAFTA Chapter 11.[57] Moreover, apart from a somewhat lackluster "10(6) working group" involving trade and environment officials from the NAFTA countries, there is no concrete joint work program between the Free Trade Commission and the CEC.

The lack of CEC involvement in Chapter 11 dispute prevention and resolution was repeatedly discussed at the CEC's October 2000 Trade and Environment Symposium, with comment from nongovernmental organizations in all three NAFTA countries urging CEC involvement. Nevertheless, the Chapter 11 disputes, many involving important environmental laws and principles, are still being played out in secret arbitration panels with no input or expertise from the CEC. Without participation in NAFTA Chapter 11 disputes or the development of a meaningful joint work program with the NAFTA Free Trade Commission to avoid future trade and environment disputes, the CEC's Trade and Environment program will, unfortunately, not meet its full potential.[58]

Notes

1. For a description of the current elements of this program, see *http://www.cec.org/programs_projects/trade_environ_econ*. For convenience, this program is hereinafter referred to as the Trade and Environment program.

2. CEC, Environment and Trade Series 6—*Assessing Environmental Effects of the North American Free Trade Agreement (NAFTA): An Analytic Framework (Phase II) and Issue Studies* 1–64 (1999) (hereafter *Analytic Framework*).

3. CEC, *Free Trade and the Environment: The Picture Gets Clearer* 2 (2001). See also Frank Ackerman, Kevin Gallagher, and Alejandro Nadal, *The Limits of Economic Modeling in the FTAA Environmental Review* 4 (Jan. 2001), available at *http://ase.tufts.edu/gdae* (discussing the limits of economic modeling for the environmental review of the proposed Free Trade Area of the Americas, and, by contrast, the benefits of the CEC framework).

4. The Free Trade Commission's purpose is to supervise the implementation of NAFTA and resolve disputes about NAFTA's interpretation and application. It is comprised of the three trade ministers of the NAFTA parties. North American Free Trade Agreement (NAFTA), Dec. 17, 1992, arts. 2001–22, 32 I.L.M. 642. See generally Howard Mann and Konrad von Moltke, *NAFTA's Chapter 11 and the Environment: Addressing the Impacts of the Investor-State Process on the Environment* (2001), available at *http://iisd1.iisd.ca/trade/chapter11.htm*; see also ch. 10, infra.

5. CEC, *Agenda for Action: 2002–2004*. This document and other CEC documents are available at the CEC website, *http://www.cec.org*. More details on each of the programs can be found at *www.cec.org/programs_projects/trade_environ_econ*.

6. This element combines NAFTA effects analysis work with a newer project aimed at identifying emerging environmental trends.

7. This focus coincides with what is one of the most controversial issues of the current globalization debate: the effects of liberalized trade on the environment in both developed and developing countries.

8. North American Agreement on Environmental Cooperation (NAAEC), Sept. 14, 1993, art. 10(6)(c), 32 I.L.M. 1480.

9. CEC, *Agenda for Action*, supra, 9.

10. CEC, Environment and Trade Series 2—*NAFTA Effects: A Survey of Recent Attempts to Model the Environmental Effects of Trade: An Overview and Selected Sources* (Apr. 1996).

11. CEC, *Analytic Framework*, supra, app. A (providing a summary of findings from the experts workshop).

12. CEC, *Analytic Framework*, supra.

13. See *http://www.cec.org/symposium* for a listing of and access to the fourteen papers prepared for and presented at the symposium. The final papers have recently been published in a single volume, CEC, *The Environmental Effects of Free Trade: Papers Presented at the North American Symposium on Assessing the Linkages between Trade and Environment*, Oct. 2000 (2002). Claudia Schatan's chapter in the present book (ch. 8, infra) grows out of a paper she prepared for the October 2000 symposium.

14. ICF Consulting, "North American Trade and Transportation Corridors: Environmental Impacts and Mitigation Strategies" (Feb. 21, 2001); Kevin Parris, "Envi-

ronmental Impacts in the Agricultural Sector: Using Indicators as a Tool for Policy Purposes" (Jan. 2002); Frank Ackerman et al., "Environmental Impacts of the Changes in U.S.-Mexico Corn Trade Under NAFTA" (Jan. 2002); Chantal Line Carpentier, "Trade Liberalization Impacts on Agriculture: Predicted vs. Realized" (Dec. 20, 2001). All these papers are available on the publications page of the CEC website, *http://www.cec.org*, under the Environment, Trade and Economy subheading.

15. For a description of the electricity project, see *http://www.cec.org/programs_projects/other_initiatives/electricity*. This study has been initiated under Article 13 of the NAAEC, which provides that the Secretariat may "prepare a report for the Council on any matter within the scope of the annual program."

16. The CEC convened an experts' workshop on this issue on Jan. 17–18, 2002. The agenda for the conference can be found at *http://www.cec.org/programs_projects/trade_environ_econ*.

17. William Nitze, former EPA Assistant Administrator for International Affairs and U.S. Alternate Representative to the Council, telephone interview with the author, Feb. 2002; Greg Block, then Director of Programs, CEC, telephone interview with the author, Feb. 2002.

18. Nitze interview, supra.

19. Id.

20. The CEC's selection of the three initial case studies to test the framework (maize production in Mexico, cattle feedlots in the U.S. and Canada, and electricity production in all three countries) did "give the governments some heartburn," according to Nitze. Nitze interview, supra. Again, however, the CEC staff's careful, objective, and participatory approach to selecting the case studies helped carry the day. See CEC, *Analytic Framework*, supra, app. B, "Rationale for Sector and Issue Selection," app. C (experts participating in 1997 Issues Studies Workshop), and app. D (Results of Expert Consultations on General Framework and Agriculture and Energy Issues).

21. These elements are discussed in some detail in the framework document itself. CEC, *Analytic Framework*, supra, 5–40.

22. The physical infrastructure includes such items as transportation infrastructure and water and wastewater treatment infrastructure.

23. CEC, *Analytic Framework*, supra, 5–11.

24. See, e.g., U.S. Trade Representative, "Trade Policy Staff Committee; Public Comments on Environmental Review of Proposed Free Trade Agreement of the Americas," 65 Fed. Reg. 233 (Dec. 4, 2000).

25. CEC, *Analytic Framework*, supra, 26.

26. Alejandro Nadal, "Maize in Mexico: Some Environmental Implications of the North American Free Trade Agreement (NAFTA)," in CEC, *Analytic Framework*, supra, 65–182.

27. Id., 123. See generally *The Transformation of Rural Mexico: Reforming the Ejido Sector* (Wayne A. Cornelius and David Myhre eds., 1998). As the major agricultural crop in Mexico, involving millions of producers, many of whom are small, subsistence farmers, corn was a central issue in the NAFTA debate. Opponents of eliminating barriers on U.S. imports of corn to Mexico were concerned that a flood of

imports would undermine Mexican corn production, threatening the country's food self-sufficiency and forcing producers off the land. Proponents saw Mexico as an important new market for U.S. corn. The chapter in this book by Alejandro Nadal (ch. 9, infra) grew out of his initial analysis of the potential impacts of NAFTA on corn production in Mexico using the CEC framework. His chapter examines in greater detail the issues of genetic resources and, in particular, analyzes some of the more recent developments, including recent findings confirming the presence of transgenic constructs in Mexican landraces.

28. Mexico is of worldwide importance as a reservoir of genetic diversity for corn. Nadal, "Maize in Mexico," supra, 75 ("Nowhere in the world is the spectrum of variation of maize as great as it is in Mexico, and nowhere is it as deeply entwined with the social and economic life of people.").

29. CEC, *Backgrounder on the Status of Agricultural Negotiations at the WTO Focusing on the NAFTA Parties and the Key Trade Liberalization Provisions of the WTO Uruguay Round Agreement on Agriculture* (Dec. 21, 2001); see also Parris, supra.

30. Ackerman et al., "Environmental Impacts of the Changes in U.S.-Mexico Corn Trade," supra.

31. Genetically modified corn includes corn that has been modified to produce a bacterium (*Bacillus thuringiensis*), which acts as an insecticide to the corn borer pest. This particular type of corn is often referred to as Bt corn. Mexico, unlike many other countries, has been willing to accept genetically modified corn. The study did not address whether the NAFTA trade rules had any direct effect on Mexico's willingness to continue accepting imports of genetically modified corn.

32. John Paul Moscarella et al., "Electricity in North America: Some Implications of the North American Free Trade Agreement (NAFTA)," in CEC, *Analytic Framework*, supra, 259–384. This study did not examine whether NAFTA would increase demand for electricity or the potential environmental effects of increased demand. That issue is, however, included in the current Article 13 study.

33. Information on this project can be found at *http://www.cec.org/programs_projects/other_initiatives/electricity*. Issues to be examined include: (1) the environmental effects of the North American integrated energy market, including the effects of restructuring, development, and increased trade; (2) the challenges and potential of "green electricity" in North American markets; (3) trade and environment issues relating to the evolving North American electricity market; and (4) enhanced cross-border/regional environmental planning and assessment.

34. Secretary of Energy Spencer Abraham, prepared remarks, Fifth Hemispheric Energy Initiative Ministerial Conference, Mexico City, Mar. 8, 2001, available at *http://www.pi.energy.gov/initiatives.html*; "Secretary Abraham Promotes Regional Energy Cooperation at Hemispheric Energy Ministers' Conference in Mexico," press release, Mar. 9, 2001, available at *http://www.energy.gov/HQpress* (describing formation of North American Energy Working Group); *http://www.americasenergy.org* (discussing hemispheric energy initiatives arising out of the 1994 Summit of the Americas). Favorable circumstances for making the CEC work policy-relevant include: timely release of the studies; an organized constituency, particularly in the public interest sector, to publicize and advocate for policy recommendations; and receptive government agencies. For an instance where these factors did converge, see the dis-

cussion in this chapter on North American transboundary hazardous waste movements.

35. CEC, *Free Trade and the Environment*, supra, 4, annex 1; Rachel M. Poynter and Sheila A. Holbrook-White, "NAFTA Transportation Corridors: Approaches to Assessing Environmental Impacts and Alternatives," in CEC, *The Environmental Effects of Free Trade*, supra, 299–331.

36. ICF Consulting, "North American Trade," supra, 47–49.

37. For example, emission reductions related to requirements for trucks to use low-sulfur diesel fuel.

38. This last alternative could have significant highway safety and highway maintenance implications.

39. Marisa Jacott, Cyrus Reed, and Mark Winfield, "The Generation and Management of Hazardous Wastes and Transboundary Hazardous Waste Shipments between Mexico, Canada and the United States, 1990–2000," in CEC, *The Environmental Effects of Free Trade*, supra, 161–212.

40. Id., 170, 208 (referring in particular to a NAFTA Chapter 11 challenge against Mexico in reference to the Metalclad hazardous waste disposal facility near San Luís Potosí, Mexico). See also Howard Mann, "Assessing the Impact of NAFTA on Environmental Law and Management Processes," in CEC, *The Environmental Effects of Free Trade*, supra, 221–39 (full discussion of NAFTA Chapter 11 cases, including the Metalclad case).

41. For an example of the press coverage, see Martin Mittelstaedt, "Canada Becomes Haven for Toxic Waste: Weakest Regulations in North America Lead to Increase in Dumping, Report Says," *Globe and Mail* (Toronto), June 18, 2001.

42. CEC Council Communiqué, June 29, 2001, at 2. The work plan for this project is set out in CEC, *Agenda for Action*, supra, 102–4.

43. Ontario Ministry of the Environment, "Strengthening Ontario's Hazardous Waste Framework," Dec. 18, 2001, available at *http://www.ene.gov.on.ca/envision/land/Hwframework.htm*.

44. See U.S. Trade Representative, "Public Comments," supra, for the proposed "core analysis" approach using macroeconomic models. This approach has received critical comments. See, e.g., Ackerman, Gallagher, and Nadal, *The Limits of Economic Modeling*, supra. See also OECD, "Workshop Summary: Methodologies for Environmental Assessment of Trade Liberalisation Agreements," Report of the OECD Workshop held Oct. 26–27, 1999, OECD Doc. No. COM/TD/ENV(99)92/FINAL, 1–6 (discussing various aspects of assessments and modeling methodology). For a listing of "case study"–type approaches that more closely reflect some aspects of the CEC *Analytic Framework*, see *http://www.balancetrade.panda.org/casefiles/casereg.html*.

45. CEC, *Free Trade and the Environment*, supra. The findings discussed in this document were also confirmed in the authors' interviews with some of the people most closely involved with the CEC's trade and environment program. Block interview, supra; Nitze interview, supra; Scott Vaughan, CEC, correspondence with author, Feb. 2002.

46. This could include the available transportation or border crossing infrastructure or water, wastewater, and waste disposal infrastructure.

47. CEC, *Free Trade and the Environment*, supra, 2. Of course, the argument that benefits from liberalized trade would make Mexico richer and thus more able to deal with environmental issues was a central argument in favor of NAFTA. See, e.g., Roberto Salinas-León, "Green Herrings: NAFTA and the Environment," 16 *Regulation* 1 (1993) ("Mexico's problem with environmental protection is not its low level of regulation; rather, the problem is Mexico's financial inability to implement its high environmental standards. But Mexico's economy stands to gain from participating in NAFTA. In fact, Mexico will enjoy greater income gains than will the United States or Canada. A 6 percent real annual growth rate is realistic and realizable in the context of free access to the largest market in the world. Such economic growth will enable Mexico to allocate more resources to environmental enhancement and enforcement."). As Kevin Gallagher points out in a recent analysis, however, data from Mexico indicates that "every major environmental problem has worsened since Mexico began liberalizing its trade policies in the 1980s" and that these trends have developed despite rising incomes, with the cost of environmental degradation "far outstripping" the benefits of trade-led growth in Mexico. Kevin Gallagher, "Fast Track: Fix It or Nix It," *Foreign Policy in Focus* (Jan. 25, 2002), available at *http://www.fpif.org/americas/commentary/2002/0201fasttrack_body.html*; see also ch. 7, infra.

48. This issue was a focal point in the debate over NAFTA's potential effect on the environment of the U.S.-Mexico border and Mexico's environment in general. The need for additional resources for border environmental infrastructure was at least partially addressed through the creation of the Border Environment Cooperation Commission and the North American Development Bank, though additional funds in the form of grants were required to make projects financially viable. Texas Center for Policy Studies, *The BECC and the NADBank: Achieving Their Environmental Mandate* (July 2001). During the NAFTA debate, some environmental organizations suggested that a small fee on cross-border trade be used to generate a continuing source of funding for environmental infrastructure needs, particularly in the interior of Mexico. Mary E. Kelly, *NAFTA's Environmental Side Agreement: A Review and Analysis* (Sept. 1993).

49. Some of the CEC's projects may help address these data gaps, including the Environmental Trends project under the Environment, Economy and Trade program; the recent report on North America's environment, entitled *The North American Mosaic: A State of the Environment Report* (2001); and the annual *Taking Stock* reports compiling and comparing emissions data.

50. In fact, the nature of the CEC's own process, which has been quite transparent, open, and participatory, helped overcome the initial resistance and skepticism of the three NAFTA governments.

51. Jacott, Reed, and Winfield, "The Generation and Management of Hazardous Wastes," supra.

52. CEC, *Backgrounder on the Status of Agricultural Negotiations*, supra; Vaughan interview, supra; OECD, "Methodologies for Environmental Assessment of Trade Liberalisation Agreements," OECD/COM/TD/ENV(99)92/Final (Nov. 1999).

53. See Ackerman, Gallagher, and Nadal, *The Limits of Economic Modeling*, supra.

54. The four main goals of the "Americas Integration" process, arising from the

1994 Summit of the Americas in Miami, are: (1) to preserve and strengthen the community of democracies of the Americas; (2) to promote prosperity through economic integration and free trade; (3) to eradicate poverty and discrimination in our hemisphere; and (4) to guarantee sustainable development and conserve the natural environment for future generations. International Institute for Sustainable Development, International Centre for Trade and Sustainable Development and United Nations Environment Program, *Trade Rules and Sustainability in the Americas Project* (2001).

55. See, e.g., OECD, "Checklist of Issues for Ex Ante Environmental Assessments of Trade Liberalisation," COM/TD/ENV(2001)42/FINAL, at 6 (Jan. 15, 2002)(identifying "flanking measures, including enhancement/mitigation options" that should be part of or parallel to the assessment process for future trade agreements).

56. For broader discussions of development and trade, see, e.g., Hemispheric Social Alliance, *Competing Visions for the Hemisphere: The Official FTAA Draft versus Alternatives for the Americas* (Jan. 2002), and Robert A. Pastor, *Toward a North American Community: Lessons from the Old World for the New* (2001).

57. Mann and von Moltke, *NAFTA's Chapter 11*, supra; see also ch. 10, infra. At the last meeting of the Free Trade Commission, the ministers took up the issue of Chapter 11 and issued certain interpretive statements, while continuing to examine its interpretation and implementation. U.S. Trade Representative, "Joint Statement of the NAFTA Free Trade Commission: Building on a North American Partnership," press release, July 31, 2001, available at *http://www.ustr.gov/releases/2001*. The CEC was not involved in the interpretive statement or the follow-up work, however. See also National Advisory Committee to the U.S. Representative to the Commission for Environmental Cooperation, "Trade-Environment Issues and Article 10(6)," NAC Advice no. 2001-4 (recommendations for enhanced cooperation between the CEC and the NAFTA Free Trade Commission).

58. For a description of the CEC's relationship with the Free Trade Commission, see CEC, Environment and Trade Series 5—*NAFTA's Institutions: The Environmental Potential and Performance of the NAFTA Free Trade Commission and Related Bodies* 5 (1997).

KEVIN P. GALLAGHER 7

The CEC and Environmental Quality

Assessing the Mexican Experience

THIS CHAPTER evaluates the extent to which the North American Commission for Environmental Cooperation (CEC) serves as a model for more effective trade and environmental institutions by examining its role in assisting in the abatement of environmental degradation in Mexico. Despite some notable improvements, the environmental costs of trade-led economic growth in Mexico have remained high since the entry into force of the North American Free Trade Agreement (NAFTA). Moreover, the CEC is not playing a significant role in channeling this growth toward sustainable levels of development. However, this chapter argues that the CEC has a number of exemplary elements of an institution that could facilitate the balance of economic growth and environmental protection. An outline is provided regarding how these elements could be developed in the context of other trade agreements, such as the proposed Free Trade Area of the Americas (FTAA).

There is now an emerging consensus that "increased trade and growth without appropriate environmental policies in place may have unwanted effects on the environment."[1] While the debate over the most appropriate mechanisms to couple trade-led growth with environmental policy is still hotly contested, many advocate the creation of new institutions as a partial solution.[2] The CEC, along with the North American Development Bank and the Border Environment Cooperation Commission, is the first institution of this kind in the Western Hemisphere. As debates over the trade and environmental linkages of the proposed FTAA continue, it is useful to ask whether the CEC serves as a model for a hemispheric institution that could be charged with mitigating the effects of economic integration on the environment in the Americas.

This chapter is divided into four parts. The first section examines whether increased economic growth in Mexico led to the hypothesized improvements in environmental quality. The second section outlines the results of various studies that have delineated the determinants of sustainable environmental policy for Mexico and juxtaposes these determinants with the performance of efforts by the Mexican government to abate pollution. The third section examines the extent to which the CEC's work is augmenting those efforts and highlights elements of the CEC that could serve as the basis for trade and environmental institutions for other trade agreements. In a brief final section, the arguments are summarized and lessons are drawn for the FTAA.

Economic Integration and Environmental Quality in Mexico

Through a number of successive changes during the 1980s and 1990s, Mexico dismantled its industrial policy of Import Substituting Industrialization (ISI) to become one of the most open economies in the world.[3] These policy shifts dramatically changed levels of production, trade, and investment in Mexico. One of the most significant changes has been the emergence of industrial manufacturing as both Mexico's chief exporter and its largest recipient of foreign direct investment (FDI). These changes have not proved to benefit the environment in Mexico.

Preceding NAFTA, some argued that the economic growth derived from economic integration in Mexico would eventually lead to improved environmental conditions. This notion is a generalization of the so-called environmental Kuznets curve (EKC) hypothesis. The name evokes the original Kuznets curve, a theory that growth in per capita income at first increases inequality, then later decreases it. In a cross section of countries at different levels of development, Grossman and Krueger showed that environmental contamination rose in the early stages of economic development, but the rise in per capita income over a certain "turning point" gradually reduced environmental impacts.[4] The turning point was approximately $5,000 Gross Domestic Product (GDP) per capita (in 1985 terms).

The explanation for why such a turnaround may occur is threefold. First, economic integration can trigger compositional shifts in production away from heavy, more polluting manufacturing activities and toward more environmentally benign economic activity such as services. Second, multinational corporations that invest in developing countries could bring cleaner technologies with them. Third, increased income may eventually trigger citizens to demand a cleaner environment.

A number of EKC studies have been conducted since that earlier work. The majority of studies find the EKC only to be true for a limited number of pollutants and nations, namely criteria air pollutants in developed coun-

Figure 7.1. Environmental Kuznets Curve for Mexico, 1985–1999 (1985 = 100)

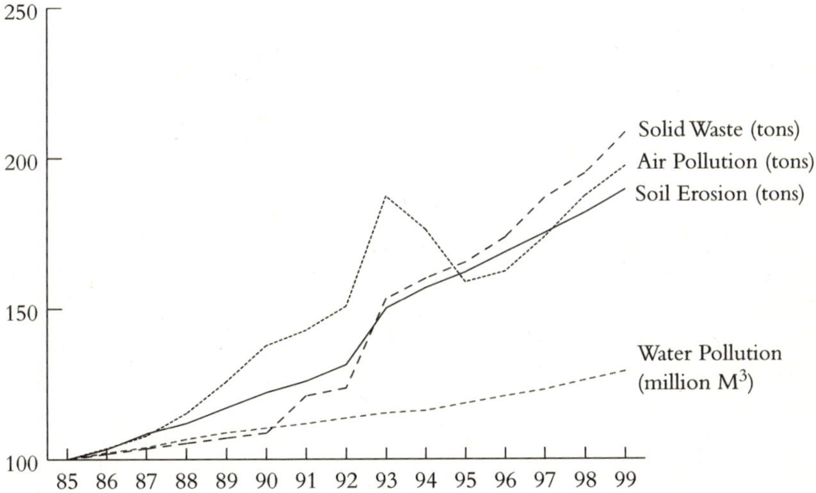

SOURCE: Mexican National Institute of Statistics, Geography and Information (INEGI), *Sistema de Cuentas Económicas y Ecológicas de México* (2000); estimates calculated in Kevin P. Gallagher, "Stuck at the Bottom? The Development of Mexico's Environmental Policy, 1985–1999," Global Development and Environment Institute working paper no. 02-02 (2002).

tries.[5] In addition, the turning point estimates fall well beyond $5,000 GDP per capita.[6] Mexico serves as a perfect laboratory to examine the EKC hypothesis, because it had a $5,000 income level in 1985, exactly the period when it began to integrate its economy.

For the majority of key environmental indicators, there is no sign of a turnaround regarding environmental degradation in Mexico. As Figure 7.1 shows, negative environmental trends have grown faster than (and despite) rising incomes in Mexico. Although GDP grew by 38 percent between 1985 and 1999 (10 percent in per capita terms), rural soil erosion grew by 89 percent, municipal solid waste by 108 percent, water pollution by 29 percent, and air pollution by 97 percent. Disaggregating air pollution, sulfur dioxide grew by 42 percent, nitrous oxides by 65 percent, hydrocarbons by 104 percent, carbon monoxide by 105 percent, and particulate matter by 43 percent.[7]

The economic costs of this environmental degradation in Mexico during this period have been severe. According to estimates derived by the official Mexican statistical agency, the annual environmental costs of economic growth amount to 10 percent of annual GDP in Mexico from 1985 to 1999.[8] Ten percent of Mexican GDP over that period equates to $36 billion each year. These costs overwhelm the value of economic growth in Mexico, which was just 2.5 percent annually over the same period, or $14 billion a year.

Air pollution accounts for more than half of the environmental damage estimates in Mexico—the equivalent of $27 billion worth of damage in 1998. Mexico City has long been one of the most polluted cities in the world. While significant reductions in levels of carbon monoxide (CO), lead (Pb), and sulfur dioxide (SO_2) have occurred, serious problems persist for ozone (O_3), nitrogen dioxide (NO_2), and particulates. Standards for particulate matter are the most frequently violated in Mexico City, followed by violations in ozone standards, which are surpassed 80 percent of days each year since 1988.[9] The shifts in Mexican industrial policy outlined above are changing the regional distribution of production in Mexico, bringing alarming levels of air pollution to industrial centers. For example, air pollution standards are now exceeded 90 percent of days each year in Guadalajara.[10]

Exposure to particulate matter and ozone have the most severe effects on human health among air pollutants in Mexico.[11] A consistent finding among those examining the health effects of air pollution in Mexico is that each 10 µg/m3 increase in levels of PM10 (particulate matter of 10 microns or less) causes an increase of daily mortality of 1 percent. Therefore, a 10 percent reduction in levels of PM10 could avert as many as 1,000 deaths per year.[12]

While many people equate rising levels of air pollution with increases in the use of motor vehicles, industry is also a significant contributor to levels of air pollution in Mexico's industrial centers. As shown in Table 7.1, industry contributes 41 percent of the particulate matter emissions in Mexico City, 89 percent in Monterrey, and 21 percent in Guadalajara. Industry is also a significant NO_x polluter, ranging from 8 to 35 percent of total NO_x emissions in some cities. NO_x not only causes its own health and environmental problems but along with SO_2 contributes to the secondary formation of particulate matter and ozone. Industry is the most significant SO_2 polluter, at 64 percent of SO_2 emissions in Mexico City, 92 percent in Monterrey, and 68 percent in Guadalajara. Industrial activity also causes significant environmental problems other than air pollution in Mexico, water pollution key among them.

Industry is indeed a significant contributor to air pollution in Mexico, but this is not because "dirty" industries are flocking from the United States—in other words, there is no "pollution haven" effect for Mexico. The share of "dirty" industries in U.S. manufacturing (based on the costs of pollution abatement and in terms of actual emissions) was 17 percent in 1988 and just over 15 percent in 1998. In Mexico, however, the share of dirty industries declined as well, from 30 percent in 1988 to 26 percent by 1998.[13] If the pollution haven hypothesis were to have held true for Mexico, declining shares of dirty industry in the United States would have corresponded with rising

Table 7.1. Industrial Air Pollution as a Percentage of Total Air Pollution in Four Mexican Cities

	PT	SO_2	CO	NO_x	HC
Guadalajara	21%	68%	0.15%	8%	3%
Monterrey	89	92	0.36	35	4
Toluca	34	82	0.08	10	7
Mexico City	41	64	0.39	24	3

SOURCE: Mexicali Inventory Group Binational Advisory Committee, *Estadisticas del Medio Ambiente*, vol. 2 (Mexico: 1999).

shares in Mexico. Rather than pollution havens, the Mexican environment is worsening because the public sector has fallen short of adequately addressing the environment-related market failures that became associated with manufacturing growth in Mexico. To this subject I now turn.

The Development and Effectiveness of Mexican Environmental Policy

Earlier examinations by the Organization for Economic Cooperation and Development (OECD) and the World Bank praise Mexico for developing an adequate environmental regime of laws and institutions. Indeed, Mexico's standards are quite similar to those of the United States and other OECD countries on paper. However, these same institutions often criticize Mexico for not providing their environmental regime with the proper resources and commitment.[14] This is not to say there have not been improvements and significant successes. Drawing from those successes, this section outlines the key factors that are understood to lead to improvements in levels of pollution in Mexico and reviews Mexican efforts toward these ends. These factors can be grouped into three broad categories: (1) increased levels of enforcement; (2) new funds for modernization, pollution-control equipment, and environmental management systems; and (3) public scrutiny of environmental practices. With a few very positive exceptions, Mexico's record toward these three ends has been inadequate.

ENFORCEMENT

Consistent with global comparisons, a number of studies have found that firms that are subject to government enforcement and inspection measures are likely to be significantly "cleaner" than their counterparts. Based on surveys of 236 industrial firms in Mexico, the World Bank found that in 60 per-

Figure 7.2. Plant-level Environmental Inspections, 1987–1999

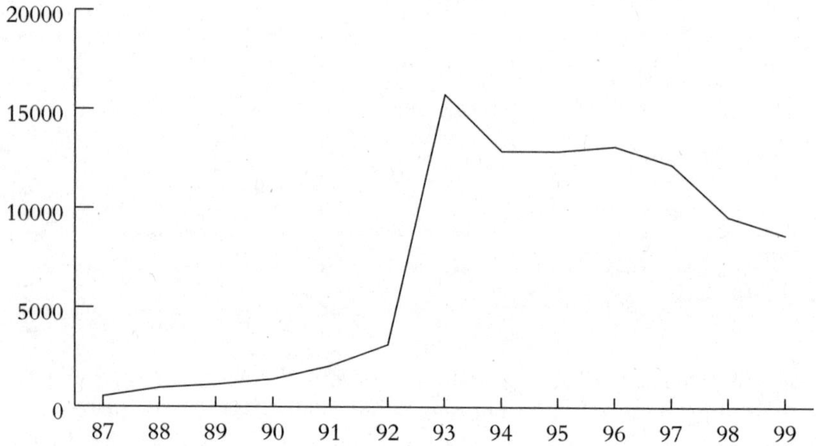

SOURCE: PROFEPA (2000), available at *http://www.profepa.gob.mex* (web page of the Mexican environmental enforcement division).

cent of the firms surveyed, regulatory requirements and enforcement were the primary reasons why those firms were in compliance with environmental regulation.[15]

Mexico's overall record on enforcement and inspections has been very poor. Figure 7.2 shows that after years of very scant amounts of plant-level environmental inspections, Mexico began to emphasize enforcement during the NAFTA negotiations, presumably due to pressure from its negotiating partners. Although the trend was going in the right direction, reaching its highest point in 1993, plant-level environmental inspections peaked at only 6 percent of all firms in the country.[16] What is worrisome is that after NAFTA was passed, the number of plant-level inspections began to diminish precipitously, suggesting that, since NAFTA, Mexico has become less serious about enforcement.

Although the overall trends in enforcement in Mexico are disappointing, there are a few success stories. There is evidence that the majority of inspections were concentrated in a few industries, mainly the chemical-petrochemicals, metal mechanics, and pulp and paper industries. Positive results have been documented in the chemical fibers and steel industries. In addition to government enforcement, such gains were also due to external influences and market pressure. In these two industries, changes in environmental management were also in part because their foreign owners, customers, or governments in foreign markets demanded such measures.[17]

Figure 7.3. Real Spending on Environmental Protection, 1985–1998 (1985 = 100)

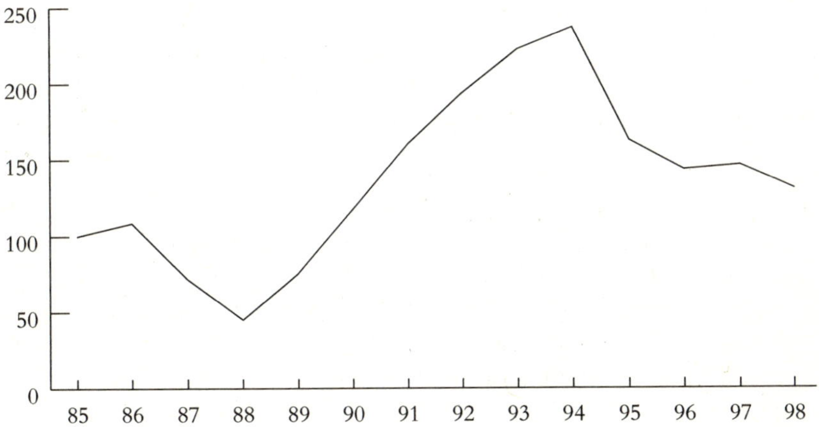

SOURCE: Mexican National Institute of Statistics, Geography and Information (INEGI), *Sistema de Cuentas Económicas y Ecológicas de México* (2000).

APPROPRIATION OF ADDITIONAL FUNDS

Another key determinant of firm-level compliance with environmental regulations in Mexico has been whether firms can mobilize or gain access to the necessary funds to modernize their energy and production equipment, install end-of-pipe technologies, switch to less environmentally damaging fuels, initiate cogeneration programs, and establish environmental management systems.[18]

Mexico's Ley General del Equilibrio Ecológico y la Protección al Ambiente (LGEEPA) sets out general guidelines for reducing pollution and refers to Normas Oficiales Mexicanos for specific regulations. Budgetary support has slightly increased for environmental programs in Mexico.[19] At the federal level, however, Mexico provides little funding for firms to come into compliance with the law. Figure 7.3 presents spending on environmental protection from 1985 to 1999. Spending grew impressively between 1988 and 1993 but then tapered off by 45 percent after NAFTA went into effect. Although spending on the environment has grown considerably, it remains the lowest of all OECD countries. In relation to GDP, the average OECD country spends three times more than Mexico on the environment. In per capita terms, the average OECD country spends six times more than Mexico.[20] Firms therefore have been left to their own devices to comply. For this reason, the record has been mixed.

The firms that are most likely to appropriate necessary funds for environmental controls are large ones.[21] Large firms are easier for governments and citizen groups to monitor and should have lower costs for environmental compliance at the margin. Larger firms are also more apt to be the recipients of FDI, which can bring newer environmental technologies.[22] However, only 2 percent of all firms in Mexico are categorized as large, and many smaller firms are more pollution intensive.[23] The rate of growth in value-added production for all of Mexican industry from 1988 to 1998 was 4.3 percent annually, approximately the same rate as the economy as a whole. However, this average is masked by large increases in production and investment in a few industries, such as automobiles and electrical machinery, while others declined sharply during the period.

Many firms could not voluntarily increase levels of compliance—many industries were falling behind and simply could not afford to step up environmental protection. An example is the Mexican textiles industry. Textiles production dropped during the period of trade opening, and funds were not available for environmental management. Any funds appropriated for environmental management in the textiles industry were a function of government and community policing activities.[24]

COMMUNITY PRESSURE

Scrutiny by local communities has also been found to exert significant influence over the environmental behavior of Mexican industry. The World Bank study shows that public scrutiny has been an effective tool to steer industrial firms toward environmental compliance. Indeed, these factors were reported to be important drivers of environmental compliance in 25 percent of the firms in the sample showing improvements.[25] This effect was particularly strong for firms that were publicly traded. The logic is that firms that are publicly traded are held more accountable because "news" of environmental performance can more easily affect their stock performance.[26] Because of data limitations, it is difficult to gauge the level of community pressure on industry in Mexico. Some case study evidence has shown that community pressure has been a key driver of environmental compliance in Mexico and may be growing.[27]

This section has outlined the state of Mexican efforts toward improving compliance toward environmental regulation. The overall trends are quite poor. Levels of enforcement are decreasing, and few additional funds are available for pollution control. However, there are signs of improvement in a few key polluting sectors, such as chemicals and steel. In these two cases, a blend of enforcement, private investment, and community pressure has been the driver of increasing levels of environmental performance.

CEC: Elements of an Effective Trade and Environment Institution

The evaluation of the EKC earlier in this chapter confirms hypotheses suggesting that developing countries may remain "stuck at the bottom" if they are not equipped with assistance that will allow them to develop the necessary environmental policies to steer trade-led growth in a sustainable manner. While the CEC falls short of filling that role, it does offer a number of promising models that could help serve in such a capacity.

A number of authors have shown that the demands of integrating into the global economy are so costly that they can crowd out the development of the social programs that are needed to mitigate the negative effects of economic integration.[28] Other authors have argued that this could be the case in the environmental realm. Lyuba Zarsky has stated that market-driven and political pressures related to economic integration can slow the development of environmental policy.[29]

Confirming these hypotheses, this chapter has shown that environmental conditions continued to worsen in Mexico during the post-NAFTA period, at considerable cost to Mexican society. Mexico was not equipped to steer the benefits of economic integration into increasing environmental protection. Here is a clear role for the development of environmental institutions as part of trade and investment treaties. If a fully equipped environmental institution was established to help Mexico meet its own environmental goals, Mexico might be able to enjoy more of the benefits of economic integration.

The CEC is largely ill-equipped to help solve Mexico's significant environmental problems because it lacks the resources to counter these problems. By its very nature, an institution with an annual budget of $9 million can hardly make a dent in a series of problems that cost the Mexican economy over $40 billion annually.

The actual amount of funds spent on environmental projects is less than half of the $9 million; the projects budget is closer to about $3 million per year. Additionally, another $500,000 supports the North American Fund for Environmental Cooperation (NAFEC), discussed later in this chapter. Remembering that the environmental costs of air pollution in Mexico amount to over $25 billion annually, I conducted an analysis of CEC budgets to estimate the amount of funds earmarked for air projects. Since the CEC's inception, I estimate that about $2 million of CEC funds have gone to air-related projects.

On the other hand, the CEC has set an important precedent for trade policy. Because of NAFTA's incorporation of environmental considerations, trade policy is no longer seen as separate from environmental policy.[30] Although the CEC does not have sufficient resources to significantly reverse the environmental consequences of economic growth in Mexico, it serves as a pilot project to examine how effective institutions could be designed for Mexico and other nations where trade-led growth needs to be channeled in a more environmentally benign manner.

As discussed earlier in the chapter, reducing the environmental costs of growth entails providing new funds for environmental management, enforcing existing standards for environmental policy, and empowering citizens to exert pressure on firms to comply with those standards. The CEC performs three tasks that are essential for any such institution: it provides additional funds for environmental management for small and medium-sized enterprises and for communities; it provides a mechanism for citizen groups to challenge whether nations are enforcing their environmental standards; and it convenes essential research and policy discussions among governments and civil society in Mexico and its North American trading partners. This section of the chapter discusses these elements in greater detail.

DEFRAYING THE ENVIRONMENTAL COSTS OF ECONOMIC GROWTH

For Mexico to develop a sustainable economy, it needs additional funds to defray the environmental costs of economic growth, which now amount to over $40 billion each year. The CEC's Fund for Pollution Prevention (Fondo de Prevención de la Contaminación, or FIPREV) and its NAFEC are both new sources of funds for industry and communities. Although these funds do not have adequate resources to significantly reduce the environmental costs of industrial growth in Mexico, they serve as models for Mexico and for mechanisms that could be established in the context of the FTAA.

Created in 1996, FIPREV is a pilot fund for pollution prevention projects in small and medium-sized enterprises in Mexico. After an initial period of assessment, the fund now has over $2 million and has given over twenty-five loans amounting to $610,000. Not only did the CEC provide funds for FIPREV itself, but the CEC was able to leverage funds from other sources.

FIPREV was established through a collaboration with the Mexican Foundation for Innovation and Technology Transfer in Small and Medium-Sized Enterprises (FUNTEC), a nongovernmental organization (NGO) linked to the Mexican Federation of Industrial Associations (CONCAMIN). FIPREV was founded to "promote the use of pollution prevention techniques and technologies among small and medium-sized Mexican industrial establishments and support them in the development of their environmental management capacities" and to "facilitate the application of pollution prevention measures in industry through the timely and appropriate offering of technical assistance, information, and financing for projects of this nature."[31] The administration of FIPREV brings together members of business, academia, government, and representatives of the CEC Joint Public Advisory Committee (JPAC).

Based on a series of preliminary needs assessments, the majority of FIPREV's projects are in the tanning industry, but other loans have been granted to firms in the food, metalworking, electroplating, chemicals, foundry, dry cleaning, and other manufacturing sectors. FIPREV's low-interest loans can amount to $30,000, or 80 percent of an investment project. They are most often offered in Mexican pesos but can come in the form of U.S. dollars if the firm is exporting its goods or services. To date, most of these loans have come in the form of technical assistance to firms to make process-based technological changes to reduce water and raw materials usage. Impressively, both the credit and the interest of all of the twenty-five loans thus far granted by FIPREV have been repaid according to schedule. Based on the annual savings of approximately 1,465 tons of chemical substances, FIPREV estimates that the economic benefits of these environmental programs have amounted to $646,000 each year since their inception.

NAFEC was also established by the CEC in 1996, and its mission is to provide grants to community-based NGOs for social and environmental projects in the three countries. Since its inception, NAFEC has issued over 142 grants for a total of $5.4 million. The average grant is approximately $30,000.

Relatively few grants have been issued to help communities monitor Mexican industry. Little more than $200,000 has gone toward projects related to industrial pollution in Mexico. However, the grants that have been issued for community-based monitoring of industrial activity have been quite effective. In 1998, $50,000 was given to the U.S.-based Environmental Health Coalition for a U.S./Mexico Comparable Industries Study on pollution prevention. Under this grant, a number of U.S. and Mexican NGOs worked together to identify the toxic chemical uses at three *maquiladoras*. Short fact sheets were put together based on the findings and distributed to the public to encourage their involvement in subsequent negotiations with the companies. The groups then entered into negotiations with those firms to reduce emissions and to implement pollution prevention strategies.

In 2000, grants totaling $45,000 were issued to a Mexican NGO named Enlace Ecológico in Agua Prieta. The grant was given for the community use of the pollutant release and transfer registry (PRTR) in Mexico. Enlace Ecologico created a pilot project in Agua Prieta and Nogales to test how NGOs can monitor and list pollutant releases in their communities. The groups will then work with 100 *maquiladoras* to assist them in reporting their pollutant releases. Industry leaders and community members will then be encouraged to create ongoing monitoring systems and dialogue concerning abatement strategies.

MONITORING THE ENFORCEMENT OF ENVIRONMENTAL LAWS

The CEC has two mechanisms that provide additional means to monitor the enforcement of environmental laws in North America. Articles 14 and 15 of the NAAEC allow citizens to make submissions to the CEC regarding the failure of a Party to enforce its environmental laws, and Part Five of the NAAEC allows any of the three Parties to request the CEC Council to approve (by a two-thirds vote) creation of an arbitral panel to resolve a dispute over whether another Party has persistently failed to enforce its environmental laws.[32]

Under Articles 14 and 15, a submission can lead to a factual record but not to any legal requirement for the Party to take action. However, it is hoped that increased public attention to the matter will trigger government action. There is evidence to suggest that such public attention can induce change. The NGO that issued the submission that resulted in the factual record to investigate alleged violations due to the development of the Cozumel Pier has gone on record to say that the factual record led to improvements in environmental impact assessment and the eventual establishment of a fund for reef protection. Part Five does provide for the possibility of sanctions, but thus far no Party has attempted to trigger it.

Since the Article 14 and 15 processes are covered in great detail in other parts of this volume, all that will be presented in this chapter is an illustration of a submission that has been filed regarding industrial pollution in Mexico. A Mexico-based human rights NGO has filed a submission charging that the Molymex corporation, a company that processes residues generated by copper-smelting firms, has violated environmental impact and air pollution standards in Mexico. According to the LGEEPA, all firms must file an environmental impact statement upon establishing operations. Once a firm is in operation, there are a number of standards that it must meet, including a series of "norms" for air pollution. The submitters allege that Molymex failed to conduct an environmental impact assessment of its operations. In addition, the submitters claim that the plant is violating Mexican standards that establish limits for SO_2 and PM10.

A factual record will be conducted for this submission. Regardless of its outcome, it serves as a clear example of citizen-based efforts to supplement enforcement activities regarding industrial pollution in Mexico. Earlier in this chapter, Figure 7.1 exhibited how Mexican efforts toward environmental inspections are on the decline. Articles 14 and 15 offer a way to counter that trend.

COOPERATION, RESEARCH, AND INFORMATION

In addition to providing additional funds and an additional forum to monitor environmental enforcement efforts, the CEC also serves as a meeting place for cooperation, research, and information sharing among the three countries. Before NAFTA, there were limited opportunities for trilateral activities of this nature.[33]

Given its limited budget, perhaps the CEC's largest contribution is in the realm of enhancing environmental cooperation among the three governments. The CEC's four program areas (Environment, Economy and Trade; Conservation of Biodiversity; Pollutants and Health; and Law and Policy) have all served as forums for governments and civil society to convene on their respective issues.

Highlights among these projects have been the development of a framework methodology for assessing the environmental impacts of NAFTA, which resulted in a number of commissioned studies that were presented at a NAFTA Effects Conference held by the CEC in 2000;[34] the development of a North American Biodiversity Information Network;[35] work toward the development of a North American PRTR as well as a North American Air Emissions Inventory;[36] the development of a capacity-building program for pollution prevention that links the work of FIPREV with similar activities in the United States and Canada; and a North American Regional Enforcement Forum that brings together experts to discuss efforts to create better incentives for environmental enforcement.

While these efforts are positive, they have been criticized as being too disparate. Although many of these programs could be synergistic, they often are not coordinated with each other. Because of this, it has been recommended that the CEC focus on a narrower range of issues.[37]

Foundations for an Environmental Component of the FTAA

This chapter has emphasized two points. First, it is well documented that overall levels of environmental degradation are not improving in Mexico and that industry continues to be a significant contributor to such degradation. Second, while it has been shown that the CEC is ill-equipped to combat the environmental costs of industrial growth in Mexico, it does have a number of positive elements that can serve as a basis for future institutions. Such elements could be broadened to lay the foundation for an effective institution that could manage the environmental component of the economic integration process in the Western Hemisphere. Decoupling industrial growth from environmental degradation entails the development and enforcement of environmental regulations, the allocation of additional funds for new technologies and management systems for industry, and the enhancement of community-based efforts to monitor industrial environmental behavior. If given the needed resources, the positive elements of the CEC outlined above could be part of an effective hemispheric institution. Estimates of the environmental damage costs for the entire hemisphere do not exist, but it can be safely assumed that billions of dollars are needed to couple economic integration with sustainable development. Indeed, the World Bank and the Inter-American Development Bank pledged over $20 billion in loans, grants, and credits to prepare for the FTAA. If an agreement is finally reached on an FTAA, many more resources will be needed to make it work.

With adequate resources, FIPREV- and NAFEC-like funds could be part of larger efforts to link the FTAA with sustainable development. Upgrades in core technology, especially in firms that are both capital and energy intensive, are among the best strategies for pollution abatement in industry. A well-funded FIPREV-like fund could provide assistance for efforts to modernize core technologies within firms as well as give assistance for process-based changes that FIPREV already provides. Like FIPREV, such a fund could leverage funds from other sources. The World Bank's Guadalajara Environmental Management Pilot can serve as an additional model. Under this project, the World Bank matched funds issued by larger companies to help "green" their small and medium-sized suppliers.

Coupling support for industry with community-based monitoring systems in a NAFEC-like fund could be an important strategy to ensure environmental compliance in the hemisphere. NAFEC-like grants could be administered for PRTR and similar programs to local communities to monitor firms' environmental behavior, educate their communities regarding such behavior, and enter into negotiations with industries over compliance strategy. If noncompliance continued and was well documented by these community groups, additional funds could be obtained to assist NGOs in Article 14- and 15-type citizen submissions.

At minimum, provisions like Articles 14 and 15 of NAAEC should be included in an FTAA. This chapter and others in this volume show that enhancing the rights of citizens in this manner has proved to be effective under the CEC in the few cases when it has occurred. However, as other chapters in this volume stress, factual records and the Article 14–15 process are themselves in much need of clarification and strengthening.

A hemispheric institution should also serve as a clearinghouse for research, cooperation, and collaboration among governments and civil society. Providing technical assistance, monitoring environmental progress, and serving as a forum for the exchange of information and ideas should all be part of such a strategy.

Notes

1. Per Fredriksson, *Trade, Global Policy, and the Environment* 1 (1999).

2. See Dan Esty and Bradford Gentry, *Foreign Direct Investment and the Environment* (1998); see also C. Ford Runge, *Freer Trade, Protected Environment* (1994).

3. ISI is a development policy, practiced by many developing countries, that established domestic industries behind tariff and quota barriers. For a history of Mexico's trade policy, see OECD, *Trade Liberalization Policies in Mexico* (1996).

4. Gene Grossman and Alan Krueger, "Economic Growth and the Environment," 110 *Quarterly Journal of Economics* 305–48 (1995).

5. Criteria air pollutants are those for which national ambient air quality standards have been established by U.S. EPA under § 109 of the Clean Air Act, 42 U.S.C. § 7409. They include particulates, ozone, sulfur dioxide, nitrogen dioxide, carbon monoxide, and lead.

6. David Stern, "Progress on the Environmental Kuznets Curve?" 3 *Environment and Development Economics* 173–96 (1998).

7. See Kevin P. Gallagher, "Stuck at the Bottom? The Development of Mexico's Environmental Policy, 1985–1999," Global Development and Environment Institute, working paper no. 02-02, 2002.

8. Mexico's National Institute of Statistics, Geography and Information (INEGI), *Sistema de Cuentas Económicas y Ecológicas de México* (2000); World Bank, *Mexico: A Comprehensive Development Agenda* (2001).

9. Mario Molina and Luisa Molina, *Integrated Strategy for Air Quality Management in the Mexico City Metropolitan Area* (2000).

10. U.S. Department of Energy, "Mexico: Environmental Issues," available at *http://www.eia.doe.gov*.

11. Sergio Margulis, "Back of the Envelope Estimates of Environmental Damage Costs in Mexico," in *Pricing the Planet: Economic Analysis for Sustainable Development* (Peter May ed., 1996).

12. See Molina and Molina, supra, 2000.

13. For an in-depth analysis of this question that reaches a similar conclusion, see the following chapter by Claudia Schatan.

14. OECD, *Mexico: Environmental Performance Review* (1998); World Bank, supra.

15. Susmita Dasgupta, Hemamala Hettige, and David Wheeler, "What Improves Environmental Performance? Evidence from Mexican Industry," 38 *Journal of Environmental Economics and Management* 39–66 (1999).

16. "PROFEPA," available at *http://www.profepa.gob.mex* (web page of Mexican environmental enforcement division).

17. L. Dominguez-Villalobos, "Environmental Performance in the Mexican Chemical Fibres Industry in the Context of an Open Market," in *Industry and the Environment in Latin America* (Rhys Jenkins ed., 2000).

18. F. Brown, "Environmental Performance and Trade Liberalization in the Mexican Textile Industry," in id.; Samudra Vijay, "Non-Transportation Energy-Related Sources of Air Pollution in the MCMA: Emission Implications and Mitigation Options" (2001) (discussion paper for the Mexico City project at MIT); Anthony Bart-

zokas and Masaru Yarime, "Technology Trends in Pollution-Intensive Industries: A Review of Sectoral Trends," UNU-INTECH discussion paper no. 9706 (Dec. 1997).

19. Jeanne Logsdon and Bryan Husted, "Mexico's Environmental Performance Under NAFTA: The First 5 Years," 9 *Journal of Environment and Development* 4 (2000).

20. OECD, *Compendium of Environmental Data* (1999).

21. Dasgupta, Hettige, and Wheeler, supra.

22. Brad Gentry, *Private Investment and the Environment* (1996).

23. Francisco Aguayo and Kevin Gallagher, "Dirt Is in the Eye of the Beholder: The World Bank Air Pollution Intensities for Mexico," Global Development and Environment Institute, working paper no. 01-07 (2001).

24. See Brown, supra.

25. See Dasgupta, Hettige and Wheeler, supra.

26. Id.

27. Red Mexicana de Acción Frente al Libre Comercio (RMALC), *El Tratado de Libre Comercio de Norteamérica y el Medio Ambiente en México* (2000); RMALC, *The Social and Environmental Impacts of NAFTA* (2001).

28. Dani Rodrick, *The Global Governance of Trade As if Development Really Mattered* (2001).

29. Lyuba Zarsky, "Stuck in the Mud? Nation-states, Globalization, and the Environment," in OECD, *Globalization and the Environment* (1997). See also Garesh Porter, "Trade Competition and Pollution Standards: 'Race to the Bottom' or 'Stuck at the Bottom,'" 8 *Journal of Environment and Development* 2 (June 1999).

30. Pierre Marc Johnson and André Beaulieu, *The Environment and NAFTA* (1996); see also RMALC, supra.

31. CEC, *Fund for Pollution Prevention Projects in Mexican Small and Medium Sized Enterprises* (June 2001), available at CEC website, *http://www.cec.org*.

32. For a description of the submissions procedure, see ch. 15, infra. For additional analysis, see also chs. 13, 14, infra.

33. Steven Mumme and Pamela Duncan, "The Commission for Environmental Cooperation and Environmental Management in the Americas," 39 *Journal of Inter-American Studies and World Affairs* 41–62 (1997/98).

34. See ch. 6, supra.

35. See ch. 4, supra.

36. See ch. 2, supra.

37. CEC, *NAFTA's Institutions: The Environmental Potential and Performance of the NAFTA Free Trade Commission and Related Bodies* (1997).

CLAUDIA SCHATAN 8

The Environmental Impact of Mexican Manufacturing Exports under NAFTA

UNDOUBTEDLY, one of the most controversial issues to arise during the North American Free Trade Agreement (NAFTA) negotiations was the potential role of Mexico as a "pollution haven," given its lower environmental standards compared to its northern counterparts. It was widely believed that foreign firms would invest in Mexico to take advantage of the lax environmental law enforcement there, thus lowering their costs. That is, those firms that produce the greatest amount of emissions into the air, water, or soil per unit of output—that is, the most-polluting firms—would find fertile ground to prosper in Mexico. At the same time, these firms would enjoy the easy access to the northern markets given by NAFTA. This concern was promptly incorporated by the North American Commission for Environmental Cooperation (CEC) in its ongoing efforts to assess the environmental effects of NAFTA. In fact, one of six preliminary hypotheses of the CEC's analytic framework for assessing NAFTA's environmental effects expresses the concern that trade liberalization associated with NAFTA may increase competitive pressures, leading firms to seek cost reductions through lower environmental regulations.[1] This chapter has been inspired precisely by the possibility that freer trade in NAFTA may deepen environmental problems in Mexico.

Seven years after NAFTA entered into force, a number of changes can be perceived in the Mexican economy. Exports expanded by 18.3 percent on average between 1994 and 2000, practically doubling total sales abroad in that period. Altogether, exports of manufactured goods, including the *maquiladora* activities, grew 19.5 percent annually, and primary product exports grew by 13.7 percent. Mexican export expansion to the United States was much more pronounced than that experienced by Canada's equivalent indicator over the same period.

Table 8.1. Primary Products, Natural Resources Intensive Products, and Technology Level of Mexican and Canadian Exports to the United States (%)

	1977	1980	1985	1990	1991	1992	1993	1994	1995	1996	1997	1998	1999	2000
Mexican Exports														
A. Primary Products	59.3	60.3	51.3	28.9	27.1	23.3	19.8	17.5	15.8	14.5	12.5	11.3	11.0	11.4
B. Natural Resources Intensive Goods	13.8	13.7	11.8	9.5	8.4	7.8	7.5	7.6	8.5	8.6	7.5	6.7	6.0	5.7
C. Low Technology	8.9	6.3	7.7	12.9	13.5	14.3	14.9	15.7	17.3	18.0	18.6	18.7	17.9	17.4
D. Intermediate Technology	5.4	4.2	10.9	19.5	21.5	23.4	24.5	25.3	26.2	26.9	26.8	26.9	27.4	27.5
E. High Technology	9.9	11.6	15.7	25.3	25.9	27.4	29.5	30.2	29.3	29.6	31.2	32.8	34.0	34.2
F. Others	2.6	3.9	2.6	4.0	3.7	3.8	3.8	3.8	3.4	3.3	3.4	3.6	3.7	3.8
Canadian Exports														
A. Primary Products	30.1	25.9	19.5	16.8	17.1	16.5	15.7	14.9	15.9	15.9	15.4	14.2	14.6	14.8
B. Natural Resources Intensive Goods	32.7	34.4	26.8	28.7	27.4	26.5	25.8	25.9	26.0	25.6	24.2	23.0	21.8	21.3
C. Low Technology	6.3	7.2	7.7	8.1	8.3	8.8	9.5	10.1	10.4	11.1	11.7	12.0	11.9	11.8
D. Intermediate Technology	24.8	22.5	33.2	31.3	31.2	32.2	33.5	33.6	31.5	31.0	31.4	32.7	32.1	32.1
E. High Technology	3.2	4.8	6.5	9.2	9.8	9.7	9.2	9.3	10.2	10.6	11.2	11.5	12.5	12.7
F. Others	3.0	5.2	6.4	6.0	6.2	6.3	6.4	6.2	6.0	5.8	6.1	6.6	7.1	7.3

SOURCE: Calculations based on the Country Competitivity Analysis Program (CANPLUS) of the Comisión Económica para América Latina y el Caribe (CEPAL) and W. Péres and L. Alcorta, "Innovation Systems and Technological Specialization in Latin America and the Caribbean," *Research Policy* 26.

Both the devaluation suffered by the peso in December of 1994 and the openness of the U.S. and Canadian markets under NAFTA favored the Mexican export performance. The latter element, which is the subject of this study, was definitely important, since tariffs fell from around 2.5 percent in 1990–93 to 0.45 percent in 1998.[2] Exports were also stirred by the elimination of import quotas and the substantial increase in foreign direct investment (FDI) in manufactured export activities, which would have probably not been attracted to Mexico in the absence of NAFTA.

The central question tackled by this chapter is the impact of NAFTA on pollution generated by the production processes of Mexican manufacturing exports and whether Mexican exports have found a special comparative advantage in the most-polluting sectors. (For a list of the highest-polluting industrial sectors, see appendix A.) The first section analyzes how the manufacturing export structure has changed in Canada and Mexico in terms of its level of technological sophistication and whether the structure has become biased toward particularly polluting sectors. The second section provides an estimate of the emissions from goods produced in Mexico for export during the pre- and post-NAFTA periods. The third section focuses on the competitive position of the Mexican and Canadian most-polluting sectors in the U.S. market. The fourth section introduces FDI in the analysis of manufacturing exports and environment. Finally, some conclusions are presented in the last section.

Export Trends

The nature of Mexico's foreign trade activity has changed substantially since Mexico started a liberalization process in 1987. This tendency has increased after NAFTA entered into force in 1994. As seen in Table 8.1, in 1977, 73 percent of total Mexican exports consisted of primary products and natural resources intensive goods. In 2000, this proportion had fallen to 17 percent.[3] During the same time period, opposite trends were occurring in high- and intermediate-technology exports. Between 1977 and 2000, the high-technology sector's share of exports increased from 10 to 34 percent, and intermediate-technology participation increased from 5 to 27 percent.

These trends were much more pronounced in Mexico than in Canada. Canadian exports from the primary products and natural resources intensive goods sectors, as a percentage of total exports from Canada to the United States, fell from 63 to 36 percent between 1977 and 2000. Intermediate-technology exports rose from 25 to 32 percent, and high-technology exports reached only 13 percent of total exports by 2000 (see Table 8.1).

In Mexico, the high-technology sectors that led the export drive were mainly computers and other electronic equipment, along with the automobile industry, while it was the pharmaceutical sector and other segments of the chemical industry that did so in the intermediate-technology industry. Apparel was outstanding as to export expansion in the lower technology level.[4] With the exception of the chemical industry and, to a lesser extent, iron and steel, most of the particularly dynamic manufactured exports during 1994 to 2000 were neither intensive in natural resources nor particularly polluting.

Another important characteristic of the Mexican export profile is the increasing participation of the *maquiladora* industry. In fact, exports originating in *maquiladora* activity reached, on average, 21 percent of total exports and 36 percent of manufactured exports between 1993 and 2000.[5] Already by 1996, 83 percent of apparel exports, 75 percent of plastic products exports, 73 percent of electric machinery and electronic exports (including computers, TVs, and so forth and their parts), and 65 percent of transport industry exports (including automobiles and auto parts) came from the *maquiladora* industry.[6]

Finally, it is useful to see how exports have evolved as compared to imports in each sector in the Mexican manufacturing industry, since the comparison can give an indication of possible shifts in export specialization.[7] To a significant degree, relatively nonpolluting industries have experienced marked increases in exports vis-à-vis imports. The sectors that experienced the greatest increase in exports compared to imports between 1992 and 2000 were beverages (313), footwear (324), apparel (322), and transport equipment (384) (including the automobile industry). (The numbers in parentheses are the International Standard Industrial Classification [ISIC] Code for each category.) None of these is particularly polluting. Further, the most-polluting industries—that is, the chemical industry (351), nonferrous metals (372), leather products (323), and paper and cellulose (341), as well as oil refineries (353)—all experienced a much smaller increase in exports compared to imports than the relatively nonpolluting industries listed above. Only a few of the most-polluting sectors—for example, other chemicals (352) and iron and steel (371)—experienced a slight increase in exports compared to imports. This data suggests that there was no relative shift of pollution-intensive industries toward Mexico as a result of NAFTA but rather an intensification of trade.

The chemical sector, the most-polluting industry of all, grew at very high rates in the 1990s (on average, 16.5 percent in the case of Mexico and 14.4 percent annually in the case of Canada between 1990 and 2000), but this high growth rate does not appear to be attributable to the chemical and petrochemical industry's treating Mexico or Canada as a pollution haven. This industry has always been of a global character, and much of its international trade is intrafirm, that is, between different plants belonging to the same enterprise. In 1994, two-thirds of the U.S. industry's exports went to the foreign branches of U.S.-based companies, while more than half of U.S. chemical imports came from foreign affiliates to their parent U.S.-based companies.[8] From the beginning, the U.S. chemical industry based its competitiveness on its natural resources endowment, initially wood and mineral resources and later oil. Petrochemicals have been the greatest strength of this sector in the United States, and in 1940 the United States accounted for 71 percent of the world refining capacity.[9]

The oil shocks of the 1970s reduced demand, increased costs, and lowered the profitability of petrochemicals in the United States. Many of them, which had become "commodities"—that is, goods intensive in natural resources, of widespread use, and produced by standardized technology—started being produced in Mexico, whose abundance of oil, as well as its state-subsidized price for the petrochemical industry, made it particularly attractive. The chemical industry in the United States (as well as in other industrialized countries) has since upgraded its production toward higher value added goods, occupying new niches of international competitiveness. U.S. chemical and petrochemical enterprises are usually trying to narrow their specialization according to the comparative advantage they have been able to develop since the 1970s with high technology, while leaving mass production of commodities to developing countries.[10] The increase in exports from Mexico in this sector appears to be more attributable to these structural changes in the industry.

In sum, an initial look at the topic of exports and pollution in Mexico suggests a tendency to specialize in technologically sophisticated products, which are comparatively less polluting than more traditional manufactured export products. Hence, there does not seem to be a shift of the most-polluting industries toward Mexico. In cases where industries producing commodities, such as the chemical industry, have expanded their exports at a high rate, their imports have increased as well, which suggests a greater intensification of trade but not a shift of such production from other countries to Mexico.

Manufactured Exports as a Source of Pollution in Mexico

The purpose of this section is to estimate the polluting impact of export expansion at an aggregated and a disaggregated level in the post-NAFTA period, comparing 1992/93 to 1997/98, that is, the period just before the agreement was signed and the latest period for which data is available. A distinction will be made between the pollution expansion generated by a "scale effect" and that caused by a "composition effect" (see the following section and appendix A for an explanation of these terms).[11]

SOURCES OF INFORMATION

This section will analyze the way in which pollution may have changed for goods produced for export by twenty-eight manufacturing sectors over the period 1992/93–1997/98. The information on exports was obtained from the Data Bank on Latin Americas Foreign Trade (BADECEL) database, which uses the ISIC, second version (or ISIC Rev. 2) with a three-digit aggregation. The information on pollution by sector was taken from the Industrial Pollution Projection System (IPPS), World Bank, which is also available in the ISIC Rev. 2 classification.[12] This information consists of the number of tons that each sector emits per US$1,000 of exports. This figure, multiplied by the amount of dollars exported (in thousands), provides an estimate of the tons of pollution produced for the years considered in the study.[13]

Since after 1992 the BADECEL export information from Mexico includes the *maquiladora* industry, it was necessary to subtract this amount from each export category. The reason why this study excludes the *maquiladora* industry is that the international fragmentation of the production process does not account for the quantity of the total pollution process generated in Mexico—that is, since only the assembling of parts is done in Mexico, it is not possible to assume that this process generates the same amount and type of pollution generated by the whole process of production of such goods (which is what IPPS provides). Additionally, the fact that the *maquiladora* industry is frequently located in sites with little infrastructure and few sanitary services changes even further the profile of environmental problems of this industry if compared to the IPPS criteria. As a result, it was necessary to subtract this pollution from the BADECEL export information.

The source of information for *maquiladora* exports for each sector was taken from Instituto Nacional de Estadística, Geografía e Industria (INEGI), which uses the Standard International Trade Classification (SITC). Since it was impossible to convert the latter into the ISIC Rev. 2 classification, the percentage of *maquiladora* exports in each INEGI sector where these kinds of exports exist was taken as an approximation and applied to the closest ISIC sectors for the BADECEL information. Therefore, the latter exports minus *maquiladora* are an approximation.

On the basis of this information, a "scale effect" and a "composition effect" were calculated (see appendixes A and B). The "scale effect" is that by which pollution varies exclusively as a result of a variation in the export activity, while the "composition effect" is the change in pollution emissions resulting from a structural change in export toward more- or less-polluting sectors (considering export activity unchanged).

THE SCALE AND COMPOSITION EFFECTS

The expansion of total manufacturing Mexican exports was very significant in the period 1992/93–1997/98 (171 percent, see Table 8.2). The pollution resulting from manufacturing export activity during the same period did not increase by a corresponding amount (it increased by 86.9 percent, or an increase of 30.4 million tons of pollutants) (see Table 8.3). This estimated increase in pollution was a result of the export dynamism ("scale effect"), which would have, by itself, been responsible for an increase of 59.8 million tons of pollution if it had not been offset partially by the contraction of 29.4 million tons resulting from a change in the composition of exports ("composition effect") in favor of less-polluting export sectors. In other words, if there had not been an expansion of manufacturing exports, pollution would have diminished in absolute terms, given the lesser weight of the most-polluting sectors in total exports in the last period.

It was the technologically more sophisticated manufacturing sectors—nonelectric machinery, electric machinery, and transport equipment—whose exports increased the most. In doing so, their expansion is estimated to have generated comparatively less pollution than if other sectors, with dirtier production records, had increased at such rates. In general, the most important polluting sectors—the chemical industry, oil refineries, and nonferrous metals—had a negative composition effect. Hence, they do not seem to have been favored by NAFTA over other less-polluting sectors (Table 8.3).

Competitiveness of Polluting Sectors

On the basis of the previous two sections, it is possible to conclude that, with some exceptions, Mexico's export drive in recent years has been concentrated in technologically sophisticated sectors, which are generally less polluting. Nevertheless, this does not give a complete picture of the position of polluting sectors in the international market, particularly the NAFTA market that is of main interest here. This section examines the competitiveness of twenty-five of the most-polluting Mexican manufacturing export sectors in the U.S. market. The section also examines Canadian exports as a point of reference for the Mexican experience within NAFTA.

From the data shown in Table 8.4, it is clear that Mexico has not specialized in highly polluting exports to the United States. The most-polluting exports have been decreasing as a percentage of total manufacturing exports. In fact, while 24.8 percent of Mexican manufacturing exports belonged to that category in 1990, in 1998 this share had fallen to 11.6 percent. If oil exports are excluded, then this reduction in the participation of the highest-

Table 8.2. Exports Excluding *Maquiladoras* (US$ millions, simple average)

ISIC Classification Rev. 2		xi_1 1992–93	xi_2 1997–98
311	Food products	483,560	1,405,494
313	Beverages	201,596	601,813
314	Tobacco	172,509	63,380
321	Textiles	297,831	1,182,304
322	Apparel	156,073	1,011,853
323	Leather products	111,731	280,208
324	Footwear	108,580	193,436
331	Wood products	280,268	469,469
332	Furniture	120,740	480,148
341	Paper and cellulose	327,507	433,977
342	Printed materials	133,084	303,652
351	Chemical industry	2,063,420	3,112,337
352	Other chemicals	585,162	1,662,112
353	Oil refinery	567,188	582,655
354	Oil and coal products	10,132	88,561
355	Rubber products	42,012	296,565
356	Plastic products	163,352	337,312
361	Ceramic	118,950	267,919
362	Glass	503,428	832,910
369	Other nonmetal mineral	169,854	443,669
371	Iron and steel	838,864	2,557,085
372	Nonferrous metals	991,071	1,655,353
381	Metal products	530,630	1,708,705
382	Nonelectric machinery	2,298,567	8,925,053
383	Electric machinery	2,547,612	7,901,354
384	Transport equipment	2,581,857	7,585,859
385	Scientific and professional instruments	889,660	2,595,957
390	Other manufactured products	335,521	807,914
	Total	17,630,759	47,787,054

Table 8.3. Disaggregation of Mexican Industry Pollution Change in the Period 1992/93–1997/98

ISIC Classification Rev. 2		*ti* (tons per million dollars of 1987)	$xi_1 \star ti$ (tons) 1992–93	$xi_2 \star ti$ (tons) 1997–98	Scale Effect (tons)	Composition Effect (tons)
311	Food products	0.11	53,551	155,649	91,596	10,502
313	Beverages	0.07	14,883	44,430	25,457	4,090
314	Tobacco	0.14	23,520	8,641	40,230	-55,109
321	Textiles	0.41	123,016	488,337	210,410	154,911
322	Apparel	0.01	1,238	8,029	2,118	4,672
323	Leather products	2.33	260,765	653,968	446,022	-52,819
324	Footwear	0.22	23,956	42,678	40,976	-22,254
331	Wood products	0.18	49,838	83,482	85,245	-51,601
332	Furniture	0.69	83,077	330,371	142,097	105,197
341	Paper and cellulose	1.66	543,180	719,764	929,075	-752,491
342	Printed materials	0.21	28,308	64,589	48,419	-12,138
351	Chemical industry	9.95	20,532,098	30,969,365	35,118,858	-24,681,590
352	Other chemicals	1.37	799,611	2,271,239	1,367,684	103,944
353	Oil refinery	1.46	830,423	853,068	1,420,386	-1,397,741
354	Oil and coal products	0.24	2,422	21,167	4,142	14,603
355	Rubber products	0.53	22,419	158,259	38,347	97,493
356	Plastic products	1.12	182,452	376,752	312,073	-117,773
361	Ceramic	0.55	64,952	146,297	111,097	-29,752
362	Glass	0.17	83,299	137,816	142,477	-87,960
369	Other nonmetal mineral	0.46	78,173	204,192	133,710	-7,691
371	Iron and steel	3.17	2,656,835	8,098,758	4,544,348	897,575
372	Nonferrous metals	5.00	4,956,405	8,278,523	8,477,618	-5,155,500
381	Metal products	0.81	430,825	1,387,318	736,899	219,594
382	Nonelectric machinery	0.23	529,514	2,056,038	905,700	620,824
383	Electric machinery	0.54	1,384,941	4,295,358	2,368,854	541,564
384	Transport equipment	0.36	928,692	2,728,628	1,588,469	211,467
385	Scientific and professional instruments	0.22	199,385	581,790	341,036	41,369
390	Other manufactured products	0.27	89,179	214,736	152,534	-26,976
	Total		34,976,956	65,379,243	59,825,877	-29,423,590

The addition of the scale and the composition effect is equal to the estimated variation of pollution between period 1 and period 2, i.e., $xi_2 \star ti - xi_1 \star ti$.

Table 8.4. Most-Polluting Exports as Percentage of Total Exports from Mexico and Canada to the United States

	1990	1991	1992	1993	1994	1995	1996	1997	1998
Mexico	24.8	21.4	19.8	18.2	16.7	16.9	15.8	16.0	11.6
Minus oil exports	7.2	6.3	6.3	5.9	6.3	7.4	6.5	6.2	6.0
Canada	31.3	32.0	31.3	30.4	29.3	30.7	30.8	30.4	27.5
Minus oil exports	20.5	20.7	20.5	19.8	19.5	21.3	20.0	19.7	19.1

SOURCE: MAGIC, ECLAC, 1999.

polluting sectors is much less pronounced, from 7.2 percent in 1990 to 6.0 percent in 1998.

Mexico's exports are much less specialized in pollution sectors than Canada's. In the latter case, 31.3 percent of total manufacturing exports were highly polluting in 1990, falling to 27.5 percent in 1998. If oil is excluded, then these percentages are 20.5 percent and 19.1 percent, respectively.

At a more disaggregated level, in the Mexican case, besides mineral fuels and oils, the other most-polluting sectors with the greatest weight in total value of manufacturing exports to the United States in 1998 were, in order of importance, iron and steel, plastics and articles, copper and articles, and precious stones and metals (Table 8.5). Following the same criteria, in Canada, those non-oil-polluting sectors with the greatest presence were paper and paperboard, plastic and articles, aluminum and articles, and precious stones and metals, also in order of value of exports (not shown in Table 8.5).

From a more dynamic perspective, Table 8.6 shows additional interesting information. Exports from Mexico and Canada are categorized according to whether they are experiencing (1) "retreats," that is, those exports that lose participation in a particular U.S. market, whose dynamism is lower than that of total U.S. imports market; (2) "missed opportunities," exports to the United States that lose their market participation, while such market is dynamic as compared to the total U.S. imports market; (3) "declining stars," those exports that gain a greater presence in a particular market in the United States, but this market is relatively stagnant as compared to the total U.S. imports market; and (4) "rising stars," exports that gain a greater participation in a specific U.S. goods market, which in turn is winning a greater weight in the total U.S. imports markets.

Mexico and Canada seem to have considerably different performances. While more than half of Canada's exports (53 percent) of the most-polluting goods were either retreating or missing opportunities in the U.S. markets in 1998, almost all of these environmentally unfriendly Mexican exports were gaining greater presence in these U.S. markets at the end of the 1990s.

In this way, 93 percent of Mexican most-polluting exports were either "declining stars" or "rising stars." Of these, most belonged to the category of "declining stars," that is, though these markets were declining in the United States, Mexico was maintaining a competitive stance in them (see Table 8.6).

In short, Canadian export specialization was much more pollution prone than were the Mexican exports in the 1990s. Both countries' most-polluting sectors have undergone shrinking export ratios to the United States; hence, they were not becoming more specialized in these kinds of exports. For Mexico and Canada, NAFTA seems to have promoted a greater specialization in nonpollution-intensive exports. Nevertheless, there was a qualitative difference in their competitive position, by which Mexico seemed to have been increasing its comparative advantage in several of those highly polluting markets, while Canada was leaving most of them. In other words, although in Mexico these sectors were less dynamic than the average rate of export growth, they still were considerably more dynamic than the U.S. markets to which they were being exported and therefore were gaining a greater share of them.

Investment, Export Specialization, and Pollution in Mexico

Contrary to what might be thought, the change in the Mexican manufacturing sector, excluding the *maquiladora* industry, was not very extensive in the period that followed the economic reform of the 1980s. When NAFTA was signed Mexico had a relatively stagnant manufacturing sector whose investment/production coefficient was considerably lower than that which prevailed in the 1970s and the beginning of the 1980s (under 6 percent as compared to nearly 10 percent in the former period). In fact, the net stock of fixed capital in 1994 was the same as that in 1984, though modernized to a certain extent.[14]

Although not enough information exists for the second half of the 1990s, the capital stock probably increased somewhat, driven by the very significant FDI that has entered Mexico since then. In the period 1995–2000, FDI flowing annually to Mexico (about $10.5 billion) almost doubled that of the period 1990–94 (around $5.4 billion).[15] The manufacturing sector received about 60 percent of this investment, but at the same time, an increasing proportion of the FDI went to the *maquiladora* industry, reaching 36 percent in 2000. This expansion has mainly nurtured the export industry, which in turn has been the main catalyst of the manufacturing sector's transformation in the recent period. There were not many changes in the capital stock that could be directly linked to environmental upgrading, since the specific investment on environment protection by enterprises still seems to be quite limited. In 1997, the environmental market was worth about $2 billion in

Table 8.5 U.S. Imports from Mexico, Most-Polluting Sectors (US$ thousands)

	1990	1991	1992	1993	1994	1995	1996	1997	1998
28 Inorganic chemicals; organic or inorganic compounds of precious metals, of rare-earth metals, of radioactive elements or of isotopes	236,398	182,385	195,494	181,014	243,923	240,299	246,735	279,583	223,413
29 Organic chemicals	164,442	256,821	300,656	223,233	285,916	370,732	351,901	406,324	358,580
32 Tanning or dyeing extracts; tannins and derivatives; dyes, pigments, and other coloring matter; paints and varnishes; putty and other mastics; inks	38,669	28,742	30,102	30,988	29,521	31,252	41,461	54,464	63,846
71 Natural or cultured pearls, precious or semiprecious stones, precious metals; precious metal–clad metals, articles thereof; imitation jewelry; coin	283,248	230,217	275,638	260,882	294,242	394,894	498,630	445,015	577,725
75 Nickel and articles thereof	249	596	773	452	286	383	692	636	1,004
76 Aluminum and articles thereof	107,791	104,992	122,563	121,806	172,891	280,047	259,471	300,452	319,818
78 Lead and articles thereof	25,249	15,575	32,788	17,930	18,552	36,301	46,526	45,188	35,289
79 Zinc and articles thereof	119,377	65,728	50,875	100,278	96,159	109,835	108,719	143,718	126,422
80 Tin and articles thereof	21,977	5,984	2,735	4,150	1,010	998	1,966	2,316	2,955
74 Copper and articles thereof	201,018	168,275	211,495	256,695	303,822	628,875	450,726	499,193	660,264
81 Base metals nesoi; cermets; articles thereof	12,183	11,946	9,688	10,423	9,970	9,163	10,508	10,547	10,435
27 Mineral fuels, mineral oils, and products of their distillation; bituminous substances; mineral waxes	5,288,108	4,684,933	4,736,831	4,874,777	5,106,514	5,836,865	6,798,428	8,419,663	5,308,913
39 Plastics and articles thereof	241,695	300,919	342,944	377,513	500,349	660,129	715,645	820,491	940,102
72 Iron and steel	278,900	227,713	231,742	334,478	578,310	849,110	990,254	1,136,646	1,055,984

	1990	1991	1992	1993	1994	1995	1996	1997	1998
56 Wadding, felt, and nonwovens; special yarns; twine, cordage, ropes, and cables and articles thereof	23,187	20,088	22,880	29,063	34,266	41,751	69,814	96,563	93,167
59 Impregnated, coated, covered, or laminated textile fabrics; textile articles suitable for industrial use	8,919	12,677	12,348	20,629	24,788	26,463	29,699	29,859	38,651
48 Paper and paperboard; articles of paper pulp, paper, or paperboard	193,168	120,485	135,457	124,823	161,562	351,150	304,506	367,305	432,742
31 Fertilizers	14,692	14,942	13,018	14,212	40,952	86,358	86,352	31,800	25,048
30 Pharmaceutical products	3,053	6,258	8,154	10,806	9,072	12,657	19,358	22,072	24,581
33 Essential oils and resinoids; perfumery, cosmetic or toilet preparations	16,116	13,651	18,742	20,814	26,154	45,085	51,661	63,095	87,015
35 Albuminoidal substances; modified starches; glues; enzymes	2,682	1,961	2,667	3,322	6,279	12,149	11,375	7,418	9,836
36 Explosives; pyrotechnic products; matches; pyrophoric alloys; certain combustible preparations	803	547	2,386	5,666	5,270	7,393	9,915	11,676	13,642
38 Miscellaneous chemical products	49,477	50,321	50,745	54,251	60,478	59,879	90,775	164,435	159,975
15 Animal or vegetable fats and oils and their cleavage products; prepared edible fats; animal or vegetable waxes	18,416	33,204	27,396	31,706	40,765	53,013	56,778	29,955	46,054
40 Rubber and articles thereof	112,735	95,887	116,377	136,440	187,640	253,558	282,932	346,054	399,641
Total most polluting	7,462,552	6,654,847	6,954,494	7,246,351	8,238,691	10,398,339	11,534,827	13,734,468	11,015,102

SOURCE: MAGIC, ECLAC.

See Table 8.1 and chapter 8 appendix for classification of industrial sectors from greater to lower level of pollution.

Table 8.6. Exports from Most-Polluting Sectors (% of total exports to United States)

	1990	1991	1992	1993	1994	1995	1996	1997	1998
Mexico-U.S. Exports									
Retreats	5.2	4.5	4.1	4.5	5.1	4.7	4.3	3.5	3.8
Missed opportunities	2.4	4.1	4.6	3.4	3.7	3.8	3.3	3.2	3.6
Declining stars	81.4	80.2	78.9	79.9	77.8	76.3	77.1	78.8	71.5
Rising stars	10.9	11.2	12.3	12.3	13.4	15.2	15.3	14.5	21.1
Canada-U.S. Exports									
Retreats	26.8	25.1	26.3	25.3	26.9	26.8	25.0	25.0	25.1
Missed opportunities	28.6	29.6	28.5	28.1	26.4	29.0	26.7	25.4	28.0
Declining stars	38.1	38.9	38.2	38.7	37.6	34.4	38.5	38.9	34.9
Rising stars	6.5	6.4	7.1	7.8	9.1	9.9	9.8	10.7	12.0

SOURCE: MAGIC.

Mexico, that is, about 0.6 percent of Gross Domestic Product (GDP), which is considered too limited to be able to tackle the environmental problems, but the prospects are good, since such market has been growing at a 10 to 14 percent rate annually.[16]

FDI was responsible for a large proportion of the Mexican export thrust, but both FDI and export growth concentrated mostly in a few sectors. Of the 61 percent total FDI that went to manufacturing industry between 1994 and 2000, one-third was absorbed by the automobile industry and the electronic equipment industry, which includes the computer industry; one-sixth went to chemical industry activities (especially pharmaceutical and other chemicals); and another sixth was directed toward beverages and the tobacco industries.[17]

As to the environmental impact of this investment and export profile, the first observation is mixed. The most substantial part of FDI does not seem to promote particularly polluting activities, which is encouraging. Instead, it searches for local advantages that may reduce costs in ways other than through lower environmental standards. This is consistent with other studies, which report that environmental costs are too small to determine the location of industry (approximately 2 percent of total value added in 85 percent of U.S. industry).[18] Among the elements that determine the location of these industries are the availability of natural resources, low salaries, and access to local markets. Even most of the chemical industry, which is the most polluting, does not seem to be attracted by lower environmental standards, as mentioned before. In fact, since much of it is integrated with transnational corporations or large national capital, which normally is associated with important technological partners abroad, it usually uses technology that is close to the best available internationally.[19]

A note of caution should be added to avoid an overoptimistic prospect of a country shifting its export activities toward technologically sophisticated, high value added sectors. An important part of the export boom, as was mentioned earlier, occurred in the *maquiladora* industry. In fact, the most dynamic segment of FDI went to the *maquiladora* industry. Between 1994 and 1998, FDI flowing to that industry grew 24 percent annually and reached 21 percent of total FDI in Mexico in September 2000.[20] Hence, technologically, much of this industry has developed only a small segment of this high-technology process in Mexico and usually, but not always, the part of the process that is labor intensive. Although there are some references to a second generation of the *maquiladora* industry, which in theory incorporates more advanced processes of production than the first generation, even the electronic and automobile *maquiladora* industries continue carrying out mostly assembly operations in a traditional way.[21] Therefore, the industrial technological upgrade spurred by exports is definitely shallow, and the change in the manufacturing export structure toward high-technology products can be misleading if considered a sign of the level of technological development. Consequently, the transference of technology and the possibility of building an industry that may produce greater value added per unit of output and increase workers' income is still an unaccomplished aim. Additionally, the segments of *maquiladora* production, which have been located mostly on the northern border of Mexico, lack the necessary infrastructure to dispose of solid toxic wastes in an environmentally acceptable way without causing emissions of pollutants to the air, soil, and water.[22]

Conclusions

As a result of NAFTA, Mexican foreign trade gained greater dynamism than it had experienced during the period of trade liberalization that began in 1987. The high rate of growth of imports and exports was accompanied by an increasing flow of FDI toward Mexico.

This increase in foreign trade, however, is not attributable to Mexico's becoming a pollution haven. It is the case that Mexico's most-polluting industrial sectors exporting to the United States have maintained their competitiveness in many of their markets in the United States. But these sectors are responsible for only a small fraction of total exports, and their share of exports has declined significantly under NAFTA. Thus, from an environmental point of view, the Mexican trade trends do not suggest a shift of export specialization toward more polluting sectors after 1994. The chemical sector, the most polluting of all, had a more rapid growth of imports than of exports. The trade trend data, in short, indicates an intensification of trade and a more significant increase in exports of nonpolluting sectors than exports of the most-polluting sectors; the data does not show a shift of production in the most-polluting sectors to Mexico.

Second, an estimate of pollution expansion related to manufacturing exports from a pre- to a post-NAFTA period (1992/93–1997/98) shows that it was the significant dynamism of exports that was responsible for greater emissions and not a change in the structure of exports toward more polluting sectors. In fact, if exports had not increased during that period, pollution would have diminished because of the greater weight gained by less-polluting sectors during that period. Therefore the "scale effect" and not the "composition effect" explains the pollution expansion in the period under study.

Third, the Mexican export structure experienced a shift away from primary goods and toward high-technology export products, in particular the automobile and the electronics industries. When compared to the Canadian export structure, Mexican exports changed to a much greater degree in favor of the high-technology sectors' exports after NAFTA, while within the Latin American context the Mexican experience was almost unique.

Finally, the environmentally favorable implications of relying less on natural resources and concentrating more in sectors with high technology have to be taken with reserve. Overall, investment was stagnant until 1994, and since then it has been FDI that presumably has injected greater capital for innovation purposes. The most dynamic part of FDI has flowed to the *maquiladora* industry, and this industry only is in charge of a small segment of the production process, usually that which is labor intensive. In general, the high-technology industries are not really integrated nationally, technological transfer from abroad is limited, and value added, particularly in the *maquiladora* industry, is quite low. Hence, too, the impact of this activity on incomes and standards of living, which is essential to overcome some environmental problems, is also limited. The *maquiladora* industry in itself produces a wide range of environmental problems that are far from being solved. Thus, while Mexico has enjoyed benefits from NAFTA over the past several years in terms of increased trade (including substantial increases in exports) and these positive developments are not due to Mexico's potential attractiveness as a pollution haven, the reality is that these developments have not yet transformed the Mexican economy in a sustainable way.

Appendix A
Highest Polluting Industrial Sectors

The industrial sectors are ranked according to pollution level, from highest to lowest. The categorization is based on the IPPS.

1. 28—Inorganic chemicals; organic or inorganic compounds of precious metals, of rare-earth metals, of radioactive elements or isotopes
2. 29—Organic chemicals
3. 32—Tanning or dyeing extracts; tannins and derivatives; dyes, pigments, and other coloring matter; paints and varnishes; putty and other mastics; inks
4. 71—Natural or cultured pearls, precious metals; precious metal–clad metals, articles thereof; imitation jewelry; coin

   75—Nickel and articles thereof

   76—Aluminum and articles thereof

   78—Lead and articles thereof

   79—Zinc and articles thereof

   80—Tin and articles thereof
5. 74—Copper and articles thereof

   81—Base metals nesoi; cermets; articles thereof
6. 29—Mineral fuels, mineral oils, and products of their distillation; bituminous substances; mineral waxes
7. 39—Plastics and articles thereof
8. 72—Iron and steel
9. 56—Wadding, felt and nonwovens; special yarns; twine, cordage, ropes, and cables and articles thereof

   59—Impregnated, coated, covered, or laminated textile fabrics; textile articles suitable for industrial use
10. 48—Paper and paperboard; articles of paper pulp, paper, or paperboard
11. 31—Fertilizers
12. 30—Pharmaceutical products
13. 33—Essential oils and resinoids; perfumery, cosmetic or toilet preparations

    35—Albuminoidal substances; modified starches; glues; enzymes

    36—Explosives; pyrotechnic products; matches; pyrophoric alloys; certain combustible preparations

    38—Miscellaneous chemical products
14. 15—Animal or vegetable fats and oils and their cleavage products; prepared edible fats; animal or vegetable waxes
15. 40—Rubber and articles thereof

Appendix B Methodology

The exports of period 1 of each of the twenty-eight industrial sectors was multiplied by the growth of total exports index between period 1 (1992–93 baseline) and period 2 (1997–98). This result was in turn multiplied by the pollution index, which gives an estimate of the amount of pollution that would have been emitted if all sectors had expanded at the average rate of growth of aggregate exports. The difference between this hypothetical emission and that of period 1 is the "scale effect."

If we subtract from the "scale effect" the pollution of period 2, then we obtain the "composition effect." All difference between the "scale effect" and the estimated pollution in year 2 is attributed to a change in composition of exports ("composition effect").

Notes

This chapter is based on and updates a paper entitled "Mexico's Manufacturing Exports and the Environment under NAFTA," which I prepared for the CEC North American Symposium on Assessing the Linkages between Trade and the Environment in October 2000. It is published here with the permission of the Commission for Environmental Cooperation. I am very grateful to Enrique Dussel Peters for his valuable comments and for having provided me with very useful information. I also thank René Hernandez for his very helpful comments. The opinions presented in this chapter are the author's exclusive responsibility.

1. CEC, *Assessing Environmental Effects of the North American Free Trade Agreement (NAFTA): An Analytic Framework (Phase II) and Issue Studies* (1999), available at *http://www.cec.org/programs_projects/trade_environ_econ/pdfs/frmwrk-e.pdf.* For further description of the analytic framework, see ch. 6, supra.

2. See Enrique Dussel Peters, *El Tratado de Libre Comercio de Norteamérica y el Desempeño de la Economía en México*, CEPAL, LC/MEX/L.431 (2000).

3. In 1977, 59 percent of total Mexican exports were primary goods and 14 percent were natural resources intensive products, while in 2000 these proportions had fallen to 11 percent and 6 percent, respectively (see Table 8.1).

4. M. Mortimore, R. Buitelaar, and J. L. Bonifaz, "México: Un CANálisis de su competitividad internacional," *Serie Desarrollo Productivo* 62 (CEPAL 2000).

5. Enrique Dussel Peters, "El Impacto de la IED a Nivel Micro en México," BID-INTAL and Facultad de Economía/UNAM (2002). This information refers to gross exports (i.e., exports including the value of imported inputs as well as value added) and not only the value added by the *maquiladora* industry to those imports.

6. Information from Instituto Nacional de Estadística, Geografía e Industria (INEGI), Mexico.

7. It was not possible to calculate these coefficients for Canada because BADECEL does not count with Canadian imports and exports in ISIC Rev. 2 classifica-

tion, which is necessary to identify each category with pollution emissions of the IPPS.

8. D. C. Mowery and R. Nelson, *Sources of Industrial Leadership: Studies of Seven Industries* (1999).

9. Id.

10. Id.

11. If we could count with observed information on pollution variation between the two periods under study and our estimated pollution variation, the difference would mostly be a "technological effect," i.e., the change in pollution attributable to a change in technology. This effect could not be calculated because we lack information for that purpose.

12. H. Hettige, P. Martin, M. Singh, and D. Wheeler, "The Industrial Pollution System," in *Policy Research Working Paper* 1431 (World Bank 1995).

13. It was not possible to make this estimate for Canadian exports since BADECEL information for Canada is not available in the ISIC classification, which is needed to be able to relate exports to emissions in the IPPS.

14. J. C. Moreno, "Reformas Macroeconómicas e Inversiones Manufactureras en México," *Serie Reformas Económicas* 47 (CEPAL 1999). An annual 5 percent depreciation of fixed capital is considered in that study.

15. *Foreign Investment in Latin America and the Caribbean, 1999* (CEPAL 2000).

16. CESPEDES, *Areas de Oportunidad Ambiental de la Economía* (México D.F. 1999)

17. E. Dussel Peters and M. Mortimore, "La Inversión Extranjera en México," *Serie Desarrollo Productivo* (CEPAL 2000); Mortimore, Buitelaar, and Bonifaz, supra.

18. D. Esty and B. S. Gentry, "Foreign Investment, Globalization and Environment," in *Globalization and Environment, Preliminary Perspectives* (OECD 1997); P. Low and A. Yeats, "Do Dirty Industries Migrate?" *International Trade and the Environment* (World Bank 1992).

19. J. Mattar, "La Competitividad de la Industria Química," in *La Industria Mexicana en el Mercado Mundial*, El Trimestre Económico, Lecturas 30 (F. Clavijo and J. Casar eds., 1994); *Grandes Empresas y Grupos Industriales Latinoaméricanos* (W. Péres ed., 1998).

20. Enrique Dussel Peters, "El Impacto de la IED a Nivel Micro en México," BID-INTAL and Facultad de Economía/UNAM (2002).

21. J. Gerber, "Perspectivas de las maquiladoras después del 2001," 49 *Comercio Exterior* 9 (1999).

22. EcoFrontera, "Industria Maquiladora y Medio Ambiente" (2000), available at *www.uacj.mx/cema/num3/ecofront.htm*.

ALEJANDRO NADAL 9

Corn in NAFTA Eight Years After

Effects on Mexican Biodiversity

IN 1999, CORN PRODUCTION in Mexico absorbed more than 53 percent of total cultivated land. It also occupied more than 2.5 million individual producers. These corn growers work under highly differentiated conditions in terms of technology and resource endowment. Production conditions are marked by deep differences in soil characteristics, topography, general climate, rainfall patterns, and evaporation coefficients. Differences also arise from diverse sources of biotic stress associated with fungi, bacteria, insects, and nematodes. The level of heterogeneity is associated with the extraordinary mosaic of agrological and ecosystem diversity in Mexico, which is in turn closely related to the country's geographical and physical characteristics.[1]

When the North American Free Trade Agreement (NAFTA) was negotiated, Mexico's corn sector was included. This was perhaps one of the most important single components of the new trade agreement. Access to Mexico's basic grains market had been a long-standing project of U.S. growers. Average yields and subsidies in the United States made Mexico's producers appear to be highly uncompetitive.

At the time, it was expected that the economic forces unleashed by trade liberalization (especially price reductions as a result of U.S. imports) would bring about an important reallocation of land, labor, and capital in Mexican corn production, which would allow Mexico to tap its comparative advantages in agriculture, especially in fruit and horticultural production. As a result, subsidies for corn producers would become unnecessary, a major policy goal as explicitly recognized in the two major studies supporting the decision to include corn in NAFTA.[2] A significant proportion of displaced producers would enter the national labor market and would be employed in sectors of higher productivity. The overall outcome would be a positive contribution to the trade balance and to Mexico's fiscal accounts.

On the social and environmental front, trade liberalization in corn was expected to bring about welfare gains for producers and consumers alike. Producers would reap the benefits of the productivity gains associated with the more efficient allocation of resources. Consumers would also gain from the lower prices of key consumer goods and especially of the country's staple food, tortillas and various corn products.

The reallocation of productive resources would also lead to improvements in soil management and reduced pressure on marginal land as well as cuts in deforestation rates. Other possible environmental effects on the use of pesticides and water resources were disregarded, but the general perception was that benefits would surpass any potential damages. An overshadowing assumption was that, in general, modern and more efficient technologies would be adopted and assimilated in Mexico's agricultural sector, and this would bring about beneficial effects in resource usage rates. An important caveat was that adequate investments in the form of public expenditures were required to turn this scenario into a reality.

The critical environmental dimension of genetic resources was completely ignored during the NAFTA negotiations. This is surprising, because the loss of genetic resources was already understood to be a major environmental problem. It is even more surprising if we take into account Mexico's position as the center of origin and diversity of corn and the critical role of corn's genetic variability in the production strategies of most growers in Mexico. Most agronomists, plant breeders, and geneticists were acutely aware of the strategic importance of Mexico's corn genetic resources in the future expansion of world output in this cereal. But their observations were not taken into account as trade negotiators plotted the future evolution of Mexico's corn sector and the fate of corn producers. The failure to take these into account reveals the existence of an important gap in the assessment of environmental impacts of trade agreements.

Two previous studies examined several potential environmental impacts of corn in NAFTA.[3] Those analyses identified potential effects on soil quality, water resources, pesticides, and genetic resources. This chapter examines in greater detail the issues of genetic resources and, in particular, analyzes some of the more recent developments, including recent findings confirming the presence of transgenic constructs in Mexican landraces.

The linkages between a trade agreement such as NAFTA and a specific environmental dimension are sometimes difficult to determine. The point of view in this analysis is that trade liberalization is only one aspect of a more complex package of economic policies. In other terms, trade liberalization is but one of many components of a wider economic strategy that, for want of other more apt semantics, I will call the open economy model. Thus, other macroeconomic considerations regarding interest and exchange rates, credit and monetary policies, financial liberalization, general economic deregulation, privatization, and fiscal expenditures must be taken into account in assessing the interplay of economic forces working on economic agents as the open economy model unfolds. From this vantage point, the impact of tariff reductions and quota elimination must be examined in conjunction with the effects of other accompanying economic policies. Without this type of analysis, the connection between environmental impacts and trade agreements becomes difficult to understand.[4]

The first section of this chapter briefly describes the implementation of NAFTA's corn regime. The second section analyzes the environmental implications for Mexico's corn genetic resources. This section also examines the potential impact of transgenic corn on Mexico's corn germ plasm. The final section focuses on policy recommendations.[5]

Corn in NAFTA

NAFTA'S RULES

The inclusion of corn in NAFTA was aimed at releasing productive resources that would find a more efficient allocation in other crops or sectors. But incorporating the corn sector in the free trade agreement constituted a delicate policy measure, and Mexico's government chose to envelop the deal in a long-term transition period. A tariff rate quota (TRQ) would immediately replace the old quota system and would be phased out over fifteen years.[6] The first year of implementation, the tariff-free import quota was 2.5 million tons. This import quota was to grow at a 3 percent yearly rate and would lead to a tariff-free quota of 3.5 million tons at the end of the fifteen-year transition period. By the year 2008, all corn imports would enjoy a zero tariff. A tariff of 206.9 percent was set on imports above the tariff-free quota for the first year of the agreement. This tariff would be phased out: during the first six years of NAFTA, the tariff would be reduced linearly by approximately 30 percent, and the remaining tariff was to be completely phased out during the next nine years.

The central variable in the fifteen-year transition period was the domestic price. In and by itself, the fifteen-year period would be meaningless without an adequate functioning of the corresponding price adjustment process. Price variations can, of course, be irregular and even volatile, but the TRQ mechanism is designed to provide stability to the adjustment process. For this to take place, the full tariff on imports above the tariff-free quota must be exacted.

Corn imports have increased from three million tons in 1993 to six million tons in 2001. The majority of total corn imports serve as inputs in processing industries producing feedstock for poultry and livestock (57 percent in 2001). Starch, oil, and flour industries account for another 38 percent of total imports. These industries are the direct beneficiaries of the reduced price of corn imports and of the fact that the tariff on imports exceeding the tariff-free quota has not been effectively levied, a point to which I return below.

Corn imports have exceeded the tariff-free quota since the first year of NAFTA's implementation. But Mexico's authorities have not levied the tariff. They argue that refraining from levying the tariff is necessary to ensure that tortilla prices would not increase. They also argue that charging the tariff is a discretionary power conferred by NAFTA's text and not an obligatory act. Public officials even stated that if the tariff were charged, a special subsidy would have to be provided to industrial tortilla producers in order to keep tortilla prices down. This would, in effect, mean that what would be levied to these producers through the tariff would have to be returned through a special subsidy to those same agents. Unfortunately, this rationale was flawed.

During the period since NAFTA came into force, tortilla prices have experienced a steep rise, with price increments surpassing 500 percent between 1993 and 2000. In addition, subsidies were provided to the producers of industrial tortillas, at least until 1998, when tortilla prices were completely deregulated. Thus, the lack of adequate implementation of the TRQ for corn was accompanied by the use of monopoly pricing power by industrial producers, canceling the consumer welfare gains that, in theory, NAFTA would bring about.

The allocation of the import quota is determined by a special committee under the leadership of the Ministry of Agriculture (SAGARPA) and the Ministry of the Economy (ME). Representatives of the main importers of corn sit on this committee: flour mills, industrial plants and oil refineries, high corn fructose producers, livestock and poultry producers. Mexico's corn growers have never been part of the committee. The lack of adequate representation of corn growers on the committee helps explain why the tariff on imports beyond the tariff-free quota has not been charged. This means that the main protection mechanism that was designed to define the terms of the transition period was never used.

Agricultural producers' associations have attempted to reverse this state of things. During the past five years, they have intervened during congressional debates on the federal budget. These associations and their allies in Congress secured a special article in the Federal Revenues Law for the year 2000 authorizing levying of a 30 percent ad valorem tax on corn imports exceeding the tariff-free quota established in NAFTA. However, government officials considered this article as giving them discretionary powers and decided not to exact the tax.

For the year 2001, the Federal Revenues Law included a peculiar obligation for the executive: in the case that corn imports would exceed the tariff-free quota, the level of the tariffs to be charged would be determined in consultation with producers' organizations. This time, the law explicitly stated that a tariff would be levied on these imports. A presidential decree was issued establishing a tariff of 1 percent on imports of yellow corn and 3 percent on imports of white corn exceeding NAFTA's tariff-free import quota. Thus, the real tariff charged on corn imports over the tariff-free quota remained a symbolic tax with no substantive effect on the evolution of domestic corn prices.

The TRQ on corn, like all TRQs, was not designed to stop imports, which is precisely the highly disruptive effect that is considered to arise from quotas and other quantitative barriers to trade. TRQs are intended to reduce the impact of imports on prices. But if the tariff on imports over the tariff-free quota is not levied, there is a direct impact on prices, as if the final year of the transition period had been reached. The impact of corn imports from the United States on domestic prices of corn in Mexico has been significant. The price of corn dropped from 1,600 pesos per ton in 1993 to less than 800 in 1999. During that same period, accumulated inflation surpassed 150 percent. This means that real income for corn producers dropped steeply and at a very fast rate.

Mexican domestic corn prices have been aligned with international (mostly U.S. prices) since 1996. These international prices have been at a rather low level for several reasons. U.S. agricultural policies and the level of subsidies that have been allocated are probably the most important explanatory variable. Today, production costs of corn in the U.S. Corn Belt cannot be fully recovered by prevailing prices.

During this same period, public expenditures for the agricultural sector in Mexico have maintained a steady downward trend. Direct income support, loans to agricultural producers, insurance against crop failure, and expenditures in agricultural infrastructure such as irrigation have all declined in real terms. This is unfortunate because during this period the agricultural sector was exposed to the pressures of trade liberalization. New investments were required to meet the challenge of reduced prices, increased competition from imports, and greater competition in international markets for Mexico's agricultural exports. Productivity-enhancing investments needed to reap the benefits of Mexico's comparative advantages, as well as investments to increase production intensity, have not been flowing to the agricultural sector. This helps explain why the sector's Gross Domestic Product (GDP) has stagnated and why the trade balance has not been improving.

Environmental Implications for Genetic Resources

BIODIVERSITY OF MEXICAN CORN

Perhaps the most important trait of corn production in Mexico is its high degree of heterogeneity. Production conditions are extremely varied and form a complex matrix of social, economic, technological, and natural variables. Corn shows a greater capacity than the other major cereals (wheat, rice, barley, sorghum, millet, oats) to adapt to a vast range of ecological conditions. It grows at altitudes of up to 3,000 meters above sea level but can also be found at sea level, and its mean growing season temperatures can exceed 26° C or may be as low as 12.5° C. The capacity of corn germ plasm to adapt to such a wide variety of ecosystems has turned it into an important component in the productive strategies of corn growers, especially in the case of the poorest farmers.

For many of Mexico's corn growers, the genetic variability of corn is one of their most important technological assets.[7] Mexican corn varieties are well adapted to changes in rainfall (especially to the interruption of rains at the beginning of the plant's growing cycle), humidity, climate variations, pests, winds, low nitrogen, or acid soils. Poor growers normally have to rely on soils of inferior quality, where yields are low and risks of crop failure are high. Thus, the local landraces that have undergone a long and systematic process of adaptation to the diverse agro-ecosystems in Mexico are a critical element in their resource endowment.[8] But in order to use these varieties, producers must possess refined information on the array of relations between seed characteristics and soil quality, weather and climate conditions, humidity levels and drainage patterns, topographic features, and pests. This information also covers complex intercropping systems involving several leguminosae (kidney beans and broad beans), cucurbitaceae (different types of squash), capsicum (various peppers), and a wide variety of herbs.

Growers who use corn's genetic variability as a key technological asset are the curators of this resource.[9] They have maintained and developed this resource through a continuous process of dynamic exchanges of open pollinated varieties, through local cultivars, and frequently through the adaptation (or "creolization") of improved varieties and hybrids generated in the formal agricultural research centers. The knowledge they possess of their agro-ecosystems enables them to maintain and continuously enrich this stock of genetic resources.

Figure 9.1 presents in simplified terms the relation between the presence

Figure 9.1. Genetic Variability and Productivity Trade-off in Corn Production

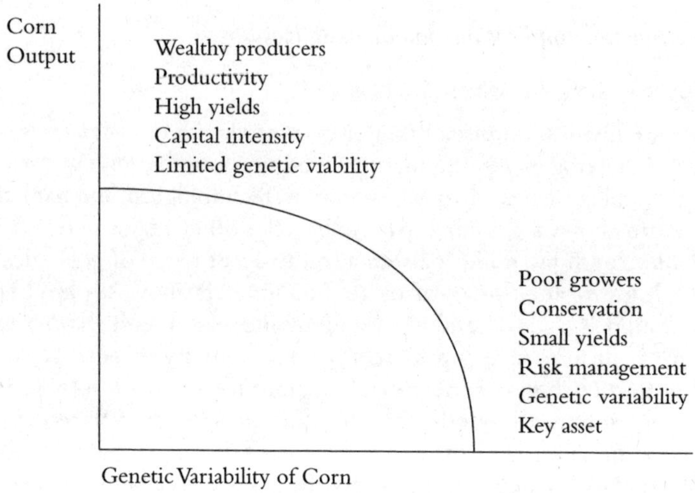

SOURCE: Adapted from Melinda Smale et al. (1999), "Farmer Management of Maize Diversity in the Central Valleys of Oaxaca, Mexico: 1998 Baseline Economic Survey," CIMMYT Working Paper 99-09 (1999). Reproduced with permission.

of rich genetic corn variability and low yields and between low variability and high yields. The case of poor corn growers who are endowed with low-quality land but rich corn variability is described by the southeast segment of the curve. The case of rich growers, with high-quality land but poor corn variability, lies in the northwest portion of the curve. The curve itself does not imply the existence of a functional relationship, but it does show the wide differences existing between these two classes of producers.

In the rationale of NAFTA's corn regime, these poor producers appeared to be noncompetitive because their yields are very low, especially if compared with yields in the U.S. Corn Belt. In addition, subsidies are required to keep these producers operating, so a significant fiscal cost, with its repercussions on the overall fiscal deficit, had also to be taken into account. Thus, these poor producers were considered to be redundant, and market forces, through trade liberalization, had to operate a reallocation of resources. This line of reasoning is inaccurate. The correct assessment of these producers' competitiveness must take into consideration their ability to provide the environmental service involved in the conservation and development of these genetic resources.

Evaluating and comparing international efficiency and competitiveness levels are complex tasks. In the case of corn growers, such a comparison cannot be limited to yield levels. This is a purely physical parameter that is prone to manifold misinterpretations because it ignores several critical variables. For one thing, it leaves out the crucial fact that yield variations originate in different agrological and ecological conditions.[10]

Thus, a farmer growing corn in the U.S. Corn Belt may attain yields on the order of twelve or fourteen tons/hectare. But this result, which appears to compete favorably with yields of Mexican producers, which barely surpass two tons/hectare, is not conclusive. The typical farmer from Nebraska, for example, will not be able to compete with the Mexican farmer if he sows his corn seed under the same harsh conditions of abiotic and biotic stresses dominating much of Mexico's agricultural landscape. In addition, at the going international price for corn (approximately $2 per bushel), the typical U.S. grower cannot recover production costs (normally around $3). This lack of competitiveness of U.S. growers is masked by federal subsidies, which will amount to more than $180 billion over the next ten years.

There are various estimates of the amount of cultivated land dedicated to corn production planted with high-yield varieties in Mexico. A recent estimate sets it at 25 percent.[11] This low rate is due to the well-known fact that landraces perform better than hybrids under stress and in poor or shallow soils.[12] Genetic erosion caused by displacement of landraces due to the massive introduction of hybrids has not been taking place in Mexico. The resilience of local landraces even in view of official policies like the "*kilo por kilo*" program (which promoted the exchange of local landraces for improved varieties and hybrids in order to attain productivity increases) has been confirmed by other analysts.[13]

During the past eight years, corn output has remained stable at levels close to eighteen million tons, although there are signs that corn production has declined in the northwestern state of Sinaloa, the country's leading producer. The price of corn has dropped dramatically, but so have the prices of other crops. Migration has continued, but the exodus of corn growers has not yet taken place. However, poverty in rural areas remains a serious problem, and there are signs that producers are operating under extreme pressure and that their capacity to conserve and develop corn genetic resources has been seriously impaired. The trend to exit the corn-producing sector may kick in in the near future, aggravating the loss of corn genetic resources.

EFFECTS OF TRANSGENIC CORN ON MEXICAN BIODIVERSITY

Genetically modified corn, using modern biotechnologies to introduce transgenic material into the plant's genome, is a subject of great interest in the context of this study. Mexico's government has declared a moratorium on the planting of transgenic corn since 1998, but imports of genetically modified corn continue. There are three closely related questions when considering this theme. The first is related to the use of transgenic corn in Mexico's agricultural sector in response to economic pressure to use new production techniques. This pressure comes from NAFTA-related imports of corn. If growers in the commercial sector use this technology, it may result in risks to biodiversity in corn production.[14] The second question concerns imports of transgenic corn from the United States. Beyond the debate concerning impacts to human health, imports of transgenic corn can pose risks for local landraces and their wild relatives, as well as for the integrity of the stock in germ plasm banks if sown by growers in Mexico. The third question concerns the risks that sowing of transgenic corn may pose for biodiversity in Mexico's ecosystems.

Effect of Transgenic Corn on Biodiversity of Corn Production

What will be the rate of adoption of transgenic corn by Mexican growers if the use of genetically modified corn is deregulated? The diffusion process of any given technological innovation is a function of the rate of imitation, and this depends on profitability, competition patterns, the structure of the branch or sector, and the expansion or contraction rate of the sector's output. Profitability is closely dependent on the appropriateness of the technology to local conditions. Transgenic corn would be no exception to this well-known rule: its diffusion rate in Mexico's agriculture will depend on its degree of appropriateness to local conditions.[15] Typically, the producers more apt to introduce this technology are not users of traditional varieties, so the adoption of transgenic corn will not threaten to initiate a process of genetic erosion by displacement of the older varieties. But another aspect of the diffusion of this technology that must be taken into account is related to the dispersal of transgenic material through cross pollination with other maize varieties and maize's wild relatives. I return to this point below.

In order to analyze how well suited transgenic corn is to Mexican conditions, we need to know more about its potential benefits to growers. The assessment of the risks and potential benefits arising from the presence of transgenic corn in Mexico's rural landscape involves examining whether the technology of transgenic corn is appropriate for Mexico. But the diffusion of this technical innovation depends on its adaptability to Mexico's agrological ecosystems and, more specifically, to the different varieties of biotic and abiotic stress that mark Mexico's countryside.

So far, transgenic corn has not been designed for use in the agro-ecosystems that prevail in Mexico. Transgenic corn comes basically in two varieties: so-called Bt corn and herbicide-resistant corn. The first incorporates the gene of the *Bacillus thuringiensis* and was specifically designed for a pest that is frequent in temperate regions, the European corn borer (*Ostrinia nubilalis*), an insect from the genus lepidoptera, which abounds in the U.S. Corn Belt. But the most important insect pests affecting Mexico's corn growers are the larvae of two insects: the southwestern corn borer (*Diatraea grandiosella*), known in Mexico as *gusano cogollero*, and the fall armyworm (*Spodoptera frugiperda*), both from the genus coleoptera. These two pests are normally attacked by direct spraying of pesticides by crews walking through the cornfields, because the larvae of these insects are well lodged inside the plant's stalk or penetrate deep inside the whorl. Application of pesticides requires precise targeting, and this can only be attained by spraying with crews of workers walking through the rows in the planted fields. This method maximizes the effects of the sprayed chemicals but poses a serious problem of direct exposure to acutely toxic pesticides. The introduction of corn varieties effectively reducing the need for these pesticides would have significant positive human health effects.

Before 1998, Mexico's government authorized experimental testing for Bt corn in order to test for the expression of the Bt gene. These tests were carried out under strict conditions of isolation, and the complete maturity of the plants was interrupted so there was no pollination. However, during the tests it was found that the *Diatraea* pests, which are predominant in Mexico, showed resistance to the Bt gene.[16] Although it is possible that these pests may be affected by other Bt proteins, this research is still to be carried out.

It has been stated by some analysts that Bt corn may reduce the risk of aflatoxins in corn. However, the vectors of the fungi that bring about the presence of these toxins are from the order coleoptera and not lepidoptera. This means that Bt corn is not an effective response to these insects, and therefore the fungi associated with aflatoxins will not be affected by Bt corn.

Altieri reports that

> recent experimental trials have shown that genetically engineered seeds do not increase the yield of crops. A recent study by the USDA Economic Research Service shows that in 1998 yields were not significantly different in engineered versus nonengineered crops in 12 of 18 crop/region combinations. In the six crop/region combinations where Bt crops or herbicide-resistant crops fared better, they exhibited increased yields between 5–30%. Glyphosphate tolerant cotton showed no significant yield increase in either region where it was surveyed. This was confirmed in another study examining more than 8,000 field trials, where it was found that Roundup Ready soybean seeds produced fewer bushels of soybeans than similar conventionally bred varieties.[17]

These results remove a critical incentive to adoption of this innovation.

If transgenic corn, such as Bt corn or herbicide-resistant corn, is not an appropriate technology given Mexico's conditions, then the diffusion of this technology will not threaten local landraces. Genetic erosion through the displacement of local landraces by transgenic corn will probably not happen if the transgenic material is limited to Bt and herbicide resistance.

On the other hand, there are many other transgenes in the pipeline of agro-biotechnology firms and their laboratories.[18] Whether these transgenes are better suited for conditions in Mexico remains to be seen. Obviously, more research is required to determine this and to assess risks for local corn landraces and biodiversity in general.

Imports of Transgenic Corn from the United States

The second question concerning transgenic corn is related to the composition of total corn imports under NAFTA's regime and the final destiny of imported transgenic corn. Mexico's corn imports from the United States probably contain significant amounts of transgenic corn. It is impossible to quantify in precise terms the amount of transgenic corn that has been imported. The amount of transgenic corn produced in the United States probably surpasses 30 percent of total output, but this does not mean that transgenic corn imported into Mexico from the United States is 30 percent of total imports. It could be more or less. Taking into account the fact that European countries have imposed prohibitions and various restrictions on imports of transgenic corn, it is not altogether unreasonable to suppose that the proportion of transgenic corn in Mexican imports is probably more than 30 percent. If this is so, then Mexico may have imported more than two million tons of transgenic corn in 2001.

Imported corn from the United States is basically destined for direct and indirect human consumption, not for seed. However, nothing will prevent growers who buy these seeds in local or regional markets from using them as seed stock if the need arises. Because transgenic corn will be mixed with nontransgenic corn, it is reasonable to expect that some of the transgenic corn will find its way into Mexican cornfields. If this happens, transgenic corn and local landraces will interact, and a two-way gene flow will be established. This will also happen with corn's wild relatives, teosinte and *Tripsacum*.

In 2001, two independent studies confirmed the presence of transgenic material in local landraces in Oaxaca and Puebla. A study by Quist and Chapela reports the presence of introgressed transgenic DNA constructs in native maize landraces grown in the southern state of Oaxaca.[19] The research sampled whole cobs of native landraces from four fields in two locations in the Sierra de Juárez, north of the city of Oaxaca, during October and November of 2000. The fields are more than twenty kilometers away from the main highway that connects Oaxaca city with Tuxtepec in the state of Veracruz. An additional grain sample was obtained from the local stores of the federal agency Diconsa, which distributes subsidized food in poor localities throughout the country. Negative controls were cob samples from the Cuzco Valley in Peru and a twenty-seed sample from a historical collection in the same region dating from 1971. The positive controls were provided by samples of Yieldgard *Bacillus thuringiensis* (Bt1) maize and the Roundup-Ready (RR1) maize, both from the Monsanto Corporation.

The study relied on a polymerase chain reaction approach and tested for a common element present in transgenic constructs currently on the market: the 35S promoter (p-35S) from the cauliflower mosaic virus, which has a widespread use in synthetic vectors used to incorporate transgenic DNA in the process of genetic modification of plants. The p-35S is not known to exist naturally in the genome of maize. The Quist and Chapela study was able to obtain positive polymerase chain reaction amplification for the p-35S in five of the seven Mexican samples that were tested. In addition, four local landrace samples showed weak but positive polymerase chain reaction amplification. The sample from the Diconsa stores yielded very strong amplification comparable in intensity to transgenic-positive Bt1 and RR1 controls.

Because the sequences adjacent to the p-35S element were diverse, the analysis suggests that the promoter was inserted into the local landrace genome at multiple loci. The diversity of transgenic DNA constructs present in local landrace samples is an indicator of multiple introgression events that may have been mediated by pollination. Some of these events were associated with introgressed DNA that had retained its integrity as an unaltered unit. However, in other events the transgenic DNA construct seemed to have been reassorted and introduced into different genomic settings, possibly during the recombination or transformation process.

Quist and Chapela summarize some of their conclusions. First, there is a high level of gene flow from maize that has been genetically modified through the incorporation of transgenic material to populations of local landraces. This conclusion coincides with other analyses.[20]

Second, the study's discovery of high rates of transgene insertion into a diversity of genomic contexts indicates that introgression events are relatively common and that the transgenic constructs are probably maintained in the population from one generation to another. If this hypothesis is corroborated, transgenic material will be present in the DNA of local landraces even if farmers do not seek to use transgenic corn.[21] The central conclusion here is that once transgenic corn is deregulated, its genetic contents will be incorporated in the genetic pool of Mexican maize germ plasm.

Third, because the samples used in the study originated in remote areas, the authors conclude it is reasonable to expect that more accessible regions will be exposed to higher rates of introgression. In Oaxaca, 1997 and 1998 were not very good years for corn production. Normally, if a single producer suffers from crop failure, the producer can go to his or her neighbors and borrow or buy the required seed stock for the next year's harvest. But if drought or frost affects all producers alike, then the only source of seed will be producers in other localities or a Diconsa store. For many poor growers, going to Diconsa stores may have been the only way to replenish their original seed stock. This pattern could be repeated in any region where a crop failure event takes place and a Diconsa store happens to operate. Thus, local landraces can be exposed to high rates of introgression in accessible or faraway regions alike.

As the Quist and Chapela results were subjected to peer review, two federal agencies, the National Institute of Ecology (INE) and the National Commission of Biodiversity (CONABIO), commissioned their own studies on transgenic corn in Mexican fields. Although the complete studies have not been published, we know through official press releases that the research confirms the presence of transgenic material in the DNA of local landraces in localities of the states of Oaxaca and Puebla. The fields studied in localities in Oaxaca were near the area examined by Quist and Chapela, and in those samples the new study confirmed the relatively low abundance of transgenic DNA in these areas.

A preliminary report was made available in March 2002. The research was initiated collecting cob samples in twenty localities in Oaxaca and two in Puebla and a sample of corn seeds in the Diconsa store in the town of Ixtlán de Juárez in Oaxaca. Grains were then randomly selected and sent to the Institute of Ecology (of the National Autonomous University [UNAM]) and to the Center for Research and Advanced Studies. The seeds were planted, and DNA was obtained for processing through polymerase chain reaction techniques. A total of 800 seeds were examined to search for the 35S promoter, the *nos* terminator segment, as well as the ribosomal agent 16S used to evaluate the quality of the analysis.[22]

No evidence of transgenic sequences was found in seven of the twenty-two localities included in the study. All of these seven localities are in the Sierra de Juárez in Oaxaca, not far from the area studied by Quist and Chapela. But in eleven localities (in the valley of Tehuacán, Puebla, and in the Sierra de Juárez, Oaxaca), between 3 and 13 percent of seeds revealed transgenic sequences. In the sample taken from the Diconsa store in Ixtlán, 37 percent of the seeds that were planted showed positive results for 35S. Finally, in four localities in Oaxaca higher frequencies (20–60 percent) of transgenic introgression were found.

According to this preliminary report, the research confirms the results of the study carried out by Quist and Chapela. These results suggest that contamination with transgenic material is not an isolated problem confined to the Sierra de Juárez but could be generalized to other regions in Mexico. It is important to note that the studies carried out so far focused on the 35S promoter and the *nos* terminator of the transgenic sequences. Therefore, these studies have not been able to identify the actual transgenes whose presence is indicated by the promoters and terminators. It is not yet possible to identify the exact functions (Bt toxins or herbicide resistance) of these transgenes. The study conducted by the Institute of Ecology aims to clarify this crucial point.

The preliminary data generated by the Institute of Ecology's study suggests a low frequency of contaminated seeds but, on the other hand, a vast geographic extension. Thus, although the presence of transgenic constructs was detected in many separate fields, in the majority of these fields the frequency of contaminated plants did not dominate the traditional varieties. Even with these frequencies of transgene introgression, the study appears to confirm that these events are relatively common and that the transgenic constructs are probably maintained in the population from one generation to another.[23]

The official position of the Mexican government concerning these important findings is expressed through the Intersecretarial Commission on Biodiversity and Genetically Modified Organisms (CIBIOGEM), which has stated that although there have been no studies proving that organisms genetically modified through modern biotechnology harm human health, it will not liberate transgenic corn seed because of uncertainty regarding the environmental risks that may be involved. The moratorium that has existed since 1998 on planting transgenic corn does not affect scientific research. However, out of 115 projects on genetically modified organisms that had been submitted to CIBIOGEM for approval by April 2000, only two had been approved. There are currently 40,000 hectares of commercial transgenic cotton planted in northern Mexico and 100 hectares of experimental soy. But the CIBIOGEM has also announced that the studies required to liberate transgenic corn could take between four and six years, and during this period it plans to work with congressional authorities to develop a regulatory framework for the application of biotechnology. CIBIOGEM also plans to undertake studies focusing on specific genes, crop characteristics, regions, and ecosystems in order to enable it to assess risks that could be involved from commercial release of transgenic crops. CIBIOGEM officials have announced that one important risk that will be evaluated concerns the generation of disease-resistant organisms.

The International Center for the Improvement of Maize and Wheat (CIMMYT) issued an official statement that the results of the Quist and Chapela study are extremely important due to the fact that Mexico is the center of origin of corn. The CIMMYT also considers it necessary to evaluate the repercussions of this finding on biodiversity, on the ecology in general, and even in the socioeconomic context.[24]

The Risks Transgenic Corn May Pose for Biodiversity in Mexico's Ecosystems

Concerning the long-term environmental effects of the presence of transgenes in local maize as a result of genetic flow, one of the first elements that must be considered is that the level of ignorance is rather important. The studies that are currently being carried out by INE and the National Institute of Forestry, Agriculture, and Livestock Research (INIFAP) are designed precisely to start bridging the gap in basic knowledge concerning the magnitude of the problem we are encountering.

The key question in this regard has been aptly put by Antonio Serratos, an INIFAP biologist, in the following terms: what is the evolutionary pattern of a transgene in a living community in an ecosystem?[25] Unfortunately, the state of the art of scientific information is still too weak to provide a definitive answer.

Transgenic corn may present yet other risks for Mexican landraces and for their wild relatives, the teosintes. These wild relatives are believed to have been the origin of corn. In fact, maize may have evolved rapidly from teosinte in a process involving just a few genes.[26] The individual teosinte seed is enclosed in a hard-shelled fruit case, and it is dispersed naturally when the fruit case is separated from the main body of the plant. The capacity of this nondomesticated plant to self-sow is one of the most important differences between teosinte and maize.

Today there is a collection at INIFAP's gene bank in Chapingo of 144 individual teosinte accessions, representing populations from approximately 110 sites in different regions of Mexico.[27] Teosintes are important repositories of genetic resources, and their value for future improvements of corn varieties cannot be underestimated. In certain cases, corn producers tolerate the presence of teosinte in their cornfields because it contributes to improved maize performance. In other cases, teosinte is used as green forage to feed cattle. Some farmers state that in three or four years teosintes can deliver new maize that has a better response than hybrids or even their traditional varieties. In other cases, however, teosintes are perceived as weeds by growers. These two views sometimes coexist in communities that are close to each other. For example, near the Sierra de Manantlán Biosphere Reserve, growers find that teosintes have both positive and deleterious effects.[28]

Teosinte is a highly variable wild plant with both annual and perennial varieties. Naturally occurring populations of teosinte populations are present in the western slope of Mexico and Central America in a dry, subtropical zone ranging from 500 to 1,800 meters above sea level (masl) and in Mexico's Central Plateau between 1,650 to 2,000 masl. There are other populations in the Valley of Mexico, Puebla, and the Valley of Toluca, which are considered to be anomalous.[29] Teosinte's growing season begins with the summer rains and runs from June to October, but by September the plants reach the midflowering stages, paralleling that of the local maize landraces.

Teosinte and corn can produce fertile hybrids, and both plants continuously exchange genetic material in many regions of Mexico and Guatemala. In many cases, the habitats of teosinte are located in proximity to or within good agricultural land. It is clear that when transgenic corn is planted, as it has been, pollen containing transgenic material will move into the germ plasm of the local teosinte populations.

The risks for teosinte populations are identified in the pioneering work of Rissler and Mellon.[30] Transgenic corn may enhance the resistance of certain teosinte subpopulations, for example, if Bt transgenes are introgressed into these plants, making them more resistant to pests. This would give one teosinte subpopulation a decided advantage, which could lead to the extinction of other subpopulations, thus reducing the diversity of teosinte varieties.

The threat of extinction of teosinte subpopulations is difficult to assess. In a 1993 publication, Hernández Xolocotzi stated that teosinte populations have been negatively affected over the past five hundred years by the arrival of cattle and the introduction of mechanical tillage systems.[31] These two events destroy spontaneously generated plants and make their recovery very difficult.

Wilkes proposes the use of the criteria established by the Species Survival Commission of the International Union for the Conservation of Nature.[32] Use of these criteria reveals that there are clear signs that certain varieties of teosinte are endangered. One example is a population in southern Guatemala that cannot be expected to persist for long without the assistance of in situ protection mechanisms. Most of the other populations of teosinte are considered to be vulnerable, meaning that their rate of declining populations is such that if nothing is done they will become endangered. Populations thought to be rare (for example, in Nobogame, Durango, and Oaxaca) are currently under no immediate threat and are more or less stable but are scarce enough that they could be eliminated easily. There are several indeterminate populations that have been significantly depleted over the past decades but appear to persist. They could be threatened by changes in land-use patterns, especially if urban growth continues in and around eastern Mexico City. Finally, there are other stable populations, mainly in the Balsas River basin in the state of Guerrero, in Michoacán, and in the state of Jalisco (Ameca). Based on observations over the last twelve years, Sánchez González and Ruíz Corral conclude that all teosinte populations in Mexico are threatened except for those in the Balsas Basin.[33] The risks posed by the presence of transgenic material are significant, and an adequate policy response is required.

In June 2002, the CEC Secretariat informed the governments of Canada, Mexico, and the United States that it intends to prepare a special Article 13 report upon the potential effects of transgenic corn on traditional varieties of maize in Mexico. The CEC now recognizes that this issue is a source of public concern and has decided to identify the precise scope of the threat to the environment. It is important that as the CEC proceeds with this study, it does not relegate the other central issues to the back burner. Even if the diffusion of transgenic constructs into Mexican corn germ plasm can be stopped, the risk of a massive loss of genetic erosion will persist as long as the economic and social pressures on corn growers continue to increase. From this viewpoint, the CEC's study is a race against time.

Conclusion: Some Policy Issues

The most important environmental impact of trade liberalization in corn identified so far relates to the possible loss of corn genetic variability. If a negative impact is to be avoided, the welfare of corn producers who rely most on this genetic variability has to be improved. One immediate step in this direction is that the original NAFTA tariff rate quota system for corn needs to be implemented if the undesirable environmental effects on corn genetic variability are to be avoided. But in addition, there is a clear need to recuperate the levels of investment in infrastructure, research and development, and technical assistance that were programmed at the time of the NAFTA negotiations. The concept of infrastructure needs to be extended in order to include not only dams, drainage canals, and soil-management structures (terracing and use of vegetative technologies) but also social welfare constructions (sewage and municipal piping, clinics, schools, and housing). This is important in order to improve living conditions in the very short term. In addition, temporary employment programs should also contemplate maintenance operations on existing infrastructure that have a short-term impact on productivity. A combination of credit, crop insurance for poor producers, and technical assistance should also be used to improve investment conditions and increase yields.

An important alternative that requires deeper analysis is to use the price mechanism to enhance the welfare of these poor producers. Avoiding price distortions should be a critical guideline here, but attaining fairness is of paramount importance if environmental objectives are to be reached. One possibility is to design a mechanism through which the poorest producers, who must rely on corn genetic variability, could sell a predetermined amount of their crops at prices higher than those prevailing in their local or regional markets. In the case of subsistence farmers who need to replenish their stock at various intervals, purchases could be carried out at lower-than-market prices. Subsistence producers would be able to sell part of their stock up to a limit to be determined by identifying the average output of a class of subsistence producers in a given region. Or it could be determined through a system of certification through appropriate authorities or new institutions.

To summarize, an array of policy instruments are needed to prevent the continued deterioration of production conditions of poor corn growers. The fact that aggregate output has remained rather stable during the past six years should not be interpreted as revealing that these growers are enjoying adequate welfare levels. On the contrary, poverty continues to be pervasive among the weaker corn producers, and lack of adequate government support is aggravating their plight. Trade liberalization has had unfavorable implications for their livelihood in terms of income and wealth effects. Already their capacity to continue working as curators of corn genetic resources has been seriously impaired. If these trends are not reversed, the probability of losing corn genetic resources will increase over time.

Notes

This chapter is based on a May 2002 paper prepared for the Commission for Environmental Cooperation (CEC). It and other CEC documents are available at *http://www.cec.org*. The chapter is included here with the permission of the Commission. The author wishes to thank Frank Ackerman for comments on an earlier draft. The help of Israel Macías, who assisted in processing data, is gratefully acknowledged. All errors are, of course, the sole responsibility of the author.

1. Its extraordinary geographical and physical diversity explains why Mexico is the fourteenth-largest country in the world in terms of total surface but ranks third in biological diversity. See R. A. Mittermeier, "Primate Diversity and the Tropical Forest: Case Studies from Brazil and Madagascar and the Importance of Megadiversity Countries," in *Biodiversity* (Edward Wilson ed., 1988). Because of its topography and climate regions, which include a Nearctic realm in the north and a Neotropical realm in the south, Mexico hosts a wide variety of species in both flora and fauna. Jerzy Rzedowski, "Diversity and Origins of the Phanerogamic Flora of Mexico," in T. P. Ramamoorthy, Robert Bye, Antonio Lot, and John Fa, eds., *Biological Diversity of Mexico: Origins and Distribution* 129–44 (1993). Thus, with only 1.4 percent of the world's surface, Mexico is host to almost 12 percent of the total number of known species. Victor Manuel Toledo and María de Jesús Ordóñez, "The Biodiversity Scenario of Mexico: A Review of Terrestrial Habitats," in Ramamoorthy et al., supra, 757–77. Together with China and India, Mexico is a country where megadiversity coexists with a center of agricultural origin within the gene belt, the band that circles the world within the Tropics of Cancer and Capricorn. Ramamoorthy et al., supra.

2. Santiago Levy and Sweden van Wijnbergen, "Transition Problems in Economic Reform: Agriculture in the North American Free Trade Agreement," 85 *American Economic Review* 738 (1995).

3. Alejandro Nadal, *The Environmental and Social Impacts of Economic Liberalization on Corn Production in Mexico* (2000) (study commissioned by Oxfam and World Wildlife Fund International); Alejandro Nadal, *Maize in Mexico: Some Environmental Implications for the North American Free Trade Agreement (NAFTA)* (1999) (prepared for the CEC "NAFTA Effects" program).

4. The first study of corn in NAFTA commissioned by the CEC (and published in 1999) was used to prepare *Assessing Environmental Effects of the North American Free Trade Agreement (NAFTA): An Analytic Framework (Phase II) and Issue Studies*. See ch. 6, supra. Unfortunately, the need to fully integrate macroeconomic policies into the evaluation of the environmental impact of trade liberalization was not adequately recognized in the final version of the *Analytic Framework*.

5. The May 2002 paper on which this chapter is based also provides an overview of recent economic trends for Mexico's agricultural sector, more analysis of the implementation of NAFTA's corn regime, description of trends in the Mexican corn sector, and an examination of poverty and social marginalization in Mexico's rural sector.

6. NAFTA Annex 302.2 in Schedule for Mexico, tariff item 1005.90.99.

7. Nadal, *Environmental and Social Impacts*, supra; Nadal, *Maize in Mexico*, supra.

8. A landrace is a locally adapted strain of a species that has been bred through traditional methods.

9. Nadal, *Environmental and Social Impacts*, supra; Nadal, *Maize in Mexico*, supra.

10. It also ignores the role of subsidies and other economic considerations, such as the availability of credits and insurance against crop failure. Some of these elements may be considered as part of an economic system against which local producers must compete in international trade, but others, like direct and indirect subsidies, cannot be factored into the comparison in this manner. This is why the international trade system incorporates control mechanisms and legal instruments to rid the playing field of these unfair elements.

11. Antonio Serratos-Hernández, Islas Gutiérrez, Fabian Berthaud, and Julien Berthaud, "Maize Production, Landrace of Maize and Teosinte Distribution in Mexico: Elements for Gene Flow Scenarios and Risk Assessment of Transgenic Maize Release," mimeograph (2001). This estimate is consistent with other assessments considered in Nadal, *Environmental and Social Impacts*, supra, and with the data from the 1991 Agricultural Census.

12. See Nadal, *Environmental and Social Impacts*, supra, and references therein.

13. Jim MacMillan and P. Aquino, "Impacts on the Mexican Hybrid Maize Seed Industry: Progress Report" (1996); Ortega Paczka, personal communication with author (1997). This viewpoint is further confirmed by the description of maize landraces in Mexico presented in Serratos-Hernández et al., supra. Summarizing, these analysts report on landraces that were described and collected since the 1940s and conclude that in most of Mexico's macroregions there exist, in varying degrees of mixture, the landraces of maize described in the classic Wellhausen et al. study of 1952 and summarized in the database of LAMP (Latin American Maize Program of the CIMMYT). This stock of germ plasm, which so far has been conserved and developed in situ by Mexico's producers, will exchange genetic information with transgenic maize should this technology be deregulated and used in Mexico.

14. Risks to human health must also be evaluated. I shall return to this point in my future research.

15. Profitability will also depend on the relation between Mexican cost structures, as well as existing subsidies, and the usual comparison with final market prices.

16. Antonio Serratos, personal communication with author (May 2002).

17. Miguel Altieri, "The Environmental Risks of Transgenic Crops: An Agroecological Assessment," in *Proceedings of an Associated Event of the 5th Annual World Bank Conference on Environmentally and Socially Sustainable Development* (Ismail Serageldin and J. Martin Brown eds., 1998).

18. *Gene Flow among Maize Landraces, Improved Maize Varieties, and Teosinte: Implications for Transgenic Maize* (proceedings of a forum held at the CIMMYT, Mexico, 1995) (J. Antonio Serratos, Martha C. Wilcox, and Fernando Castillo eds., 1995). These include aluminum tolerance, apomixis, vaccines, degradable plastic products, quality protein genes, and mutator regulating elements from various landraces (for example, Zapalote Chico).

19. David Quist and Ignacio H. Chapela, "Transgenic DNA Introgressed into Traditional Maize Landraces in Oaxaca, Mexico," 414 *Nature* 541–43 (2001).

20. Serratos-Hernández et al., supra.

21. This is consistent with the results of a simple model of diffusion using a typical logistic function in Serratos-Hernández et al., supra, and in which the speed of diffusion (dispersal) of transgenic maize once it is deregulated depends on the size of the area planted to corn and the number of transgenics planted in that area.

22. The 35S promoter is derived from the cauliflower mosaic virus and is commonly used as an indicator of the genetic expression of transgenes introduced into maize. The *nos* segment is derived from the nopaline synthase of *Agrobacterium tumefaciens* commonly used as an eucaryotic terminator for the RNA transcription. The Quist and Chapela study tested for the synthetic vector 35S promoter due to its widespread use during plant transformation.

23. This also corroborates the results in Serratos-Hernández et al., supra.

24. The CIMMYT has been working with growers in Oaxaca for a long time and has been concerned with the necessity to conserve their corn's genetic diversity and increase their productivity. It has also analyzed the flow of genetic material between individual farmers and communities, as well as the impact of these flows on corn genetic variability and its wild relatives, teosintes and *Tripsacum*. In addition, the CIMMYT has carried out its own experiments with transgenic corn, in full compliance with norms and official protocols on biosafety in Mexico. Its last trial with transgenic corn sown in an open field, which ended in September 1999, involved planting transgenic corn in its experimental field in Tlaltizapán, in the state of Morelos, under the supervision of Mexican officials. Today, the CIMMYT continues to carry out research on transgenic plants within the confines of its biotechnology laboratories and greenhouses.

25. Antonio Serratos, personal communication with author (Jan. 8, 2002).

26. Elizabeth Culotta, "How Many Genes Had to Change to Produce Corn?" 252 *Science* 1792–93 (1991).

27. José de Jesús Sánchez González and José Ariel Ruíz Corral, "Teosinte Distribution in Mexico," in Serratos, Wilcox, and Castillo, supra.

28. One example of beneficial effects from teosinte presence in cultivated fields arises from the hard enamel cover of *Zea diploperennis* kernels. This is why many growers like to have this wild relative of corn in their fields. Open pollination and two-way genetic flow allow for the incorporation of some traits from teosinte into maize, making it more resistant to insects that are postharvest pests and bore tunnels into the individual kernels. Ezequiel Ezcurra, personal communication with author (1998).

29. Garrison Wilkes, "Teosinte in Mexico: Personal Retrospective and Assessment," in Serratos, Wilcox, and Castillo, supra.

30. Jane Rissler and Margaret Mellon, *The Ecological Risks of Engineered Crops* (1996).

31. Quoted in Sánchez González and Ruíz Corral, supra.

32. Wilkes, supra.

33. Sánchez González and Ruíz Corral, supra.

SANFORD E. GAINES **10**

Protecting Investors, Protecting the Environment

The Unexpected Story of NAFTA Chapter 11

THE INVESTMENT PROVISIONS of the North American Free Trade Agreement (NAFTA), Chapter 11 of the Agreement, have implications for environmental protection measures that most advocates and commentators overlooked during the NAFTA debates of the early 1990s. As an international agreement on the treatment of foreign investors, Chapter 11 represents the mutual consent of governments to put limits on their freedom to determine domestic policies affecting economic behavior in order to facilitate cross-border investments. Environmental rules commonly affect economic activities, so domestic environmental decisions are bound to intersect on occasion with NAFTA's protections for foreign investors. In particular, the Chapter 11 language on compensation for expropriation evokes U.S. jurisprudence on regulatory "takings" and thus opens the door to claims for compensation by foreign investors that local environmental decisions have effectively expropriated their investment. This possible avenue of challenge to local environmental regulation largely escaped the attention of environmental organizations at the time of NAFTA negotiation and approval; nor did environmentalists identify the risk in offering foreign investors the opportunity to have their claims arbitrated by independent tribunals.[1]

As it has turned out, about a third of the North American investor claims for compensation filed under Chapter 11 through mid 2002 have involved environmental activities or environmental protection measures.[2] Three such claims to date have resulted in awards or settlements in favor of the investor. Even though two other claims have been turned aside, environmental organizations, some government officials, and prominent journalists have raised the alarm that Chapter 11 is unduly inhibiting governments from taking steps to protect the environment.[3] Leaving aside clearly hyperbolic reactions

("What we can envision here is a wholesale overturning of the regulatory state, which took 100 years to build.")[4] even temperate environmental voices have construed the Chapter 11 awards as insidious threats to domestic environmental regulations.[5]

The current popular reaction against Chapter 11 stems in part from misunderstandings about its provisions and their place in international law. The first part of this chapter therefore briefly describes the core elements of Chapter 11 and their historical and international law genesis. More important, public debate about Chapter 11 is informed mostly by simplified accounts of the facts. The second part of this chapter gives more detailed accounts of the major cases, which show that the Chapter 11 cases are volatile controversies over competition between foreign and domestic firms, conflicts between federal and subfederal officials, and exercises of regulatory power that, even if taken at face value, were disputable in terms of domestic environmental law and largely devoid of public input.

Nevertheless, the cases raise significant questions about the substantive and procedural relationship between Chapter 11's protection of investors and the broader patterns of environmental cooperation provided by the North American Agreement on Environmental Cooperation (NAAEC) and the Commission for Environmental Cooperation (CEC). Can the CEC play a role in helping the governments and peoples of North America reconcile investment protection with environmental protection? The third part of the chapter will try to answer that question and consider the broader implications of Chapter 11 in terms of North American environmental policy. The chapter concludes with a look to the future of Chapter 11 and its lessons for other trade and investment agreements.

Overview of NAFTA Chapter 11

PURPOSE

A misapprehension persists that NAFTA Chapter 11 was an innovation in trade and economic policy. In fact, "what was produced in Chapter 11 . . . was actually nothing terribly novel. . . . [T]here was an enormous volume of precedent."[6] It builds directly on the Canada-U.S. Free Trade Agreement of 1989 and the bilateral investment treaties (BITs) with developing countries negotiated by the United States, Canada, and many European countries during the 1980s.[7] The BITs encourage foreign direct investment by giving foreign investors rights against discriminatory treatment and uncompensated expropriations of their investments and offering them legal recourse against illegal host government actions under international law norms concerning government treatment of aliens through channels other than host country courts.

The promotion of cross-border investments was an "essential element" for the United States, Canada, and Mexico in negotiating NAFTA.[8] Mexico understood that it could attract significant new investment to promote economic development only if it guaranteed transparent legal rules and fair treatment for foreign investors so as to overcome its historical legacy of expropriation (most memorably, the 1938 expropriation of foreign oil companies) and doubts about the integrity of its domestic judicial processes.[9] Domestically, Mexico adopted a new foreign investment act in 1993 that expressed a "clear policy to promote, not regulate, foreign investment."[10] NAFTA Chapter 11 confirmed that new spirit of liberalization and made it into an international commitment, marking "a major departure from Mexico's previous position on foreign investment and international economic relations."[11]

Canada had dual objectives. Like Mexico, it wished to become an attractive destination for foreign investment as part of its economic development policies. At the same time, Canada also wanted to promote direct investment abroad by Canadian companies as "part of its strategic effort to increase market share and stay competitive in foreign markets."[12]

The United States had goals complementary to both Canada and Mexico. Already having a liberal regime for accepting incoming foreign direct investment, it wanted NAFTA to assure that the investments of Americans in Mexico and Canada would be protected from expropriation or unfair treatment.

SUBSTANTIVE PROVISIONS

Chapter 11 has a broad, but not unlimited, scope. It applies to any government "measures" (understood in trade law to include procedures and practices) relating to "investors" or "investments" from another NAFTA country (which are broadly defined in Article 1139 to encompass enterprises, equity or debt securities in enterprises, loans, rights to a share of profits, real estate and tangible and intangible property, and contractual or other interests associated with capital commitments).[13] In an important ruling, the arbitral tribunal in *Methanex v. United States* interpreted the "relating to" link between "measures" and "investors/investments" to mean that the measure in question must have a "legally significant connection" to the foreign investor or investment.[14]

For the measures to which it applies, Chapter 11 imposes three fundamental disciplines on government action, disciplines that are routine elements of international law. First, NAFTA Articles 1102 and 1103 enunciate familiar nondiscrimination obligations: government measures should not discriminate between domestic and foreign investors, and they should not discriminate between foreign investors from different countries. Second, Article 1105 assures a "minimum standard" of "fair and equitable" treatment for foreign investors. Third, Article 1110 sets forth a rule against uncompensated expropriation. Expropriation itself is not forbidden by NAFTA or by any rule of international law.[15] What Article 1110 disallows is expropriation or any "measure tantamount to nationalization or expropriation" *unless* it is "(a) for a public purpose; (b) on a non-discriminatory basis; (c) in accordance with due process of law and Article 1105(1); and (d) on payment of compensation in accordance with paragraphs 2 through 6." All four conditions must be satisfied; that is, even a measure for a public purpose applied with due process of law and without discrimination gives rise to a claim for compensation if it results in expropriation.

The key interpretive question about Article 1110(1) is the meaning of "expropriation" and the phrase "measure tantamount to . . . expropriation." Four points are reasonably clear, though they only reframe the interpretive challenge. First, NAFTA Article 1110 restates a prevalent international law norm. Second, an important influence on the international law of "indirect" expropriation (analogous to the NAFTA phrase "tantamount to expropriation") is the American jurisprudence on regulatory "takings" under the Fifth and Fourteenth Amendments to the U.S. Constitution.[16] Third, under both international law and U.S. constitutional law, regulatory exercises of the "police power" of the government are in principle excluded from the notion of "expropriation," leading to the further question of what "police power" means and whether a particular environmental measure is an exercise of that power.[17] These last two matters are muddled at best in both U.S. and international law, meaning that any evaluation of compensation claims based on environmental regulatory "expropriations" of investments under NAFTA Chapter 11 will be fractious and legally complex.[18] The fourth point about Chapter 11 is that the international law of expropriation it invokes differs substantially from Mexican and Canadian domestic legal norms about government compensation for takings of property.[19] Thus, NAFTA Chapter 11 contradicts settled expectations in two of the three NAFTA countries and adds insult to that injury by creating a two-tiered legal system in which foreign investors in Canada or Mexico obtain international law protections greater than those available to comparable national investors under domestic law.

PROCEDURE

North American foreign investors can seek monetary compensation from a NAFTA government for violations of Chapter 11 through binding international arbitration. NAFTA's investment chapter thus brings Mexico and Canada into an investor-state arbitration system that already exists for other countries through many bilateral agreements.[20]

The investor initiates the claim by filing a statement of the claim. The challenged government responds, and the parties are encouraged first to settle the claim. If settlement is not successful, the investor then files a notice of intent to submit the claim to arbitration. An arbitral tribunal is then appointed, typically by a process in which each disputing party names one arbitrator and the two so named agree on a third person, who is the presiding arbitrator. The other NAFTA governments may, and regularly do, participate in briefings and legal argumentation on matters of interpretation of Chapter 11. The tribunal rules on all issues of procedure and jurisdiction as well as on the merits of the claim. The "awards" of the tribunal are final, except that under the three arbitral systems the disputing parties can appeal on matters of law to a national court of the site of the arbitration, as happened in the *Metalclad* case described below.

The three international systems for investor-state arbitration available under NAFTA, which were designed for commercial arbitrations where confidentiality can promote resolution of disputes, are inherently secretive in nature and thus not well suited to quasi-public disputes where a government measure is at issue.[21] Even environmental officials and trade officials in the federal governments may not learn until after the fact that an investor intends to submit a claim, thwarting any chance to invoke the trade-environment intergovernmental consultation procedures under Article 10(6) of the NAAEC.[22] Once a tribunal has been appointed, the tribunal handles the submissions of the parties confidentially, and the arguments before the tribunal take place behind closed doors.

Joan Claybrook of Public Citizen has said of these procedures, "What we're talking about here is secret government."[23] The NAFTA Free Trade Commission, made up of the three trade ministers, responded to such criticism in July 2001 with a statement expressing their authoritative policy that there is no "general duty of confidentiality" with respect to Chapter 11 filings of the governments and other parties and committing the governments to publication of all documents submitted to or issued by tribunals.[24] Nevertheless, the Commission's statement recognizes that the arbitral tribunals have control over their own procedures and must comply with the requirements of the organizations under whose auspices they operate, which leaves the door open for a tribunal to decide that the customary confidentiality of arbitral proceedings must be observed. In a recent decision, for example, one arbitral tribunal refused to allow Canada to release to the public the transcripts of oral arguments before the tribunal.[25] In the case of *Methanex v. United States*, on the other hand, nongovernmental organizations secured an interim ruling that neither Chapter 11 nor the international arbitration rules bar amicus curiae briefs, though the tribunal postponed a final decision on whether it would accept such briefs in the *Methanex* case.[26]

A more subtle concern about the closed nature of arbitration is the oblique representation of the real parties in interest. Provincial/state and local government actions have given rise to several Chapter 11 claims, but because the federal government is the defending entity, the states and localities are unable to fight their own battles. It is reasonable to worry that the federal governments may not aggressively or effectively represent regional or local interests.[27] A subfederal jurisdiction might also have interests contrary to the federal government defending a federal action. Despite these worries, the provincial or state governments have not raised public complaints about their federal representatives in the cases to date.

Environmental Issues in Chapter 11 Arbitrations

The regulations at issue in the several Chapter 11 "environmental" cases fall into three distinct environmental policy categories. All three cases resolved on the merits by arbitral tribunal awards—*Azinian v. Mexico*, *Metalclad v. Mexico*, and *S. D. Myers, Inc. v. Canada*—involve the always controversial matter of government decisions that prevented the claimant company from providing otherwise lawful waste disposal services at specific sites. Two other prominent Chapter 11 cases, one settled (*Ethyl Corp. v. Canada*) and one still pending (*Methanex v. United States*), concern the regulation of particular products (both of which happen to be gasoline additives) on claimed grounds of preventing risks to the health of the general population arising from their use. They present classic issues of how governments deploy their regulatory authority in the face of scientific uncertainty, issues that have been much mooted in domestic and international environmental regulation. A third pair of cases, not discussed here, are unresolved cases based on claims of discrimination in the economic terms or conditions of access to natural resources (water and timber) in British Columbia.

WASTE DISPOSAL SERVICES CASES

Azinian v. Mexico

Mexican municipal officials rescinded a contract with Azinian for waste collection and recycling on the grounds that he and his partners (all U.S. nationals) had misrepresented their qualifications and capabilities. Azinian sued for breach of contract in Mexican court, which found that the municipality had acted within the scope of its authority. Azinian then filed a claim under Chapter 11. In its award on the merits, the arbitral tribunal noted that it was not its role to act as a court of appeal from a domestic court. Therefore, it framed the Chapter 11 question as one of whether the local court's decision was contrary to Mexico's obligation to afford fair and equitable treatment to foreign investors. Having no evidence that the Mexican court proceedings had breached that obligation, the tribunal denied the investors' claim.[28]

Metalclad v. Mexico

Metalclad, a California-based waste disposal company, has received over $16 million in compensation from Mexico for its direct costs in constructing a federally permitted hazardous waste landfill that it was prevented from operating by subsequent site-specific decisions of state and local officials. Environmental critics of Chapter 11 see *Metalclad* as a case where a company failed to win local consent to the siting of its facility, built the facility anyway, and then claimed compensation when the local officials used their executive authority to block operation of the facility because of its threat to the local environment. The full story, though, as described in the tribunal award and the decision of a Canadian court on appeal, is more ambiguous.

Metalclad contracted for an option to buy a Mexican waste disposal company that was already operating a hazardous waste transfer facility in Guadalcazar, San Luis Potosí, at a site remote from populated areas of the municipality. A considerable amount of hazardous waste was temporarily stored on the surface at the site. After the Mexican company applied for and obtained from the federal environmental agency a permit to construct a modern hazardous waste landfill on the same site, Metalclad exercised its option and bought the Mexican company. Meanwhile, however, the governor of the state of San Luis Potosi began to oppose Metalclad. In another complication, the municipality of Guadalcazar insisted that Metalclad apply for a local construction permit but then, because of disagreements with Metalclad about cleanup of the waste already on the site, declined to act on the application.

Upon the advice of the federal environmental agency, Metalclad proceeded with facility construction without the local construction permit. When construction was complete, the federal environmental authorities audited the facility and entered into a written agreement (*convenio*) under which Metalclad was granted a five-year permit to operate the facility on the condition that it clean up the waste remaining on the site from the site's earlier use during the first three years and that it establish an environmental buffer zone around the facility. Two weeks later, the municipal council of Guadalcazar voted to deny the long-pending municipal construction permit. (The authority of the municipality to deny the permit on environmental grounds under Mexican law is disputed.)[29] Metalclad and the municipality then engaged in a round of litigation and negotiation that proved fruitless on all sides, and Metalclad filed its claim under Chapter 11. Nearly two years after the *convenio*, the governor of San Luis Potosi, as one of his final acts before leaving office, issued an ecological decree declaring a 189,000-hectare zone in Guadalcazar for the protection of certain rare cactus species. The zone completely surrounds and includes the Metalclad facility site. The Chapter 11 arbitral tribunal concluded that the surface disturbance restrictions in the decree precluded Metalclad from operating its facility. Finding that this was "tantamount to expropriation" of Metalclad's good-faith investment in its facility, the tribunal awarded compensation for the costs of construction, at the same time denying any compensation for lost profits.

The reasoning of the arbitral tribunal on certain issues of law left much to be desired, so Mexico appealed, as provided by the arbitral mechanism, to the courts in Vancouver, the official site of the arbitration.[30] A British Columbia lower court upheld most of the award because it found no fault with one of the tribunal's key conclusions—that the governor's ecological decree, which effectively denied Metalclad any use of the constructed facility, constituted an act tantamount to expropriation.[31] Mexico made the required payment to Metalclad late in 2001.

S. D. Myers, Inc. v. Canada

S. D. Myers, Inc. (SDMI) offers remediation of polychlorinated biphenyl (PCB) contamination and destruction (by incineration) of PCBs being taken out of service. Eastern Canada was an attractive market area for SDMI; many eastern Canadian utilities and manufacturers were holding PCB-contaminated wastes, and disposal by SDMI in Ohio would be less expensive for them than cross-country shipment to the sole Canadian disposal facility, Chem-Security of Swan Hills, Alberta.

At the beginning of the story, Canadian law under the bilateral agreement on hazardous wastes between the United States and Canada allowed export of PCBs from Canada to the United States, but U.S. Environmental Protection Agency (EPA) regulations pursuant to the Toxic Substances Control Act prohibited the import of PCBs into the United States.[32] In 1993, SDMI began a concerted effort to obtain the eastern Canada PCB business by incorporating a separate company, Myers Canada, and lobbying U.S. officials for a relaxation of the ban on movements of PCBs from Canada to the United States. Canadian environmental officials and the Chem-Security firm monitored these developments closely. In July 1995, before final EPA action, the Minister of Environment Canada, Sheila Copps, responded to a parliamentary question by enunciating a government position that "the handling of [Canadian] PCBs should be done in Canada by Canadians." On October 26, 1995, the EPA issued SDMI a written notice of "enforcement discretion" under which EPA would allow import of PCBs from Canada for disposal (by destruction) in the United States between November 15, 1995, and December 31, 1997. Chem-Security immediately wrote to Minister Copps urging a quick Canadian response. On November 16, 1995, just as the new EPA policy became effective, she signed an Interim

Order (later made into a permanent Order in Council of the Governor General) amending Canada's PCB Waste Export Regulations to prohibit the export of PCBs. In February 1997, a new Environment Minister rescinded the Order in Council and once again allowed PCB exports to the United States. (This window of opportunity for SDMI closed five months later when a U.S. court held EPA's import allowance to be contrary to the Toxic Substances Control Act.)[33] SDMI filed a claim under Chapter 11 for the loss to its investment during the fifteen months of the Canadian ban on PCB exports on the ground that the ban was discriminatory, favoring the Canadian investor over the like U.S. investor.

Whether Canada's export ban was bona fide environmental regulation depends on the environmental risks from the transboundary movement of PCB wastes and on Canada's environmental interest in maintaining domestic capacity for PCB incineration and disposal. These two environmental considerations are articulated in the Basel Convention on the Control of Transboundary Movements of Hazardous Wastes and Their Disposal.[34] Article 4(2)(d) commits governments to "ensure that the transboundary movement of hazardous wastes and other waste is reduced to the minimum consistent with the environmentally sound and efficient management of such wastes." Article 4(2)(b) calls on parties to "ensure the availability of adequate disposal facilities, to the extent possible, within its own boundaries."

Canada's export ban defied written advice to the minister from the senior staff of Environment Canada to the effect that an export ban was contrary to Canadian policy on the Basel Convention as expressed at various international meetings. It had been Canada's consistent view that the Basel provisions did not bar waste exports when those exports would facilitate environmentally sound management of the waste. Moreover, on an objective assessment of the relative environmental risks of shipment of PCB wastes from Quebec or Ontario to Ohio as compared to Alberta, shipment to Ohio was environmentally preferable under the proximity principle.

Viewing "the documentary record as a whole," including the minister's repeated statements that PCBs should be handled "in Canada by Canadians," the arbitral tribunal found that it "clearly indicates that the Interim Order and the Final Order were intended primarily to protect the Canadian PCB disposal industry from U.S. competition." It also concluded that "there was no legitimate environmental reason for introducing the ban." The strongest environmental policy argument for the Canadian export ban is the Basel obligation of Article 4(2)(b) to assure adequate domestic disposal capability. If Canada had allowed its eastern Canada inventory of PCB wastes to be shipped to Ohio, the Alberta-based Chem-Security might have been left with an insufficient volume of Canadian waste to justify its continued operation. On this point, the arbitral tribunal simply asserted that Canada's objective "could have been achieved by other measures." The tribunal's position is firmly rooted in the law in all jurisdictions for evaluating trade restrictions applied in the name of environmental policy. Within Canada itself as well as within the United States and the European Union, trade restrictions in pursuit of environmental goals are not allowed to pose undue (or disproportionate) burdens on the free movement of goods and services or to impose economic costs disproportionate to the environmental gain to be achieved.[35] The government's burden of justification is particularly heavy where the economic burden of its action falls on a single firm. The scrutiny is heightened further when that single firm happens to be foreign.

REGULATION OF PRODUCTS ON GROUNDS OF PUBLIC HEALTH

Ethyl Corp. v. Canada

The *Ethyl* case, the first to result in payment of compensation (Canada settled the case), has a particularly complex background.[36] Ethyl Corporation, a U.S. company, manufactures the manganese-based gasoline additive methylcyclopentadienyl manganese tricarbonyl (MMT), an octane booster that enhances fuel efficiency. Throughout the story, Ethyl was the sole supplier of MMT to the Canadian market. There were two potential problems with MMT. First, scientists had expressed concern about health effects from inhalation of manganese; however, a number of health effects studies in both Canada and the United States did not substantiate these concerns. Second, there was a hypothesis that manganese would interfere with the operation of pollution-controlling catalytic converters. Scientific studies also failed to confirm these hypothesized effects. At just the time of Canada's initiative, the EPA had withdrawn a long-standing prohibition on MMT based on the catalytic converter concern and had judged the health effects evidence too weak to go forward with health-based regulation even under the Clean Air Act's precautionary authority to prohibit fuel additives that "may reasonably be anticipated to endanger the public health."[37]

Notwithstanding the evolving regulatory situation in the United States, the Minister of Environment Canada, Sheila Copps (involved at about the same time in *S. D. Myers*), announced her intention to have MMT removed from Canadian gasoline by August 1995, apparently in response to public health concerns. Given the inconclusive results of health effects studies, however, Copps lacked the necessary science-based justification to use her authority under Canadian environmental law to impose a federal ban on MMT on health grounds. Instead, the government invoked federal authority over foreign and interprovincial commerce, enacting the Manganese-based Fuel Additives Act to ban the importation or interprovincial sale of MMT. Because Ethyl imported MMT, blended it in Ontario, and then sold it to refiners in other provinces, the law effectively prevented Ethyl from continuing to sell MMT in Canada. Ethyl submitted a claim against Canada under Chapter 11 for losses to its investment in Canada in blending and distributing MMT.

While the Ethyl claim was pending, four provinces initiated a domestic challenge to the interprovincial trade ban under Canada's Agreement on Internal Trade (AIT). A Canadian panel ruled in favor of the provinces in June 1998, holding the interprovincial ban to be an undue burden on internal commerce in Canada.[38] The domestic panel recognized protection of the public health as a legitimate objective that could justify an internal restriction on trade under the AIT but found that there was no urgency to the health concerns and therefore the federal government could have met its legitimate objective through less trade restrictive means.[39]

A month after the AIT ruling, the Canadian government settled Ethyl's Chapter 11 claim. It rescinded the trade ban on MMT and paid Ethyl a reported US$13 million for its legal expenses and lost profits during the period the ban was in effect. As part of the settlement, the federal government publicly conceded that there was no scientific basis to prohibit MMT on health grounds. Meanwhile, MMT remains a legal product in the United States, though many large refiners, responding to public and environmental group pressure, have voluntarily agreed not to use it in their gasoline products.

Methanex v. United States

Methanex is a Canadian-based manufacturer of methanol, with operations in the United States and other countries. Its methanol is the basis for the production of the gasoline additive methyl tertiary butyl ether (MTBE), an oxygenate widely used in the reformulated gasolines devised to meet air quality goals under the Clean Air Act. When leaked into the soil from gasoline tanks, MTBE moves very rapidly through the soil and into groundwater or surface water, including sources of drinking water. The mobility of MTBE in the environment has caused considerable concern, because some recent scientific studies link it to tumors and nervous disorders in rats and mice, and it has been classified a possible cancer-causing agent by the EPA. In light of these studies, California Governor Gray Davis issued an executive order on March 25, 1999, ordering steps to phase out the use in California of MTBE by December 31, 2002. California is the largest single market in the United States for MTBE. Methanex is making a claim under Chapter 11 for over $900 million, its estimate of lost profits and also lost stock value as a result of the impending ban.[40]

The decision of the *Methanex* tribunal in August 2002 all but rejected Methanex's claim.[41] The tribunal agreed with arguments advanced by all three governments that NAFTA Chapter 11, which covers only claims against measures "relating to" an investor or investment, means that the challenged measure must have a "legally significant connection" to the investor or investment. In this case, the tribunal noted that the governor's executive order addressed MTBE, and Methanex does not make or distribute MTBE. Rather, Methanex merely supplies methanol to the MTBE makers. The tribunal concluded that, even though a ban on MTBE obviously affects the market for methanol, that effect is indirect. The executive order therefore does not "relate to" methanol, so the tribunal lacks jurisdiction over Methanex's basic claim. The tribunal left a small door open to Methanex: Methanex may file a "fresh plea" with some evidence that substantiates its later claim that Governor Davis acted purposely to discriminate against Methanex as a "foreign" producer at the behest of U.S. ethanol-maker Archer Daniels Midland. If Methanex can support such a claim, there may be a Chapter 11 case involving a government measure taken with intent to discriminate against the foreign investor and to advantage a competing domestic investor. On the other hand, a new executive order by Governor Davis extending the deadline for MTBE phase-out indefinitely because supplies of other oxygenates are not sufficient for the California market will make it more difficult for Methanex to show injury or intentional discrimination.[42]

Investment and Environment in the Broader Context

A central premise of sustainable development holds that effective environmental protection requires a foundation in sound economic development. In recent decades, foreign direct investment has dwarfed official development assistance as an engine of development throughout the world, so development policies in countries like Mexico have focused on attracting foreign investment.[43] The sustainable development challenge is to assure that the private investments are used in the destination countries in an environmentally sound manner.

Chapter 11 of NAFTA was an early effort to reduce obstacles to investment flows, on the one hand, while attending to the environmental context for investments, on the other. Environmentalists identified two salient concerns with NAFTA's investment provisions during the negotiations. One was the possible creation of "pollution havens" if governments used the lure of lowered environmental standards to attract new investment. To meet that concern, the trade negotiators included a policy statement against a pollution haven strategy in Article 1114(2), committing themselves not to lower standards as a means of attracting or retaining investments.[44] The other prominent environmental concern was that the scale and intensity of foreign investment, especially in Mexico, would overwhelm the public environmental protection system and aggravate pollution and ecosystem degradation. Article 1114(1) of NAFTA, which explicitly reserves the right of each government to adopt laws or policies of general application controlling, regulating, or restricting investments in order to preserve or protect the environment, only partly addresses this concern.[45] The call for further environmental oversight of investment flows was a major impetus behind the campaign by environmental organizations for the creation of a trinational environmental commission parallel to NAFTA that could reinforce environmental programs in all three countries, an idea that ultimately took shape in the CEC.

The wild card for investment and environment turned out to be the Chapter 11 provisions for investor-state arbitration. Everyone seems to agree with the observation of a Canadian lawyer who has been involved in two of the Chapter 11 proceedings: "No one quite understood or anticipated where it would go."[46] The CEC embodies a vision of collective effort toward a better environment throughout the continent, including an impartial assessment of the environmental effects of economic liberalization, policy reforms to mitigate those effects, and mechanisms for open inquiry into circumstances where environmental laws are not being enforced. The Chapter 11 arbitration regime stands in stark contrast to this vision of continental collaboration. It gives a select group of economically motivated private parties (foreign investors) leverage to resist or deflect the economic impositions of environmental regulation by bringing claims (with no threshold standard of good faith) against national governments for compensation, and it resolves those claims in closed hearings of politically unaccountable ad hoc tribunals. Despite requests from the environmental community, neither the environmental ministers who constitute the Council of the CEC nor the trade ministers who make up the NAFTA Free Trade Commission have established mechanisms to bridge the gap between environmental cooperation and investor compensation or to promote explicit consideration of the environmental and economic ramifications of the Chapter 11 disputes. Recent joint meetings of trade and environment officials of the three countries have at least created a forum for discussion of the investment-environment issues, but they have not led toward new policies or procedures.

The lack of policy or institutional reform would be a serious matter if the Chapter 11 arbitrations were presenting a serious threat to national and cooperative environmental protection. To date, however, only two "environmental" Chapter 11 cases, *S. D. Myers* and *Metalclad*, have resulted in awards of compensation on the merits. As we have seen, both cases concerned disposal of hazardous wastes, though it is worth noting that *S. D. Myers* involved final disposal in the home country of the investor, so only *Metalclad* involved regulation of final disposal in the host country. It would be a mistake to draw broad conclusions about the environmental threat of Chapter 11 from the two awards.

Nor do the cases support the claim that Chapter 11 presents a threat to democratic choice and autonomy of governments. In *S. D. Myers*, a federal minister for the environment made a decision by executive decree against the uniform advice of the career officials in the ministry. The only non-governmental organization that participated in the making of that decision was the commercial firm that benefited from the export ban. In *Metalclad*, there was a conflict between national environmental officials and state and local officials. Mexico is free to empower local communities to reject unwanted facilities, and nothing in NAFTA changes that power. As reflected in the *Metalclad* facts, however, Metalclad dealt in good faith with the federal environmental authorities and had every reason to accept their assurances that they had full and exclusive power to authorize the construction and operation of the landfill. Mexican law allowed the state governor, in the face of these federal permits, to declare an ecological zone that has the effect of preventing the facility's operation. Nothing in the record indicates any public input or consultation process related to the decree, which was issued by an outgoing governor in his last days in office. Metalclad did not challenge the propriety of the ecological decree, which remains in effect. Metalclad only asked that it be compensated for this last-minute, site-specific exercise of a state governor's unreviewable executive power to override a federal environmental permit granted after several years of environmental planning and government oversight.

Putting these Chapter 11 cases in the broader, cooperative North American context, both *Metalclad* and *S. D. Myers* have significant environmental policy implications. Hazardous waste disposal in North America requires national commitments to proper disposal of wastes generated in the national territory without, however, ignoring the possibility that the environmentally sound management of certain wastes may be best accomplished by their transfer across a border for treatment or disposal. Each nation faces difficulties in convincing particular local communities to host the treatment and disposal facilities necessary to provide national waste management capacity. *Metalclad* shows the special difficulties in Mexico, where foreign service providers may be the ones offering the requisite technical skill and financial capital for such facilities. Mexico recognizes that it can benefit from foreign investment in environmental technology and services; the federal authorities encouraged Metalclad as part of that strategy. After the ecological decree abruptly prevented operation of its facility, Metalclad announced that it was discontinuing all operations in Mexico, and at least six other foreign environmental investment projects were delayed or discontinued.[47] The message is clear: unless Mexico can improve the predictability and accountability of its regulation at all levels of government, foreign investors will be reluctant to invest in highly regulated businesses like hazardous waste disposal despite the obvious need for such investments in Mexico.

S. D. Myers presents the complementary problem, the tendency of both Canada and the United States to "go it alone" in hazardous waste treatment, discouraging or prohibiting cross-border transfers of many such wastes. Yet with waste, as with air pollution, the environment knows no national boundaries. Assuming that the final treatment or disposal systems are equivalent, environmentally sound management generally prefers shipment to the nearest suitable facility because it reduces the risk of accidental release during transfer and transportation. Neither the absolute ban of the Toxic Substances Control Act on importation of PCBs into the United States nor the temporary ban on exports of PCBs that Canada imposed by decree promoted a cooperative, continental approach to the environmentally sound disposal of PCBs. In this respect, the efforts of S. D. Myers to provide cost-effective PCB disposal services to Canadian companies holding PCB wastes should not be construed as an effort to create or take advantage of regulatory loopholes, nor should the Canadian action at dispute in *S. D. Myers* be construed as a measure of "environmental protection."

The CEC's efforts to promote the control and elimination of certain hazardous chemicals throughout North America represent the better approach of cooperative environmental policy-making, eschewing the chimerical autonomy of national action for the tangible collective benefits of collaboration. The policy flaw in Chapter 11 is that it treats an arbitration as strictly a matter of resolving a private claim about government treatment of a specific investment. The tribunals have neither the authority nor the expertise to think about the broader environmental implications, much less to shape their legal judgments with these implications in view. The NAFTA governments have not made full use of the CEC to fill this policy gap. The *Metalclad* and *S. D. Myers* cases should have been the inspiration for a mandate to the CEC to study and report on the continental scale of hazardous waste generation, disposal capacity availability and needs, facility siting problems and prospects, and the potential role of cross-border investments and cross-border waste transfers to alleviate environmental problems. As Mary Kelly and Cyrus Reed report in Chapter 6, the CEC Council did vote in 2001 to initiate "a North American approach to the environmentally sound management of hazardous wastes," though that initiative focuses on tracking and proper disposal and does not directly address issues of investment, siting, and cross-border collaboration in finding the best solutions to waste disposal.

CEC intervention would avail less in product regulation cases exemplified by *Ethyl* and *Methanex*. Although the two cases seem superficially similar and thus suggestive of a possible common approach throughout North

America, the differences between the two cases are more vivid than their similarities and are likely to bring distinctly different outcomes under Chapter 11, diminishing the value of any broader investigation or policy recommendation by the CEC.

The preceding review of Chapter 11 cases teaches that the environmental protection claims for regulatory actions by governments cannot always be accepted at face value. In *Ethyl*, the environment minister deliberately avoided making a science-based regulatory decision, and the government publicly renounced any health justification for the challenged trade ban. But that does not mean that all environmental regulations affecting investors are disingenuous. In the *Methanex* case, MTBE is clearly shown to be a groundwater contaminant, and the scientific evidence of its potentially serious health effects, though preliminary and disputable, provides ample legal foundation for the governor's executive order grounded in state law and in the international environmental law principle of precaution.

The cases also teach that commercial and regional interests within the host country can distort internal decisions and encourage government officials to sacrifice the interests of foreign investors in the pursuit of local political and economic advantage. One reason for international protections for foreign investors is that they are not effectively represented in the political processes of the host country that may affect their interests. The trade ban in *Ethyl* left open the possibility that a Canadian producer in a single province where refiners were located could manufacture and sell MMT within the province. In *Methanex*, by contrast, the challenged regulation targets the product itself, regardless of the country or state of its manufacture or sale.[48] Moreover, the California governor's original order allowed three years for an orderly withdrawal of MTBE from the market, affording Methanex the chance to shift production or investments to other markets or to products unaffected by the California action. That deadline has now been deferred indefinitely.

Finally, Canada's MMT ban was ruled illegal under internal Canadian trade law and had to be abandoned by the federal government. In the case of MTBE, other states have followed California's lead, and the U.S. Congress is debating a national ban on MTBE.[49] Cynics will note that the federal ban on MTBE is supported by corn-growing states that stand to benefit from increased use of ethanol as a substitute, but that political and economic opportunism does not contradict the original public health motivation in California and other states banning MTBE.

In short, with respect to product regulation, it is not clear that the CEC can make a meaningful contribution toward better outcomes in Chapter 11 arbitrations. The CEC has taken strong and effective action to promote continental controls on a small class of products internationally recognized as environmentally harmful, such as persistent organic pollutants. Beyond that, though, there is no firm basis for a continental products policy. On the contrary, as the *Ethyl* and *Methanex* cases vividly demonstrate, significant environmental and economic controversy persists within Canada and the United States, respectively, over the control of air pollution from vehicles and the appropriate regulation of different gasoline additives. Although the markets for these products are clearly international, the environmental effects of their use are fundamentally local rather than transboundary, so disparate state or national regulations do not undermine regional or continental environmental protection efforts. Moreover, the extended and very public debates about MMT and MTBE in each country have allowed a full airing of the scientific, technical, and economic dimensions of the policy choices being made. The CEC can add nothing distinctive to the national discourses, nor could it have done anything to prevent or resolve the specific disputes.

If, as now appears likely, the *Methanex* claim is rejected, the general value of Chapter 11's investor protections will be vindicated as compatible with the right of government officials to take nondiscriminatory action to protect health and the environment on a precautionary basis. If *Methanex* somehow results in an award of compensation, I will join the chorus of environmental critics of Chapter 11. But that remote possibility lies in the future. On the record to date as discussed in this chapter, I find the expressions of environmentalist alarm about Chapter 11 to be exaggerated at best and "fear-mongering [unimpeded] by knowledge of the facts" at worst.[50] To be sure, regulations justified or propounded on environmental grounds have been at the center of about a third of the NAFTA investor-state cases so far. In the three most prominent cases, the government has agreed to or been ordered by tribunals to pay multimillion dollar compensatory awards to the complaining foreign investors. But if one goes beneath the surface of the environmental explanations for the government actions in each of these three cases, national commercial and political interests appear to be significant drivers of the application of the supposed environmental protection measures to the foreign investor. It is notable that in every case only a single foreign investor (and no domestic investor) has been affected by the government action. In short, the cases so far better support the view that Chapter 11 is functioning precisely as intended, protecting foreign investors who, as politically vulnerable outsiders, have fallen victim to unfair or arbitrary treatment by governments acting on short-term, locally based political motivations.

Where Do We Go from Here?

The NAFTA countries and their neighbors in the Western Hemisphere have committed to the negotiation of a Free Trade Area of the Americas, drafts of which contain investor protection provisions closely modeled on Chapter 11. The United States and others supported an initiative in the Organization for Economic Cooperation and Development (OECD) to create a so-called Multilateral Agreement on Investment that also would have applied rules similar to Chapter 11 throughout the world, an idea that is being revived in the negotiating agenda of the World Trade Organization. In light of the NAFTA Chapter 11 experience, should investor protections and investor-state arbitration be adopted regionally or globally? If so, are there particular features of the investment regime or the arbitration regime that should be modified?

In my view, there is sustainable development value in rules and mechanisms that encourage direct investments in developing countries provided that those investments are environmentally sound, as determined primarily by compliance with local, national, and international environmental law and norms. To encourage direct investments, national and international rules must substantially reduce the "regulatory risk" that the investment will be treated in a discriminatory or arbitrary manner or appropriated by the host government without compensation. To ensure that investments are environmentally sound, national and international rules must allow governments the freedom to adopt environmental protection laws and procedures, to insist that foreign investors comply with those requirements at the time of the investment, and to revise those requirements after the investment in light of new information or new social ideas about the appropriate standard of performance. NAFTA Chapter 11 makes an effort to deal with all of these issues and provides an appropriate basic framework for a multilateral regime.

The most acute substantive concern about Chapter 11 for environmental interests is the meaning of "expropriation [or] tantamount to expropriation." Some environmentalists embrace the view expressed by David Schorr, then Director of the World Wildlife Fund's Sustainable Commerce Program, who said of *Methanex*: "To call a country's effort to protect the environment 'an expropriation' is absurd. It's like saying we should pay polluters every time the government asks them not to pollute."[51] That statement, though, leads to the simplistic idea that environmental regulation should never give rise to a claim for expropriation, which would negate the protection that investors need from extreme regulatory risk. International law has left behind the formalistic distinction between "direct" or "total" expropriations and "indirect" effects on investors that are equivalent to expropriation. Once the notion of "indirect expropriation" is accepted, no amount of linguistic legerdemain in redrafting or interpreting Chapter 11 can create bright-line distinctions between noncompensable exercises of regulatory authority and exercises of that same regulatory authority that effectively expropriate an investment. By the very nature of "takings" law, judgments must be made, case by case, about the nature of the investment interest, the form and purpose of the regulation, and the degree to which the regulation has impaired the value of the investment.

The irreducible indeterminacy of rights to compensation, though, means that claims for compensation should be resolved through procedures that are open to input by representatives of the environmental, economic, and social considerations at stake and fully transparent to the public and to the private interests concerned with those matters. The international arbitration systems available under Chapter 11 lack the necessary procedures and infrastructure to vindicate rights of public participation and access to information. Revising those systems would be counterproductive; they have established traditions and significant value for commercial arbitration. The NAFTA governments should instead devise a new investor-state arbitration system with the public profile and procedural openness of national judicial systems. Such a revamped arbitration process would go a long way to enhance the public legitimacy of Chapter 11 arbitration outcomes and bolster support at home and abroad for the multilateral extension of investment protection rules in the Free Trade Area of the Americas and the World Trade Organization.

Notes

1. Among the public interest commentaries on NAFTA before it was approved, only a Canadian group perceived that Chapter 11 might put limits on a "government's ability to initiate new public programs" and would "reduce democratic control of the economy." Canadian Centre for Policy Alternatives, *Which Way for the Americas?* 127 (1992). The otherwise excellent analysis of environmental issues in NAFTA by Johnson and Beaulieu is more typical, omitting almost entirely any consideration of Chapter 11 or its arbitration procedures. Pierre Marc Johnson and André Beaulieu, *The Environment and NAFTA: Understanding and Implementing the New Continental Law* (1996).

2. One tabulation indicated that nine of the sixteen Chapter 11 claims filed by the end of 2000 involved environmental questions (disregarding one claim that is a duplicate of an earlier claim that was dismissed). International Institute for Sustainable Development, *Private Rights, Public Problems: A Guide to NAFTA's Controversial Chapter on Investor Rights* (2001) (hereafter IISD). But since then another eleven claims have been filed, only one of which implicates environmental policy.

3. Bill Moyers, "Trading Democracy," *NOW with Bill Moyers*, PBS broadcast, Feb. 5, 2002, transcript available at *http://www.pbs.org/now/transcript/transcript_tdfull.html.*

4. Daniel Seligman, Director of the Sierra Club's Responsible Trade Program, quoted in Dennis Pfaff, "Trade Winds," *California Lawyer* 25 (Sept. 2000).

5. E.g., IISD, supra.

6. Daniel M. Price, "NAFTA Chapter 11–Investor–State Dispute Settlement: Frankenstein or Safety Valve," 26 *Canada-U.S. Law Journal* 107, S-2 (2001). Price was the lead U.S. negotiator of Chapter 11.

7. For a brief synopsis, see David A. Gantz, "Resolution of Investment Disputes under the North American Free Trade Agreement," 10 *Arizona Journal of International and Comparative Law* 335, 336–41 (1993).

8. Hon. Pierre Pettigrew, Minister for International Trade, remarks to the House of Commons (Canada), May 1, 2001, available at *http://www.dfait-maeci.gc.ca/tna-nac/Min_S_Inv-e.asp* (Mar. 27, 2002). Minister Pettigrew's comment applied to "[t]he chapter [11] and in particular investor-state dispute settlement."

9. For example, Mexico and most other countries in Latin America have subscribed to the so-called Calvo Doctrine, which holds that foreign investors should have only the same rights as citizens of the country. Gloria L. Sandrino, "The NAFTA Investment Chapter and Foreign Direct Investment in Mexico: A Third World Perspective," 27 *Vanderbilt Journal of Transnational Law* 259, 285–86 (1994). NAFTA Chapter 11 preempts the Calvo Doctrine for North American investors. Canada had constitutional concerns of its own. Donald S. MacDonald, "Chapter 11 of NAFTA: What Are the Implications for Sovereignty?" 24 *Canada-U.S. Law Journal* 281 (1998).

10. Jorge Vargas, "Mexico's Foreign Investment Act of 1993," excerpted in Ralph H. Folsom, Michael Wallace Gordon, and David Lopez, *NAFTA: A Problem-Oriented Coursebook* 298 (2000).

11. Sandrino, supra, 327.

12. Pettigrew, supra.

13. Only claims to money and sales of goods and services or credit associated with such sales are specifically excluded. North American Free Trade Agreement (NAFTA), Sept. 17, 1992, art. 1139, 32 I.L.M. 642.

14. *Methanex v. United States*, Preliminary Award on Jurisdiction, Aug. 7, 2002, ¶ 147.

15. Jason L. Gudofsky, "Shedding Light on Article 1110 of the North American Free Trade Agreement (NAFTA) Concerning Expropriations: An Environmental Case Study," 21 *Northwestern Journal of International Law and Business* 243, 252 (2000). The authority to expropriate private property is, indeed, often considered a central attribute of the territorial sovereignty of states.

16. American Law Institute, *Restatement (Third) of Foreign Relations Law* § 712, reporters n.6. But a Canadian scholar argues that the *Restatement* view is "generally regarded as articulating a lower threshold as to what constitutes a compensable taking than is often accepted as customary international law." Chris Tollefson, "Games without Frontiers: Investor Claims and Citizen Submissions under the NAFTA Regime," 27 *Yale Journal of International Law* 141, 161 n.109 (2002).

17. Martin J. Wagner, "International Investment, Expropriation, and Environmental Protection," 29 *Golden Gate University Law Review* 465 (1999). Confiscation of money or property in connection with a criminal arrest exemplifies a confiscation of property clearly within the "police power" rule, but there is confusion in the cases and scholarly commentary about whether a rule against production of a particular product by a legitimate business is an exercise of the police power, even if the rule is designed to guard against a risk to health.

18. The muddle and controversy continue in the majority and dissenting opin-

ions in the latest U.S. Supreme Court takings opinion, *Tahoe-Sierra Preservation Council, Inc. v. Tahoe Regional Planning Agency*, 122 S.Ct. 1465 (2002). Poirier argues that the lack of clarity is not only irreducible but to some extent socially useful. Marc R. Poirier, "The Virtue of Vagueness in Takings Doctrine" (Jan. 2002, draft paper).

19. MacDonald, supra, 282–83.

20. Investor-state arbitration is neither exclusive nor mandatory; it is initiated at the option of the investor. In submitting a claim under Chapter 11, the investor must consent to the arbitration procedure and must waive his or her right to initiate or pursue any administrative or judicial process involving the same claim. NAFTA, supra, art. 1120. There is a three-year statute of limitations on submitting a claim to arbitration.

21. The three systems are the World Bank's International Center for Settlement of Investment Disputes (ICSID), the ICSID "Additional Facility," and the United Nations Commission on International Trade Law (UNCITRAL). Because the ICSID requires both parties to be members and neither Canada nor Mexico have agreed to it, the ICSID option is not currently available. Under the Additional Facility provisions, however, much the same process is available when one party has agreed to the system and thus can be selected if the United States is either the respondent or the home of the claimant. The UNCITRAL process is open for all NAFTA disputes. See Anthony DePalma, "NAFTA's Powerful Little Secret," *New York Times*, Mar. 11, 2001 (reporting the views of international arbitration officials ["'The whole thing here was to have a mechanism to give a base level of comfort to foreign investors,' said Ko-Yung Tung, secretary general of (the) International Center for Settlement of Investment Disputes."] and environmental advocates ["'The fact that the drafters of NAFTA chose this secretive process to resolve these disputes is further evidence that they weren't foreseeing matters of broad social concern coming before these panels,' said Martin Wagner, director of international programs for Earthjustice Legal Defense Fund."]). See also IISD, supra.

22. Article 10(6)(c) calls upon the CEC Council to cooperate with the NAFTA Free Trade Commission in "contributing to the prevention or resolution of environment-related trade disputes." It is far from clear, though, whether Chapter 11 arbitrations even fall within the "trade disputes" about which CEC and the FTC are to consult (as compared with state-to-state trade disputes under NAFTA Chapter 20).

23. Quoted in DePalma, supra.

24. U.S. Trade Representative, "Joint Statement of the NAFTA Free Trade Commission: Building on a North American Partnership," press release, July 31, 2001, available at *http://www.ustr.gov/releases/2001*.

25. *Pope & Talbot v. Canada*, Decision and Order of Mar. 11, 2002, available at *http://www.dfait-maeci.gc.ca/tna-nac/Decision-Order-11Mar02.PDF*. The tribunal cited UNCITRAL Rule 25(4) and the tribunal's own procedural order that "hearings are to be held *in camera* unless the parties agree otherwise." The tribunal noted explicitly that the July 2001 clarification by the FTC recognized that specific requirements for confidentiality would override the general policy of publication.

26. The International Institute for Sustainable Development, a Canadian organi-

zation, and Friends of the Earth separately petitioned the tribunal for permission to file amicus curiae briefs. After briefing on the issue from all three governments, the tribunal issued its ruling on January 15, 2001. *Methanex v. United States*, Decision of the Tribunal on Petitions from Third Persons to Intervene as "Amici Curiae," available at *http://www.naftaclaims.com/*.

27. In the July 31, 2001, "Clarifications," though, the FTC expressly agreed that governments are free to share all documents and information with officials of their respective federal, state, or provincial governments in the course of a Chapter 11 proceeding.

28. Emmanuel Gaillard, "NAFTA Dispute Arbitration under Auspices of the International Center," *New York Law Journal*, Aug. 3, 2000 (discussing the award in *Azinian v. Mexico*). David Gantz has remarked that this case is "of no direct relevance to the issue of environmental takings or the possible application of Article 1110 to such actions." David A. Gantz, "Potential Conflicts between Investor Rights and Environmental Protection under NAFTA's Chapter 11," 33 *George Washington International Law Review* 651, 702 (2001).

29. The arbitral tribunal accepted the view that the local construction permit may cover only technical and safety factors of design, materials, and construction methods and not the environmental effects of postconstruction operation of the site.

30. In particular, some have commented with concern on a paragraph of the award in which the tribunal construed "tantamount to expropriation" to include "covert or incidental interference with the use of property which has the effect of depriving the owner, in whole or in significant part, of the use or reasonably-to-be-expected economic benefit of property." Certainly it would be alarming to think that every "incidental interference" by governments with the use of property should be compensated. Read in context, however, the reference to "incidental interference with property" goes inseparably with the following qualification: "which has the effect of depriving the owner, in whole or in significant part, of the use or reasonably-to-be-expected economic benefit of property." This brings the tribunal's interpretation within the realm of well-accepted understandings of expropriation, which recognize the notion of the investor's reasonable expectations and the idea that regulation that deprives an owner of all or nearly all use of the property is functionally equivalent to its physical appropriation by the government.

31. *United Mexican States v. Metalclad Corp.*, 2001 B.C.S.C. 0664 (per Tysoe, J.).

32. Agreement Between the United States and Canada Concerning the Transboundary Movement of Hazardous Waste, Oct. 28, 1986, T.I.A.S. 11099; Toxic Substances Control Act, § 6(e), 15 U.S.C. § 2605(e); 40 C.F.R. § 761.93.

33. *Sierra Club v. EPA*, 118 F.3d 1324 (9th Cir. 1997).

34. Basel Convention on the Control of Transboundary Movements of Hazardous Wastes and Their Disposal, Mar. 22, 1989, 28 I.L.M. 657.

35. Daniel C. Esty and Damien Geradin, "Market Access, Competitiveness, and Harmonization: Environmental Protection in Regional Trade Agreements," 21 *Harvard Environmental Law Review* 265 (1997); Daniel A. Farber and Robert E. Hudec, "Free Trade and the Regulatory State: A GATT's Eye View of the Dormant Commerce Clause," 47 *Vanderbilt Law Review* 1401 (1994).

36. For a full account, see Julie A. Soloway, "Environmental Trade Barriers under NAFTA: The MMT Fuel Additives Controversy," 8 *Minnesota Journal of Global Trade* 55 (1999).

37. The decision not to regulate MMT came after a U.S. court held that the EPA lacked statutory authority to invoke generalized public health concerns to block MMT under a specific fuel additives waiver provision of the Clean Air Act, and at the same time upheld the EPA's decision that the latest evidence no longer supports continued prohibition of MMT as a fuel additive based on the supposed interference of manganese with catalytic converters. *Ethyl Corp. v. EPA*, 51 F.3d 1053 (D.C. Cir. 1995).

38. In addition to Soloway, supra, see Gudofsky, supra.

39. The ruling in Canada's AIT proceeding is similar to rulings in the United States in cases involving environmental regulation affecting interstate commerce and cases in Europe involving the balance between local environmental jurisdiction and the Europe-wide effort to promote the "free movement of goods." See Esty and Geradin, supra; Farber and Hudec, supra.

40. "NAFTA Used to Attack Clean Water Move," *Environment News Service* (June 24, 1999), *http://ens.lycos.com/ens/jun99/1999L-06-24-04.html.* It is noteworthy that Methanex has suffered a general reversal of fortunes in recent years: the world price of methanol declined in the late 1990s, and Methanex share prices were in steep decline just prior to the Chapter 11 action.

41. *Methanex v. United States*, Preliminary Award on Jurisdiction, Aug. 7, 2002, available at *http://www.naftaclaims.com.*

42. California Executive Order D-52-02, Mar. 14, 2002.

43. In 2000, foreign direct investment flows were $800 billion, of which $120 billion went to developing countries. That compares with approximately $55 billion in official development assistance.

44. Gary C. Hufbauer and Jeffrey J. Schott, *NAFTA: An Assessment* 95–96 (1993). Article 1114(2) is not mandatory; rather, it declares the common policy of the three governments that "it is inappropriate to encourage investment" by relaxing standards and that they "should not," therefore, "waive or otherwise derogate from . . . such measures [or offer to do so] as an encouragement for the establishment, acquisition, expansion or retention" of investments.

45. "Nothing in this Chapter shall be construed to prevent a Party from adopting, maintaining or enforcing any measure *otherwise consistent with this Chapter* that it considers appropriate to ensure that investment activity in its territory is undertaken in a manner sensitive to environmental concerns" (emphasis added). The investor-state disputes under NAFTA all involve claims that the government environmental measures in question were *not* consistent with Chapter 11's substantive provisions.

46. Evelyn Iritani, "Trade Pacts Accused of Subverting U.S. Policies," *Los Angeles Times*, Feb. 28, 1999 (quoting Barry Appleton).

47. "Large U.S. Handler of Toxic Wastes to End Mexican Operations after NAFTA Suit," 29 *Environment Reporter* (BNA) 2578 (Mar. 30, 1999).

48. Of course, like most product bans, the governor's order mandates the end of sales of the product. But a ban on all commercial transactions involving the product

is markedly different from the Canadian restrictions on MMT, which prohibited only interprovincial sale or import.

49. David E. Rosenbaum, "Senate Passes an Energy Bill Called Flawed by Both Sides," *New York Times*, Apr. 26, 2002. The Senate energy bill, S. 517, calls for a ban on MTBE within four years. As of August 2002, the legislation was in House-Senate conference.

50. Gudofsky, supra, 304 (quoting Sergio Marchi, then International Trade Minister of Canada, to Maude Barlow of the Council of Canadians).

51. Quoted in "NAFTA Used to Attack California Clean Water Move," *Environment News Service* (June 24, 1999), *http://ens.lycos.com/ens/jun99/1999L-06-24-04.html.*

PART 3

Toward an International Civil Society

JOHN D. WIRTH 11

Perspectives on the Joint Public Advisory Committee

OF THE THREE BRANCHES of the North American Commission for Environmental Cooperation (CEC), the Joint Public Advisory Committee (JPAC) is arguably the most innovative. The fifteen citizens on JPAC—five from each country—are appointed by their governments to give advice to the CEC Council, to comment on the Secretariat's work plan, and to consult with the public in open meetings on aspects of the CEC's program. Depending on their expertise and areas of interest, individual JPAC members also serve on various advisory committees and expert groups engaged in developing projects in the work plan. JPAC's scope is broad, allowing room for flexibility as the Committee carries out its role to facilitate public participation in the CEC. Not surprisingly, there has been friction at times between nongovernmental JPAC members and the deputy ministers and other federal officials who staff the Council, particularly over the rules and procedures for addressing citizen complaints over nonenforcement of environmental laws. In fact, a certain creative tension is built right into JPAC's role. In the nearly eight years since it was constituted in 1994, JPAC has become an effective, visible, and respected branch of the CEC. It continues to evolve as the CEC itself evolves as an institution.

As Johnson and Beaulieu point out, "there are few precedents in international law for such formalized nongovernmental participation."[1] Citizen participation emerged as an artifact of the environmental consciousness that swept through Canadian and American civil society in the late 1960s and took hold in Mexico two decades later.[2] The idea for JPAC emerged in the context of negotiations leading to the North American Agreement on Environmental Cooperation (NAAEC) in the early 1990s. This Agreement reflected the concerns of the environmental community that with the passage of the North American Free Trade Agreement (NAFTA), Mexico, especially, would become a "pollution haven." In particular, the Green Group supporting NAFTA—Natural Resources Defense Council, Environmental Defense Fund, National Wildlife Federation, and the National Audubon Society—and certain key individuals working on the Agreement were concerned about enforcement and public participation. After discussing the relative merits of granting the new Commission subpoena power and the ability to levy fines up-front, they decided these would be deal-breakers and settled instead for a citizen right to question instances of nonenforcement of environmental laws in any of the three countries. They also wanted citizen participation to be a constituent part of the Commission. In this way JPAC became part of the basic architecture of the Agreement.

Conceptually, JPAC owed much to the yeasty climate of the United Nations Conference on Environment and Development (UNCED), the 1992 environmental conference in Rio where nongovernmental organizations (NGOs) gathered in their thousands to discuss trade and environment issues, sound each other out, and form coalitions. In the words of Kathleen Rogers, then head of migratory birds and wildlife counsel at Audubon, "1992 was a revolutionary year, with globalization hitting people over the head. In Rio, we all caught on at the same time that civil society was emerging, [manifested] in civil participation and talking about trade at the grass roots level. All of a sudden trade, the environment and the Internet came together."[3] Spurred by this momentum, the JPAC model came out of the NGO community and it happened fast, in the first months of the new Clinton administration. As well, the JPAC model was heir to the advisory councils set up to discuss education and trade in the last years of the first Bush administration. Public consultation was in the air.

Informants do not recall any specific Canadian agency on the origins of JPAC, although as Dan Magraw, a former U.S. Environmental Agency (EPA) official, recalls, "Canada didn't much like it but it wasn't a big deal with them; they had other issues." As for the Mexicans, they really didn't like it, not because they were against the idea of having an advisory body but because they believed that Mexican nationals should not be in the position of advising other governments. On sovereignty grounds, they thought it should be national and not trinational.[4] (In advising their own ministers, National Advisory Committees [NACs] in all three countries play this role today.)

Headed by Administrator Carol Browner, who came out of the environmental movement herself, the new team at the EPA welcomed the JPAC model and worked closely with Katy McGinty at the White House–based Council on Environmental Quality, who vetted all the ideas coming in from the environmental community. In fact, Browner recalled, "I knew I would be better served by having people of stature behind me. It never would have worked with just the three ministers." That the first U.S. JPAC members were drawn from a large applicant pool helped to assure a strong group, especially when the EPA succeeded in making the selections instead of the White House, which had certain political needs. JPAC soon proved its utility to Browner, who used it to build consensus among her two colleagues and their staffs on the new Council. "And because JPAC talked with one voice," she added, "it was a voice ministers had to listen to."[5]

At their first meeting in Washington, D.C., in July 1994, JPAC members made two decisions that set the style and tone of their modus operandi. For one thing, they chose to interact as North Americans rather than see themselves as advocates or defenders of national positions or as representatives of any particular private voluntary organization or interest group. Realizing that JPAC was something really new, they sensed that it might be an early harbinger of an emerging North American community and in this spirit wrote their vision statement (see Appendix A at the end of this chapter). For another, they decided that the elected chair would rotate yearly and sequentially among the countries, starting with a Canadian, followed by an American and then a Mexican.[6]

The consequences of these decisions were beneficial. A cooperative style of decision-making developed and persisted over the ensuing years despite the turnover in JPAC members, principally the Canadian and Mexican members whose governments chose to rotate members more frequently than the Americans did. (To date, three of the original five Americans still serve on JPAC).[7] Undoubtedly, not taking national positions did facilitate making decisions by consensus, which promoted and reinforced cooperation. And also it bolstered the ability to stand together in the face of pressure from another branch of the CEC, as will be discussed below. Rotating the chair yearly and sequentially helped to address the asymmetries in power between the three countries and neutralized it, in that with this procedure the JPAC could and in fact did make decisions on the basis of equality. The Parties' decision to name an equal number of members from each country also helped in this respect.

One of JPAC's tasks is to comment on the Secretariat's work plan, which in the early days tended to mushroom across a range of projects that soon pushed against the Commission's small budget ($15 million, which soon dropped to $9 million; the three countries also support their own programs through their national efforts). Alarmed, the Council asked JPAC to advise on how the work plan might be trimmed and systematized under the rubric of a few key areas, such as migratory birds and biodiversity, toxics and the sound management of chemicals, and capacity-building and compliance issues.[8] This effort bore fruit, and in the meantime the Secretariat continued to build what became an outstanding trinational staff.

These first years also saw an evolution in JPAC's ability to engage the public in consultations. The first such effort, based on two-minute presentations by interested individuals, was highly unsatisfactory, as were the small roundtables attempted at the second formal meeting of the Council held in Oaxaca in 1995. However, the public was given the opportunity to interact directly with the three ministers, which was well received, and this became a feature of Council meetings from then on. More recently, JPAC has become both more experienced and adept at engaging the public in three or four simultaneous sessions during Council meetings, each session dealing with an aspect of the work plan. Over these first years, JPAC members were gratified to see the process of public participation wax ever stronger in Mexico.

Running an effective consultation process for the public turned out to be no simple matter, given the different national styles of public participation: the Canadians, with their well-tuned ear for process and procedure; the Americans, impatient to obtain results, attending sporadically; and the Mexicans reveling in the opportunity to participate openly in a democratic forum with their North American counterparts. Since JPAC, with only fifteen members, could in no way claim to represent all the NGOs, business and professional groups, academics, and state and local governments involved, it had to earn its legitimacy and acceptance as a facilitator of open public dialogue. This it did in cooperation with the U.S. NAC, a multistakeholder group advising the EPA, and the Governmental Advisory Committee (GAC), representing subfederal and tribal officials. (The Canadian and Mexican counterpart organizations were and are less institutionalized.) Clearly, JPAC has been heavily invested into running public meetings. JPAC has learned how to engage the public, although in truth there will always be room for improvement and fine tuning of this central function of its mission.

Power of the purse has not been available to JPAC. Phrasing this more precisely, the early and persistent willingness of JPAC to give advice to ministers on budgets has had no effect. For several years running, JPAC advised the Council that the funding allocated to the CEC was insufficient to grow the operation. This shortfall problem was exacerbated by the ministers' tendency at times to add on more tasks without the requisite increase in funds to carry them out. Especially problematical was the decision taken in 1995 at Oaxaca to create the North American Fund for Environmental Cooperation (NAFEC), a granting program, which under excellent leadership soon engaged scores of grass-roots NGOs in environmental projects but at the cost of carving US$1 million out of the overall total budget of US$9 million. NAFEC is a jewel, another first in continental cooperation. But in 2000, even as applications grew into the hundreds, its annual budget was cut drastically, to $500,000.[9] Knowing that the overall budget for the CEC was anemic, the EPA offered to double its contribution, but the other two nations chose not to follow suit, and the budget remains inadequate. JPAC's one budgetary success was in obtaining a modest line item in the CEC budget to cover its own operating expenses, including a small staff and the not inconsiderable costs of the public consultations, including a modest travel fund for representatives of the public to attend meetings.

If JPAC failed to become a burr under the Council's budgetary saddle, it soon demonstrated its utility to Council in the Silva Reservoir case. Ducks migrating south from Canada and the United States died by the tens of thousands after alighting on the toxic waters of a lake in Guanajuato. The Audubon Society and Mexican associates responded by bringing the first citizen submission to the CEC. Had they chosen to do so, they could have brought the submission pursuant to Article 14, under which the CEC can consider allegations that a Party has failed to effectively enforce its domestic laws. But in consultation with Victor Lichtinger, then Executive Director of the Secretariat, the environmental groups decided instead to request the Secretariat to prepare a report under Article 13, which gives the Secretariat broad authority to investigate environmental problems related to the CEC work plan, which includes programs on migratory birds. Accordingly, a trinational experts panel was authorized to report on the Silva Reservoir die-off. Highly embarrassing to Mexico, the Silva Reservoir case was defused by a scientifically sound report that not only pinpointed the cause (botulism, rather than heavy metals from tanneries upriver) but also finessed the clumsy efforts of some local officials to cover up the die-off. JPAC was asked to assess the report in draft and, if it passed muster, to endorse it, which JPAC did. With this report (*Presa Silva*, 1995) the CEC proved its utility to the then governor of Guanajuato, Vicente Fox, and reaped favorable publicity in the Mexican press. Julia Carabias, the Mexican minister, was praised for meeting with angry petitioners from the start and for supporting the investigation. For its part, the Council was grateful to JPAC for helping to legitimize the CEC's science-based approach to this highly charged environmental issue.

JPAC members participated actively in the preparation of subsequent Article 13 reports, including *Pollutant Pathways*, a study of the long-range transport of air pollution in North America, issued in 1997. The individual studies of pollutants in this report played in nicely with a program called the Sound Management of Chemicals (SMOC), an ongoing program of the CEC, on which JPAC members have also served. For example, the problem of persistent organic pollutants getting into the food chain of native peoples was the subject of a joint meeting with the Arctic Council JPAC held in Anchorage. Barry Commoner served on this panel, among others.

The author of this chapter was privileged to be a member of the advisory committee on the San Pedro Project, which examined ways to preserve migratory bird habitat on the U.S. side of the San Pedro River, which flows from Sonora north into Arizona. The report, *Ribbon of Life* (1997), which included an experts' report as well, suggested ways that residents of rapidly growing Sierra Vista and environs in Arizona could calibrate water use with habitat conservation. They were presented with a classic choice: take corrective action and the birds would survive; continue their unsustainable water mining practices and Sierra Vista would be known as the town that killed the birds migrating between Canada and Central America on the last unchannelized river in the American Southwest. The report was the product also of extensive public consultations. Subsequently, stakeholder groups have formed on both sides of the border to address the findings and recommendations in the report.[10]

Electricity and the Environment (2001) is the latest and the most ambitious of the Article 13 reports. With this well-crafted investigation the CEC has truly come of age, and the report itself has been well received in Ottawa, Washington, and Mexico City. A JPAC member sits on the expert panel of this wide-ranging and revealing study of the increased pollution loadings that can be expected from the surge of power plant construction on the U.S.-Mexican border.

In recent years, regular JPAC meetings have sometimes been held in conjunction with one of the working groups. The above-mentioned session in Anchorage is a good example. Another was the 2001 meeting in Winnipeg held with the working group on Green Trade Corridors, the study of major north-south highway linkages and ways to manage their environmental impacts. And in April 2002, JPAC met with the Children's Health and the Environment working group in Mexico City. These joint meetings are another way to provide public access to the ongoing work of the Commission.

The range and variety of interactions bespeak a close and comfortable relationship between JPAC and the Secretariat, with its trinational staff of scientists, lawyers, communication specialists, and experts in community development. JPAC itself is ably staffed by the Secretariat, which has become adept at fielding four JPAC meetings a year, including JPAC's participation in the yearly meeting of the Council. Moreover, the flow of information between these two branches is robust, as exemplified by the regular briefings to JPAC given by the Director and her deputy, the Director of Programs, and the frequent networking between JPAC individual members and the Secretariat.

In contrast, relations with Council, while cordial at the ministerial level, have a tendency to become strained and even confrontational with the Alternate Representatives (called Alt Reps), deputies at the subministerial level who meet regularly during the year to oversee the work of the Commission when the Council is not in session. As is abundantly clear, the CEC is not an independent body; rather, it reports to three governments that do not always agree among themselves. Here the role of nationality is central and pervasive. It falls to the Alt Reps to translate national interest into collective policy for approval by their principals. When the Alt Reps themselves do not agree, the bureaucratic response is to hunker down and narrow down. The contrast with the nongovernmental JPAC and its broad and flexible mission is striking. In fact, the JPAC's nickname for the Alt Reps is the "B team." That the framers of the CEC saw fit to put two such different entities cheek by jowl in the new Commission is a cause for wonder. But, to be sure, with one significant exception, it works.

Frustrated in the initial years by the "B team's" predilection for decision-making behind closed doors, JPAC petitioned to be included and soon won access to their meetings. Initially, the JPAC chair attending could only observe, but today he or she is a full participant when the agenda turns to matters concerning JPAC. Yet relations remain wary, in part because of the structural differences that divide two such different branches of the CEC but in part, also, because of the persistent and troubling dispute over how to implement the right for any citizen to petition any government in North America for nonenforcement of environmental law under Article 14 of the NAAEC.[11] Because the three governments have never reached agreement on all aspects of this submission procedure—which is arguably the most innovative process in the NAAEC—the Alt Reps' discomfort with it has drawn in JPAC. As a group, these volunteers would rather spend their time on other things, but they find themselves by fate and by duty playing a central role in the Article 14 imbroglio. Because dealing with this issue has taken up a good deal of JPAC's time, it is well to probe it in some detail.

As is abundantly clear to readers of this book, the CEC is much less an environmental watchdog than it is a vehicle for discussing, studying, and hopefully inspiring cooperative solutions to some very controversial issues. To the extent that it deals with enforcement at all, the NAEEC provides for large fines down the road for a nation failing to rectify a persistent pattern of pollution. Such a finding would apply only if the ministers accepted it by majority vote. The obstacles, including a large measure of political realism, militate against such an outcome.[12] Nonetheless, Canada evidently fears that a finding of a persistent pattern of nonenforcement in that country might open it to a large liability down the road or might even conceivably be used against it by the United States as a trade weapon. This would explain why Canada has sought to narrow the scope of factual records to a single instance of failure to enforce. As for Mexico, it has been concerned with the potential for disclosure of proprietary information and business secrets during the discovery process when the Secretariat prepares what is known as a factual record. Neither country much likes the Article 14 process, seeing it as having the potential to escape government control. As well, the citizen submission right under NAAEC is broader than rights granted under Mexico's new environmental law, and even Canada is less accommodating to citizen complaints. By contrast, the United States has been more comfortable with this right, which resonates with its political culture. If truth be known, Article 14 is a very American idea, and given the asymmetries in the relations among the North American countries, it is perhaps inevitable that the other NAFTA partners would balk when it came to simplifying and facilitating the process of citizen submissions and making the guidelines more transparent. It is no accident that the large majority of submissions have come from Mexican and Canadian groups seeking redress, often in partnership with American groups.

Not everything in the side agreement had been negotiated and agreed upon when NAAEC came into effect in 1994, the implementation of Article 14 being the most prominent example. In fact, there were still gaps in the language on citizen submissions in the final text. At first the sides were so far apart that the prospect of a prolonged deadlock loomed. To avoid this outcome, which would have put the fledgling Commission at risk and would certainly have alienated the environmental NGOs, the Council turned to JPAC. Validating Silva Reservoir was easy; drawing up the first operating guidelines for the citizen submission process was hard. After nearly a year of effort, including sustained consultations with the public, JPAC produced a workable document, and the Council accepted it.

However, these first JPAC guidelines were complex, in part to pass muster with the Alt Reps and their lawyers and in part to protect the Secretariat from frivolous or poorly prepared submissions. For its part, the Secretariat was slow to gear up its legal staff to process the submissions, so that after three years of operation only one factual record had been prepared by the Secretariat and approved by the Council. And as the number of submissions in the pipeline increased, public confidence in the process weakened.

Meanwhile, the Alt Reps continued to raise objections in detail, to the point where JPAC concluded that efforts were under way (particularly by the Mexican Alt Rep) to bureaucratize the submission process and to make it less transparent.[13] Additional public consultations revealed strong support for the guidelines, coupled with a demand to speed up the process, not slow it down.

Matters came to a head at the June 2000 meeting of the Council in Dallas, when JPAC protested a move by certain of the Alt Reps to change the guidelines behind closed doors while threatening the independence of the Secretariat to prepare factual records. The protest succeeded. This was a defining moment for the CEC, with the ministers backing JPAC.[14] However, the upshot was that JPAC was again charged by the Council to examine the guidelines and suggest improvements, again in consultation with the public. The process played out, and on June 6, 2001, JPAC submitted its report, entitled *Lessons Learned; Citizen Submissions under Articles 14 and 15 of the North American Agreement on Environmental Cooperation.*

In addition to recommending that the process of preparing factual records be speeded up, JPAC also advised the Council to modify the guidelines to include due process with respect to the submission of evidence and measures to enhance transparency. In keeping with its charge from the Council, JPAC reaffirmed that public consultations be held before the Council decided upon any future changes in the guidelines. This report was taken under advisement at the Council meeting held in June 2001 at Guadalajara.

Here things stood, but not for long. Surprisingly, the Alt Reps again met in closed session (in November 2001) to fine-tune the guidelines more to their liking. At issue were the terms of reference for the Secretariat in preparing factual records. To ease the backlog, the Council directed the Secretariat to prepare factual records for five submissions, but for four of these the Alt Reps dramatically limited the scope of the Secretariat investigation to a specific incident or incidents and decided not to allow a broader review of whether regulations are routinely violated. In other words, submitters will now find it more difficult to base their submission on a representative case from which implications of a persistent pattern could be drawn. Furthermore, the Secretariat was now required to submit a plan of work to the Alt Reps for review before preparing a factual record. And for the first time, the U.S. Alt Rep voted with her Mexican and Canadian counterparts to narrow the guidelines.[15]

JPAC's chair then raised strong objections at the next Alt Rep meeting. Having been charged twice before by the Council—first to develop and then to fine tune the guidelines—JPAC asked the Alt Reps to explain their changes to the guidelines in public and then asked to submit the matter to public consultation once again before resolution at the 2002 Council meeting in Ottawa.[16] Given all that had transpired, why did the Alt Reps narrow the factual records, especially in light of the fact that JPAC, the U.S. NAC, and the U.S. GAC had given specific advice to the contrary? Specifically, when a pattern of failure to enforce was alleged, what was the rationale for limiting the factual record?[17] Would the Alt Reps then use their review of the *Lessons Learned* report over time to erode the independence of the Secretariat, especially given the troublesome history that had gone on before? For its part, how could JPAC not be troubled by this latest action by the "B team"? Eager to move on to other issues, JPAC found itself once again protecting the integrity of the submissions process and also protecting the independence of the Secretariat. And through it all, the JPAC consensus has always held.

Having said this, JPAC's continued engagement in the issue was clearly important to the Council. Operating on the pragmatic principle that "where there's a will there's a way," hopefully the three governments will find agreement on this issue and then reach closure. Or could one say that with the change in U.S. administration and the effects of September 11, 2001, there appears to be less support for transparency and public participation? If so, this would be closure of a different sort.

Several examples of what these citizen-volunteers would prefer to be doing instead reflect their individual areas of expertise. A JPAC member assisted Mexican companies to become certified at the ISO 14000 level. He secured support from the U.S. Council for International Business and its Canadian counterpart in conjunction with CONCAMIN, the Mexican business council. Another JPAC member is arranging to cosponsor a multistakeholder workshop with the CEC to discuss and comment on the work of an expert group that is recommending market mechanisms to abate greenhouse gases in North America. Recently, three JPAC members attended a meeting of the NAFTA Effects group, which seeks to anticipate the next issues arising from the nexus of free trade and the environment.

A frustration to date has been JPAC's inability to move forward the long, difficult negotiations to achieve a Transboundary Environmental Impact Assessment (TEIA) treaty by the three governments. While few would deny the need for TEIA in the border regions, complex jurisdictional issues with respect to state and federal responsibilities remain to be resolved. It is possible that the current momentum for state/provincial agreements will converge and will later be incorporated into a treaty at the federal level. To date, however, the oft-expressed desire of JPAC and of the author of this chapter in particular to see TEIA through to conclusion has not borne fruit.[18]

A signal achievement was JPAC's success in convincing the Council of the need for a study of market-based mechanisms—principally a continental trading system—to address climate change.[19] The Council accepted this advice at the Guadalajara meeting in 2001 and authorized the CEC to form an expert group which, as mentioned, will soon present its findings in a workshop. After more fine-tuning, an action plan will then be presented to the public. In light of the fact that the three governments do not agree on the Kyoto Protocol, JPAC's success in putting economic instruments on the North American agenda was important. Furthermore, given the income disparities, it would seem that using North America as a regional laboratory to gain experience with a trading regime and the clean development mechanism with respect to Mexico is a very good idea.

JPAC has also been a strong supporter of making the yearly *Taking Stock* reports on toxic releases in Canada and the United States into a trinational pollution release transfer registry. Up to now, Mexican reporting has been voluntary, with spotty results. A bill to require mandatory reporting, which would be harmonized with Canadian and U.S. practice, was passed by the Mexican Congress in December 2001.[20] JPAC also played a helpful role in generating guidelines for the NAFEC as a cooperative effort, even though, as discussed above, JPAC was unable to protect NAFEC's budget.

As of current writing, an issue looming large in the minds of everyone at the CEC is what to do about Chapter 11. This is the "takings" clause in the main NAFTA treaty, now being used in ways never intended by the framers. The Chapter 11 issue is described in detail elsewhere in this book.[21] Suffice it to say here that the controversy impinges on the work of the CEC to explore the linkages between trade and environment. Indeed, some might characterize Chapter 11 as "the mother of all trade-environment issues." With this in mind, JPAC held a public consultation on the matter in Ottawa at the June 2002 meeting of the Council and provided advice to ministers.

Given the broad scope of its mandate, it is clear that in nearly eight years of operation JPAC has risen to the challenge. Throughout its engagement in many different projects and activities, it has continued to act cooperatively as a group and to make decisions by consensus. The idealistic mission statement it wrote in 1994 became operational from the start and informs what might be called the institutional culture or spirit of JPAC. JPAC's achievements owe much to the quality and diversity of the five members appointed by each government. The large majority of members have come from business, the law, NGOs, and universities. The one state government official (appointed by the White House for political reasons) did not work out, preferring to build his résumé without coming to meetings. In any case, for the United States at least, officials at the subfederal level are best represented on the GAC.

JPAC was fortunate indeed to have elected Jacques Gérin, a Quebec engineer, to serve as its first chair. In addition to drawing on his considerable experience in government, Gérin had a strong affinity for decision-making by consensus and helped set the tone of JPAC from then on. He was followed by Jonathan Plaut, former vice president for environmental management at Allied Signal and currently professor of environmental management at Penn State. Plaut's corporate experience and forceful personality enabled him to get things done, and such was his effectiveness that members elected him three times to the rotating chair. The first Mexican chair was María Cristina Castro, representing an NGO from Yucatán. She was followed by Mary Simon, who was also Canada's ambassador to the Arctic Council. Regina Barba, a publisher and prominent environmentalist in Mexico City, served her turn as chair and is now an undersecretary at SEMARNAT, the Mexican Environment Secretariat. Most recently, Liette Vasseur, a conservation biologist who holds the K. C. Irving Chair in Sustainable Development at the University of Moncton in New Brunswick, served as chair.

In a brief chapter it is not possible to mention everyone who has served or is now serving on JPAC (see Appendix B), yet touching on a few of them will indicate the range and variety of members. Jorge Bustamante, a prominent Mexican sociologist and first president of the Colegio de la Frontera Norte, also served as the first chair of the Border Environment Cooperation Commission. Mike Apsey represented the Canadian forest products industry in British Columbia. Peter A. A. Berle, former New York State Commissioner of Environment and past President of the National Audubon Society, has served on JPAC since its inception. Jean Richardson, an environmental law professor at the University of Vermont, helped spearhead JPAC's effort to develop the initial guidelines for citizen submissions under Article 14. And Ernesto Enkerlin, formerly of Pronatura, now serves as director of wildlife refuges and protected areas in the Fox administration.

Finally, the JPAC model has legs. In Santiago, Chile, the author was privileged to attend the installation of a six-member JPAC under the Canada-Chile Agreement on Environmental Cooperation, signed in 1998. Modeled on NAAEC, this new agreement went forward when it became clear that the U.S. Congress would not vote for a free trade agreement with Chile. For its part, JPAC was ready to welcome Chileans to the JPAC table. But this was not to be, and the Canada-Chile agreement went forward instead.[22]

On the other hand, the JPAC model and even something resembling the CEC is noticeably absent in the emerging architecture of the Free Trade Area of the Americas.[23] In fact, most Latin American officials want nothing to do with this model, based as it is on transparency and public participation. A political culture of paternalism and control still exerts a strong pull. Traditional trade–types dislike linking trade with the environment—the Mexican trade ministry worked against the CEC during the Zedillo administration. They exaggerate the risks, while failing to take notice of the diverse and useful roles that a strong citizen group like JPAC can play.

"There is nothing like the CEC in the world," concludes Bill Nitze, the former U.S. Alt Rep. JPAC is a creative way to get society involved, he continues, "and because of its history and structure in theory maintains a certain independence of government. But it is fragile. Governments should have the self-confidence to respect this independence, even if they don't agree with the Secretariat and JPAC."[24] In addition to the quality of its members, a good deal of JPAC's effectiveness has been its access to the ministers. Were this to be downgraded to the deputy minister level, it is doubtful that JPAC would get such a strong level of participants or be as effective. "Power comes only if the ministers choose to listen," Carol Browner concludes.[25] As well, JPAC is also still evolving internally—especially by the more effective use of subcommittees, which will strengthen its ability to contribute.

In this chapter I have attempted to relate the highlights of JPAC's activities since its formation in 1994. Still a young organization, the CEC has made extraordinary progress in addressing environmental issues that until recently had little or no resonance across all three countries. With its broad and flexible mandate, JPAC has contributed to this process of dialogue and discovery, while linking ministers to the broader public. Undeniably, much remains to be done. Through it all, JPAC members have continued to act as North Americans, cooperatively, by consensus. No small achievement.

Appendix A
Joint Public Advisory Committee Vision Statement

The Joint Public Advisory Committee (JPAC), together with the Council and the Secretariat comprise the North American Commission for Environmental Cooperation (CEC), a unique institution charged with seizing an historic opportunity.

The North American Agreement on Environmental Cooperation sets a precedent as a formal environmental agreement adopted in parallel with a trade agreement, and the Commission it created also set a precedent by including a public, nongovernmental advisory group as one of its components.

JPAC was established as a cooperative mechanism to advise the Council in its deliberations and to advise the Secretariat in its planning and activities.

Our vision is to promote continental cooperation in ecosystem protection and sustainable economic development, and to ensure active public participation and transparency in the actions of the Commission.

While we come from three different nations, and have different institutional connections, we serve on the JPAC as individual citizens of the North American continent, joined in a commitment to preserving and enhancing our common environment and to achieving a sustainable society.

JPAC will work to provide firm leadership and constructive contributions to build a trinational model of collaboration, consensus building, and consensus-based results. JPAC is, in effect, a model for the future in a process which is without precedent, and which presents a great opportunity for cooperative progress.

26 July 1994
Washington, D.C.

Appendix B
Joint Public Advisory Committee Members

CANADA

Mike Apsey	July 1994–March 1998
Cam Avery	June 2000–December 2003*
Ann Bourget	April 2001–December 2004*
Dan Christmas	February 2003–
Michael Cloghesy	July 1994–December 1998
Louise Comeau	July 1994–June 1997
Jacques Gérin	July 1994–December 1999*
Rosemarie Kuptana	July 1994–July 1996
Merrell-Ann Phare	April 2001–December 2004*
Jonathan Scarth	November 1998–August 2000*
Mary Simon	March 1997–December 2000*
Donna Tingley	April 1998–December 2004*
Liette Vasseur	April 1999–December 2002*

MEXICO

Gustavo Alanís-Ortega	May 2001–
Regina Barba	March 1999–December 2000
Francisco Barnés	July 1994–January 1997
Guillermo Barroso	July 1994–March 1999
Mindahi Crescencio Bastida Muñoz	March 2002–
Daniel Basurto	March 1999–March 2002
Jorge Bustamante	July 1994–March 1999
María Cristina Castro	July 1994–March 1998
Adriana Nelly Correa Sandoval	March 2002–
Jesús Druk	June 1998–April 1999
Ernesto Enkerlin	December 1999–January 2001
Exequiel Ezcurra	October 1997–January 1998
Ivan Restrepo	July 1994–March 1999
Carlos Sandoval Olvera	March 2002–
Laura Silvan de Durazo	May 2001–
Raúl Tornel	June 1998–March 2002
Blanca Torres	March 1999–March 2002

UNITED STATES

Peter Berle	July 1994–January 2003
Patricia Clarcy	February 2003–
Dinkerrai Desai	February 2003–
Arturo Duran	February 2003–
Jane Gardner	February 2003–
Patricia McDonald	February 2003–
Dan Morales	July 1994–September 1998
Steve Owens	September 1999–January 2003
Jonathan Plaut	July 1994–January 2003
Jean Richardson	July 1994–June 1999
Serena Wilson	April 2000–February 2003
John Wirth	July 1994–June 2002

*Fixed mandate.

Notes

1. Pierre Marc Johnson and André Beaulieu, *The Environment and NAFTA: Understanding and Implementing the New Continental Law* 140 (1996). In preparing this chapter I am grateful for comments by the editors, Peter Berle, Jacques Gérin, and Jonathan Plaut.

2. *Environmental Management on North America's Borders* 3–11 (Richard Kiy and John D. Wirth eds., 1998).

3. Kathleen Rogers, interview with author, Feb. 14, 2002.

4. Daniel Magraw, phone conversation with author, Mar. 27, 2002.

5. Carol Browner, interview with author, Feb. 14, 2002; William Nitze, former Assistant Administrator for International Affairs at the EPA, phone conversation with author, Feb. 14, 2002.

6. This model followed a practice developed by the North American Institute to facilitate discussion by having a Canadian make the first presentation, then an American would speak, followed by a Mexican presenter. By advocating cooperation instead of fines and sanctions ("guns 'n' badges"), the North American Institute also contributed to the architecture of the CEC. Mario Aguilar, Mexico's environmental representative, endorsed this approach at the February 12–14, 1993, forum held in Santa Fe, New Mexico. See NAMI, "The North American Environment: Opportunities for Trilateral Cooperation," Feb. 12–14, 1993.

7. John Wirth wrote this chapter in spring 2002, shortly before his death. In early 2003, the Bush administration appointed an entirely new slate of U.S. members—Eds.

8. Today the program concentrates in four areas: Environment, Economy and Trade; Law and Policy; Conservation of Biodiversity; and Pollutants and Health.

9. Attempts to interest foundations in partnering with the CEC to support NAFEC did not bear fruit.

10. For a discussion of the San Pedro report, see ch. 12, infra.

11. For additional analysis of the citizen submissions procedure, see chs. 13–15, infra.

12. Part Five of the NAAEC allows one country to seek a finding from an arbitral tribunal that another country has engaged in a persistent pattern of failure to effectively enforce its environmental laws, which in theory could result in sanctions if the Party does not change its ways, but the process depends on a two-thirds vote by the Council. Under Article 14, citizens may allege that one of the countries is failing to effectively enforce its laws, but the allegation can result in at most a factual record prepared by the Secretariat under Article 15. Moreover, the Council must approve, by a two-thirds vote, the Secretariat's request to prepare such a factual record and its publication after it is completed. There is no formal link between factual records and sanctions under Part Five, and the Secretariat cannot trigger the Part Five procedure. However, the preparation of a factual record can and does attract press attention and public scrutiny, the effect of which can generate a powerful beam of "intrusive sunshine."

13. As Peter Berle relates: "The pattern has been that when a filing is made against a government its apparatchiks go into overdrive to change the submission rules." Peter Berle, memo to the author, Mar. 17, 2002.

14. Put another way, Administrator Browner "made full use of JPAC to prevent Canada and Mexico from shutting down the submission process." Nitze interview, supra. On Nitze's own pivotal role Berle writes: "I think Bill Nitze's tireless efforts year after year to stop the Article 14 processes from being eviscerated through procedural rule changes should be noted. Also a group of NGO lawyers has weighed in heavily, as well as the US and Canadian NACs." Berle memo, supra.

15. For a description and analysis of the November 2001 resolutions, see ch. 15, infra.

16. JPAC, Advice to Council No. 01-07 re: Citizen Submissions on Enforcement Matters under Articles 14 and 15 of NAAEC, Oct. 23, 2001. See also Stephen Porter, Center for International Environmental Law, to JPAC, memorandum re: US Position on Migratory Bird Submission, Oct. 17, 2001.

17. As reported in the *Globe and Mail* (Toronto) (Nov. 21, 2001), Noreen Smith, the Canadian Alt Rep, "defended the action, saying it is better to look at a single accusation that a country has not applied environmental rules, rather than having open-ended investigations involving many such allegations. [She said,] 'I think it's a lot more powerful to investigate what happened in a particular instance than it is to look at more general allegations.'" As for Judith Ayres, the new U.S. Alt Rep, she was responsive to strong objections from the U.S. Department of Interior to the terms of reference in the migratory bird submission.

18. See ch. 5, supra; see also John D. Wirth, "If So, Then What: The Struggle for TEIA," unpublished paper, Feb. 18, 2002 (on file with editors).

19. JPAC, Advice to Council No. 01-04 re: Climate Change, June 28, 2001.

20. See ch. 3, supra.

21. See ch. 10, supra.

22. For information on the Canada-Chile Agreement on Environmental Cooperation Joint Public Advisory Committee, see *http://can-chil.gc.ca/English/Profile/JPAC/Default.cfm.*

23. In these negotiations, the Committee of Government Representatives on Civil Society is said to be "unique in that it is the first group specifically created in a trade negotiation to receive directly input from members of civil society for use in those trade negotiations." As yet, however, no mechanism for direct and unfiltered public advice has been created. FTAA, Office of NAFTA and Inter-American Affairs, "Free Trade Area of the Americas," Jan. 2002, *http://www.mac.doc.gov/ftaa2005/participation.htm.* Meanwhile, in these FTAA discussions, the environment languishes. What a contrast with debates in the run-up to NAFTA, as described by John J. Audley, *Green Politics and Global Trade: NAFTA and the Future of Environmental Politics* (1997).

24. Nitze interview, supra.

25. Browner interview, supra.

A. DAN TARLOCK AND JOHN E. THORSON 12

Coordinating Land and Water Use in the San Pedro River Basin

What Role for the CEC?

NAFTA IS A "trade law plus" regime because it tries to integrate the promotion of free trade and environmental protection through environmental and labor side agreements. The North American Agreement on Environmental Cooperation (NAAEC) created the Commission for Environmental Cooperation (CEC), which can pressure the member countries to enforce existing environmental laws and generate an information base to stimulate new environmental protection initiatives.[1] The CEC Secretariat can perform two important information and assembly functions reaching below the national level into the activities of subsidiary governmental units. First, under Articles 14 and 15, the Secretariat can accept and review citizen submissions alleging that one of the three countries is not enforcing its existing environmental laws. If the Secretariat recommends the preparation of a nonbinding factual record, only two of the three members of the cabinet-level Council must agree. A factual record sets out the evidence for and against the allegation without drawing explicit legal conclusions.[2]

Second, under Article 13, the Secretariat may undertake a wide range of studies, including on transboundary environmental problems, to disseminate scientific information on environmental problems common to Canada, Mexico, and the United States. Article 13 authorizes the preparation of Secretariat reports "on any matter within the scope of the annual program" without Council approval. (The Secretariat may prepare reports on other matters—except ineffective enforcement—unless the Council objects.) The scope of the annual program is broad and always includes projects aimed at biodiversity conservation, among other areas. Article 13 reports are broader in scope than the Article 14–15 submission process because, as the San Pedro River case study presented here illustrates, they may inquire into the adequacy of existing domestic laws—not simply whether they are underenforced. The relationship between Article 13 reports and Article 14–15 submissions is not always clear, but they can play off each other, and parties may substitute one for the other. For example, the San Pedro report was undertaken after an Article 14 submission by the Southwest Center for Biological Diversity, which alleged that the U.S. Army had failed to enforce the U.S. National Environmental Policy Act (NEPA) in expanding Fort Huachuca, was withdrawn and an Article 13 report requested in lieu of a factual record. John Knox has suggested that the two processes should be seen as complementary alternatives to promoting compliance with the NAAEC.[3] There are examples of Articles 13 and 14–15 processes that have triggered similar changes in party behavior. Our case study of the San Pedro River suggests that Article 15 factual records are likely to shine a more powerful light on undesirable environmental behavior compared to Article 13 studies but that such studies can help change user attitudes and indirectly support more concrete environmental protection actions.

The three countries have not yet adopted the model of the European Union and created both supranational legislative and judicial authorities with the power to enact binding legislation and the power to review and invalidate domestic laws.[4] Under the NAAEC, the three countries retain their sovereign right to decide which environmental laws to enact and do not need to harmonize them to a supranational standard. NAFTA only curtails the use of domestic environmental laws to restrain trade. Nonetheless, the CEC is an important legal evolution because it is a hybrid agency combining elements of two competing theories of how to achieve compliance with international norms. More broadly, it can be seen as an effort to escape the confines of existing theories of international law and enforcement that play almost no formal role in the development of transnational environmental law regimes.

Article 13 can be characterized as an example of postmodern, "soft" or "reflexive" international law because it seeks to influence public and private behavior without the threat of the enforcement of traditional, sanction-based "hard" law.[5] Lawyers find it hard to imagine that law can exist without coercive enforcement. Followers of H.L.A. Hart's positivist theory of law argue that supranational adjudication is the most effective mechanism for obtaining compliance with international law.[6] Hart's followers have the better jurisprudential argument, but this narrow definition of international law suffers from many defects and does not take into account the numerous changes that have occurred in international law since the end of World War II, such as the roles of nonstate actors and multinational organizations (including the ubiquitous nongovernmental organizations, or NGOs) in the law-making process. The net result of post–World War II international law is that proponents of increased fidelity to international norms and processes have to settle for messier, imperfect forms of enforcement. Otherwise, international law would be a static rather than a dynamic body of law. In this spirit, others argue that there are managerial alternatives to supranational adjudication, such as the informal settlement of disputes and domestic compliance capacity building.[7] Scholars searching for alternative forms of compliance with these norms have borrowed from the human rights experience the idea of disclosing embarrassing information to shame states into compliance. Many students of the evolution of both domestic and international environmental law have suggested that the assembly and dissemination of environmental impact information can be an important regulatory policy instrument.[8]

The CEC has considerable power to shine a bright light into places that all three countries would rather remain dark through its power to study selected cases of nonenforcement and to collect and disseminate information about existing resource laws and policy. This chapter tests the effectiveness of this role by examining the impact of a 1999 Commission report, *Ribbon of Life: An Agenda for Preserving Transboundary Bird Habitat on the Upper San Pedro River.*[9] The San Pedro River is an excellent case study to examine the potential newly emerging "soft" and reflexive international law regime, using information disclosure to influence well-entrenched domestic water allocation and land-use regimes long operating free of international constraints. *Ribbon of Life* concluded that groundwater depletion in Arizona threatens to destroy a broadleaf riparian forest and recommended an altered pumping regime. The specific recommended changes were not enacted by the state of Arizona, which restricts groundwater pumping only in highly stressed urban and agricultural basins. The report did produce important attitudinal changes in the basin and widespread agreement among basin residents and key American and Mexican decision-makers about the nature of the basin's environmental problems.[10] Enabling people to view a landscape as a functioning ecosystem is an essential first step toward biodiversity conservation. This chapter examines the theory of information dissemination as a substitute for direct regulation, assesses why it was not more effective in Arizona, and speculates about the success of future "sunshine" studies and reports that require substantial changes in domestic law and policy.

San Pedro River Valley

THE RESOURCE, ITS CONSTITUENTS, AND THE BROADER ISSUES

The San Pedro River is a small, international river arising in Sonora, Mexico, and flowing northward into the state of Arizona. It joins the Gila

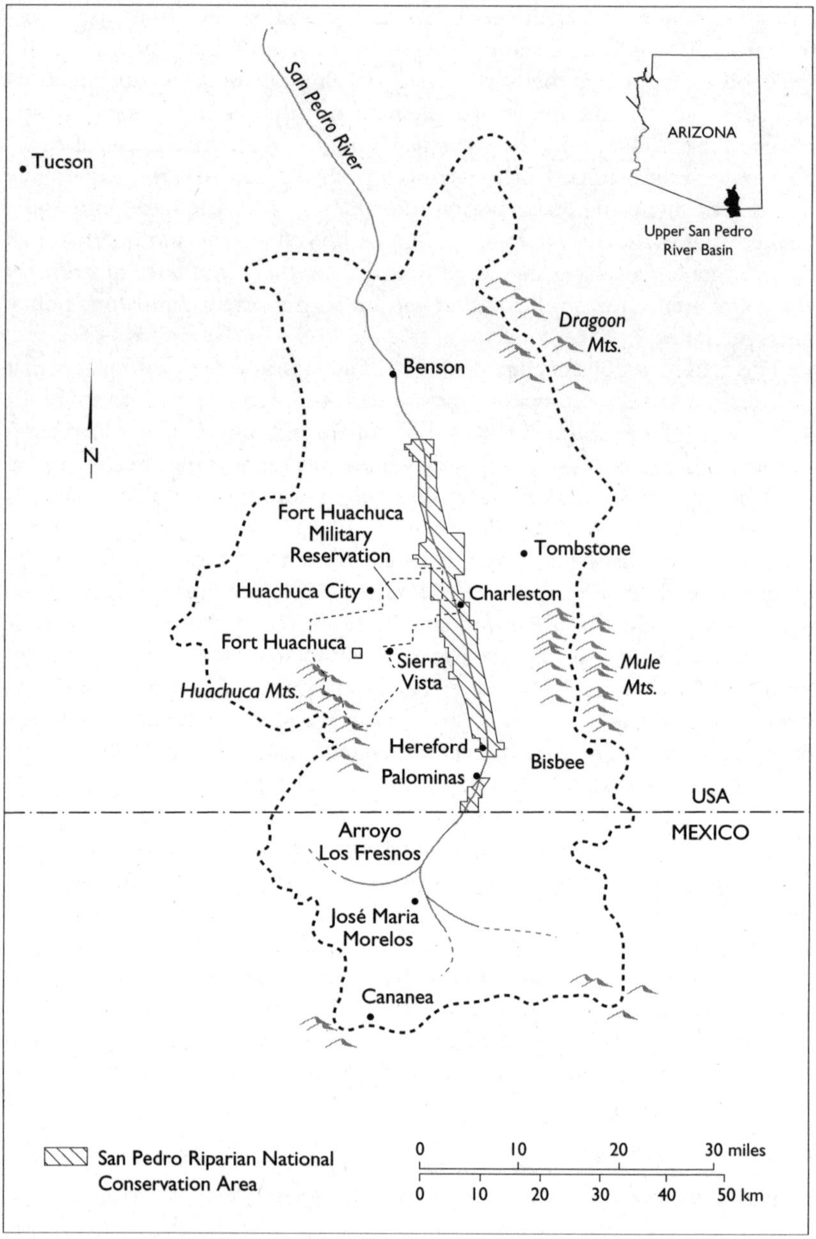

The Upper San Pedro River Basin

River, itself a tributary of the Colorado River, near Winkelman. The river has a total length of 151 miles, with its headwaters 30 miles south of the international border. The basin, with a north-northwest orientation, comprises 4,485 square miles of semiarid land. Mexico's portion of the basin is approximately 696 square miles. The Babocomari River and Aravaipa Creek, both rising in Arizona, are the river's two main tributaries. A regional alluvial aquifer consisting of older basin fill materials is the largest source of groundwater. The water supply of the basin is about 160,000 acre-feet per year.[11]

Unlike most western United States rivers, the Upper San Pedro is undammed from its headwaters to its confluence with the Gila. The river's hydrograph is typical of small western rivers in semiarid regions. Its highest flows are during winter and spring floods, and its lowest flows are from April to June before the arrival of the desert monsoon season.[12] April to June flows are supported by the Sierra Vista subbasin aquifer. This transnational aquifer holds some 50 million acre-feet of water.

Although not one of the world's major contested rivers, the small, narrow San Pedro basin is a microcosm of the water and related land-use conflicts faced in many areas around the world.[13] The fundamental conflict is between those who hold existing rights, or the expectation of rights, acquired in an era when development was the sole objective of the water allocation and land-use law and more contemporary values emphasizing the maintenance or restoration of ecosystem functions.[14] Thus, the San Pedro can be simultaneously characterized as a "transboundary heritage resource or biodiversity reserve," a source of water for agricultural and expanding urban uses in the United States, and a sink for copper mining wastes in Mexico.[15] To complicate matters, the conservation of the San Pedro as a biodiversity reserve is both a problem of water use and land use. In both countries, the law has served to detach water rights from their watersheds by favoring exploitation over environmentally sustainable use.[16] This detachment has also been facilitated by the long tradition of regulating the use of land and water by two separate, unintegrated legal regimes. In the United States, water rights are administered by the state while land-use control is delegated to local government. In Mexico, Article 27 of the federal constitution specifies that the original ownership of land and water belongs to the nation. While the nation may transfer these resources to private persons, it may at any time impose restrictions favoring fair distribution of wealth, conservation, and the public interest.[17]

The basin's fate is currently shared between in-basin entitlement holders and local governments and out-of-basin actors. The most important out-of-basin actors are the federal Bureau of Land Management, manager of the San Pedro Riparian National Conservation Area (SPRNCA), and the U.S. Department of the Army, operator of the 120-year-old Fort Huachuca Military Reservation. The San Pedro's biological resources have been well documented, and biodiversity conservation in the San Pedro does not lack for advocates. Mexican and U.S. NGOs and government agencies are heavily involved in studying the evolution of the basin and in devising biodiversity conservation strategies.[18]

The Commission report states that "the San Pedro River riparian ecosystem is of critical importance in maintaining regional biodiversity at the ecotone between the Sonoran and Chihuahuan Deserts and Plains grassland."[19] The San Pedro's location in the uplands of these two ecosystems allows it to maintain a high level of biodiversity. The Upper San Pedro, from its origin to Benson, contains over twenty different biotic communities. Three of these, cottonwood and willow forests, river marshlands or cienegas, and big sacaton grasslands, are considered endangered. In Mexico, four biotic communities, two forests and two grasslands, provide "outstanding" biological values. Together, the binational biotic communities constitute one of the most important migratory bird habitats in North America and contain some eighty species of mammals and forty species of reptiles and amphibians. Three species, the Huachuca water-umbel, the southwestern willow flycatcher, and the jaguar, are listed as endangered under the U.S. Endangered Species Act, and twelve bird species are classified as Wildlife of Special Concern by the state of Arizona. An internationally important wintering area for birds, the SPRNCA extends along the river for thirty-six miles northward from the international border. The area comprises 47,668 acres and was acquired by the Bureau of Land Management in the 1980s. The reserve was formally dedicated on May 6, 1989, as America's first Riparian National Conservation Area.[20]

HYDROLOGIC BALANCE IN THE BASIN

The Upper San Pedro hydrologic balance has long been crucial to the maintenance of the river's ecosystem services, but this balance is threatened by increased water use. Data collected by the Arizona Department of Water Resources suggests that the basin is in overdraft by as much as 22,000 acre-feet per year.[21] One of the major teachings of the rapidly developing science of large river ecology is that rivers must be seen in the context of the landscapes through which they flow. This may seem obvious, but it was not always so.[22] Specifically, rivers are connected to adjacent floodplains and forest areas, and anthropocentric changes breaking the connectivity pose great environmental risks. This is precisely the situation on the Upper San Pedro with respect to groundwater withdrawals.

The natural state of the basin is one of dynamic equilibrium. Precipitation recharges the groundwater supporting the riparian vegetation crucial to biodiversity maintenance. Like other desert rivers, the San Pedro's flows vary seasonably and over time. Base or spring flows provide the basic support necessary to sustain riparian plants when the floodplain is dry. These flows are sustained by the system's deep aquifer. Riparian vegetation needs both base flows and periodic flood pulses. Brief floods, which generally occur in the summer monsoon season, wet the soil and permit species such as cottonwood and willow trees to regenerate. Desert vegetation is well adapted to long dry periods and to flood pulses but is put at risk when the dynamic water balance is permanently altered. A small decrease in groundwater discharge from the principal aquifer of one cubic foot per second (cfs) would cause the river to go dry for forty-five days in a dry year.[23] Permanent groundwater declines of one meter or more could cause a loss of vigor or even death of cottonwoods. In the San Pedro, a decrease in groundwater depth of one to two meters below the thalweg (the middle of the river) would result in an unacceptable "ecologically degraded state."[24] Most marshland avian species would be lost, and migrating songbirds would decline substantially.

GROUNDWATER PUMPING ACTIVITY

Pumping is increasing in the San Pedro Valley. If recharge is less than the rate of extraction, groundwater levels will permanently fall. This is the story of Arizona's long history of groundwater use. The problem is complicated in the basin because there is extensive pumping in both the Mexican upper basin and the U.S. lower basin. The overall effect of Mexican groundwater pumping is not thought to reach the Sierra Vista subbasin in the United States, but "[t]he transborder connections between groundwater sub-basins of the upper San Pedro basin are not well known."[25] Historically, the largest groundwater user in the lower basin was Fort Huachuca, but the base's extractions are declining due to aggressive conservation measures and the loss of personnel.

Irrigated agriculture is a minor but not unimportant use in the basin, since most of the American irrigated acreage is supplied by wells. In 1990, approximately 21,000 acres were irrigated in Arizona and 5,100 acres in Mexico. Depending on methodology, estimates of water diverted for agricultural uses range from 70,000 to 100,000 acre-feet per year.[26] Irrigated acreage decreased by 3,170 acres between 1970 and 1992 in the United States but increased by 390 acres in Mexico.[27] After the establishment of the SPRNCA, the Bureau of Land Management and the Nature Conservancy purchased all existing water rights in the area. The buyout triggered the expansion of new center-pivot irrigation on acreage adjacent to the SPRNCA for high-water-use pasture crops fluctuating widely in price. The retirement of existing water rights is an extremely cost-effective strategy, given the relatively low contribution of irrigated agriculture to the local economy compared to the increasing revenues from birding tourism. *Ribbon of Life* expressed concern that some landowners may be engaging in classic strategic behavior: putting previously fallow land into production for the sole purpose of being bought out.

Mining has also been a large user of water on the American side of the border. In 1991, one company, the largest user of water in the basin, used eleven wells (five close to the river) to pump an estimated 23,000 acre-feet per year.[28]

The largest potential source of future groundwater use is urban development. Forty-four municipal systems and private water companies now operate in the Arizona portion of the basin, pumping over 8,000 acre-feet per year from wells and springs.[29] The city of Sierra Vista is a typical rapidly growing southwestern community. However, the impact of future urban development on groundwater levels is difficult to predict because urban communities can both be a source of further depletion and new recharge through treated sewage releases or the construction of improved storm water catchment basins. Mexican use is not as significant as U.S. use. Mexico maintains some 209 wells for irrigation, livestock maintenance, and municipal and industrial use. The largest town in the basin is Cananea with a population of 30,000. A copper mine, Mexicana de Cobre, is located over the Cananea aquifer, but the current consensus is that pumping from the aquifer does not have a significant impact on upstream base flows.[30]

THE FUTURE OF THE BASIN

Ribbon of Life considered three options: (1) the reduction of present water consumption below current levels; (2) transbasin imports from either the Douglas Basin or the Central Arizona Project, bringing Colorado River water as far as Tucson; and (3) the continued mining of the aquifer to meet current and future demands and to supplement San Pedro base flows. Reduced water consumption would require eliminating agricultural uses on 500 acres of land near Hereford, Arizona, which the report describes as of marginal local economic benefit.[31] Three other approaches were considered. The first was voluntary sales or state-federal land exchanges. The second was the use of existing regulatory instruments, such as the Arizona Groundwater Management Act or the federal Endangered Species Act. The third was to file and claim instream flows, based on the federal reserved water rights doctrine, in the Gila River general stream adjudication.

The Legal Framework for Land and Water

Aside from control of its retained public lands and specific problems such as the reclamation of mined coal lands, the American federal government has not directly invoked its potential powers to regulate the use of land.[32]

Within American states, land-use power has been delegated to cities and counties, and interjurisdictional coordination remains weak. Arizona has no statewide land-use planning, and the state exerts almost no influence on local land-use controls. Nations face almost no international constraints on the control of land, except for land uses that are the site of transboundary pollution. The passage of NAFTA has focused attention on the disparity among the parties' legal regimes and their levels of development and environmental protection, but as of yet formal transborder coordination of land and water use is rare.

The allocation of water has been a jealously guarded territorial prerogative. American states must surrender their exclusive control only to federal programs based on the Commerce Clause or other federal powers. State governments in America have yielded their exclusive right to allocate water only when an interstate stream has been involved, Native American water rights must be satisfied, a federal reclamation or environmental mandate exists, or the United States has assumed treaty obligations to Canada or Mexico. Nations have been even more reluctant to surrender their water allocation prerogatives. International water law is premised on a minimal state duty to share international rivers and associated groundwater to allow each riparian to use its equitable or fair share of a stream.

Mexico allocates water through a national allocation law, while in the United States, the state of Arizona has effective control of the basin's water resources. The Mexican constitution declares that both surface water and groundwater are the property of the nation, and the Regulation of National Waters Law provides that both surface water and groundwater users must apply to the National Water Commission for a permit.[33] The Commission has almost total discretion to decide to issue a fifty-year permit.

Surface water rights in Arizona are governed by the doctrine of prior appropriation, and appropriative permits must be obtained from the state Department of Water Resources. Arizona has the most stringent groundwater conservation program in the country, but it is limited to four areas of the state, called Active Management Areas (AMAs).[34] The San Pedro basin falls outside the geographic boundaries of the AMAs because it is neither populous nor a major agricultural area. In addition, AMAs are designed to conserve water for human uses, not to sustain ecosystems. As a result, groundwater use in the San Pedro is allocated by a rule of capture subject to minimal "reasonable use" limitations.

CEC's San Pedro River Initiative

The CEC's interest in the San Pedro River commenced in 1996, when the Commission recognized the watershed as important habitat for the conservation of North American birds, a protection program previously launched by the CEC Council.[35] In May 1997, the CEC Secretariat launched under Article 13 of the NAAEC a more specific initiative to preserve and enhance the ecology of the binational Upper San Pedro River.

The CEC's Upper San Pedro River initiative had three objectives:

(1) initiate a process for diverse stakeholders to "develop and implement economically and environmentally sustainable strategies" for protecting the riparian ecosystem of the Upper San Pedro watershed;

(2) develop a model of cooperation of possible relevance to other regions facing similar transboundary ecological problems; and

(3) provide public information about the challenges and opportunities in conserving valued transboundary resources such as migratory birds and their habitat.[36]

The initiative proceeded in three steps. A team of scientific and legal experts was dispatched to study the basin's ecology and legal, economic, and institutional context. This was followed by a public input process coordinated for the CEC by the Udall Center for Studies in Public Policy at the University of Arizona and review by a thirteen-person public advisory committee. In summer 1999, a final report was submitted to the CEC Council. The Council publicly accepted and released the report and modestly agreed to study possible future CEC roles, "including identification of possible funding mechanisms, in any potential implementation of the report's recommendations."[37] At that time, the Council members were Carol M. Browner for the United States, Julia Carabias Lillo for Mexico, and Christine Stewart for Canada.

The expert study team impaneled by the CEC consisted of six individuals, only one of whom was from Mexico.[38] The areas of expertise represented included hydrology, resource economics, ornithology, watershed management, plant ecology, and law–public policy. The team's independent work occurred during 1997–98, and it resulted in a public review draft in June 1998 and a revised final report in March 1999.[39] The report included a careful examination of the important ecological features of the upper river; the hydrologic requirements of riparian habitat; surface water, groundwater, and their interrelationship in this water-short basin; water-use trends; and possible solutions. The study team employed what it described as "cascading analysis" by identifying the habitat resources that need to be sustained for the benefit of migratory birds, the surface water and groundwater resources necessary to maintain habitat, and the options to reduce the 7,000 acre-foot per year overdraft in groundwater pumping that threatens riparian habitat (projected to increase to 12,000 acre-feet per year in a decade).[40]

The study team discovered "[s]ubstantial consensus . . . as to the nature of the hydrologic problem. Solutions in the basin are inhibited not so much by conflicts over hydrology as concerns over the allocation of the costs and benefits of the remedies."[41] The study team described the hydrologic problem as steadily declining base flows and the loss of groundwater-surface water connectivity in existing perennial reaches of the river. The culprits are a recent resurgence in irrigated agriculture (despite the Bureau of Land Management's cessation of irrigated agriculture within the SPRNCA and the Nature Conservancy's purchase and retirement of 500 acres of irrigated acreage in the vicinity), urbanization around Sierra Vista and Fort Huachuca, and domestic wells in surrounding rural areas.[42]

The study team explored numerous solution opportunities—some hydrologically and economically promising, some with uncertain hydrologic potential, and others that are economically problematic—but declined to recommend a "wholly in-basin strategy that would bring the aquifer into balance."[43] Without importing water, the only route to the sustainability of riparian vegetation, in the study team's view, would be to move the protected riparian area southward into Mexico (by restoring flows there), thereby avoiding the groundwater pumping effects of the Sierra Vista–Fort Huachuca complex.[44] In effect, this would be an application of conservation biology to identify the minimum area of a larger landscape that must be protected to sustain at-risk species. Water importation was itself discounted because of its expense (in the case of a possible extension of the Central Arizona Project from its present terminus at Tucson) or adverse impact on potential areas of origin (in the case of possible imports from the even more arid Douglas Basin to the east).

Rather than recommending these controversial measures, the study team concluded by recommending a reduction in irrigation pumping on both sides of the border and a series of water conservation and recharge efforts in the Sierra Vista–Fort Huachuca area. The report tacitly acknowledged these steps may be inadequate, over the long term, to protect riparian vegetation. Institutionally, the report suggested improved coordination through binational organizations that might be precursors of a binational river basin commission and said that such binational efforts might be more effective if they were created through presidential proclamations by the two countries.[45]

The University of Arizona's Udall Center performed a commendable job during the summer of 1998 in soliciting public comment on the study committee's draft report. Fifteen hundred copies of the report were distributed to libraries, public officials, and opinion-makers. A tabloid summary of the CEC initiative and study team report was printed and inserted in all newspapers distributed in the Sierra Vista–Cochise County area. Public service ads were run on local radio. Udall Center staff held focus group meetings with concerned organizations and hosted other open houses and public workshops. Eventually, a summary of public comments was prepared for the CEC.[46]

These public comments indicated less certainty than held by the study team about the hydrologic understanding of the San Pedro River and how different management options might assist in preserving flows. The public expressed support for water conservation and recharge measures but opposition to water imports or a relocation to the south of the protected riparian zone. Public comment was emotionally divided on the reduction of irrigated agriculture. Sentiment was even less settled on the potential effectiveness of creating an AMA under Arizona groundwater law. Many public members suggested a greater emphasis on growth management options.[47]

During the third phase of the CEC's San Pedro initiative, the Secretariat formed a thirteen-member Upper San Pedro Advisory Panel to consider the study team's findings and recommendations, as well as the public comment. This binational "blue ribbon" panel was chaired by Pedro Carlos Guillén Rodríguez, Director General of Ecological Regulation and Environmental Impact at Mexico's Instituto Nacional de Ecología (INE), and Jack Pfister, former general manager of the powerful Salt River Project (a water and electricity distributor), with other influential members such as the director of the Arizona Department of Water Resources. Generally, the advisory panel recommended a multiplicity of voluntary initiatives implemented at the local level and an increased involvement of Mexican stakeholders in the binational process. While seconding many of the expert study team's recommendations and the public preferences, the advisory panel did offer some informed insights to enrich the dialogue. For instance, the panel suggested that the state corporation commission allow water companies to recoup conservation improvements through rate increases. The panel also recommended that the state buy and retire development rights on state school trust lands in order to reduce water consumptive development in the basin. The panel did acknowledge the possible eventual need for painful or expensive measures such as a cap on groundwater withdrawals or transbasin diversions. However, the advisory panel was most comfortable with conventional measures such as federal and state funding for land and water right retirement, urban conservation measures, growth management, and augmented supplies (for example, capturing storm water runoff).[48]

The CEC Secretariat also added its own emphasis before the results were submitted to the CEC Council. In particular, the Secretariat underscored the procedural aspects of the study, noting that the study methodology had pioneered new approaches for addressing transboundary problems and highlighted the continuing need for a comprehensive basinwide plan involving stakeholders on both sides of the border. The Secretariat recommended continuing CEC work on the San Pedro River, including the appointment of an interagency working group, direct support of local efforts, sponsorship of a workshop on models for transboundary water management, and a pilot project on increasing the value of sustainable tourism in natural areas.[49] In considering the final report at its June 1999 meeting, the Council was much more ambiguous about the CEC's future involvement in the San Pedro. It agreed only to examine the report for future CEC roles, such as identifying funding sources for implementing some of the report's recommendations.[50]

Analysis of CEC's Role

The San Pedro River initiative was among the CEC's first efforts under Article 13 of the NAAEC, and the assessment of its work must be considered in that context. On the positive side of the ledger, the CEC did achieve, in the words of the advisory panel, "a process that we believe has narrowed the bounds of discussion for finding sustainable solutions to ensuring that future generations can enjoy the cultural, scenic, historic and ecological bounty" of the river system.[51] The focusing of discussion is no minor achievement in public deliberative processes. The study team's report is to be especially credited for this result. In many instances, *Ribbon of Life* succinctly addresses an issue without overwhelming the reader with data (as it readily does by comparing numerous institutional options, such as water importation, utilizing a table). The iterative process, involving an expert study team, public comment, and advisory panel of knowledgeable and influential members, allows the refinement of promising options and the critique of others. None of the principal options are omitted in the process, and they remain to be evaluated independently by others. Finally, the CEC impaneled an exceptionally talented expert study team and advisory panel. The public input process on the American side of the border was quite extensive and yielded valuable information and insights for the study.

On the negative side of the ledger, the CEC process is not that exceptional, and it certainly has not resulted in many improvements to the San Pedro River. A public policy process involving independent scientific study, public comment, and advisory group components is certainly not an innovation in American resource policy. Similar procedures have been used in many resource areas, such as in developing salmon mitigation strategies in the Columbia River Basin. However, the CEC was extremely open and seems to have broken new ground by taking on such a politically charged issue. The CEC was warranted to test this public policy process in an international setting, such as the San Pedro, and the professionalism demonstrated and experience gained there will benefit future CEC initiatives.

At its foundation, the CEC emphasis on the San Pedro River may have been misplaced. While the San Pedro is an international river with environmental threats on both sides of the border, the CEC's principal concern—maintaining riparian habitat for migratory birds—is essentially a U.S. problem. Groundwater decline threatening river flows and dependent species is due to urban, military, and agricultural pumping north of the border. Unless the protected riparian area is actually moved south into Mexico, Arizona and the U.S. government themselves will have to wrestle with the solutions. The CEC would have addressed a more characteristically transboundary environmental problem if it had studied, for instance, the Colorado River Delta, where ecological degradation in Mexico is the result of upstream water diversions principally in the United States.

The expert study team and advisory committee have enumerated many options, and it appears certain that water importation must be part of any long-term solution. None of the options are self-executing. They all rely upon public support and the political will of local, state, and U.S. government officials—and, thus far, there is precious little of either. Recent improvements, if any, are incremental. The Sierra Vista area remains a magnet for retirees and others who seek a high-quality but relatively inexpensive place to live. Farmers, such as those living in the Mormon communities of St. David and Pomerene, where families have worked the land for more than a century, resist threats to their agriculturally based culture. Many basin residents resent governmental intrusions into their lives, and they oppose the imposition of a bureaucratic AMA under the state groundwater statute. Some groundwater pumping might be curtailed to provide water for more senior downstream surface water uses, with accompanying benefits to the riparian area, but the Arizona courts have struggled for decades to regulate tributary groundwater outside the relatively few AMAs. Evidenced by the efforts of numerous private and public groups (many of which preceded the CEC initiative), there is no shortage of concern about the San Pedro River.

Action-forcing pressures, however, are lacking. If the CEC had the accumulated prestige of a century of diligent, quality work, its mere pronouncement on the San Pedro's needs might be enough to galvanize action. Though its San Pedro effort was very professional, the CEC is new, is unknown to many, and lacks such legitimacy. The fact that the CEC is an international body itself goes against the grain of many basin residents. Other forces may bring about needed change, though at a cost to deliberative processes. The U.S. Endangered Species Act emerges as the prime candidate with the potential to apply the brakes to many forms of development in the lower basin, but such a development would signal both institutional failure and an environmental "last stand" on behalf of threatened or endangered species.

More generally, the San Pedro experience illustrates the two major problems that new multinational institutions face when they try to influence domestic biodiversity conservation regimes. The first is the lack of adequate domestic laws to implement the CEC's recommendations, and the second is the lack of incentives to complement the information disclosure.

One of the many paradoxes of environmental law is that we are entering our fourth decade of environmental regulation, but the legal regime, which initially came before an understanding of the basic nature of many of the problems, has not kept pace with our understanding of the scientific and institutional issues. Biodiversity conservation is a case in point. Scientific views of the nature of environmental protection have radically changed. Modern biodiversity conservation relies more on the dynamic nonequilibrium paradigm than the previous static one and is less concerned with simply fencing "nature" from humans. Institutionally, biodiversity conservation is an important objective, but it has a limited legal foundation at all levels of government, and it requires that all levels of government cooperate to preserve it.[52] In addition, environmental law is evolving, at least in the eyes of many observers, from a centralized command-and-control and planning model to a more decentralized, inclusive system that increasingly relies on markets and voluntary compliance with environmental norms.[53]

The San Pedro experience clearly shows the limitations of information disclosure as an environmental policy instrument when it is applied to small-scale biodiversity conservation. Information disclosure is a policy instrument of the field of reflexive law.[54] Reflexive law tries to align systematically legal rules with norms that the relevant actors will internalize. It builds on the realization that the reasons why people actually obey law ultimately lie outside formal adjudication and the power of the state to enforce rules.

Information disclosure works well when people have both the incentives and the capacity to modify their behavior in response to what is disclosed.[55] Most of the case for information disclosure is based on the experience with voluntary industry efforts to reduce both conventional and toxic pollution streams or from efforts, such as eco-labeling, to change consumer choice. This experience reveals two powerful incentives at work: shame and the desire to be virtuous while saving money or increasing profit margins. In a post-Holocaust world, human rights NGOs have effectively used shame to induce compliance with universal human rights norms. Also, voluntary pollution reduction has been achieved when it is internally profitable for an industry to reduce its discharges or an industry anticipates increased regulatory or public pressure to reduce them from the disclosure, such as through public shaming. Shaming works well with pollution, especially toxic pollution, because it draws on deep, perhaps irrational, fears of exposure to the risk of serious illness and an innate abhorrence of bodily impurity.

The marginal legal status of biodiversity conservation and the misfit between its objectives and available policy instruments help explain why the

CEC's San Pedro intervention had limited immediate success. The widespread acceptance of the "biodiversity" construct as a general policy objective came long after the major land and water management programs were put in place. As of yet, there is comparatively little shame in failing to practice biodiversity conservation, so noncoercive information disclosure is not enough. A credible threat of sanctions and a mix of positive incentives to avoid them must also exist.

Two concrete incentives that have successfully induced landowner cooperation under the U.S. Endangered Species Act are fear of a worse regulatory outcome and immunity from liability for changed conditions. Large-scale habitat conservation plans under the Act provide landowners opportunities to avoid a worse regulatory outcome (civil and criminal liability for taking protected species). To induce landowner cooperation, the Department of Interior took a bold risk-reduction step by issuing a "no surprises" policy protecting the landowner from future consequences under the Act if the requirements of a habitat conservation plan were implemented on the owner's land.[56] The policy shifted the financial responsibility for remedying unforeseen species to the federal government. Controversial as it is, a "no surprise" policy is useful in large, multispecies protection efforts because it encourages landowner participation. The policy offers a positive reward, risk minimization, and lower transaction costs rather than direct regulation, sanctions, and a negative perception in the community.

It is too early to judge whether new forms of information assembly such as the Article 13 process will be a positive force to improve the North American environment. It is likely that reports such as *Ribbon of Life* will be only one of many factors that may influence future actions. Since the publication of the report, the most dramatic action concerning the San Pedro environment is a federal district court decision that the U.S. Army violated the Endangered Species Act in its expansion plans for Fort Huachuca.[57] The court held that the army failed to reduce sufficiently groundwater pumping to protect the Huachuca water-umbel and the southwestern willow flycatcher. For the present time, "rule of law" litigation that holds federal agencies to strict environmental duties may be the most effective catalyst for action. However, reports such as *Ribbon of Life* serve as an important reminder that more comprehensive ecosystem-wide solutions that involve the major stakeholders are the best long-run hope for effective biodiversity conservation.

Notes

Since 1999, A. Dan Tarlock has served as a special legal adviser to the Submissions Unit of the CEC Secretariat but has had no involvement, direct or indirect, in the CEC's work on the San Pedro River. From 1990 to 2000, John E. Thorson served as the special master for the Arizona General Stream Adjudication, which includes the determination of water rights in the Arizona portion of the San Pedro River basin. We wish to thank Greg Block for his willingness to share his insights about the San Pedro study with us. The chapter was greatly improved by his helpful comments.

1. North American Agreement on Environmental Cooperation (NAAEC), Sept. 14, 1993, 32 I.L.M. 1480.

2. For description and analysis of the CEC submissions procedure, see chs. 13–15, infra. See also David L. Markell, "The Commission for Environmental Cooperation's Citizen Submission Process," 12 *Georgetown International Environmental Law Review* 545 (2000).

3. John H. Knox, "A New Approach to Compliance with International Environmental Law: The Submissions Procedure of the NAFTA Environmental Commission," 28 *Ecology Law Quarterly* 1, 117 (2001).

4. See "European Environmental Law," §§ 1–5, *International Encyclopedia of Laws* (Kurt Deketelaere ed., 1998).

5. Positivism has limited classic international law to obligations that the international community has accepted as binding since these are the closest approximation to the command of the sovereign. See note 6, infra. It is often impossible to achieve the necessary degree of consensus through a treaty, state practice, or universal norm to call an obligation binding. Thus, the international community increasingly relies on "soft," or nonbinding, law. The conditions under which soft law can be effective are discussed in Edith Brown Weiss, "Conclusions: Understanding Compliance with Soft Law," in *The Role of Non-Binding Norms in the International Legal System* (Dinah Shelton ed., 2001). "Reflexive" law is a concept developed by Gunther Teubner. Gunther Teubner, "Substantive and Reflexive Elements in Modern Law," 17 *Law and Society Review* 239 (1983). Reflexive law posits that there are cognitive limits to the capacity of formal common law rules as well as more direct positive regulation to be understood by key societal actors. Thus, we must seek ways to encourage more direct citizen participation in the achievement of the underlying goals of legal rules.

6. See H.L.A. Hart, *The Concept of the Law* (1961); H.L.A. Hart, *Essays on Bentham* (1982). Modern English jurisprudence derives from John Austin, who defined law as the command of the sovereign and thus created the positivist paradox. According to Austin, international law cannot be positive law because there is no supranational sovereign. John Austin, *The Province of Jurisprudence Determined* 201 (1832, 1954 ed.). To overcome the paradox, international law has developed narrow categories of binding obligations.

7. See Knox, supra, 27.

8. Harold K. Jacobson and Edith Brown Weiss, "Assessing the Record and Designing Strategies to Engage Countries," in *Engaging Countries: Strengthening Compliance with International Environmental Accords* 543 (Edith Brown Weiss and Harold K. Jacobson eds., 1998). For an argument that the submission process will empower Mexican NGOs and give them increased leverage with the government to address internal environmental issues, see Margaret Wilder, "Border Farmers, Water Contamination, and the NAAEC Environmental Side Accord to NAFTA," 40 *Natural Resources Journal* 873 (2000).

9. CEC, *Ribbon of Life: An Agenda for Preserving Transboundary Migratory Bird Habitat on the Upper San Pedro River* (June 1, 1999), *http://cec.org/pubs_docs/documents.*

10. Interview with Greg Block, CEC Director of Programs, Nov. 2001.

11. Arizona Department of Water Resources, *Hydrographic Survey Report for the San Pedro River Watershed* 31, 55, app. F-2 (Nov. 20, 1991).

12. CEC, *Ribbon of Life*, supra, 15.

13. World Commission on Dams, *Dams and Development: A New Framework for Decision-Making* (2000), is a good introduction to the intense social and environmental conflicts in many of the world's river basins.

14. See Gilbert White, "Reflections on Changing Perceptions of the Earth," *Annual Review of Energy and the Environment* 19 (1994). The underappreciated value of ecosystem services has emerged as a primary justification for objectives such as biodiversity conservation and ecosystem restoration because it fits well within a scientific and welfare economics policy framework and avoids the hard philosophical issues such as the rights or intrinsic worth of natural systems. See James Salzman, Barton H. Thompson Jr., and Gretchen C. Daily, "Protecting Ecosystem Services: Science, Economics, and Law," 20 *Stanford Environmental Law Journal* 309 (2001).

15. According to the Nature Conservancy, the San Pedro River is one of the "Last Great Places" because it "provides a crucial stopping ground for many species of birds that migrate from South and Central America to North America and back again" and "is one of the most biologically diverse areas in the world." See *http://lastgreatplaces.org/SanPedro/Index.htm* (providing a "virtual tour" of the San Pedro).

16. See A. Dan Tarlock, "Reconnecting Property Rights to Watersheds," 25 *William and Mary Environmental Law Review* 69 (2000).

17. Héctor Fix-Zamudio and Francisco Ruíz-Massieu, "Mexico," 1 *International Encyclopedia of Comparative Law* M-63, M-70 (Viktor Knapp ed. [L/M], 1973).

18. See Hector M. Arias, "International Groundwaters: The Upper San Pedro River Basin Case," 40 *Natural Resources Journal* 199 (2000).

19. CEC, *Ribbon of Life*, supra, 14.

20. Arizona Department of Water Resources, supra, 465–67.

21. Id., app. F-2.

22. For example, what we now call essential riparian vegetation was historically classified as phreatophytic (water-loving) vegetation. Phreatophytes were targets of opportunity to increase river flows, and much research was done to support the thesis that clearing them would increase river flows. But later research shows that temporary flow gains are offset by losses caused by replacement vegetation. CEC, *Ribbon of Life*, supra, 21.

23. Id., 35.

24. Id., 26.

25. Id., 40.

26. Arizona Department of Water Resources, supra, 147, 169, 145.

27. CEC, *Ribbon of Life*, supra, 44.

28. Arizona Department of Water Resources, supra, 163.

29. Id., 162.

30. CEC, *Ribbon of Life*, supra, 48.

31. Id., 54, 58.

32. See *Solid Waste Association of Northern Cook County v. U.S. Army Corps of Engineers*, 121 S.Ct. 675 (2001).

33. Constitution of the United Mexican States, art. 27.

34. See A. Dan Tarlock, *Law of Water Rights and Resources* (1988 with annual updates), for an analysis of the Arizona Groundwater Management Act.

35. CEC Council Resolution 96-02, Feb. 8, 1996. For a description and analysis of the CEC's biodiversity programs, see ch. 4, supra.

36. CEC, *Upper San Pedro River Initiative* 2 (July 1998) (public information tabloid prepared by the Udall Center for Studies in Public Policy at the University of Arizona).

37. CEC Council Resolution 99-04, June 28, 1999.

38. Expert team members included John Bredehoeft (hydrologist), Ronald Lacewell (economist), Jeff Price (ornithologist), Hector Arias Rojo (watershed management), Julie Stromberg (plant ecology), and Greg Thomas (law and public policy).

39. San Pedro Expert Study Team, *Sustaining and Enhancing Riparian Migratory Bird Habitat on the Upper San Pedro River* (Mar. 1999) (report prepared for the CEC).

40. CEC, *Ribbon of Life*, supra, 114.

41. Id., 13.

42. Id., 16–17.

43. Id., 18.

44. "It entails maintaining a riparian habitat zone comparable in quality and extent to the SPRNCA by shifting the protected area southward to straddle the US-Mexico border. . . . [I]t is possible to re-establish the riparian habitat zone within the Mexican reach of the San Pedro to a level comparable to that of the SPRNCA by restoring flows, retiring irrigated agriculture and restricting grazing access. . . . [I]t seems likely that the effects of groundwater pumping on the reach of the San Pedro in the vicinity of Charleston that currently has perennial flow can be ameliorated by shifting the pumping north of the valley out of the Sierra Vista sub-basin." Id., 54.

45. Id., 22.

46. Udall Center for Studies in Public Policy, *Public Input Digest for the Upper San Pedro River Initiative* (Sept. 1998).

47. Id., iii, 18–20.

48. CEC, *Ribbon of Life*, supra, 25–31.

49. Id., 7, 10.

50. Council Resolution 99-04, supra.

51. CEC, *Ribbon of Life*, supra, 28–29.

52. See generally Richard B. Stewart, "A New Generation of Environmental Regulation?" 29 *Capital Law Review* 21 (2000).

53. See Daniel C. Esty and Marian R. Chertow, "A Vision for the Future," in *Thinking Ecologically: The Next Generation of Environmental Policy* 231 (Daniel C. Esty and Marian R. Chertow eds., 1997). See also Daniel A. Farber, "Triangulating the Future of Reinvention: Three Models of Environmental Protection," 2000 *University of Illinois Law Review* 61.

54. See Stewart, supra, 127; Eric W. Orts, "Reflexive Environmental Law," 80 *Northwestern University Law Review* 1227 (1995).

55. See Bradley C. Karkkanien, "Information as Environmental Regulation: TRI and Performance Benching, Precursor to a New Paradigm?" 80 *Georgetown Law Journal* 257 (2001).

56. The rule was initially adopted as a policy statement, but the Department issued it as a federal regulation after the policy was challenged on procedural and substantive grounds. The final rule and comments can be found at 63 Fed. Reg. 8859–73 (Feb. 23, 1998) and 50 C.F.R. pt. 17.

57. *Center for Biological Diversity v. Rumsfeld*, 198 F. Supp. 2d 1139 (D.Az. 2002).

DONALD MCRAE 13

Trade and the Environment

The Issue of Transparency

THE CREATION of the Commission for Environmental Cooperation (CEC) has to be placed within the ferment that followed the *Tuna-Dolphin* decision by an arbitral panel in 1991.[1] There, a ban on the importation of tuna imposed by the United States, which was designed to achieve the environmental objective of protecting dolphins, was declared to be contrary to U.S. obligations under the General Agreement on Tariffs and Trade (GATT).

The outcry that followed had repercussions far beyond GATT. The trading regime came under greater scrutiny. There was an impact on the negotiation of the North American Free Trade Agreement (NAFTA), which contributed to a side agreement: the North American Agreement on Environmental Cooperation (NAAEC). There was a lesser, but nevertheless perceptible, effect on the Uruguay Round of multilateral trade negotiations leading to the creation of the World Trade Organization (WTO). And, more broadly still, there has been a questioning of the compatibility of trade obligations not just with environmental protection but also with other social values, including labor standards and human rights.

Although the NAAEC and the institution it created, the CEC, have as a rationale the "conservation, protection and the enhancement" of the environments of the United States, Mexico, and Canada both within their territories and as a whole—a rationale that is, in a sense, independent of trade—the trigger for the conclusion of the NAAEC was a trade agreement, NAFTA.[2] Moreover, the NAAEC is explicitly linked to trade. Article 1 of the Agreement includes among the objectives of the NAAEC to "support the environmental goals and objectives of the NAFTA" and to "avoid creating trade distortions or new trade barriers." Furthermore, under Article 10 of the NAAEC, the CEC Council is given responsibility to cooperate with the Free Trade Commission set up under NAFTA in a number of environmentally related functions, including the broad mandate of "considering on an ongoing basis the environmental effects of the NAFTA."

Moreover, the principal mechanism for achieving the objectives of the NAAEC, that is, ensuring that states properly enforce their own laws, was also the foundation for the regime for antidumping and countervailing duty that was set out in Chapter 19 of the Canada-U.S. Free Trade Agreement (FTA) and was carried over almost identically into NAFTA.[3] The citizen submission procedure of NAAEC Articles 14 and 15 takes the same approach. It seeks to ensure that Parties are properly applying their own environmental laws, and the government-to-government dispute settlement process in Part Five of the NAAEC is founded on the obligation of each Party to enforce its own environmental laws.

The various links between environment and trade in the NAAEC invite comparisons between the effectiveness of the NAAEC in dealing with environmental issues and the effectiveness of NAFTA and the WTO in dealing with environmental issues. In critical respects, the institutions adopted in the trade organizations are quite different from the institutions of the environmental organization. Allegations that a state is not complying with its obligations under NAFTA or under the WTO are dealt with in an adjudicative forum. Although some allegations that states are not complying with their obligations under the Agreement are dealt with in an adjudicative forum in the NAAEC,[4] the principal process under the NAAEC for dealing with allegations of noncompliance is the citizen submission process set out in Articles 14 and 15, which is not—at least, would not commonly be perceived to be—an adjudicative process.

Effectiveness can be measured in a variety of ways.[5] In respect of environmental institutions, one aspect of effectiveness involves the extent to which the institutions are perceived as having legitimacy, particularly in relation to whether the actions of the institutions are public, known, and open to external input. The question is frequently phrased in terms of the transparency of the institution and of its activities.

Transparency in International Environmental Regulation

The concept of transparency has become of increasing importance in the development of international law. It has a wide currency in the fields of trade and investment law, where it refers to the need for laws, regulations, and standards established by governments to be ascertainable and readily understood. In this sense it is a fundamental principle of GATT and finds its articulation in Article X. In the field of international environmental regulation, the concept of transparency is related to access to information and participation in the processes of environmental decision-making, and it is linked to the role played by nontraditional international actors. The role of nongovernmental organizations (NGOs) in the development of international environmental regulation is a central part of any discussion of the topic.

The role played by NGOs in the development of international environmental laws, practices, and procedures is part of a broader question of public participation in these processes. Public participation in environmental regulation has been accepted to some degree at the international level, although hardly on a par with domestic processes.[6] International organizations grant NGOs observer status, and in some instances this includes the right to address the intergovernmental organ during debates.[7] In other areas, the role of NGOs in international law-making processes continues to be enhanced. The negotiations leading to the conclusion of the Land-Mines Convention and the agreement creating the International Criminal Court are particular examples of this.[8]

The right of public access to information relating to environmental decision-making has been increasingly finding its way into international environmental conventions.[9] Although there is no customary rule of international law guaranteeing transparency in international environmental decision-making, there is a developing expectation that such transparency will be provided. Principle 10 of the Rio Declaration provides that "environmental issues are best handled with the participation of all concerned citizens."[10] More recently, the 1998 Aarhus Convention provides in Article 6 for public participation in specific areas of environmental decision-making as well as more broadly when decisions have a "significant effect" on the environment.[11] Daniel Bodansky has argued that although it has several limitations, public participation in environmental decision-making could be "an important source of legitimacy" for international governance in the field of environmental law.[12]

Public participation in environmental decision-making might take a number of forms.[13] Five will be identified here: (1) the opportunity to initiate processes that will lead to decision-making or that will contribute to ensuring compliance with environmental standards; (2) access to information; (3) the opportunity to contribute information to an environmental decision-making process; (4) participating in forums in which decision-makers consider information and hear arguments; and (5) participating in the making of the actual decision that has an environmental impact.

If transparency through public participation in these various ways contributes to the legitimacy of environmental decision-making processes, then this becomes a useful measure for considering the effectiveness of the processes of the WTO and NAFTA, on the one hand, and the CEC, on the other, in respect of environmental issues. Processes that are not perceived to be legitimate are not likely to be effective nor will they endure. Thus, in considering the processes of these institutions, a central question to ask is the extent to which their approaches to transparency have affected perceptions of their legitimacy as well as their ability to deal with environmental issues effectively.

It is proposed to look at the institutions of the WTO, NAFTA, and the CEC that deal with allegations of violations of legal obligations that involve environmental issues.[14] In each case, the focus will be on the extent to which transparency through public participation is possible. Thus, this chapter will provide an assessment of the state of transparency in these institutions.

Environmental Issues in WTO and NAFTA Dispute Settlement

THE WTO

How the Issues Arise

Issues affecting the environment do not come up directly in WTO dispute settlement.[15] An environmental issue would typically arise when there is an allegation that a measure taken by government violates its obligations under one of the WTO agreements, principally GATT, and the member concerned seeks to absolve itself on the ground that the measure in question was designed to attain an environmental objective. It may be a measure that is alleged to be discriminatory and hence a violation of either the most favored nation (MFN) provision, GATT Article I, or of the national treatment provision, GATT Article III. Or it may be a measure that bans or restricts importation or exportation contrary to GATT Article XI. In any of these cases, the member may rely on environmental grounds to show that there has not been a violation of the relevant GATT obligations.

The use of an environmental justification might arise in two different ways.[16] The first approach deals with the nature of the product that is affected by the impugned measure. A defending WTO member may claim that it was not discriminating either in relation to other foreign products (MFN) or in relation to domestic products (national treatment) because the products in question are not "like." Under GATT Articles I and III, the obligation not to discriminate is an obligation to treat a product no less favorably than other "like" products. It might be claimed, therefore, that two products are not "like" when the production of one product causes environmental harm that is not caused in the production of the other. Or it might be argued that two products are not "like" when there is environmental harm resulting from the use of one of the products that does not result from the use of the other.

The second way in which a justification for violating trade obligations for environmental reasons arises is when the exceptions set out in GATT itself are invoked. There are two provisions of Article XX that are relevant. Paragraph (b) focuses on health and paragraph (g) more generally on the environment. The approach of GATT Article XX is to permit WTO members to deviate from their obligations provided that they have a justification that fits within one of the listed heads of the article and provided that, as set out in the chapeau to Article XX, the measure has not been applied in an arbitrary or discriminatory manner and that the measure is not just a disguised restriction on international trade.

The Process for Dealing with Environmental Issues

Ultimately, the determination of whether there is an environmental justification for a trade restrictive measure is to be made under the process set out in the WTO Dispute Settlement Understanding (DSU). It consists of a determination by a three-person ad hoc panel established by the WTO Secretariat in consultation with the parties, with the possibility of an appeal to a standing Appellate Body. Unless there is a consensus in the WTO Dispute Settlement Body (DSB) to reject the decision of a panel that is not appealed or to reject the decision of the Appellate Body, the decision in any particular case must be adopted by the DSB.[17] Since a consensus of all members of the DSB—a plenary organ—is virtually impossible, in practice the decision of the panel or the Appellate Body is binding.

WTO dispute settlement is limited to states—WTO members. Only a WTO member can challenge the actions of another member for its conformity with the WTO. Thus, an environmental justification for violating a WTO provision would be advanced by a government in a government-to-government dispute settlement process. How a government organizes itself domestically to prepare for that process is a matter for the government alone. There is no obligation of transparency or for any form of public participation in the way in which individual governments approach WTO dispute settlement.

Moreover, continuing the GATT tradition, WTO dispute settlement is conducted in private. The decisions of panels and of the Appellate Body are made public, and parties may make their own pleadings public.[18] But hearings are in private, and no transcript of the proceedings is ever made public. In short, there is no formal basis for public participation in the WTO dispute settlement process. Thus, under the rules for WTO dispute settlement, decisions about whether distinctions in the "likeness" of a product can be made on the basis of environmental factors or whether a measure meets the criteria of Article XX(b) or XX(g) are to be made without any form of public participation and in that sense without transparency.

NAFTA

How the Issues Arise

As a regional free trade agreement, NAFTA is based on the same principles as the WTO—nondiscrimination and the prohibition of restrictions on importation and exportation. GATT Articles III and XI are incorporated into NAFTA, as are the exceptions set out in GATT Article XX.[19] Thus, in this respect, issues relating to the environment arise in the same way under NAFTA as they arise under GATT: a state seeks to support a measure it has taken that is arguably contrary to its obligations under NAFTA by invoking an environmental justification. Again, that justification might relate to nondiscrimination, or it might involve the application of the environmental exception in GATT Article XX.

However, environmental issues arising under NAFTA are dealt with in a regulatory environment that is, in principle, more sensitive to environmental issues than that of the WTO. The preamble to NAFTA speaks of its provisions operating in a manner that is consistent with environmental protection and conservation. Under NAFTA Article 104, the provisions of certain environmental conventions are given priority in the event of inconsistency between them and NAFTA.

NAFTA also goes further in its regulatory sphere than the WTO, providing a regime to protect the investors of each of the NAFTA Parties in the territory of another.[20] Again, there is a potential for environmental issues to be raised. A NAFTA Party accused of violating its obligations toward the investor of another NAFTA Party may wish to claim that its actions were justified on environmental grounds.

The Processes for Dealing with Environmental Issues

NAFTA has several different dispute settlement mechanisms, in two of which environmental issues might be raised. The first is Chapter 20, the procedure for government-to-government disputes. The process is an adjudicative one, resembling the WTO's, except that the panel is composed of five individuals, and there is no possibility of a further appeal to an appellate body. Moreover, panel decisions are not automatically binding on the NAFTA Parties, although the Parties are expected to agree on a resolution of the dispute that normally will "conform with the determinations and recommendations of the panel."[21] As in the WTO, however, although each party is free to make its own pleadings public, the oral proceedings are held in private. The final report of the panel is made public unless the NAFTA Free Trade Commission decides otherwise,[22] and, in practice, panel reports are routinely made public.

The second dispute settlement arena in which environmental issues might be raised is the mechanism for dealing with investment disputes established under NAFTA Chapter 11. Here the process differs from either that of the WTO or of NAFTA Chapter 20. Under NAFTA Chapter 11, an investor of a NAFTA Party can bring a claim directly against another NAFTA Party for violation of the obligations set out in Section A of Chapter 11. These relate to national treatment, MFN treatment, treatment that does not accord with the minimum standard under international law, the setting of performance requirements, or expropriation.[23]

Thus, the NAFTA Chapter 11 process avoids the need for a state-to-state claim and allows the investor direct access in bringing a claim against a government. The mechanism that is used for such claims is a form of international commercial arbitration under the arbitral rules of the International Centre for Settlement of Investment Disputes (ICSID), the ICSID Additional Facility, or the United Nations Commission on International Trade Law (UNCITRAL).[24] It involves a complaint to a three-person tribunal, which considers written and oral pleadings and then reaches a decision. The decision is binding on the parties and is enforceable under the domestic law of the party against which the claim is brought.[25] Although the decision is made public, the pleadings of the parties and the oral hearing all remain private unless the parties by agreement and with the approval of the arbitral tribunal decide otherwise.[26]

In practice, some NAFTA Parties have by operation of their domestic freedom of information laws provided pleadings in Chapter 11 cases to the public. Moreover, in July 2001, the NAFTA Free Trade Commission issued an interpretative statement that nothing in NAFTA imposes a general duty of confidentiality on disputing Parties to a Chapter 11 arbitration and agreed to make public all documents submitted to a Chapter 11 tribunal or issued by it subject to the protection of business confidential information.[27] Nevertheless, a Chapter 11 tribunal has ordered a NAFTA Party not to release information under its freedom of information laws, even though the law required release of the material in question.[28]

OPENING THE TRANSPARENCY DOOR IN THE WTO AND NAFTA

The move to grant more transparency in WTO dispute settlement came from a somewhat unlikely source—the WTO Appellate Body. In *Shrimp/Turtle*, several NGOs, concerned that a WTO panel was to make a determination on the compatibility of U.S. laws purporting to protect sea turtles with the U.S. obligations under the WTO, sought to put their own views forward directly to the panel.[29] The United States also attached the brief of an NGO to its own submission. The panel took the view that there was no legal basis for considering such submissions, but the Appellate Body disagreed. Relying on the power of a panel under Article 13 of the DSU to seek information from any individual or body it deems appropriate, the Appellate Body took the view that a panel had the power to consider whatever material it wished, including material submitted by an NGO or by anyone else for that matter.

Thus, the concept of an amicus brief found its way into the WTO. An amicus brief in the WTO sense is an unsolicited brief; it does not have to be requested by a panel. The Appellate Body's decision in *Shrimp / Turtle* therefore provided a certain degree of transparency. It enabled the views of those outside government to be placed before a panel. But transparency stopped at that point. The Appellate Body imposed no obligation on a panel receiving such information to consider it. Nor would there be any way of knowing how the information has been appreciated or understood, or whether it has had any direct or indirect impact on the panel's decision. Thus, there is no guarantee that a panel will look at information submitted in an amicus brief, let alone take it into account.

Furthermore, the Appellate Body's decision related only to the panel stage, not to the Appellate Body itself. Nevertheless, the Appellate Body was prepared to take the next step. In *Hot-Rolled Lead and Bismuth Carbon Steel*, it concluded that since there was no prohibition in the DSU against the receipt of amicus briefs, and the Appellate Body had the power to set its own working procedures, then it could decide to receive such briefs.[30] It then went a further step in *Asbestos* and notified potential submitters of briefs of the conditions under which it would receive and consider such briefs.[31] The fact that the Appellate Body granted a right to submit such briefs did not mean that the Appellate Body was likely to be influenced by their content. In fact, it rejected all of the briefs submitted in *Asbestos* and did not take them into account.

The receipt of amicus briefs by the Appellate Body was widely criticized by WTO members in a special session of the WTO General Council called to consider the issue. Many states, particularly developing countries, considered that the Appellate Body had exceeded its powers and essentially revised the rules of dispute settlement, granting entities that were not members rights not contemplated in the Uruguay Round negotiations. Nevertheless, no action was taken by the WTO members to overturn the position of the Appellate Body, and thus the power to receive amicus briefs remains.

Although no attempts have been made to submit amicus briefs in cases arising under NAFTA Chapter 20, the amicus model has now been raised in NAFTA Chapter 11 proceedings. In *Methanex*, a Canadian supplier of a gasoline additive brought a claim against the United States, arguing that a ban placed on the additive by the state of California was an expropriation of its property contrary to NAFTA Article 1110.[32] Concerned that the case would involve issues of importance to future environmental regulation, a

Canadian NGO, the International Institute for Sustainable Development (IISD), made a request to the tribunal hearing the case for the right to make written and oral submissions, to receive all of the pleadings of the parties, and to be present throughout the oral hearing. That request was followed by a similar joint request from two American environmental NGOs, Communities for a Better Environment and the Earth Island Institute.

The tribunal invited the parties to comment on the request and then ruled that in principle it could hear the views of NGOs, although it could not permit the presence of such entities in its oral proceedings in the absence of agreement from the parties. Such agreement was not forthcoming from the claimant in that case, so the tribunal concluded that it could only receive written briefs.[33] However, it postponed the determination of the modalities of receiving such briefs until it had reached a decision on the jurisdictional phase.[34]

The approach taken under NAFTA Chapter 11 differs from that taken in the WTO. In the latter, NGOs may of their own volition send written briefs to panels or to the Appellate Body and hope that they will be taken into account. The approach taken by the IISD in the *Methanex* case was to seek authority from the tribunal to submit an amicus brief. Acceptance by the tribunal of the submission of such a brief carries with it the implication that the tribunal will consider the brief and take it into account, something that will not necessarily happen in the WTO.

Transparency under the WTO and NAFTA, in the sense of public participation, is extraordinarily limited. The WTO parties saw no need for it when the agreements were negotiated, and they have generally been opposed to the efforts of the Appellate Body to provide a limited form of transparency. The pressure for that transparency came with the increase in WTO dispute settlement of trade issues with environmental implications, although the possibility of submitting an amicus brief in the WTO is not limited to environmental cases. Under NAFTA Chapter 11, the fact that a tribunal was to deal with an environmental issue also triggered the request for amicus status before the tribunal.

Environmental Issues in the CEC's Citizen Submission Procedure

HOW THE ISSUES ARISE

Environmental issues are at the core of the citizen submission procedure of the NAAEC. The process is triggered, in accordance with Article 14, by the action of a "non-governmental organization or person." The basis of the submission is an allegation that a NAFTA Party is failing to effectively enforce its environmental law. The submission is then reviewed by the Secretariat for admissibility and to determine whether it merits a response by the NAFTA Party. If a response is requested, then, in accordance with Article 15, the Secretariat has to determine in the light of that response whether to recommend to the CEC Council that a "factual record" be prepared. If the Council determines that a factual record is to be prepared, that is done by the Secretariat. After the Secretariat completes the factual record, the Council decides whether the report should be made public.

The objective of the process is not for the Secretariat to make a determination of whether there has been a failure to enforce environmental laws. Such a determination can be made only under the process set out in Part Five of the NAAEC, which involves complaints by one NAFTA Party about a "persistent pattern of failure" by another NAFTA Party to effectively enforce its environmental law. Instead, the process under Articles 14 and 15 is designed to provide information that can eventually be made public about specific allegations of failure to effectively enforce environmental laws. The role of the Secretariat is to provide information that would allow a conclusion to be reached as to whether a state was enforcing its environmental law effectively. In that sense, the very nature of the process is transparency—the disclosure of full information about the practices of a NAFTA Party in the enforcement of its environmental laws.

THE PROCESS FOR DEALING WITH SUBMISSIONS

Submissions under Article 14 are made by individuals or NGOs residing in the territory of a NAFTA Party.[35] Article 14 sets out certain formal criteria for a submission to be deemed admissible, including that it is in writing, that it identifies the person or organization making the submission, and that it provides sufficient information to enable the Secretariat to review the submission. There are two more substantive requirements. The submission must also be aimed at promoting enforcement, not at harassing industry, and it must show that the matter had been communicated in writing to the relevant authorities of the Party concerned and the nature of the reply by those authorities, if any.

The Secretariat has the task of reviewing submissions and determining their admissibility. It does this through the application of the provisions of the NAAEC and of guidelines adopted by the CEC Council in 1995 and revised in 1999. In determining admissibility, the Secretariat exercises an interpretative function in respect of the provisions of the Agreement and of the guidelines. It has had to determine what falls within the scope of the term "environmental law" and decide what constitutes an allegation of noneffective enforcement. It has also had to consider the temporal scope of submissions.[36] In addition, the Secretariat decides whether the formal and substantive requirements referred to earlier have been met.

The Secretariat considers only the written submission of the person or NGO bringing the complaint. The Secretariat can ask the submitter to rectify minor errors or can request clarification, but there is no basis for oral submissions to the Secretariat.[37] Indeed, the approach of the Secretariat is that this is an initial screening process and "is not intended to be unduly searching."[38] It is certainly not an in-depth analysis of the complaint. If the Secretariat determines that the submission is not admissible, it must notify the submitter and provide reasons for not considering the submission. The submitter then has thirty days to submit a revised submission. If the Secretariat again determines that the submission cannot be considered, it must again provide reasons to the submitter, and the process is then terminated.[39]

Once having determined that a submission is admissible, the Secretariat has to make a further determination. It must decide whether to request a response from the Party against which the complaint has been made. In considering this, the NAAEC gives the Secretariat guidelines rather than formal criteria to follow. These guidelines relate to whether harm to the submitter is alleged, whether further study of the matter would advance the NAAEC's goals, whether private remedies have been pursued, and whether the submission has been drawn exclusively from mass media reports.[40] In practice, the Secretariat treats these as guidelines and considers them individually and collectively in determining whether to request a response from the Party, but it does not require that they all be fulfilled.[41]

A decision to request a response or a decision not to request a response must be accompanied by reasons, which are provided both to the Party and to the submitter. If the decision is not to request a response, the submitter has thirty days to submit new or additional evidence to the Secretariat. If no such evidence is forthcoming or the Secretariat decides that the new evidence provided does not justify requesting a response from the Party, the submitter is notified that the process is terminated.[42]

The response of a Party, where one is requested, is not forwarded to the submitter.[43] However, the submitter is advised if the process is to be terminated because the submission is the subject of pending judicial or administrative proceedings or because the Secretariat concludes that, in light of the response, the development of a factual record is not warranted. In the latter case, the Secretariat must provide reasons for not proceeding further. The submitter is also advised if the Council decides not to direct the preparation of a factual record.[44]

The submitter has no specific role in the Secretariat's preparation of a factual record. However, since the Secretariat is specifically authorized to consider "relevant technical, scientific or other information" submitted by "interested nongovernmental organizations or persons," the submitter is able to provide the Secretariat with any information it deems appropriate.[45] Indeed, the Agreement clearly contemplates substantial nongovernmental input into the preparation of a factual record. In addition to receiving submissions from NGOs or persons, the Secretariat can receive information from the Joint Public Advisory Committee (JPAC), which itself is composed of nongovernmental representatives, and the Secretariat can also receive information from "independent experts."[46]

The process of preparing a factual record by the Secretariat has involved a wide-ranging search for information, including in one case meetings involving experts, the submitters, and the government.[47] Although the Secretariat canvasses widely in its search for information, it does not make drafts of its factual record available for comment, except to the Council. Public dissemination of the final version of the factual record depends upon the decision of the Council, which can decide not to release the factual record at all or to release it only to the JPAC. If a decision is made not to make the factual record public, the submitter is so advised.[48]

TRANSPARENCY UNDER THE CITIZEN SUBMISSION PROCESS

There are two aspects to the citizen submission process: the process leading to the determination whether a factual report should be prepared and the preparation of the factual report. The former is a process whereby a series of determinations are made by the Secretariat that lead either to the termination of the complaint or to a decision by the Council whether to direct the preparation of a factual record. The process is initiated by a person or an NGO in the form of a fifteen-page submission.[49] Although the submitter is kept informed and may receive requests from the Secretariat for clarification, the submitter essentially has no further role in the process. Even though a determination of admissibility, a determination of whether to request a response from the Party concerned, and a determination to recommend to the Council that a factual report be prepared all involve potential issues of the interpretation of the NAAEC, there is no formal opportunity for the submitter to make any submissions on these points.[50] Equally, no opportunity is provided for other interested NGOs or persons to make submissions on such issues, although there appears to be no prohibition against the Secretariat receiving such material.

By contrast, the process for the collection of information for the preparation of the factual report is one in which there is a full opportunity for persons and NGOs to submit information and to provide input. The difference between the prefactual report preparation stage and the preparation stage itself is in part explained by the fact that, in the case of the former, these are not generally issues where further factual information would be useful. They involve the interpretation and application of more technical criteria for determining whether a submission is admissible and whether ultimately the preparation of a factual report is to be recommended. Nevertheless, these issues are crucial, because through this process the ambit of the citizen submission process is determined.

In the past, while the Secretariat has been praised for interpreting Article 14 broadly, there has also been criticism of the rules for citizens' submissions, on the grounds that the submitter is essentially excluded from the process after the Secretariat decides that the submission is admissible.[51] In particular, the fact that the Secretariat decides whether to recommend the preparation of a factual report on the basis of a response by the government on which the submitter has no chance to comment diminishes the transparency of the process.

Nevertheless, taken as a whole, the citizen submission process is one where there is substantial transparency. Some have seen the object of this process to be the involvement of the public in the enforcement of environmental obligations, and the preamble to the NAAEC emphasizes "the importance of public participation in conserving, protecting and enhancing the environment."[52] To a large extent this is achieved both through the submitters' right to bring complaints and the Secretariat's ability to draw widely on information from nongovernmental sources in the preparation of the factual record.

Transparency in the WTO, NAFTA, and the CEC: An Evaluation

As pointed out earlier, it is difficult to make comparisons on matters of process between adjudicative and nonadjudicative processes. Although the WTO and NAFTA are clearly adjudicative processes, the citizen submission process would generally not be so regarded. Yet it is a mistake to characterize the CEC process as completely nonadjudicative. The first part of that process does involve a form of adjudication. It involves determinations by the Secretariat on the basis of provisions of the Agreement and the guidelines. These determinations have legal consequences, because they can have the effect of terminating a submission or of moving it through to the recommendation that a factual report be prepared.

Five types of public participation and transparency were identified earlier: initiating the process; gaining access to information; providing information; having access to oral proceedings; and being involved in actually making the decision. How do these processes measure up in these terms?

INITIATING THE PROCESS

There is no opportunity under the WTO or NAFTA Chapter 20 for anyone other than the WTO members or the NAFTA Parties to initiate proceedings. Under NAFTA Chapter 11, it is a private and not a governmental entity that initiates the process. But this can hardly be described as public participation. It is a complaint brought by an investor of a NAFTA Party alleging infringement of its own private interests.

Under the NAAEC citizen submission process, the right of the public to initiate the process exists. Indeed, only individuals or NGOs have the right to initiate the process. Thus, in this respect, the CEC's process clearly provides transparency.

ACCESS TO INFORMATION

Under the WTO and NAFTA processes, some information is made available, but it is not complete or necessarily timely, and in some cases it is not systematically available.

WTO panel and Appellate Body decisions are made available promptly on the WTO website, but the availability of the written pleadings of parties depends on the release by each party of its own pleadings. Transcripts of oral proceedings are not made available unless a particular state decides to release its own oral pleadings. The situation is similar in respect of disputes decided under NAFTA Chapter 20. The decisions of panels are posted on the NAFTA Secretariat website, and each party is responsible for the release of its own written pleadings. Cases decided under NAFTA Chapter 11 have generally been less accessible. Decisions rendered under the ICSID rules are published by ICSID. Those rendered under the UNCITRAL rules become available if the parties decide to release them. The parties may also decide to release their written pleadings as well. It remains to be seen whether the NAFTA Free Trade Commission's July 2001 interpretation on confidentiality will result in more transparency.

In short, although the results of WTO and NAFTA decisions generally become known, there is little information available during the course of the dispute. In this respect, there is little transparency.

In the case of the NAAEC citizen submission process, the submitter is kept informed of the progress of the submission, and the CEC website maintains a record of the status of submissions. However, information gathered during the preparation of the factual report that is ultimately included in the report becomes available only at the end of the process when a factual record is published.

PROVIDING INFORMATION

The acceptance by the WTO dispute settlement organs of a right to submit amicus briefs provides in fact a degree of transparency that is lacking in the formal provisions of the DSU. No such right has been accepted so far under NAFTA Chapter 20, but it is emerging in the practice of tribunals set up under NAFTA Chapter 11. However, under the WTO, this transparency is significantly curtailed. There is no obligation on a WTO panel or on the Appellate Body to consider an amicus brief or to take it into account in reaching its decision. It is too early to determine whether NAFTA Chapter 11 tribunals will adopt the same approach.

In the citizen submission process, a substantial opportunity exists for the provision of information. The Secretariat makes its decisions on admissibility, requesting a response, and recommending that a factual record be prepared on the basis of information provided by the submitter—a person or an NGO. Throughout the preparation of a factual report, NGOs and other persons have the opportunity to provide information to the Secretariat.

However, in respect of the CEC process, there still appears to be a gap in the opportunity to submit information. Public participation in the Secretariat's first phase determinations is limited to the submission of the complaint by a person or an NGO. Unless it decides to request further information from the submitter, the Secretariat essentially determines the ambit of the submission process itself. There is no provision in the Agreement or in the guidelines for the Secretariat to look elsewhere, either for information or to gain assistance in the interpretation of the provisions relating to admissibility, requesting a response, or recommending the preparation of a factual report. Could the Secretariat nevertheless consider submissions provided by other persons or NGOs on these issues? Could it consider further information provided by the submitter? In short, the question arises whether there is any scope for amicus briefs being received by the Secretariat in the first phase of the citizen submission process.

The preparation of a factual report, largely an information-gathering and fact-identifying process rather than a process of determination whether particular provisions of an agreement have been complied with, has less in common with the adjudicative process of the WTO and NAFTA. However, under Article 13 of the DSU, WTO panels have authority to seek information, and there is no reason why they could not seek information from NGOs as the CEC Secretariat does in preparing a factual report. So far, WTO panels have used this power very infrequently, and it remains to be seen whether the CEC's approach will provide any guidance to the application of the WTO provision.[53]

ACCESS TO ORAL PROCEEDINGS

In none of the dispute settlement proceedings under the WTO or NAFTA is there any provision for public access to oral proceedings. The amicus brief process provides an opportunity to make written submissions but no opportunity for making oral submissions. Under the CEC citizen submission process, the Secretariat does not conduct any oral proceedings in the phase leading to a recommendation that a factual record be prepared. The meetings held in the context of preparing the factual submission in *BC Hydro* involved a controlled presentation of information by stakeholders to experts, rather than a formal oral proceeding.

PARTICIPATION IN DECISION-MAKING

None of the processes under the WTO, NAFTA, or the CEC provide for public participation in actual decision-making. If draft factual reports were circulated to NGOs for comment before the preparation of the final factual report, the NGOs would play a greater role than just providing information, although it would not reach the level of a decision-making role.

Conclusions

The purpose of this chapter has been to provide an assessment of the state of transparency in respect of public participation in WTO and NAFTA dispute settlement affecting environmental issues and in the CEC citizen submission process. Clearly the CEC provides significant opportunities for public participation in environmental decision-making through allowing the public the opportunity to initiate the process, to obtain access to information, and to provide information. By contrast, the WTO and NAFTA processes provide limited opportunities for public participation. Access to information is limited, and there are only marginal opportunities for the provision of information from nongovernmental and other nonstate sources. Thus, if public participation in environmental decision-making is to be taken as a measure of the legitimacy of institutions making such decisions, then both the WTO and the NAFTA dispute settlement processes have serious problems in this regard.

However, this assessment of the state of transparency in these institutions raises questions about the appropriate level of public participation in forums dealing with environmental issues. Is the level of public participation in the CEC process appropriate for the WTO and NAFTA dispute settlement processes? And what is the appropriate level of public participation within the CEC process itself? These are issues that require consideration as the idea of transparency gains further stature in international environmental law and international law more generally.

Notes

I am grateful for the research assistance of Katherine Frankl.

1. *United States—Restrictions on Imports of Tuna*, Aug. 16, 1991, 39 GATT B.I.S.D. 155 (39th Supp.), 30 I.L.M. 1594 (1991).

2. See North American Agreement on Environmental Cooperation (NAAEC), Sept. 14, 1993, preamble, 32 I.L.M. 1480.

3. See North American Free Trade Agreement (NAFTA), Dec. 17, 1992, cha. 19, 32 I.L.M. 642.

4. NAAEC, supra, pt. 5.

5. See generally Laurence R. Helfer and Anne-Marie Slaughter, "Toward a Theory of Effective Supranational Adjudication," 107 *Yale Law Journal* 273 (1997).

6. David Wirth, "Public Participation in International Processes: Environmental Case Studies in National and International Law," 7 *Colorado Journal of International Environmental Law and Policy* 1 (1996).

7. Alexander Gillespie, "Transparency in International Environmental Law: A Case Study of the International Whaling Commission," 14 *Georgetown International Environmental Law Review* 333 (2001).

8. Frank Loy, "Public Participation in the World Trade Organization," in *The Role of the World Trade Organization in Global Governance* 117 (Gary P. Sampson ed., 2001).

9. Philippe Sands, *Principles of International Environmental Law* 616 (1995).

10. UN Conference on Environment and Development, Rio Declaration on Environment and Development, June 14, 1992, UN Doc. A/CONF.151/5/Rev.1, princ. 2, 31 I.L.M. 874.

11. Convention on Access to Information, Public Participation in Decision-Making and Access to Justice in Environmental Matters, June 25, 1998, available at *http://www.ece.org/env*.

12. Daniel Bodansky, "The Legitimacy of International Governance: A Coming Challenge for International Environmental Law?" 93 *American Journal of International Law* 619 (1999).

13. See David A. Wirth, "Re-examining Decision-Making Processes in International Environmental Law," 79 *Iowa Law Review* 769 (1994) (identifying three minimum requirements for public participation in intergovernmental negotiations: access to interim drafts, the right to comment, and the right to attend negotiating sessions as an observer).

14. There are many instances of allegations of violations of trading obligations that do not have any overt environmental impact. These kinds of violations are outside the scope of this chapter.

15. This chapter will deal only with the WTO dispute settlement process and not with the work of the WTO Committee on Trade and the Environment.

16. See generally John H. Jackson, *The World Trading System, Law and Policy of International Economic Relations* 235–38 (2d ed., 1997).

17. WTO Dispute Settlement Understanding (DSU), arts. 16(4) and 17(14), available at *http://www.wto.org/english/tratop_e/dispu_e/dsu_e.htm*.

18. As soon as a panel or Appellate Body decision is released to WTO members it is placed on the WTO website, *http://www.wto.org*.

19. See NAFTA, supra, arts. 301, 309, 2101.
20. Id., ch. 11.
21. Id., art. 2018(1).
22. Id., art. 2017(4).
23. Id., arts. 1102–6, 1110.
24. Id., art. 1120.
25. Id., art. 1136(4).
26. Id., Annex 1137.4.
27. "Notes of Interpretation of Certain Chapter 11 Provisions," available at *http://www.dfait-maeci.gc.ca/tna-nac/NAFTA-Interpr-e.asp*.
28. *Pope & Talbot Inc. v. Government of Canada*, Decision and Order of the Tribunal of Mar. 11, 2002, available at *http://www.dfait-maeci.gc.ca/tna-nac/Decision-Order-11Mar02*.
29. *United States—Import Prohibition of Certain Shrimp and Shrimp Products*, Report of the Appellate Body, Oct. 12, 1998, AB-1998-4.
30. *United States—Imposition of Countervailing Duties on Certain Hot-Rolled Lead and Bismuth Carbon Steel Products Originating in the United Kingdom*, Report of the Appellate Body, May 10, 2000, AB-2000-1.
31. *European Communities—Measures Affecting Asbestos and Asbestos-Containing Products*, Report of the Appellate Body, Mar. 12, 2001, AB-2000-11.
32. *Methanex v. United States*. All information is derived from the IISD website, *http://www.iisd.org*, which includes copies of its submissions and the decision of the tribunal. The author was counsel to IISD in its submission.
33. Although the decision of a NAFTA Chapter 11 tribunal has no precedential value for other tribunals, another Chapter 11 tribunal in *UPS v. Canada* has also decided to accept amicus briefs.
34. At the time of writing, the jurisdictional decision was still pending.
35. NAAEC, supra, art. 14(1)(f).
36. David L. Markell, "The Commission for Environmental Cooperation's Citizen Submission Process," 12 *Georgetown International Environmental Law Review* 551–53 (2000).
37. CEC, Guidelines for Submissions on Enforcement Matters under Articles 14 and 15, guideline 3.10, available at *http://www.cec.org*; Markell, supra, 557.
38. Id., 558.
39. Guidelines, supra, 6.1, 6.2, 6.3.
40. NAAEC, supra, art. 14(2).
41. Markell, supra, 568.
42. Guidelines, supra, 7.2, 8.1.
43. However, the response is kept in a file by the Secretariat that is available for public access and is placed on the Secretariat's website. Id., 16.1(b).
44. Id., 9.4, 9.6, 10.4.
45. NAAEC, supra, art. 15(4).
46. Id.
47. *BC Hydro*, SEM-97-001, Factual Record, ¶¶ 42–49, *http://cec.org/files/pdf/sem/97-1*.

48. Guidelines, supra, 13.1, 13.3, 13.2.

49. Id., 3.3.

50. The interpretations made by the Secretariat are discussed in Markell, supra.

51. Christopher N. Bolinger, "Assessing the CEC on Its Record to Date," 28 *Law and Policy in International Business* 1107 (1997); Beatriz Bugeda, "Is NAFTA Up to Its Green Expectations? Effective Law Enforcement under the North American Agreement on Environmental Cooperation," 32 *University of Richmond Law Review* 1604 (1999).

52. However, it should be noted that the objectives of the NAAEC as set out in Article 1 include "transparency and public participation" only in respect of the "development of environmental laws, regulations and policies," not in respect of their enforcement.

53. In cases involving the Agreement on the Application of Sanitary and Phytosanitary Measures (SPS Agreement), panels are expected to seek advice on scientific and technical issues from experts chosen by the panel in consultation with the parties. SPS Agreement, Apr. 15, 1994, Marrakesh Agreement Establishing the World Trade Organization, Annex 1A, *Legal Instruments: Results, Uruguay Round*, vol. 31, also available at *http://www.wto.org/english/tratop_e/sps_e/spsagr_e.htm.*

KAL RAUSTIALA 14

Citizen Submissions and Treaty Review in the NAAEC

THE NORTH AMERICAN Free Trade Agreement (NAFTA) helped usher in the contemporary "trade and environment" era. In an effort to assuage environmental organizations that feared NAFTA's impact on the North American environment, the United States, Canada, and Mexico negotiated the North American Agreement on Environmental Cooperation (NAAEC). The NAAEC commits the Parties to ensure that their domestic laws provide high levels of environmental protection and are effectively enforced. This chapter explores a key aspect of the NAAEC: its provisions for the review of these international commitments.

The review of treaty commitments is a critical issue because international agreements are frequently plagued by collective action problems. While the parties to these accords evidently desire cooperation, they face incentives to renege or behave opportunistically with regard to their international commitments. Consequently, a key component of many contemporary treaties is a system for the regularized review of state performance. I call these systems "review institutions."[1] Review institutions typically review treaty implementation, but they also may review treaty compliance or even effectiveness.

The mechanism created by Articles 14 and 15 of the NAAEC, commonly known as the citizen submissions procedure, is an example of a review institution. The citizen submissions procedure permits any individual or group in Canada, Mexico, or the United States to allege that one of these states is failing to effectively enforce a domestic environmental law. If successful, a submission can compel a response from the Party in question and lead to the publication of a "factual record" of the situation. The procedure's aim is to ensure that the NAFTA Parties and their political subunits, such as municipalities, effectively enforce their environmental laws. The political subtext that led to the procedure's creation was the fear that liberalized trade under

NAFTA would produce pressures to lower domestic environmental standards and weaken enforcement.[2]

In this chapter I argue that we can usefully distinguish two fundamental modes of treaty review: "police patrols" and "fire alarms."[3] The police patrol–fire alarm metaphor is drawn from the study of administrative oversight in U.S. domestic politics. Rather than rely solely on investigative police patrols by a centralized bureaucracy, the NAAEC creates a fire alarm: it permits private actors to trigger an investigation by the Commission for Environmental Cooperation (CEC) when they allege that a NAFTA Party is failing to uphold its treaty obligations. The use of fire alarms in treaty review, while not unknown, is unusual: international law rarely permits private actors to challenge states. As a result, the choice to employ a fire alarm structure in the NAAEC raises two important questions. First, why, and under what conditions, do states choose to rely on fire alarms, police patrols, or some combination when designing treaty review institutions? Second, what outcomes flow from this choice?

The focus of this chapter is primarily on the second question—the implications of empowering private actors. I argue that under the NAAEC the creation of a fire alarm yields important positive and normative benefits. However, I do not claim that the anticipation of these benefits explains the decision to create a fire alarm in this case. Prevailing rationalist theories of treaty design argue that the functional benefits that flow from international institutions largely explain the treaty design choices states make.[4] But unintended consequences, uncertainty, and domestic political pressures often play important roles as well.[5] For the NAAEC, domestic politics, rather than rational treaty design, best explains the choice of review institution. The submissions procedure was created because of political pressure from U.S. environmental organizations. Nonetheless, the benefits that flow from this choice may in time encourage states to employ more fire alarms as they learn which review institutions work best in differing contexts and as the political barriers to fire alarms—based largely on concerns about sovereignty—weaken.

The benefits that flow from the creation of a fire alarm review fall into three categories: effectiveness, efficiency, and participatory governance. Because it involves the citizenry of the NAFTA Parties, the submissions process draws on the private information about environmental enforcement that individuals possess, which makes it more effective than a pure police patrol system. It is also likely that, in the context of the NAAEC, a fire alarm is more efficient than a police patrol model. And because fire alarm review directly involves individuals, it upholds—however weakly—normative values concerning participatory democracy.[6] While the citizen submissions procedure is a small step in this regard, it does enhance participation in the process of international economic liberalization, which is an increasingly important issue as popular protests mount over the rising role of international institutions.[7] From a domestic law perspective, the review provisions of the NAAEC are feeble. But in the context of international law they are groundbreaking. By creating a direct role for individuals, the submissions process challenges the state-centric orientation and sovereignty focus of international law.

The first part of this chapter elaborates the police patrol–fire alarm dichotomy. In the second part I describe the details of the NAAEC procedure. Then in the third part I show how the police patrol–fire alarm distinction applies to the NAAEC, describe the advantages of fire alarms in this case, and argue for its significance as a component of institutional design. The fourth part concludes.

Two Models of Treaty Review

Treaty review institutions are defined here as institutions that gather, assess, and make decisions based on information relevant to the implementation of, compliance with, and effectiveness of commitments in international agreements. While empirical studies are few, most treaties appear to contain no review provisions whatsoever, whereas a few employ elaborate, variegated review institutions. In the study of American politics, scholars of the congressional oversight of administrative bureaucracies have argued that two basic models of review exist: police patrols and fire alarms.[8] Police patrols are efforts by centralized authorities (in the congressional context, committees) to search actively and systematically for problems or violations through hearings, audits, inspections, and the like. Fire alarms are procedures that private actors trigger to signal that a violation or problem has occurred. Like real fire alarms, these procedures are reactive and decentralized, and they rely on individual stakeholders who have economic or political incentives to pursue such claims.

The core distinction is one of information provision: does the system of review rely upon central authorities to search for and reveal information about performance, or does it delegate that role to other actors? A review institution that empowers private actors to bring forward claims about state performance, as the NAAEC does, I term a fire alarm. One that permits a central authority to inspect and review state performance, such as under the Chemical Weapons Convention, is a police patrol. In police patrols, central authorities (congressional committees; an international organization) bear the costs of searching for noncompliance. Fire alarms, by contrast, shift search costs away from governments and international organizations to individuals and other private actors.[9]

These two models represent distinct but not mutually exclusive institutional strategies. Review institutions can and do blend elements of both police patrols and fire alarms. (Under the NAAEC, for example, the CEC Secretariat can initiate studies of its own on a wide range of topics.) Review institutions can also eschew both models. That is, the review institution may rely only on self-reporting by the states party to the treaty, or there may be no reporting or review process at all. In many treaties, states do not wish to have any review of their performance. This may be because the treaty addresses a coordination problem (and hence is basically self-enforcing), because the agreement is largely symbolic, or because the states involved are fearful of "relinquishing sovereignty," in the sense of relinquishing autonomy and control. When states do create treaty review institutions, fire alarms are often shunned, seemingly because by empowering private actors they threaten state sovereignty and have the potential to embarrass governments sufficiently to offset the gains in compliance.

It is important to underscore that the police patrol–fire alarm dichotomy refers to the manner in which treaty relevant information is gathered and signaled, not the response to that information. Responses can vary independently of the mode of the review. In the context of international treaties, responses to noncompliance typically range from mild shaming strategies to authorized trade sanctions. A second distinction worth noting is that in domestic systems legislators make law that applies primarily to other actors. In the international system, by contrast, states typically create legal obligations by negotiating treaties, which by definition apply to their own behavior. In this sense treaties are more like contracts than statutes. As a result, states face incentives both to review the performance of other states and to behave opportunistically. These sometimes conflicting incentives, coupled to the sovereignty concerns associated with fire alarms, help explain why treaty review is generally so weak when compared to congressional oversight.[10]

I argue that the advantages of police patrol or fire alarm review vary given the structure of relevant information and the politics of the issue addressed. (For example, I suggest below that where compliance-relevant information is well hidden or confidential, police patrols should be more effective than fire alarms.) I argue more specifically that fire alarm review likely possesses effectiveness, efficiency, and participatory advantages in the context of North American environmental cooperation. In other words, for the NAAEC, the creation of a fire alarm was not just a good political choice, it was a good policy choice.

The NAAEC Citizen Submissions Procedure

The NAAEC's aim is to enhance environmental protection in North America and increase cooperation among the NAFTA Parties. Environmental organizations, particularly in the United States, had two chief fears about NAFTA. First, they feared that the increased trade that NAFTA would produce would exacerbate environmental problems in the border regions. Second, and more important, they feared that NAFTA would induce a decline in environmental protection generally. Many environmentalists believe that trade liberalization undermines environmental protection not only in terms of a race to the bottom in regulatory standards but also in a race to the bottom in implementation and enforcement.[11] In the NAFTA context, this concern was particularly salient because Mexican environmental law, while formally strict, was in practice poorly enforced.[12] Due to the relatively tepid political support for NAFTA in Congress in the early 1990s, environmental groups were able to successfully demand that the Clinton administration negotiate an agreement that would address this alleged race-to-the-bottom problem.[13] Clinton, concerned that NAFTA would not pass if environmentalists opposed it, pressed for the creation of the NAAEC. Canada and Mexico ultimately accepted this as the price of NAFTA. As a result, the NAAEC was negotiated with the core objective of the "improvement of environmental laws, regulations, procedures, policies, and practices" and the enhancement of "compliance with, and enforcement of, environmental laws and regulations."[14]

The citizen submissions procedure of the NAAEC, which in many ways is the agreement's centerpiece, permits any individual or nongovernmental organization (NGO) residing in the territory of the three Parties to file a submission with the Secretariat of the CEC alleging that a Party is "failing to effectively enforce its environmental laws."[15] This provision is unique in international environmental law because it focuses not on the enforcement of *international* law but rather on that of *domestic* law. In this sense, the NAAEC creates a means for the international "enforcement of enforcement."[16] There are minor threshold requirements submitters must meet, but, unusually, submitters need not reside in or be a citizen of the Party whose enforcement practices they challenge. Thus, the process is truly transnational: Mexican NGOs can complain about enforcement failures in Nova Scotia, and—what was critical from the political perspective of securing the overall NAFTA package—U.S. NGOs can complain about enforcement failures in Tijuana.[17]

When a submission is made, the Secretariat determines whether to request a response from the Party that is challenged. After receiving the government's reply, the Secretariat then decides whether to recommend the creation of a "factual record." The Council—the environment ministers of the three NAFTA Parties—must approve the decision by a two-thirds vote. When the factual record is complete, the Council votes again on its public release.

From the inception of the process in 1995 through February 2003, the Secretariat has received thirty-six submissions. Of the fourteen cases where preparation of a factual record was recommended, the Council has approved ten and refused two. The remaining decisions are pending. Three records have been published—one concerning the construction of a pier in Cozumel, Mexico, near a coral reef; one concerning threats to fish from dams in British Columbia; and a third concerning a lead smelter in Tijuana.[18] The records are comprehensive but generally neutral in tone; indeed, a recurring critique of the current procedure is that the Secretariat may not make any explicit recommendations, nor does it have the power to reach affirmative conclusions as to whether the Party in question is in fact "failing to effectively enforce" its law.[19]

The NAAEC citizen submissions procedure is, as a result, primarily an information-forcing mechanism. There are no direct sanctions employed; rather, the NAAEC employs a regulatory strategy of "sunshine."[20] By forcing Parties to respond to complaints and through the creation of factual records, the procedure generates information about environmental enforcement. It forces states to explain, and to give reasons for, their conduct and administrative choices.

From an administrative law perspective, the lack of a meaningful remedy and the low number of submissions (about five a year) might suggest that the significance of the process is minimal. But when viewed in the context of international law, the procedure is highly unusual. It both addresses domestic legal enforcement through an international agreement and empowers individuals—even those from other jurisdictions—to bring claims against a sovereign state. And while it is not a form of supranational adjudication, it shares some important characteristics of adjudication.[21]

Nonetheless, the empirical impact of the submissions process remains unclear. In the *Cozumel Pier* case, the submitters deemed their effort a success.[22] Other observers agree, arguing that due to the factual record "in Cozumel . . . the reef is now declared as a protected area, the development project was downsized, there have been legal changes and a management plan is in place."[23] In the *BC Hydro* case, local NGOs claim that commitments made by Canada in response to their submission, and recorded in the factual record, have "proven extremely valuable . . . those commitments have become a very potent tool for us."[24] With only a few years of operation, it is too soon to convincingly gauge the effectiveness of the submissions process. Perhaps the best evidence to date on this question is the reaction of the NAFTA Parties themselves. In 2000, the Parties, apparently led by Canada and Mexico, considered curtailing the submissions process but backed off under NGO pressure. Nonetheless, as discussed in David Markell's chapter in this volume, recent actions and resolutions of the NAFTA Parties circumscribe the process in potentially significant ways—ways that may go beyond the permissible bounds set by the treaty text.[25] If the NAAEC submissions process were truly toothless, these efforts, which have been the subject of considerable controversy, would not make sense.

Treaty Review in the NAAEC

The NAAEC submissions process, like all fire alarms, shifts the search for noncompliance away from central actors (such as government officials or international organizations) and toward private actors. My primary argument in this chapter is that the choice to create a fire alarm review institution yields certain benefits but also creates problems and risks. My aim is to detail these benefits and costs. By highlighting the outcomes that flow from one or the other model, the police patrol–fire alarm typology also provides a potential explanation of the choice of review institution in the NAAEC: rational states designed the optimal system for gathering information about compliance with the NAAEC's environmental standards. This rationalist explanation, while consistent with prevailing theories of institutional design in international relations, is largely unpersuasive, however. There is no evidence that the NAFTA Parties sought to create a fire alarm as the optimal institution to deter and reveal violations of international commitments. Rather, the U.S. government demanded it in order to assuage critical domestic interest groups. Because NAFTA was perceived to be a close vote in Congress, these groups posed a credible threat to NAFTA's ratification (and were key campaign supporters of Bill Clinton). Mexico and Canada, as weak states deeply interested in access to the U.S. market—and cognizant of the congressional politics over NAFTA—acquiesced to the U.S. demand. At the time, few knew what to expect of this procedural innovation. Now, as the impact has become more clear, the NAFTA Parties have sought to weaken the submissions system. They can do so at the margin since green groups' political leverage is now much lower: NAFTA is the status quo rather than a proposal. In short, the existing evidence, as well as the negotiating history of the NAAEC, supports the conclusion that the creation of the citizen submissions process was largely a product of domestic political incentives.

The NAAEC submissions procedure is unusual in its formal role for private actors, but it is not unique—the World Bank Inspection Panel and even NAFTA's Chapter 11 investor protection provisions are examples of the growing access of private actors within international law. Where the NAAEC is most distinctive is in its substantive focus on *domestic* environmental law enforcement. By providing private actors with a formalized role in the international regulation of domestic enforcement, the NAAEC breaks new ground in international environmental law.[26] In the remainder of this chapter, I explore the advantages of fire alarm review in the NAFTA-environment context.

THE ADVANTAGES OF FIRE ALARMS

Under the NAAEC submissions process, factual records are prepared by the CEC Secretariat, a centralized body. The search for treaty violations and initiation of the submissions process, however, are triggered by private actors. This fire alarm structure, in the context of North American environmental cooperation, yields several important benefits. I group these into three categories: effectiveness, efficiency, and participatory benefits. The first two are closely linked and relate to the structure and distribution of compliance-relevant information. The last advantage is distinct and relies on a particular normative vision of liberal democracy. That vision can be defended directly or, more strategically, as a means to blunt opposition to economic liberalization. There are also countervailing disadvantages to the fire alarm approach.

EFFECTIVENESS AND EFFICIENCY

One of the perennial challenges in environmental regulation is enforcement. Enforcement is difficult partly because information about environmental violations is often hard to obtain.[27] In theory, members of the CEC Secretariat could simply ask governments about their enforcement patterns or could even patrol around the United States, Canada, and Mexico seeking to uncover failures to effectively enforce domestic laws. By creating a fire alarm, the NAAEC instead accesses private information about both legal violations and enforcement efforts.

Reliance on private information is beneficial because of the structure of information in this area. Information about environmental enforcement and its failure is often widely diffused, in the sense that numerous actors may possess it, though it may be costly to collect in many instances. To be sure, governments often possess the best information about their own enforcement efforts and those of related entities (such as municipalities that share a watershed). Nonetheless, in their normal activities, private actors can discover instances of environmental violations that governments may miss or may not choose to act upon. They may also detect patterns of enforcement or nonenforcement that government officials do not. There is no reason to think the information private actors possess is systematically better than that of governments; rather, it is likely to be different than that possessed by governments. The diffusion of information about environmental enforcement is one reason citizen suit provisions and private monitoring efforts (such as the many bay- and river-keeper organizations now popular in the United States) have been so successful in U.S. environmental law.[28]

Private parties may search for relevant information on environmental enforcement for economic reasons, such as a firm concerned about competitors. While private parties may make special efforts to search for and uncover enforcement failures for the express purpose of drafting a NAAEC submission, it is reasonable to assume that at least some of these search efforts would occur in the absence of the NAAEC process. In addition, some relevant information will be uncovered even without explicit searches. Those who live near or fish on a river, for example, directly observe water quality, fish catches, development changes, and the like while engaging in their normal routines. Information thus can arise as the by-product of other activities rather than the product of a specific search. The relatively diffuse structure of information about the environment is sometimes furthered by particular domestic statutes, such as the U.S. Clean Water Act, which, by allowing individuals to access information relevant to enforcement, are explicitly information forcing. In short, the structure of information about environmental enforcement is one in which information is relatively dispersed and is sometimes a collateral benefit of other, exogenous activities that private actors engage in. A fire alarm provides a pathway for this wealth of private information to flow to decision-makers.

Even for private search efforts that are completely additional—that is, searches that would not have occurred but for the NAAEC—centralized international authorities, such as the CEC Secretariat, will not always be lower-cost information providers. Private actors may be better placed to discover relevant information about environmental enforcement, and to discover it more cheaply, than are official actors because of proximity or because of specialization.[29] By proximity I mean that individuals and NGOs are often on the ground in places and situations where violations occur. This is particularly true for environmental violations. This proximity to environmental sites (for example, a protected forest) should permit these actors to readily discover at least some types of enforcement failures. By specialization I mean that some private actors focus on the issue of monitoring environmental amenities and enforcement. Private actors such as bay-keepers are a good example of specialized monitors.

Again, it is important to underscore that governments possess significant information about enforcement failures and will be motivated to act on that information under some conditions. My claim is only that private actors possess relevant information as well, and sometimes possess *different* information—information that governments do not possess and perhaps can only acquire at high cost.

Possessing information, however, is not the same as revealing it. What are the incentives for private actors to reveal information—in other words, to pull the fire alarm? Some private actors will face economic incentives to reveal relevant information. For example, shellfish harvesters working in an estuary face an economic incentive to reveal information about illegal water discharges from an upstream factory, as do rule-compliant competitor factories. Hikers and boaters similarly face incentives to reveal relevant information because of the potential harm to their leisure activities. Environmental NGOs, which often specialize in such monitoring, are organizationally motivated to reveal information they possess. Collective action problems will surely restrict the gathering and revelation of information, but there is no reason to think such dilemmas will stem the flow of information totally.[30]

Consequently, in the context of environmental protection, this analysis suggests that a treaty review institution incorporating a fire alarm may be more efficient than a pure police patrol system in at least two ways. First, the fire alarm model taps into information already possessed by private actors and therefore entails no or low additional search costs in some instances. Second, a fire alarm capitalizes on the ability of low-cost private-information providers to uncover new, additional compliance-relevant information. The question of whether a fire alarm or police patrol is more efficient in a given treaty turns on the relative marginal cost of government actors obtaining the information private actors possess or obtain as a by-product of their normal activities. That relative efficiency calculus is complex and beyond the scope of this chapter. Here my claim is only that, for the reasons given, there is a good theoretical case that fire alarms are relatively more efficient than police patrols in uncovering environmental enforcement failures. It is important to emphasize that I am not arguing that fire alarms are efficient in the sense of yielding the optimal amount of enforcement. In fact, as I discuss below, fire alarms may be structurally disposed not to yield the optimal amount of enforcement.

Fire alarms can thus create a collective cost savings from a social-welfare perspective: more violations uncovered for the same aggregate expenditure. But fire alarms may also be cost-saving from an individual state perspective. Fire alarms transfer search costs off-budget. While states must collectively supply the institutional structure of the "alarm" (in the NAAEC, the unit in the CEC Secretariat that receives citizen submissions) and must bear the costs of responding to alarms (the expense of responding to submissions and preparing factual records), the direct costs of discovering enforcement failures are borne by private actors. Moreover, the costs of translating facts into legal claims—the preparation of a submission that alleges enforcement failures—are borne by the submitters as well.

Finally, the same structure of information—wide dispersal among many private actors—that I suggest may make fire alarms efficient in a cost-per-violation-detected sense in the NAAEC context is also likely to make them more effective than pure reliance on police patrols.[31] All else equal, fire alarm systems can be much more comprehensive than police patrols. As McCubbins and Schwartz argue in the congressional context, fire alarms involve private actors who can cover more territory than centralized authorities are capable of covering.[32] Centralized agencies engaged in police patrol monitoring inevitably spend considerable time monitoring actions, actors, and places that do not yield violations—in other words, they engage in wasted search efforts. Fire alarms minimize the likelihood of wasted search efforts.[33] Private actors, because their information is often a by-product of other activities, do not incur the substantial search costs that centralized monitors do. And these private actors are able to monitor a wide range of government enforcement efforts, a much wider range than even a tremendously expanded CEC Secretariat could.

The problem of wasted search efforts is rendered more complex when one considers that police patrols, even when they fail to uncover violations, have deterrent value. Police patrols consequently yield some benefits even when they fail to successfully uncover violations. Similarly, the threat of private actors pulling fire alarms also has deterrent value. The key question, again, is under what conditions is the deterrence produced by one model more effective, or cheaper, than that of the other model? One plausible hypothesis is that the deterrent value of a police patrol is likely highest where noncompliant actors can escape attention and/or readily hide the evidence of their malfeasance ex post. This is consistent with the fact that real police officers patrol for crime rather than merely responding to calls. Fire departments do not generally patrol, precisely because fires do not run away or burn out without a trace. The relevant information about fires is physically fixed. Because the failures to enforce environmental laws that are at issue in the NAAEC are often ongoing, and because these failures are readily documented and the actors relatively easily identified, the relevant information is better thought of as fixed rather than mobile.[34] This analysis suggests that fire alarms are likely to be more effective at the margin than are police patrols in the context of the NAAEC.

ENHANCING PARTICIPATION IN INTERNATIONAL LAW

When employed in international treaties, fire alarms can also provide greater legitimacy and perceived political accountability than pure police patrols. Indeed, this may be their most important impact. In contemporary debates over global governance and international institutions, critics have focused on accountability and public participation. As international institutions have increasingly encroached on traditionally domestic policy spheres, many individuals have questioned their democratic pedigree and lack of access for the public.

The NAAEC submissions process is a response to these critiques. Private actors concerned about environmental protection now need not rely solely on domestic law to ensure that environmental laws are adequately enforced. The citizen submissions procedure thus enhances political responsiveness, and this enhancement goes beyond NAFTA's potential impact on environmental enforcement. Submitters need not prove or even allege that an enforcement failure has resulted from NAFTA. *Any* failure to effectively enforce environmental laws, whether putatively NAFTA driven or not, is a permissible focus of a submission under the NAAEC.

The use of a fire alarm may also enhance the legitimacy of the NAAEC by enhancing public participation. Citizen participation is a mantra of many advocates of good global governance. It is also a central component of contemporary administrative law in the United States, the chief architect of the NAAEC.[35] A key facet of fire alarms is that they permit individuals to drive the substantive caseload of the review institution. By engaging in the citizen submissions process, private actors can at the margin both influence the actions of the Secretariat and of the Parties. To be sure, this influence is not large: many critics of the NAAEC procedure argue that it lacks teeth, addresses peripheral issues, and creates many obstacles to effective participation.[36] But for all its weaknesses, the NAAEC is an important step in the democratization of international environmental law. However small the current scope for citizen participation in the NAAEC, the NAAEC is a major advance over most environmental treaties, in which direct public participation nears zero. This advance in participation may be normatively preferable on its own terms or merely instrumentally useful from the perspective of gaining support for economic liberalization. As the NAFTA history illustrates, the NAAEC substantially smoothed NAFTA's prospects within a key domestic interest group.

THE DISADVANTAGES OF FIRE ALARMS

Fire alarms are not a panacea. Many of the disadvantages of fire alarm systems are related closely to the advantages. I have argued above that the structure of information is an important determinant of whether a fire alarm is effective as a tool of treaty review in a given case. I hypothesized that fire alarms are ill-suited to situations where information is not widely dispersed among many actors or where information is not "fixed"—where violators can readily hide evidence or move quickly. That is one reason fire alarms are unlikely to be effective in a treaty such as the Chemical Weapons Convention, which is aimed at the hidden development of chemical weapons by governments.

But other serious shortcomings exist. Decentralized citizen participation, because it is fundamentally driven by disconnected individual choices, can entail unfocused, reactive compliance management. Fire alarms may also systematically skew responses by centralized review bodies because the fire alarms are monopolized by actors with particularistic preferences.[37] Ultimately, the fire alarm model depends crucially on the interests and behavior of private actors. These interests may be particularistic and/or may promote goals that are not in the collective interest of the broader cooperative community.

This helps explain citizen-triggered fire alarms have been avoided in the World Trade Organization (WTO), despite repeated calls for access by private actors. Because trade liberalization entrains so many particularistic economic interests, the state must engage in a large degree of interest aggregation. Permitting individuals to bring claims directly would disrupt the often delicate political balances that trade liberalization demands. Relatedly, fire alarms may pressure governments to enforce the law beyond what they consider optimal levels. This issue goes beyond the sometimes reflexive sovereignty costs that governments fear. Even when governments welcome public oversight in principle, enforcement is not free. The fire alarm driven diversion of funds toward particular enforcement efforts—enforcement that the government has explicitly or implicitly chose to ignore—risks misallocating scarce resources. Thus, providing private actors with a means to pressure officials creates risks of both overenforcement and poorly targeted enforcement.

Fire alarms may also yield underenforcement. Procedure is the primary throttle on the use of fire alarms, and procedures can be incorrectly "set." The cost-benefit ratio for potential users is critical: if the benefit gained from pulling the fire alarm is too low relative to the costs of doing so, the system will not work optimally. Many commentators have argued that the NAAEC submissions process, resulting in at best the release of a factual record, is too weak to make a meaningful difference in behavior. This weakness may undermine the system's effectiveness both for submissions brought and submissions not brought. In other words, the weakness of the remedy, when coupled to the cost of preparing a submission, may discourage otherwise-worthy submissions from being made.

This issue of underenforcement is worth a brief detour. The relative weakness of the remedy in the NAAEC, when balanced against the costs associated with bringing forward a submission, is one possible interpretation of the low number of citizen submissions so far: as of February 2003, thirty-six in eight years. There is clearly no objective way to determine whether this is a high or a low number, but I would submit that, given the size and population of North America, this is not a high figure. The preceding analysis also suggests an explanation for the great disparity in the number of challenges to each NAFTA state. Controlling for population, the United States is markedly underrepresented. On a per capita basis, complaints against Canada are more than 1200 percent higher and complaints against Mexico more than 500 percent higher than complaints against the United States. The United States, with nearly ten times the population of Canada, has had fewer submissions filed against it than has Canada even in absolute terms.

One plausible explanation for this marked disparity are differences in the suite of domestic remedies across North America. Domestic measures obviously act as substitutes for the NAAEC submissions procedure and are often more attractive because they are more comprehensive and involve stronger remedies. Since the U.S. legal system provides a wealth of access for aggrieved citizens—in particular via the many citizen suit provisions contained in U.S. environmental statutes—the disparity in citizen submissions probably reflects the existence of better alternatives in U.S. domestic law.[38] The interesting question, still unanswered, is why Canada has a much higher per capita rate of submissions than does Mexico.

Conclusion

Review institutions play an important role in promoting treaty implementation, monitoring performance, and ensuring that states comply with treaty obligations. The NAAEC citizen submissions procedure is one example of a growing set of treaty review institutions. The police patrol and fire alarm dichotomy, used here to delineate two models of review, helps to illuminate the core of the NAAEC procedure and to underscore its distinctive features.

I have argued that there are compelling deductive reasons to believe that fire alarm review institutions have some efficiency, effectiveness, and normative advantages in the context of North American environmental cooperation. These advantages largely flow from the fact that information about environmental enforcement and environmental violations is widely dispersed. These advantages are not overwhelming, but they are nontrivial. I have also argued, however, that there is little evidence that the NAAEC submissions process was created, in a functional manner, to capture these benefits explicitly. Rather, the causal relationship is more indirect: powerful environmental interests in the United States demanded the NAAEC citizen submissions procedure as a tool and political statement, and their political leverage in the NAFTA debate led to its negotiation.

The submissions procedure has been criticized for its weaknesses, in particular with regard to the outcome: a factual record rather than a legal ruling or even authoritative recommendation. Strengthening the remedy would likely increase the number of submissions, just as enhancing the remedy in the WTO dispute settlement process appears to have raised the number of claims in that setting. At the moment, however, the United States, Canada, and Mexico seem more inclined to weaken the procedure than to strengthen it. Nonetheless, when viewed against the backdrop of other international environmental treaties, the NAAEC, by further involving private actors in public regulation, represents an innovative step in the design of international institutions.

Notes

I thank Stuart Banner, Larry Helfer, John Knox, Dave Markell, and especially Jody Freeman for helpful comments on earlier drafts.

1. In previous work with David Victor and Gene Skolnikoff, we used the phrase "systems for implementation review." *The Implementation and Effectiveness of International Environmental Commitments* (David G. Victor et al. eds., 1998).

2. This fear was particularly salient for Mexico. See Betty Ferber, Janine Ferretti, and Lynn M. Fischer, "Building an Environmental Protection Framework for North America: The Role of the Non-Governmental Community," *Green Globe Yearbook* (1995); Pierre Marc Johnson and André Beaulieu, *The Environment and NAFTA: Understanding and Implementing the New Continental Law* (1996).

3. I borrow the police patrol and fire alarm metaphor from Mathew D. McCubbins and Thomas Schwartz, "Police Patrols and Fire Alarms: Congressional Oversight Overlooked," in *Congress: Structure and Policy* (Mathew D. McCubbins and Terry Sullivan eds., 1987).

4. Functional theories evaluate causes in terms of effects. As Robert Keohane argues, "Functional explanations in social theory are generally post hoc in nature. We observe such institutions and then rationalize their existence. Rational-choice theory, as applied to social institutions, assumes that institutions can be accounted for by examining the incentives facing the actors who created and maintained them. Institutions exist because they could have reasonably been expected to increase the welfare of their creators." Robert O. Keohane, *After Hegemony* 80 (1984). See also "The Rational Design of International Institutions," 55 *International Organization* 761–1103 (Barbara Koremenos, Charles Lipson, and Duncan Snidal eds., special issue, 2001).

5. As the emerging literature on treaty effectiveness illustrates, we know relatively little about the effects of different institutions, and hence the assumption that states are rationally designing institutions may be valid, but the information they possess is severely limited, and thus these choices occur in an atmosphere of significant uncertainty.

6. Thompson argues that the citizen suit, from which the NAAEC process is broadly derived, bolsters democratic values in a similar fashion. See Barton Thompson Jr., "The Continuing Innovation of Citizen Enforcement," 2000 *University of Illinois Law Review* 185.

7. The democratic deficit in international institutions is much lamented and commented upon. See, e.g., "Symposium: Trends in Global Governance: Do They Threaten American Sovereignty?" 1 *Chicago Journal of International Law* 323 (2000); Daniel Bodansky, "The Legitimacy of International Governance: A Coming Challenge for International Environmental Law?" 93 *American Journal of International Law* 596 (1999); David Wirth, "Reexamining Decision-Making Processes in Interna-

tional Environmental Law," 79 *Iowa Law Review* 769 (1994).

8. For example, McCubbins and Schwartz, supra.

9. John Knox has used the phrase "complaint-based monitoring." John H. Knox, "A New Approach to Compliance with International Environmental Law: The Submissions Procedure of the NAFTA Environmental Commission," 28 *Ecology Law Quarterly* 1, 11 (2001).

10. See also Andrew Guzman, "The Cost of Credibility: Explaining Resistance to Interstate Dispute Resolution Mechanisms," 31 *Journal of Legal Studies* 303 (2002).

11. The race-to-the-bottom notion is explored in David Vogel, *Trading Up: Consumer and Environmental Regulation in a Global Economy* (1998); Richard Revesz, "Rehabilitating Interstate Competition: Rethinking the 'Race to the Bottom' Rationale for Federal Environmental Regulation," 67 *New York University Law Review* 1210 (1992); Kirsten Engel, "State Environmental Standard-Setting: Is There a 'Race' and Is It 'to the Bottom'?" 48 *Hastings Law Journal* 271 (1997).

12. The U.S. General Accounting Office conducted a study of Mexican law that significantly fed this concern; see GAO, "US-Mexican Trade: Information on Environmental Regulations and Enforcement," No. GAO/NSIAD-91-227. See also "North American Free Trade Agreement Greeted with Suspicion by Environmental Groups," 15 *International Environmental Reporter* (BNA) 561 (Aug. 26, 1992).

13. "Green Groups Press Kantor for Powerful NAFTA Environmental Commission," *Inside US Trade* (Mar. 5, 1993). The U.S. Trade Representative had already been pressured into preparing a report on the environmental issues. U.S. Trade Representative, *Review of US-Mexico Environmental Issues* (1992).

14. North American Agreement on Environmental Cooperation (NAAEC), Sept. 14, 1993, art. 1, 32 I.L.M. 1480. See ch. 1, supra.

15. NAAEC, supra, art. 14.

16. Kal Raustiala, "International 'Enforcement of Enforcement' under the North American Agreement on Environmental Cooperation," 36 *Virginia Journal of International Law* 721 (1996).

17. Often there are coalitions. *Metales y Derivados*, SEM-98-007, involving a lead smelter in Tijuana, was brought by a Tijuana-based NGO and a San Diego-based NGO.

18. *Cruise Ship Pier Project in Cozumel, Quintana Roo*, SEM-96-001, Final Factual Record (1997), *http://www.cec.org/pubs_info_resources/publications/pdfs/english/cozumel.pdf*; *BC Aborginal Fisheries Commission, et al.*, SEM-97-001, Final Factual Record, *http://www.cec.org/files/english/Fr97001e.pdf*. For discussions of the Cozumel process and report, see Beatriz Bugeda, "Is NAFTA Up to Its Green Expectations? Effective Law Enforcement under the North American Agreement on Environmental Cooperation," 32 *University of Richmond Law Review* 1591 (1999); Paul Kibel, "The Paper Tiger Awakens: North American Environmental Law after the Cozumel Reef Case," 39 *Columbia Journal of Transnational Law* 395 (2001); David Schiller, "Great Expectations: The North American Commission on Environmental Cooperation Review of the Cozumel Pier Submission," 28 *University of Miami Inter-American Law Review* 437 (1997). For a chart showing the disposition of all of the submissions, see the appendix to Chapter 15.

19. JPAC, Final Report to the Council of the CEC: Lessons Learned: Citizen

Submissions under Articles 14 and 15 of the North American Agreement on Environmental Cooperation. The JPAC report and other CEC documents are available at *http://www.cec.org*.

20. "Sunshine strategies are intended to bring the behavior of parties and targeted actors into the open for appropriate scrutiny, and thereby to encourage compliance." Harold Jacobson and Edith Brown Weiss, "Assessing the Record and Designing Strategies to Engage Countries," in *Engaging Countries: Strengthening Compliance with International Environmental Accords* 543 (Edith Brown Weiss and Harold K. Jacobson eds., 1998).

21. On supranational adjudication, see Laurence Helfer and Anne-Marie Slaughter, "Towards a Theory of Effective Supranational Adjudication," 107 *Yale Law Journal* 273 (1997).

22. Bugeda, supra. See also Gary C. Hufbauer, Daniel Esty, Diana Orejas, Luis Rubio, and Jeffrey J. Schott, *NAFTA and the Environment: Seven Years Later* 34 (2000).

23. JPAC summary report, Mexico City Meeting, Mar. 8, 2002 (reporting comments of a JPAC member).

24. "Citizen Submission Proves Valuable in BC Hydro Case," *TRIO* (fall 2001), available at *http://www. cec.org*.

25. See the discussion in ch. 15, infra; see also Knox, supra.

26. See generally Wirth, supra. Investor protection provisions in NAFTA provide even greater access. See "Symposium: NAFTA Chapter 11," 2 *University of Chicago Journal of International Law* 183–252 (2001).

27. See, e.g., Clifford Rechtschaffen, "Deterrence vs. Cooperation and the Evolving Theory of Environmental Enforcement," 71 *Southern California Law Review* 1181 (1998).

28. See, e.g., Thompson, supra.

29. While governments may discern patterns of enforcement more readily than can private actors, even this claim is not always true: some private groups, such as the Sierra Club, can marshal considerable resources across many jurisdictions.

30. Indeed, the environmental movement itself is a testament to the capacity of actors to overcome, at least intermittently, even severe collective action problems.

31. Effectiveness here refers to the ability to meet the goal of deterring and redressing violation.

32. McCubbins and Schwartz, supra, 429.

33. Id.

34. The Secretariat has often noted that there is an inherent temporal element to the legal standard of "is failing to effectively enforce." See, e.g., *BC Mining*, SEM-98-004, Notification to Council (May 11, 2001) (noting the temporal requirement inherent in Article 14(1)).

35. See, e.g., Richard B. Stewart, "The Reformation of American Administrative Law," 88 *Harvard Law Review* 1667 (1975); Jody Freeman, "The Private Role in Public Governance," 75 *New York University Law Review* 543 (2000).

36. For example, Jay Tutchton, "The Citizen Petition Process under NAFTA's Environmental Side Agreement: It's Easy to Use, but Does It Work?" 26 *Environmental Law Reporter* 10018 (1996).

37. One might view this as a variant on capture. Here, a special interest(s) captures a process that centralized bureaucrats administer. On citizen suits and shifting agency policy choices, see Jody Freeman, "Collaborative Governance in the Administrative State," 45 *UCLA Law Review* 1 (1997).

38. See Knox, supra, 107–8 (noting that "while potential submitters may see environmental remedies under U.S. law [and, to a lesser degree, Canadian law] as so effective that the submissions procedure can add little to them, the procedure may offer avenues for relief otherwise unavailable to potential submitters concerned with Mexican environmental issues").

DAVID L. MARKELL 15

The CEC Citizen Submissions Process

On or Off Course?

THE NORTH AMERICAN Agreement on Environmental Cooperation (NAAEC) citizen submissions process is an international spotlight that is intended to shine on (and thereby invigorate) the domestic environmental enforcement practices of Canada, Mexico, and the United States. Such a spotlight might be expected to have, and indeed has had, two effects on its core constituencies. It has created expectations for interested citizens (and nongovernmental organizations, or NGOs) by providing a new international forum to engage domestic government officials and to highlight concerns about domestic governance.[1] It also has created apprehension on the part of the NAAEC Parties that are its potential targets (and creators).[2]

A key issue in the operation of the NAAEC citizen submissions process involves the scope of the authority of each of the main actors: the Commission for Environmental Cooperation (CEC) Council (comprised of the environmental ministers of the three Parties); interested citizens ("civil society"); and a Secretariat created under the NAAEC to assist in implementation of the citizen submissions process, among other responsibilities.[3] In creating the process, the Parties did not reserve all of the authority and responsibility for themselves. Instead, they created a substantial role for citizens of the three North American countries by empowering them to start the spotlighting process and thereby to influence where the spotlight will shine (the process is launched with the filing of a citizen complaint, called a submission). The NAAEC also empowers citizens to contribute information about the nature and effectiveness of the government enforcement practices at issue in particular submissions. In addition, the NAAEC vests in an independent Secretariat considerable authority over administration of the spotlighting process, including the authority to dismiss submissions, request Parties to respond to submissions, recommend to the CEC Council preparation of "factual records" (the end point of, and ultimate investigative tool established by, the process) and, at the direction of the Council, develop such factual records. Thus, an important issue in the evaluation of early implementation of the citizen submissions process involves the allocation of authority and responsibility among the Parties, civil society, and the Secretariat.[4]

The considerable tension and acrimony that this question of boundaries has spawned during the early years of the process are evidence of the importance that many attach to its resolution.[5] A common theme of the NGO community and of scholarly and other commentary has been that, for the process to operate as intended (and for it to be credible with civil society), the Parties need to do a better job of adhering to the self-imposed limits contained in the NAAEC and, relatedly, to accord appropriate respect to the Secretariat's integral role in the process.[6]

This chapter considers this allocation of authority issue through a review of four resolutions that the CEC Council issued on November 16, 2001, in which the Council directed the CEC Secretariat to prepare factual records in connection with four citizen submissions. The chapter considers the nature of the allocation of authority established in the NAAEC as well as the extent to which the CEC Council's actual exercise of authority in these resolutions is consistent with the Agreement. It concludes that, in the resolutions, the Council may have exercised more authority than it possesses over the scope of factual records—the resolutions potentially give the Council more power to decide where the CEC spotlight should shine, and they give less power to determine this issue to citizens and the CEC Secretariat than contemplated in the NAAEC. Thus, the resolutions may inappropriately alter the boundary lines that the NAAEC draws concerning the respective roles of citizens, the CEC Secretariat, and the CEC Council.

The first part of this chapter provides the necessary factual context, briefly summarizing the four CEC Council resolutions. The second part explains why the resolutions potentially accrete more power to the CEC Council to direct the scope of factual records than the NAAEC contemplates—why, to be precise, these resolutions may constitute actions by the Parties that are ultra vires their authority under the Agreement. The third part offers some thoughts about the possible consequences of these Council resolutions for the future of the citizen submissions process. It suggests that the resolutions reflect that the Parties' capacity or willingness to respect the limits they set in the NAAEC on their roles in operating the citizen submissions process remains in issue. It concludes that the resolutions' potential accretion of power to the Council may undermine the credibility of the process, although only the future will reveal its actual impact on the willingness and interest of NGOs to continue to use the process.

The CEC Council's November 16, 2001, Resolutions

The CEC Council's issuance on November 16, 2001, of five resolutions to develop factual records represents an important milestone in the formative years of the citizen submissions process. As the statistics provided in the chapter appendix reflect, through these resolutions the Council authorized preparation of more factual records than it had directed be developed during the first seven years of the process.[7] The importance of these Council actions for the direction and credibility of the process is magnified because factual records are at the heart of the citizen submissions spotlighting process; they serve as its primary, and certainly its most in-depth, spotlighting mechanism. Further, the November 2001 resolutions may prove to have special value as bellwethers because they were the first major actions of the current U.S. and Mexican administrations under the NAAEC regarding specific submissions. As a result, they may be important indicators of the nature and extent of the administrations' commitment to the process and of their vision for it.

The resolutions' importance as potential indicators of the U.S. views is heightened by the fact that one of the resolutions involves the first Secretariat recommendation to develop a factual record involving the United States and therefore the first occasion for the Council to consider such a recommendation. The United States had been the only Party that had not yet voted to reject a Secretariat recommendation, and the public and, most likely, the other Parties were interested in learning whether the U.S. support for the citizen submissions process would remain firm even when the spotlight would be on its own enforcement practices. In 1994, the Clinton administration had issued an executive order in which the president committed to vote in favor of Secretariat recommendations except in extremely limited circumstances;[8] the recommendation focusing on U.S. enforcement practices arguably put this order to a stricter test than the recommendations that had preceded it.

At a superficial level, the resolutions suggest a congruity of views among Council, Secretariat, and submitters about factual records, since in each resolution the Council agreed with the Secretariat's recommendation, and the submission itself, that a factual record should be developed. But this superficial congruity of views disappears upon closer examination of the resolutions. Instead, a wide chasm is evident.

Four of the five Council resolutions dramatically change the focus of the factual records that the submitters requested and that the Secretariat recommended by substantially limiting or redefining the scope of the factual records to be developed. While the submitters asserted that broad, programmatic failures to effectively enforce particular environmental laws exist, and while the Secretariat recommended that these asserted widespread failures to effectively enforce be investigated through development of factual records, the Council resolutions decline to direct the Secretariat to develop factual records on such broad, programmatic alleged failures to effectively enforce.[9] Instead, the resolutions direct the Secretariat to develop factual records concerning some of the isolated examples of asserted failures to effectively enforce that the submitters had included as illustrations of the broader failures. A February 2002 memorandum from the director of the CEC Secretariat's submissions unit to the chair of the Joint Public Advisory Committee (JPAC) makes this clear:

> [T]he Council included instructions [in the four Resolutions] to prepare factual records regarding specific cases raised in the submissions, but did not include instructions regarding allegations in each of those submissions of widespread failures to effectively enforce environmental laws. For each of those four submissions, the Secretariat had recommended preparing factual records in regard to the widespread allegations of failures to effectively enforce.[10]

The following summaries of the respective positions of the submitters, Secretariat, and Council with respect to these submissions, taken directly from the CEC website (see Latest News, November 19, 2001), specifically draw attention to this wide gap (the headings and emphases are mine). In each case, it is by no means clear that the Secretariat would have recommended a factual record if the submission only involved the isolated examples for which the Council authorized development of factual records. Thus, there is a possibility that the resolutions may require the Secretariat to develop factual records on matters for which the Secretariat believes a factual record is not warranted or is warranted only if part of a larger inquiry.

OLDMAN RIVER II

[The Submission]

The Submitters contend that Canada is failing to effectively enforce the Canadian Environmental Assessment Act [CEAA] and sections 35, 37 and 40 of the Fisheries Act. The Submitters contend that, *as a matter of Canada-wide policy*, Canada improperly avoids subjecting projects to environmental assessments by issuing Letters of Advice to project proponents outlining measures that will avoid the need to obtain authorizations to harm fish habitat under section 35(2) of the Fisheries Act. Such authorizations ordinarily require an environmental assessment. The Submitters also contend that, *throughout the country*, Canada routinely fails to ensure compliance with or prosecute violations of the habitat protection provisions of the Fisheries Act. The Submitters described the Sunpine Forest Products Forest Access Road case *as an example* of Canada's failure to effectively enforce the two laws.

[The Secretariat's Recommendation]

On 19 July 1999, in light of the submission and Canada's response, the Secretariat recommended that a factual record be prepared regarding the full scope of the submission.

[The Council's Resolution]

In May 2000, the Council deferred voting on the recommendation in light of a pending judicial proceeding involving the Sunpine case. On 16 November 2001, rejecting the Secretariat's recommendation to prepare a broad factual record, the Council voted unanimously to instruct the Secretariat to prepare a factual record only with respect to the Sunpine case.

The Submitter of the Oldman River submission, Martha Kostuch, has echoed the CEC's description of the Council resolution as a significant modification of the type of factual record sought by the Submitters and recommended by the Secretariat:

The Secretariat [in its Recommendation] also understood that [Friends of the Oldman River's (FOR)] submission dealt with the general failure of the Government of Canada to enforce the Fisheries Act and CEAA and not a specific case. FOR's submission alleges a general failure to enforce the Fisheries Act and CEAA, not a failure in relation to any specific case.[11]

In short, it is clear from the submission and the recommendation that the submitter and the Secretariat believed a factual record was appropriate regarding Canada's generic approach to enforcing the two federal environmental laws at issue in the submission, but the Council did not direct the Secretariat to develop information about this asserted broad-based failure to effectively enforce. Instead, the Council effectively rejected the vast majority of the Secretariat's recommendation by authorizing a factual record that was limited to the Sunpine project. It is by no means clear that the Secretariat would have recommended a factual record if the submission only involved the Sunpine permit.

BC MINING

The BC Mining submission raises virtually identical issues, as the following summary from the CEC website makes clear:

[The Submission]

The BC Mining submission was filed on 29 June 1998, by the Sierra Club of British Columbia and other environmental groups. The Submitters allege that Canada systemically fails to enforce section 36(3) of the Fisheries Act to protect fish and fish habitat from destructive environmental impacts of the mining industry in British Columbia. The submitters described the Britannia, Tulsequah Chief and Mt. Washington Mines as examples of Canada's failure to effectively enforce this section of the Fisheries Act.

[The Secretariat's Recommendation]

On 11 May 2001, in light of the submission and Canada's response, the Secretariat recommended that a factual record be prepared regarding the full scope of the submission.

[The Council's Resolution]

On 16 November 2001, rejecting the Secretariat's recommendation to prepare a broad factual record, the Council voted unanimously to instruct the Secretariat to prepare a factual record only with respect to the Britannia case.

BC LOGGING

The third resolution issued on November 16, 2001, also is of the same type. Quoting from the CEC website once again:

[The Submission]

The BC Logging submission was filed on 15 March 2000, by the David Suzuki Foundation, Greenpeace Canada, Sierra Club of British Columbia, Northwest Ecosystem Alliance, and the Natural Resources Defense Council. The Submitters contend that Canada is systematically failing to effectively enforce sections 35 and 36 of the Fisheries Act in connection with logging operations on both public and private lands throughout British Columbia. The Submitters claim that the federal government relies too heavily on British Columbia's forestry regulations which, according to the Submitters, allow logging practices that harm fish and fish habitat and deposit harmful sediment in fish-bearing waters. The submission alleges that these practices result in many Fisheries Act violations that Canada is failing to address effectively. The submission also cites Canada's actions in connection with TimberWest's logging operations in the Sooke watershed as a specific example of ineffective enforcement.

[The Secretariat's Recommendation]

On 27 July 2001, in light of the submission and Canada's response, the Secretariat recommended that a factual record be prepared for the allegations regarding the province-wide failure to enforce the Fisheries Act effectively, as well as specific allegations relating to TimberWest's logging operations.

[The Council's Resolution]

On 16 November 2001, the Council instructed the Secretariat to prepare a factual record with regard to two specific cases involving TimberWest, declining the Secretariat's recommendation to prepare a factual record regarding the alleged province-wide failure to enforce the Fisheries Act effectively.

MIGRATORY BIRDS

The Migratory Birds submission, while differing from the preceding three submissions in that it involves the United States rather than Canada, raises identical issues as, again, the CEC website summary reflects:

[The Submission]

The Migratory Birds submission was filed on 19 November 1999 by nine American, Mexican and Canadian environmental groups: the Alliance for the Wild Rockies, Center for International Environmental Law, Centro de Derecho Ambiental del Nordeste de México, Centro Mexicano de Derecho Ambiental, Friends of the Earth, Instituto de Derecho Ambiental, Pacific Environment and Resources Center, Sierra Club of Canada, and West Coast Environmental Law Association. The Submitters contend that the United States is failing to effectively enforce section 703 of the Migratory Bird Treaty Act, which prohibits the killing of birds and destruction of their nests without a permit, against logging operations throughout the United States. In its response, the United States admitted that it has never enforced section 703 against a logging operation, and [contended] that nonenforcement of the Act against logging operations is a reasonable exercise of enforcement discretion and results from a bona fide allocation of enforcement resources to higher enforcement priorities.

[The Secretariat's Recommendation]

On 15 December 2000, in light of the submission and the United States' response, the Secretariat had recommended that a factual record be prepared for the submission.

[The Council's Resolution]

On 16 November 2001, the Council instructed the Secretariat to prepare a factual record with regard to two specific cases identified in the submission, but declined the recommendation to prepare a factual record regarding the allegation in the submission of a widespread failure to enforce section 703 against logging operations throughout the United States.

While, as noted at the outset of this section, these Council resolutions superficially suggest an alignment of views among submitters, Secretariat, and Council, the reality is that by authorizing factual records that are limited to specific alleged failures to effectively enforce, the Council dramatically changed the types of alleged enforcement failures to be addressed in the factual records. The following section suggests that by effecting this dramatic departure in focus from that embodied in the Secretariat's recommendations, the resolutions may accrete to the CEC Council more power than the Council possesses under the NAAEC to direct the preparation of such records.[12]

The November 2001 Resolutions May Cede More Power to the Council to Establish the Appropriate Scope of Factual Records Than the Council Is Given under the NAAEC

We begin with a brief primer on the citizen submissions process. As noted above, the primary purpose of the process is to shine a spotlight on domestic enforcement practices that North American citizens believe are less effective than they should be. The hope is that this spotlight will induce domestic governments to invigorate their approach to enforcement. The expectation is that invigorated enforcement of the environmental laws will improve compliance with these laws and thereby achieve higher levels of environmental protection (see, for example, NAAEC Article 5[1]).

In describing the citizen submissions process, it is important to explain what it is not. Among other things, it is not intended to serve as a forum for complaining about domestic environmental governance in the arena of standard-setting. That is, the process is clearly confined to allegations that a government is failing to effectively enforce an environmental law; allegations that the laws themselves are flawed (for example, because they fail to serve particular environmental values adequately) are off-limits for the process.

In many respects, quite understandably, the few pages of the Agreement devoted to the citizen submissions process do not answer questions about its implementation. These questions have been posed in submission-specific contexts, in which case the Secretariat and, in some instances, the Council have been required to interpret the Agreement in applying its terms to particular facts and allegations. In other situations, questions about the meaning of the Agreement have been raised more generically. To the extent that these issues have been addressed, or at least grappled with, this has occurred in a variety of contexts, including consultations among the Parties and engagement of the NGOs under the auspices of JPAC and otherwise. During the relatively short history of the process, the Council has adopted, and subsequently revised, guidelines intended to explicate the terms of the Agreement in different areas. For the most part, as is discussed in more detail below, the interested NGO community has been less than impressed either with the nature of these efforts or with their results.

It is clear that in creating the NAAEC the Parties intended to retain an important role in the implementation of the citizen submissions process, vesting considerable power in the CEC Council. The Parties also, however, created a Secretariat to administer the process, and they gave it significant responsibilities as well. As noted above, the NAAEC also gives citizens an essential role in directing the spotlight by vesting solely in them power to initiate the process.

Under the NAAEC's division of responsibilities, it is the Secretariat's job to conduct the initial review of a submission and decide, based on a variety of factors contained in NAAEC Article 14(1) and (2), whether to reject the submission or to ask the targeted country for a response.[13] Article 14(2)(b), for example, directs the Secretariat to consider whether the submission "raises matters whose further study in this [the citizen submissions] process would advance the goals of this Agreement." The Secretariat has exercised this initial review or filtering responsibility under Article 14(1) and (2) fairly rigorously; it has issued eighteen dismissals of submissions to date under one or the other of these provisions out of a total of thirty-six submissions filed.[14]

The Secretariat requests a response from the Party whose practices are at issue for submissions that survive the Secretariat's Article 14(1) and (2) filtering process. The Secretariat reviews the submission in light of any such response (thus far, the Parties uniformly have provided such responses). Its responsibility is to determine whether to notify the Council that, in the Secretariat's view, it would be appropriate under the NAAEC to prepare a "factual record" (factual records, as indicated above, are the end point of the citizen submission process and provide information about the nature of the Party's enforcement practices at issue and about the effectiveness of those enforcement practices). The Secretariat unilaterally may dismiss a submission at this stage if it determines that a factual record is not warranted. In either case (recommendation to proceed with a factual record or dismissal), the Secretariat must explain the rationale for its decision. As of February 21, 2003, the Secretariat had made fourteen recommendations to the Council that a factual record is warranted; it had dismissed seven submissions after receiving a Party's response (see chapter appendix).

The process creates a "check" for the Council for submissions for which the Secretariat has recommended development of a factual record. Instead of allowing the Secretariat unilaterally to determine to proceed with preparation of a factual record, Article 15(2) of the NAAEC allows the Council to decide whether to authorize the Secretariat to prepare a factual record. A potentially important feature of this check is that only a two-thirds vote of the Parties is required to go forward with preparation of such a record. Thus, the Party that is the focus of the submission cannot unilaterally terminate the process at this stage. As of February 21, 2003, the Council had directed the Secretariat to develop factual records for ten submissions; it had issued two other resolutions (Council Resolution 00-01, issued May 2000, and Council Resolution 02-13, issued December 2002) in which it rejected the Secretariat's recommendation and instead dismissed the submission (the former dismissal was by a two to one vote, with the United States voting to proceed with a factual record and Canada and Mexico voting to dismiss; the latter dismissal was unanimous). The Council, in another May 16, 2000, resolution (Council Resolution 00-02), deferred consideration of the Oldman River submission (subsequently, in one of the November 16, 2001, resolutions discussed above, the Council voted to go forward with a factual record for this submission) (see chapter appendix for more information about these Council resolutions).

If the Council directs the Secretariat to go forward, the Secretariat has the opportunity and responsibility to develop information relating to the allegations in the submission of a failure to effectively enforce and then to prepare a draft factual record that contains the results of its investigative work. Article 15(4) of the Agreement authorizes the Secretariat to consider "any relevant technical, scientific or other information" that is (a) publicly available; (b) submitted by interested NGOs or persons; (c) submitted by the JPAC; or (d) developed by the Secretariat or by independent experts. The Agreement also specifies that the Secretariat shall consider any information provided by a Party. Another provision in the NAAEC, Article 21, also gives the Secretariat authority to obtain information from the Parties, and Article 11(4) forbids Party efforts unilaterally to influence the Secretariat in the performance of its responsibilities.

The process creates two additional Party "checks" on the Secretariat's authority following the Secretariat's preparation of a draft factual record. First, the NAAEC requires that the Secretariat submit draft factual records to the Council, and it authorizes each Party to provide comments to the Secretariat on the draft. An important limitation on this Party "check" is that the Agreement specifies that Parties' comments must be confined to the "accuracy" of the draft. An additional limitation on this Party "check" is that the Agreement does not obligate the Secretariat to incorporate even these narrowly focused comments. Instead, it simply requires that the Secretariat take such comments into account as appropriate.

After the Secretariat considers the Parties' comments and incorporates them as it deems appropriate into a final factual record, the Parties' final "check" is that the Secretariat submits the final factual record to the Council, leaving it to the Council to determine whether to release it to the public (again, a two-thirds vote of the Council members is required to make a final factual record public). As of February 21, 2003, the Secretariat had submitted four final factual records to the Council. The Council unanimously approved the release of the first three; when this chapter was being finalized in February 2003, the Secretariat had just submitted the fourth, and the Council had not yet acted on it (see chapter appendix).

What conclusions may be drawn about the NAAEC's division of responsibilities between the Council and Secretariat? Initially, it is clear that the Parties have not retained plenary authority to make the decisions required under the citizen submissions process. Instead, they have given the Secretariat certain responsibilities and a significant degree of independence in the implementation of the process, and they have given submitters certain powers as well (notably, for our purposes, the power to launch the process and thereby identify alleged failures to effectively enforce for possible detailed scrutiny).

The diffusion of responsibility makes it necessary to determine the boundary lines for the respective roles and responsibilities of the three principal actors—CEC Council, CEC Secretariat, and submitters. While this issue has arisen in numerous contexts, the focus in this chapter is limited to the appropriate demarcation of responsibilities concerning the function of identifying enforcement practices and policies that are appropriate subjects for factual records. The limited conclusion offered here is that the Council lacks the authority under the NAAEC to act *sua sponte* to direct the Secretariat to develop a factual record. The Council does not have the authority, for example, to direct the Secretariat to prepare a factual record on a particular alleged enforcement failure, such as an asserted failure to effectively enforce the U.S. Clean Water Act against a particular facility regulated under that law, unless a submitter first raises this issue as one warranting such treatment and the Secretariat concurs in a recommendation to the Council. Instead, the Council only is empowered to order the Secretariat to develop a factual record concerning particular enforcement practices and/or policies if a submitter identifies them in a submission and if the Secretariat determines that development of a factual record concerning them is appropriate and makes a recommendation to that effect to the Council.

In short, the initial conclusion offered in this chapter is that while the Council retains the authority to veto shining the spotlight in particular directions, the Council cannot decide on its own where the spotlight should shine. For that affirmative decision, the Council must follow the lead of civil society, as reflected in the submissions, and the lead of the independent Secretariat created to administer the process in a neutral way. A Council failure to respect this limit in the Agreement on its authority risks serious intrusion into the independent roles that the Agreement creates for the Secretariat and submitters.

The important question the Council's four November 2001 resolutions raise involves the application of this interpretation of the Agreement to a situation in which a Council resolution departs so dramatically from the Secretariat's recommendation that the Council in effect may well be requiring the Secretariat to develop factual records on matters for which the Secretariat believes a factual record is not warranted or is warranted only if part of a larger inquiry. The point here is that this may well be the practical effect of the four November 2001 resolutions.

The Migratory Birds submission is a good example. The Secretariat recommended that a factual record be prepared concerning the United States' alleged failure on a nationwide basis to enforce the Migratory Bird Treaty Act (MBTA). The Secretariat's recommendation provides no indication at all that the Secretariat thinks that it would be warranted to develop a factual record limited to two isolated instances of alleged failures to effectively enforce the MBTA. The submitters emphasized the alleged "systematic" failure to enforce and devoted a single paragraph to these two instances in their submission, the United States did not even mention the two alleged examples in its response, and the Secretariat devoted little attention to them in its recommendation. Further, the questions highlighted in the Secretariat's recommendation as warranting in-depth review in a factual record focus almost entirely on the broad alleged failure to enforce the MBTA effectively—for example, it recommends a review of the overall numbers of migratory birds killed in logging operations, as to which the United States concedes it does not enforce the MBTA, compared to the numbers killed through activities for which the United States does take enforcement action. Thus, by directing the Secretariat to develop a factual record that focuses on two isolated instances of asserted failures to effectively enforce, the Council may well be directing the Secretariat to prepare a factual record even though the Secretariat itself would have determined that a factual record that focused only on these isolated incidents was not warranted.[15] Many of the issues that the submission raised that the Secretariat believed warranted development of a factual record may be beyond the scope of the Council resolution.

The view of this author is that the limitations on the Council's authority contained in the NAAEC raise serious questions about the legitimacy of the Council's four November 2001 resolutions. While leaving for another day the precise limits that the NAAEC imposes on the Council's decision-making authority in this area, the point offered here is that a necessary predicate for the Council to be empowered to order development of a factual record is that the Secretariat believes that development of such a factual record is warranted and that the Secretariat has informed the Council of the Secretariat's view in a recommendation.[16] Because there is no indication from these recommendations for broadly focused factual records that the Secretariat believes preparing the limited factual records contemplated in the Council resolutions is warranted other than as part of a larger inquiry, it is arguably beyond the scope of the Council's authority to direct the Secretariat to prepare them. If a fair reading of the recommendations is that the Secretariat made them because of the assertions of widespread failures to effectively enforce, the Council appears to have done what it appears to lack the power to do—it has directed the Secretariat to prepare four factual records focused on isolated alleged failures to effectively enforce without being informed by the Secretariat that the Secretariat believes that such factual records are warranted under the NAAEC.[17]

Observations and Conclusions Concerning Possible Consequences of the Council's November 2001 Resolutions on the Citizen Submissions Process

What are the possible consequences of the resolutions on the vigor and viability of the citizen submissions process? The resolutions are by no means the first apparent Council forays into territory ceded in the Agreement to other actors. Virtually since the inception of the citizen submissions process there has been considerable criticism that the Council has overplayed its role by limiting the independence and authority of the Secretariat and has thereby weakened the process. The two CEC-sponsored reviews of the citizen submissions process have raised concerns about the Parties' performance.[18] The JPAC also has expressed concerns about the Council's conduct in a series of "Advices" it has issued to the Council over the years.[19] Other advisory bodies, such as the National Advisory Committees (NACs) and the Governmental Advisory Committee (GAC), which the Parties have established under the Agreement to advise them on the implementation of the NAAEC, have also made known their discomfort with the Parties' actions in performing their responsibilities under the process.[20] Civil society, including but not limited to the submitter community, also has weighed in with considerable criticism of the countries' performance of their respective roles under the citizen submissions process. *Business Week* reported in May 2000 that during that spring more than one hundred NGOs from all three countries charged that the governments were "working together to undermine" the process.[21] A *Washington Post* June 10, 2000, editorial entitled "How to Wreck Trade" characterized the submission process as "sound[ing] rather government-controlled" and criticized the countries for "pushing ideas that might strengthen that bias by allowing governments to intervene in the experts' fact-finding work."[22] The level of concern and tension has continued, and perhaps increased, in recent years.[23]

The existence of such tension should not be surprising. As Kal Raustiala discusses in the preceding chapter, countries do not often embrace "fire alarm" review mechanisms such as the CEC citizen submissions process, in which they invest authority to review performance in actors they cannot control, in part because of concerns about the implications for state sovereignty as well as the prospect for embarrassment.[24] Raustiala also explains that in the particular context of the NAAEC, the Parties did not embrace a fire alarm approach because of an abiding desire for an international mechanism intended to invigorate domestic enforcement by spotlighting ineffectual domestic enforcement practices or policies or because of any sense of conviction that such a strategy would be especially effective in encouraging the Parties to enforce their environmental laws effectively. Instead, they were forced into it as a price for treaty enactment because of the power of domestic environmental NGOs, particularly in the United States. Thus, inclusion of the citizen submissions process does not reflect a significant investment by the Parties in the process or a significant Party commitment to its operating successfully.[25]

The structure of the citizen submissions process makes it virtually inevitable that a key flashpoint would involve the boundaries of authority of the different actors. In creating the process, the Parties agreed to serve as targets of this new international spotlight. At the same time, they reserved considerable, though by no means complete, authority over its operation. It seems entirely predictable that the evolution of the spotlight would be characterized by Party efforts to narrow its scope and by NGO efforts to extend its reach. The history of the process bears out this tug and pull.[26]

The resolutions represent another chapter in this ongoing tug and pull, but there is not yet enough information to forecast the conclusion to the citizen submission story with any great degree of confidence. It is not yet clear whether the resolutions signal an invigorated Council initiative to circumscribe the citizen spotlight or whether they more accurately should be characterized as opportunistic actions of the Council that respond to a flurry of Secretariat recommendations.[27] Gauging the extent and efficacy of civil society's response to the Council's actions similarly must await future developments. Since the inception of the process, NGOs have given considerable support to it as a highly innovative feature of international law that has the potential to enhance domestic governance and accountability.[28] In recent years, several NGO participants, among others, have begun to offer anecdotal evidence that the process is producing dividends by triggering improvements in domestic environmental governance.[29] Thus, there appears to be some level of NGO investment in and commitment to the process, which makes it more likely that NGOs will seek through various strategies to encourage the Council to respect the boundaries established in the NAAEC rather than rush to abandon the process as a result of the Council resolutions.

There is evidence that this is the case. JPAC has offered several Advices to the Council expressing dissatisfaction with the Council's actions, and submitters have registered complaints as well.[30] For example, the Sierra Legal Defence Fund (SLDF), which submitted two of the three Canadian submissions addressed by the November 2001 resolutions, sent a letter to the Canadian NAC expressing its concerns about the resolutions, characterizing them as a "clear infringement on the independence of the Secretariat" and suggesting that they "threaten to strip the citizen submission process of its integrity, utility and legitimacy."[31] Similarly, the submitter of the U.S. submission, the Center for International Environmental Law (CIEL), sent a letter to JPAC that characterizes the narrowing of the factual records as an "attempt to limit the utility of the citizen submission process."[32]

New submissions that offer the Council a mechanism to adjust its role are another form of efforts to engage the process in order to reform it. An example is the February 2002 submission in connection with logging operations in Ontario. This submission advances a creative rationale for pursuing broad-based allegations of failures to effectively enforce with respect to logging operations in Ontario and the widespread deaths to birds that these operations allegedly cause in violation of Canadian environmental law.

Assuming civil society is sufficiently invested to challenge the Council when its actions have the potential to reduce the value of the citizen submissions process, such as the November 2001 resolutions, there is the "efficacy question," notably the extent to which civil society will have sufficient leverage to influence the Parties. As Raustiala points out in his chapter, NGO leverage likely was greater prior to the adoption of NAFTA than it is now, at the implementation stage.[33] Thus, an outstanding question involves the extent to which an engaged civil society has the leverage to forestall Party initiatives to curtail the citizen submissions process.

It is too early to tell, in short, whether the resolutions represent a temporary bump in the road in the emergence of a vibrant citizen submissions process or a more significant derailment—whether NGO pressure and interest, creative approaches, and the responsive instincts of government officials will produce a convergence of views about the appropriate parameters for the process that will enable it to find, or gradually move toward, a place of rough equilibrium or whether the process will implode because of either Party discomfort or NGO frustration. Because of the process's role as an experiment in regional governance as well as its potential to influence domestic policy choices, the answers to these questions hold considerable interest for those concerned about environmental governance issues in North America and beyond.[34]

Appendix: A History of the Thirty-six CEC Submissions on Enforcement Matters, 1995–21 February 2003

	Submission received	Secretariat Article 14(1) and/or 14(2) determination continuing the process*	Secretariat Article 14(1) and/or 14(2) dismissal	Secretariat Article 21(1)(b) request for additional information from a party	Secretariat dismissal following response from a party	Secretariat notification to the Council that a factual record is warranted	Council resolution on Secretariat notification	Secretariat draft factual records	Secretariat final factual record	Council action on final factual record
SEM-95-001 Spotted Owl (US)	6/30/95	7/19/95	9/21/95, 12/11/95							
SEM-95-002 Logging Rider (US)	8/30/95		12/8/95							
SEM-96-001 Cozumel (Mx)	1/18/96	2/6/96, 2/8/96				6/7/96	#96-08 "yes" 8/2/96	4/23/97		Authorized release 10/24/97
SEM-96-002 Aage Tottrup (Can)	3/20/96	4/17/96	5/28/96							
SEM-96-003 Friends of the Oldman River I (Can)	9/9/96		10/1/96							
	Resubmitted 10/8/96	10/18/96, 11/8/96			4/2/97					
SEM-96-004 Fort Huachuca (US)	11/14/96	12/16/96, 1/22/97	6/6/97**							
SEM-97-001 BC Hydro (Can)	4/2/97	5/1/97, 5/15/97				4/27/98	#98-07 "yes" 6/24/98	3/28/00	5/30/00	Authorized release 6/11/00

*The Secretariat issued a single determination covering both Article 14(1) and (2) for several of these submissions.

**The submission was withdrawn by the submitters.

Appendix *continued*

	Submission received	Secretariat Article 14(1) and/ or 14(2) determination continuing the process*	Secretariat Article 14(1) and/ or 14(2) dismissal	Secretariat Article 21(1)(b) request for additional information from a party	Secretariat dismissal following response from a party	Secretariat notification to the Council that a factual record is warranted	Council resolution on Secretariat notification	Secretariat draft factual records	Secretariat final factual record	Council action on final factual record
SEM-97-002 Río Magdalena (Mx)	3/15/97	10/6/97, 5/8/98		9/13/99		2/5/02	#02-02 "yes" 3/7/02			
SEM-97-003 Quebec Hog Farms (Can)	4/9/97	5/8/97, 7/9/97		2/16/98		10/29/99	#00-01 "no" 5/16/00			
SEM-97-004 Canadian Env. Defence Fund (Can)	5/26/97		8/25/97							
SEM-97-005 Biodiversity (Can)	7/21/97		5/26/98							
SEM-97-006 Oldman River II (Can)	10/4/97	1/23/98, 5/8/98				7/19/99	#00-02 "deferred" 5/16/00; #01-08 "yes" 11/16/01			
SEM-97-007 Lake Chapala (Mx)	10/10/97	10/2/98			7/14/00					
SEM-98-001 Guadalajara (Mx)	1/9/98		9/13/99							
	Resubmitted 10/15/99		1/11/00							
SEM-98-002 Ortíz Martínez (Mx)	10/14/97		6/23/98							
	Revised 8/4/98		3/18/99							

	Submission received	Secretariat Article 14(1) and/ or 14(2) determination continuing the process*	Secretariat Article 14(1) and/ or 14(2) dismissal	Secretariat Article 21(1)(b) request for additional information from a party	Secretariat dismissal following response from a party	Secretariat notification to the Council that a factual record is warranted	Council resolution on Secretariat notification	Secretariat draft factual records	Secretariat final factual record	Council action on final factual record
SEM-98-003 Great Lakes (US)	5/28/98		12/14/98							
	Resubmitted 1/5/99	9/8/99		3/24/00	10/5/01					
SEM-98-004 BC Mining (Can)	6/29/98	11/30/98, 6/25/99				5/11/01	#01-11 "yes" 11/16/01			
SEM-98-005 Cytrar (Mx)	7/23/98	4/9/99			10/26/00					
SEM-98-006 Aquanova (Mx)	10/20/98	3/17/99				8/4/00	#01-09 "yes" 11/16/01			
SEM-98-007 Metales y Derivados (Mx)	10/23/98	3/5/99				3/6/00	#00-03 "yes" 5/16/00	10/1/01	11/29/01	Authorized release 2/7/02
SEM-99-001 Methanex (US)	10/18/99	3/30/00			6/30/00					
SEM-99-002 Migratory Birds (US)	11/19/99	12/23/99				12/15/00	#01-10 "yes" 11/16/01	11/28/02	2/21/03**	
SEM-00-001 Molymex I (Mx)	1/27/00		4/25/00							

*The Secretariat issued a single determination covering both Article 14(1) and (2) for several of these submissions.
**Date on which the Secretariat submitted the final factual record to the Council. The Council had not determined whether to make this final factual record publicly available when this chart was prepared.

Appendix *continued*

	Submission received	Secretariat Article 14(1) and/or 14(2) determination continuing the process*	Secretariat Article 14(1) and/or 14(2) dismissal	Secretariat Article 21(1)(b) request for additional information from a party	Secretariat dismissal following response from a party	Secretariat notification to the Council that a factual record is warranted	Council resolution on Secretariat notification	Secretariat draft factual records	Secretariat final factual record	Council action on final factual record
SEM-00-002 Neste Canada (US)	1/21/00	4/17/00 consolidated with SEM-99-001			6/30/00					
SEM-00-003 Jamaica Bay (US)	3/2/00		4/12/00							
SEM-00-004 BC Logging (Can)	3/15/00	5/8/00				7/27/01	#01-12 "yes" 11/16/01			
SEM-00-005 Molymex II (Mx)	4/6/00	10/19/00	7/13/00							
	Resubmitted 7/31/00					12/20/01	#02-03 "yes" 5/17/02			
SEM-00-006 Tarahumara (Mx)	6/9/00	11/6/01				8/29/02				
SEM-01-001 Cytrar II (Mx)	2/14/01	4/24/01, 6/13/01				7/29/02	#02-13 "no" 12/13/02			
SEM-01-002 AAA Packaging (Can)	4/12/01		4/24/01							
SEM-01-003 Dermet (Mx)	6/14/01		9/19/01							

	Submission received	Secretariat Article 14(1) and/or 14(2) determination continuing the process*	Secretariat Article 14(1) and/or 14(2) dismissal	Secretariat Article 21(1)(b) request for additional information from a party	Secretariat dismissal following response from a party	Secretariat notification to the Council that a factual record is warranted	Council resolution on Secretariat notification	Secretariat draft factual records	Secretariat final factual record	Council action on final factual record
SEM-02-001 Ontario Logging (Can)	2/6/02	2/25/02				11/12/02				
SEM-02-002 Mexico City Airport (Mx)	2/7/02	2/22/02			9/25/02					
SEM-02-003 Pulp and Paper (Can)	5/8/02	6/7/02								
SEM-02-004 El Boludo Project (Mx)	8/23/02; 9/30/02 (new information)	11/26/02	9/19/02							
SEM-02-005 Alca-Iztapalapa (Mx)	11/25/02		1/31/03							

*The Secretariat issued a single determination covering both Article 14(1) and (2) for several of these submissions.

Notes

John Knox, Kal Raustiala, Robert Glicksman, and Dan Tarlock, as well as Geoffrey Garver of the CEC, provided helpful comments on earlier drafts of this chapter. Any errors, of course, are my responsibility alone. While I previously served as director of the CEC's Submissions on Enforcement Matters Unit and currently serve as a consultant to the CEC, the views expressed here are entirely my own and should not be attributed to the CEC, including its Secretariat.

1. For a review of some of the reasons why this forum may be of particular interest and value to NGOs, as well as some of the arguable shortcomings in the process, see David L. Markell, "NAFTA's Citizen Spotlight Process," 18 *Environmental Forum* 32 (Mar./Apr. 2001).

2. For a discussion of the pressures that led the Parties to create the process despite its potential to embarrass them, see ch. 14, supra.

3. The structure of the CEC is discussed in Chapter 1, supra. In addition to the actors referenced in the text, the Joint Public Advisory Committee (JPAC) plays a role in the citizen submissions process. See ch. 11, supra.

4. This chapter does not suggest that any particular allocation of power is appropriate but instead focuses on the Parties' obligation to live up to the commitments they have made. Cf. Claude E. Barfield, *Free Trade, Sovereignty, Democracy: The Future of the World Trade Organization*, 8 (2001).

5. Some early commentators anticipated these tensions. See, e.g., Pierre Marc Johnson and André Beaulieu, *The Environment and NAFTA: Understanding and Implementing the New Continental Law* (1996); Independent Review Committee, "Four-Year Review of the North American Agreement on Environmental Cooperation: Report of the Independent Review Committee" (June 1998). Numerous observers have commented on the presence of such tensions. See, e.g., Christopher Tollefson, "Games Without Frontiers: Investor Claims and Citizen Submissions Under the NAFTA Regime," 27 *Yale Journal of International Law* 141, 175 (2001); John H. Knox, "A New Approach to Compliance with International Environmental Law: The Submissions Procedure of the NAFTA Environmental Commission," 28 *Ecology Law Quarterly* 1 (2001); Paul Stanton Kibel, "The Paper Tiger Awakens: North American Environmental Law after the Cozumel Reef Case," 39 *Columbia Journal of Transnational Law* 395 (2001).

6. See, e.g., JPAC Advice to Council no. 01-07, Oct. 23, 2001. The JPAC Advice and other CEC documents are available at *http://www.cec.org*.

7. The appendix to this chapter contains a status report on the actions taken under the citizen submissions process since its inception. Before November 2001, the Council had authorized the preparation of only three factual records.

8. Executive Order 12915, 59 Fed. Reg. 25775 (May 18, 1994).

9. The discussion in the text does not apply to one of the five resolutions the Council issued on November 16, 2001, in which the Council directed the Secretariat to prepare a factual record with respect to the Aquanova submission, because the Secretariat recommended development of a factual record relating to a particular shrimp farm, and the resolution charged the Secretariat with going forward on that basis. The chapter does not discuss this submission any further.

10. Geoffrey Garver, Director, Submissions on Enforcement Matters Unit, to Jon Plaut, JPAC Chair, memorandum, Feb. 15, 2002.

11. CEC, "Written Comments on the Public History of Submissions Made under Articles 14 and 15 of the North American Agreement on Environmental Cooperation" (Nov. 14, 2000).

12. The resolutions raise other concerns not addressed in this chapter. Perhaps of greatest importance, the resolutions potentially signal the Council's view that the citizen submissions process should be confined to allegations of specific instances of failures to effectively enforce and should exclude allegations of widespread failures to effectively enforce. Because in many situations widespread failures seem particularly suited to attention on a regional stage, a move to limit the process in this way would be unfortunate from a public policy standpoint. There also is a strong argument that such a limitation would represent an inappropriate limitation in the coverage of the process. The Secretariat's recommendation concerning the Migratory Birds submission raises this issue, and there already have been several criticisms of the resolutions on the grounds that they inappropriately narrow the scope of the process. See, e.g., Environmental Policy Alert, "EPA Backs Narrow NAFTA Inquiry to Resolve Environmental Dispute" (Oct. 3, 2001), available at *http://www.InsideEPA.com*; Environmental Policy Alert, "Parties Vote to Limit NAFTA Environmental Citizens' Suit Process" (Nov. 28, 2001), available at *http://www.InsideEPA.com*.

A second concern is that the resolutions are less transparent than they should be because of the limited Council explanation of why it rejected the Secretariat's recommendations that broad-based factual records be developed and instead opted for narrowly focused factual records. The Council's decision to direct the Secretariat to prepare and share work plans for the factual records, and to allow comment on them, also raises questions about the appropriate allocation of responsibility to administer the factual record process.

13. The review of the process provided in the text is based primarily on Articles 14 and 15 of the NAAEC. The process has been summarized in more detail elsewhere. For one such review, see David L. Markell, "The Commission for Environmental Cooperation's Citizen Submission Process," 12 *Georgetown International Environmental Law Review* 545 (2001).

14. The appendix to this chapter contains a history of the submissions process. As the appendix reflects, the Secretariat has dismissed some submissions more than once. Some submissions that were dismissed were revised and are now moving through the citizen submission process.

15. A related issue, not addressed in detail here, involves the question of how much the Council may depart from a submission in directing preparation of a factual record. The submitters for the four submissions discussed in the text uniformly opposed the Council's decision to narrow the factual records. See, e.g., SLDF to the Council (Mar. 6, 2002); CIEL to JPAC (Oct. 17, 2001).

16. For example, because of the much more limited gap between resolution and recommendation concerning the BC Hydro submission, this chapter does not address whether that resolution exceeded the Council's authority.

17. Because of space limitations, this chapter does not examine in detail possible mechanisms for addressing disagreements between the Council and the Secretariat

about the appropriate scope of factual records or ambiguities in Secretariat recommendations. One option is that the Council simply must approve or reject a Secretariat recommendation. A second would be for the Council to "remand" a recommendation for further explanation if the Council is not persuaded that a factual record is warranted, at least on the terms provided in the recommendation. Guideline 10.1 already provides authority for the Council to make such a request. Finally, the Secretariat unilaterally could seek to address some of the issues discussed in the text by proactively specifying in considerable detail in its recommendations the types of factual records it believes are warranted in connection with particular submissions and the types that are not. Fuller treatment of these questions is warranted.

18. See, e.g., "Four Year Review," supra, 20, 54, 55; JPAC, *Lessons Learned: Citizen Submissions under Articles 14 and 15 of the North American Agreement on Environmental Cooperation* (2001).

19. See, e.g., JPAC, Advice to Council no. 99-01, Mar. 25, 1999. JPAC has expressed frustration with the Council's performance of its responsibilities in connection with the citizen submissions process on numerous occasions, raising a variety of concerns. See, e.g., Regina Barba, JPAC Chair, to the Council members, Mar. 24, 2000; Regina Barba, JPAC Chair, to the Council members, May 2, 2000 (indicating that the JPAC is communicating with the Council, "once again," about "our frustration and growing unease with how matters relating to Articles 14 and 15 are being managed"). More recent JPAC Advices evince this frustration concerning the Council's actions relating to the specific issues discussed here, among others. Advice 01-09, for example, requested that the Council authorize a public review concerning the "matter of limiting the scope of factual records," among other issues. JPAC, Advice to Council no. 01-09, Nov. 30, 2001. See generally ch. 11, supra.

20. See, e.g., letter from U.S. NAC to the U.S. Representative to the CEC, May 15, 2000; NAC Advice no. 2000-2 (expressing concern about, inter alia, Council overreaching).

21. Elizabeth Malkin, "Taking the Green out of NAFTA," *Business Week*, May 29, 2000.

22. Editorial, "How to Wreck Trade," *Washington Post*, June 10, 2000.

23. Tollefson, supra; Knox, supra.

24. See ch. 14, supra. Fire alarms permit private actors to trigger an investigation, much as a private individual can pull a fire alarm to trigger a response by the appropriate fire officials. A police patrol, in contrast, involves investigations by government officials of situations that might warrant government response.

25. See id.

26. The Secretariat has a key role in defining the parameters of the process, and it also variously has been criticized for narrowing or expanding the scope of the process. See, e.g., Jay Tutchton, "The Citizen Petition Process under NAFTA's Environmental Side Agreement: It's Easy to Use, But Does It Work?" 26 *Environmental Law Reporter* 10031 (1996). An interesting observation concerning the process is contained in a 2001 CSIS/Yale report:

> The issue of citizens' complaints is presented as both a strength and a weakness for the CEC. It is a weakness only in the sense that the ample opportunity that the

> NAAEC provides for citizens to file environmental complaints against their governments has proved so contentious in Mexico, and to some extent in Canada, that at times it has stalled progress in other areas of environmental policymaking for North America.
>
> In the early years of NAFTA, the Mexican government lacked experience in making information on government activities available to the public and the country had only a short track record of involving the public in government decision-making. In fact, the first-ever public hearings by a Mexican federal environmental entity occurred only in summer 1991, when the Mexican environmental agency of that period held hearings jointly with the U.S. Environmental Protection Agency on a planned environmental improvement program for the U.S.-Mexican border area.
>
> Many government officials in all three countries agree that this lack of experience has created political problems for the CEC's Secretariat, making it difficult to implement the transparency and citizens' participation components of NAFTA's environmental side agreement, particularly the provisions of Articles 14 and 15 of the NAAEC.

Jan Gilbreath, *Environment and Trade: Predicting a Course for the Western Hemisphere Using the North American Experience* 37–38 (June 2001).

27. Jonathan Graubart suggests that the current U.S. administration may be less supportive of the process than previous administrations, particularly of an independent Secretariat. Jonathan Graubart, "Giving Meaning to New Trade-Linked 'Soft Law' Agreements on Social Values: A Law-In-Action Analysis of NAFTA's Environmental Side Agreement," 6 *UCLA Journal of International Law and Foreign Affairs* 425, 460 (2001–2). This could be significant since the United States long has been considered the primary defender of the process among the Parties. See ch. 11, supra. The prospect of multiple factual records, the key mechanism with potential to spotlight and embarrass the Parties, also could be a contributing factor in the existence of a heightened state of resolve or apprehension among the Parties. On the other hand, some commentators suggest that the current Mexican administration is more favorably disposed to support the process than its predecessor. Graubart, supra, 460.

28. There also have been claims that the citizen submissions process was not likely to have much effect because of its lack of sanctioning authority, among other perceived weaknesses in the mechanism, and there have been criticisms of its performance and impacts. See, e.g., Johnson and Beaulieu, supra, 34; Kibel, supra; John Kirton, "The Commission for Environmental Cooperation and Canada-U.S. Environmental Governance in the NAFTA Era," 27 *American Review of Canadian Studies* 459 (1997). See also Tutchton, supra.

29. A real need for systematic research in this area exists, and JPAC, among others, has called for incorporating follow-up as a part of the citizen submissions process. JPAC, *Lessons Learned*, supra, 16. See also David L. Markell, "The Commission for Environmental Cooperation's Citizen Submission Process," 12 *Georgetown International Environmental Law Review* 545 (2001). JPAC, in its 2001 *Lessons Learned* report, in which it reviews the track record of the process at the request of the CEC Council, concludes that citizen submissions "play a unique—and indispensable—

role in fostering the vigorous environmental enforcement that is a necessary component of expanded free trade under NAFTA." JPAC, *Lessons Learned*, supra, 2. JPAC observes that the "new procedure has already made [contributions] to environmental enforcement in North America" and points to several such contributions. Id., 13, 14. Also providing a positive gloss is a June 2001 study (Gilbreath, supra, 5, 12, 14, 34).

At an anecdotal level, evidence is mounting that the process is adding value in a variety of ways. The process appears to be yielding considerable information on domestic enforcement practices that might not be developed otherwise. Further, even for information that already exists, the process is serving as a mechanism that facilitates organizing this information in a way that is more responsive to citizens' interests. In addition, there is some evidence that the process has been at least a partial contributor to more "environmentally protective" behavior on the part of governments. See, e.g., Geoff Garver, "Factual Record Helped in Cozumel Pier Case, Says Submitter," *TRIO* (summer 2001); Kibel, supra, 469–70; Paul Kibel, "Awkward Evolution: Citizen Enforcement at the North American Environmental Commission," 32 *Environmental Law Reporter* 10769, 10774, 10775 (2002); *Environmental Management on North America's Borders* 252 (Richard Kiy and John D. Wirth eds., 1998); Jamie Bowman, "Citizen Submission Process Proves Valuable in BC Hydro Case," *TRIO* (fall 2001).

30. See, e.g., JPAC, Advice to Council no. 01-09, Nov. 30, 2001.

31. See also Environmental Policy Alert, "EPA Backs Narrow NAFTA Inquiry to Resolve Environmental Dispute," Oct. 3, 2001, available at *http://www.InsideEPA.com*; Environmental Policy Alert, "Parties Vote to Limit NAFTA Environmental Citizens' Suit Process," Nov. 28, 2001, available at *http://www.InsideEPA.com*.

32. CIEL to JPAC, Oct. 17, 2001.

33. See ch. 14, supra.

34. A coalition of environmental groups (Sierra Club, the Natural Resources Defense Council, and others) has developed a document entitled "Principles for Environmentally Responsible Trade" that urges policy-makers to "provide a mechanism for citizens to seek review of failures to enforce health and environmental laws (e.g., see NAFTA)." It is available at *http://www.sierraclub.org/trade/fasttrack/letter.asp*.

JOHN H. KNOX AND DAVID L. MARKELL **16**

Conclusions

THIS BOOK HAS examined the degree to which the North American Commission for Environmental Cooperation (CEC) is fulfilling its mandates as a regional environmental organization, a trade and environment institution, and a vehicle for facilitating public participation. In this chapter, we summarize the conclusions the contributors have reached in each of these respects and offer our own thoughts about the progress of and prospects for the Commission.

The CEC as a Trade and Environment Organization

We begin with the record of the CEC as an institutional way to respond to environmental concerns with economic integration, since that was the initial impetus for the creation of the organization. As we explain in the first chapter, the North American Agreement on Environmental Cooperation (NAAEC) does not speak to many of the environmental concerns with the North American Free Trade Agreement (NAFTA). Unsurprisingly, the CEC has made little or no effort to address concerns for which it did not have a specific mandate in the NAAEC. For example, the CEC has never addressed the compatibility with NAFTA (or other trade agreements) of domestic environmental laws such as the Marine Mammal Protection Act that led to the *Tuna-Dolphin* case. Nor does the CEC mission include cleaning up the U.S.-Mexico border, a task the United States and Mexico left to other institutions.

But the NAAEC does give the CEC mandates to address other NAFTA-related issues. The most important are: (a) assessing the environmental effects of NAFTA; (b) injecting environmental perspectives into the NAFTA institutions; and (c) working to prevent "pollution havens" by promoting effective enforcement of domestic environmental laws.

ASSESSING THE ENVIRONMENTAL EFFECTS OF NAFTA

Mary Kelly and Cyrus Reed describe the way that the CEC has developed an analytical framework to assess the environmental effects of NAFTA. They credit the "careful, objective, and transparent approach" of the CEC Secretariat with overcoming initial reluctance among the Parties' trade ministries to allow the CEC to examine linkages between trade and the environment. The framework that resulted encourages studies to focus on specific issues or sectors in light of their environmental, economic, and social context; to carefully identify connections to NAFTA and how NAFTA-induced changes relate to changes in other areas; and to evaluate environmental effects using specific indicators. A call by the CEC for studies applying the framework resulted in a number of papers presented at a CEC-sponsored symposium in October 2000, and the CEC held another symposium in 2003. Kelly and Reed give high marks to the framework, comparing it favorably to the "more rigid, macroeconomic modeling approaches" of the U.S. Trade Representative. They argue that studies applying the CEC framework "do not necessarily produce sound-bite results," but they "often dramatically show the inherent complexity of trade/environment linkages, the strong influence of domestic economic and social conditions, and the ability (or inability, given NAFTA-related rule changes) of the governments to employ regulation or incentives to remedy adverse environmental effects."

Alejandro Nadal's contribution gives an example of how such a study can work. Building on some of his earlier work, including a paper prepared for the 2000 CEC symposium, Nadal examines a specific economic sector—corn—and a specific environmental issue—the impact of NAFTA on genetic resources in Mexico. He describes how NAFTA has resulted in greatly increased imports of corn from the United States to Mexico but has ignored the importance of the services provided by Mexican farmers in conserving and developing an enormous variety of genetically diverse types of corn. After examining several ways that increased corn imports might adversely affect biodiversity, he concludes that Mexican farmers have not been abandoning their local varieties in favor of the hybrids used in the United States and are unlikely to adopt transgenic corn developed to resist pests and herbicides common in the United States but not in Mexico. But he describes scientific studies suggesting that transgenic corn imported from the United States has found its way into Mexican cornfields, where its modified genes have been incorporated into local varieties of corn. He also identifies risks posed by imports of transgenic corn for teosinte, a wild relative of corn.

Kelly and Reed do not suggest that these studies always produce concrete results, but they do cite one study of transboundary hazardous waste movement in North America that appears to have contributed to a decision by Ontario to strengthen its hazardous waste land disposal restrictions. They conclude that "trade effects assessment can be made relevant to policy decisions if it is combined with an organized constituency and publicity to draw the attention of the relevant national or subnational government. Standing alone, however, effects studies are unlikely to create the political will required to generate appropriate governmental policy responses."

INJECTING ENVIRONMENTAL CONCERNS INTO THE NAFTA INSTITUTIONS

Article 10(6) of the NAAEC instructs the CEC Council to cooperate with the NAFTA Free Trade Commission (composed of the Parties' trade ministers) in several ways, including through "acting as a point of inquiry and receipt for comments from non-governmental organizations and persons concerning [NAFTA's environmental] goals and objectives," contributing to the prevention or resolution of environment-related trade disputes, and "otherwise assisting the Free Trade Commission in environment-related matters," as well as through assessing the environmental effects of NAFTA. Although this somewhat vague language is far from a strong commitment to open NAFTA institutions to public participation and environmental concerns, it does provide a mandate to the CEC to raise environmental concerns within the Free Trade Commission and the procedural mechanisms created by NAFTA for resolving disputes.

One obvious test of how well the CEC has fulfilled this mandate is the extent to which its Council has established a working relationship with the Free Trade Commission. The short answer is that it has not done so. As Kelly and Reed note, "the North American governments have yet to call on the CEC's significant trade and environment experience to inform . . . the deliberations of NAFTA's Free Trade Commission." The CEC Council has never even met with the Free Trade Commission, although the Council members jointly said at their June 2001 meeting that they would "explore with [their] trade counterparts" the possibility of a meeting in 2003. The CEC has convened a "10(6) working group," composed of trade and environmental officials, but it has met only sporadically.

Another test is whether the work of the CEC on the environmental effects of NAFTA is filtering into the consciousness of the Free Trade Commission or the trade ministries that comprise it. Again, there is little sign that it is. Kelly and Reed do not point to any evidence that the CEC work has influenced the Parties' trade policies, much less led the Parties to think of trade liberalization in the context of a broader "development policy," as Kelly and Reed argue that they should.

Finally, the CEC has not played any role in influencing or even informing the resolution of environment-related disputes that have arisen under NAFTA. One reason is that there have been almost no disputes under NAFTA involving conflicts between environmental laws and trade disciplines, such as the *Tuna-Dolphin* case. But, as Sanford Gaines describes, a number of investment disputes involving environmental issues have been taken to arbitration under Chapter 11 of NAFTA, and observers have called for the CEC to be more involved in their resolution. Indeed, Kelly and Reed say that without meaningful participation in those issues, the CEC trade and environment program will not be able to meet its full potential.

Gaines casts doubt, however, on whether Article 10(6) gives the CEC much of a legal basis to play a role in investment, rather than trade, disputes. Moreover, he argues that much of the concern about the Chapter 11 cases is overblown, at least based on the cases decided so far. From his detailed examination of the facts in the decided cases, Gaines argues that they have appropriately protected vulnerable foreign investors from discriminatory treatment. In his judgment, the Chapter 11 outcomes do not present a serious threat to national and cooperative environmental protection or to democratic choice and the autonomy of governments. Nor does he believe that the CEC should become involved in all Chapter 11 disputes, most of which are highly fact-specific and do not raise larger questions of environmental governance. He does conclude, however, that the Chapter 11 cases concerning hazardous waste movement and treatment reveal the need for better continental cooperation on these issues, a task for which the Chapter 11 tribunals are unsuited but that the CEC is uniquely qualified to address.

PREVENTING POLLUTION HAVENS

As our first chapter explains, if the CEC was designed to address any concern with NAFTA, it was intended to prevent Mexico from becoming a pollution haven. In her contribution, Claudia Schatan adds her voice to those who have cast doubt on the idea that Mexico is a pollution haven. After analyzing data concerning exports of manufactured goods from Mexico, changes in pollution from twenty-eight manufacturing sectors, the relative competitiveness in U.S. markets of goods from highly polluting sectors in Mexico and Canada, and the destinations of foreign direct investment in Mexico, she concludes that the evidence does not suggest that Mexico has acted as a pollution haven by attracting foreign investment to polluting industries.

Schatan does not address the underlying causes of this result. One might suppose that the reason is that, spurred by the CEC, Mexico has improved its levels of environmental enforcement to remove or reduce any differential in this regard between it and its NAFTA trading partners. And, of course, many people have seen NAFTA and the NAAEC as an opportunity to promote better environmental enforcement and compliance in Mexico, apart from whether doing so would prevent companies from moving south in search of lower environmental standards.

But Kevin Gallagher throws cold water on these ideas in his chapter. He explains that overall levels of environmental degradation are not improving in Mexico. Reviewing three key factors that could reduce levels of pollution in Mexico (better enforcement, increased funds, and public scrutiny of environmental practices), Gallagher argues that Mexican efforts have been largely inadequate. For example, he notes that plant-level environmental inspections peaked in 1993, at the height of the NAFTA debate, and have been declining ever since, and that spending on environmental protection has dropped 45 percent over the same period. He concludes that "Mexico was not equipped to steer the benefits of economic integration into increasing environmental protection." He finds in this record a "clear role for the development of environmental institutions as part of trade and investment treaties. If a fully equipped environmental institution was established to help Mexico meet its own environmental goals, Mexico might be able to enjoy more of the benefits of economic integration."

Is the CEC that institution? Gallagher praises its elements, saying it "performs three tasks that are essential for any such institution: it provides additional funds for environmental management for small and medium-sized enterprises and for communities [through its FIPREV and NAFEC funds]; it provides a mechanism for citizen groups to challenge whether nations are enforcing their environmental standards [the citizen submissions procedure]; and it convenes essential research and policy discussions among governments and civil society in Mexico and its North American trading partners." He argues that these components, especially the citizen submissions procedure, should be a model for efforts to address environmental protection in the Free Trade Area of the Americas (FTAA). But Gallagher emphasizes that the CEC simply has too few resources to make a significant difference to the gigantic environmental problems Mexico faces. He argues that an institution with a budget of $9 million "can hardly make a dent in a series of problems that cost the Mexican government over $40 billion annually."

The CEC as a Regional Environmental Organization

As we explain in Chapter 1, the goal of preventing pollution havens by improving Mexican environmental performance may have been an initial motive for the NAAEC, but the NAAEC as it was finally concluded transformed that goal into a much broader set of mandates to take on almost any environmental issue in North America. Greg Block describes the process through which the CEC has chosen from and prioritized among the innumerable issues it could address. Although the issues chosen by the CEC could be categorized in many ways, one useful way to assess them is with respect to how successfully they meet two aims: facilitating upward harmonization of domestic environmental standards and identifying and coordinating responses to transboundary or continental issues. (Obviously, since many domestic environmental policies can have international effects, these categories blur together.)

FACILITATING UPWARD HARMONIZATION OF DOMESTIC STANDARDS

The aim of harmonizing domestic standards upward is closely related to the goal of trying to prevent pollution havens. Differences are that the former is less concerned with avoiding movement of firms, or with trade and investment at all, and is not limited to Mexico. Nevertheless, to the degree that Mexican environmental standards are lower than those of Canada and the United States, upward harmonization will result in the greatest changes in Mexican standards. Greg Block gives an important example of this process in his description of the CEC Sound Management of Chemicals (SMOC) program, through which the North American governments have taken steps toward phasing out a series of highly toxic substances. One of the first chemicals addressed was DDT, which had already been prohibited in the United States and Canada but was still used to combat malaria in Mexico. The CEC helped Mexico to institute alternative antimalaria actions, with the result that Mexico phased out DDT entirely by 2000, well ahead of schedule. The DDT program was so successful that it is being used as a model by other international organizations working in Central America.

Similarly, Mark Winfield describes how the CEC's pollutant release and transfer registry (PRTR) program helped to improve and make mandatory the Mexican PRTR system. He says that the CEC provided support to Mexico's environmental ministry for outreach and training and that it provided financial support, through NAFEC, to Mexican nongovernmental organizations (NGOs) so that they could develop the capacity to access and use PRTR data. He notes that the Council was a consistent source of pressure. Moreover, all of these efforts facilitated the emergence of a strong trinational network of NGOs around this issue. As a result, Winfield concludes that "the CEC processes provided an alternative venue for policy actors blocked domestically in Mexico on the establishment of a mandatory PRTR." Thus, while Gallagher shows that the CEC is far from able to single-handedly save the Mexican environment, Block and Winfield demonstrate that with respect to some discrete issues the CEC has made an important difference, leading to higher environmental standards than existed before.

It would be a mistake to view the CEC harmonization programs as limited to Mexico, however. As Block describes, other SMOC efforts are aimed at addressing toxic chemicals in use throughout North America, such as mercury. And Winfield explains that by providing the first comprehensive analysis of the environmental performance of Canadian provinces and facilities relative to their U.S. counterparts, the CEC's *Taking Stock* reports brought widespread attention to Canadian PRTR for the first time, resulting in its being used much more effectively by nongovernmental and governmental actors.

Winfield emphasizes that strong networks of contacts among key actors in each jurisdiction play an important part in strengthening and harmonizing environmental standards, and he underlines the central role played by the CEC in the development of such networks. He also maintains that placing jurisdictions in an explicitly comparative context, as the CEC is well suited to do, has promoted domestic policy debates in lagging jurisdictions and encouraged the upward movement of policies and requirements, especially in Canada and Mexico. He concludes that "the CEC has been a central catalyst in the evolution and convergence of PRTR systems in North America" and that the PRTR case demonstrates the CEC's success as a regional environmental organization.

ADDRESSING TRANSBOUNDARY AND REGIONAL ENVIRONMENTAL PROBLEMS

An effective multilateral organization may be most important in addressing transboundary and regional environmental problems that require a common response. How successful has the CEC been at identifying transboundary and regional environmental problems and coordinating responses to them?

Over the past century, the North American governments have created several bilateral institutions to address transboundary and border issues, such as the Canada-U.S. International Joint Commission and the Mexico-U.S. International Boundary and Water Commission. In order to assess the ability of the CEC to coordinate and fill gaps in the coverage of these institutions, John Knox examines its two specific mandates with respect to transboundary harm: promoting a trilateral agreement on transboundary environmental impact assessment (EIA) and encouraging reciprocal access to domestic legal remedies for transboundary pollution. He explains that the CEC has failed to reach an agreement on transboundary EIA despite good-faith efforts by the Council and Secretariat and that the CEC has made almost no effort at all to promote reciprocal access. He concludes that, as a trilateral institution, the CEC is ill-suited to facilitating agreement on issues that primarily raise parallel bilateral concerns, such as most transboundary pollution, and suggests that the CEC's work on transboundary harm should focus on areas that directly affect all three countries. One such "continental" problem is long-range air pollution, a problem that the CEC has begun to address on an ongoing basis.

Another continental environmental problem is the loss of biodiversity throughout North America. Robert Glicksman assesses the CEC's work in that area in light of four steps identified by Edward O. Wilson as necessary to protect biodiversity. He argues that the CEC biodiversity programs are strongest at the first step, *surveying what we have*. Many of the programs involve improving information—one project identifies 150 important bird areas, another maps marine and coastal ecosystems, a third seeks to establish an integrated North American database of biodiversity information. The CEC has also made considerable effort to address the next two steps: *defining needs* and *developing plans* to meet those needs. Glicksman says that the most difficult challenge for the CEC is the crucial fourth step, *adapting institutions* so that they can implement the plans. He criticizes the "impenetrable bureaucratese" CEC documents often employ in describing who will be responsible for carrying out the plans they describe. He also emphasizes that the CEC's limited authority to effect change in the Parties' policies "can be expected to make the final step of Wilson's four-step process the most resistant to successful CEC inroads."

Nevertheless, he argues that the CEC can play a useful role in facilitating the necessary changes, in three ways: (a) strengthening domestic environmental enforcement mechanisms through the citizen submissions process; (b) enhancing substantive domestic laws by recommending desirable changes (although he notes that this will have a limited effect because the relevant laws are often local) and using NAFEC to support biodiversity conservation efforts; and (c) helping to create international cooperative mechanisms by serving as an honest broker and facilitator. His conclusion, therefore, is mixed. He emphasizes that "the CEC is an organization of limited authority" that cannot impose its plans on the Parties. But he also says that "the CEC appears to be asking the right questions about the state of continental diversity and what is needed to avert threats to it. It is also engaged in concerted efforts to supply answers to those questions or at least to point the

Parties in the direction of the answers." In short, "it seems to be taking advantage of the authority it has in facilitating efforts to protect North American biodiversity."

The CEC as a Forum for Civil Society

The NAAEC requires and encourages the CEC to allow private individuals to participate in its work in many different ways. Some of the ways are informal but not necessarily the less effective for that. As noted above, Mark Winfield describes how the network of nongovernmental actors the CEC helped to develop around its PRTR program played an important role in improving PRTR systems in Canada and Mexico. But of particular importance are the formal mechanisms through which individuals are assured the right to participate in the CEC: the procedures through which citizens of the three countries can trigger investigative reports by the Secretariat under Articles 13, 14, and 15 and the ongoing advice given to the Council by the Joint Public Advisory Committee (JPAC) on the entire range of CEC activities.

Greg Block says that "international institutions typically influence public policy by wielding substantial resources, by exercising their adjudicative mechanisms, or by establishing an authoritative voice on a number of important issues within their mandates. Of these, only the last tool is available to the CEC, but it is an exceptionally important one." In addition to resolutions and statements by the Council, the main way that the CEC can exercise its "authoritative voice" is by issuing investigative reports on environmental issues, either under Article 13 or pursuant to the Article 14–15 procedure. The NAAEC gives the CEC a strong mandate to ensure that citizens have the ability to influence when and how that voice is used.

TRIGGERING CEC REPORTS

As Donald McRae describes, under Article 14 individuals and groups can submit a claim that a Party is failing to effectively enforce its environmental law, which can lead to a "factual record" prepared by the Secretariat under Article 15. He notes that the "role of the Secretariat is to provide information that would allow a conclusion to be reached as to whether a state was enforcing its environmental law effectively. In that sense, the very nature of the process is transparency—the disclosure of full information about the practices of a NAFTA Party in the enforcement of its environmental laws." More specifically, he compares the transparency of the Article 14–15 citizen submissions procedure to that of dispute resolution under the World Trade Organization (WTO) and NAFTA, in five respects: (1) initiating the process; (2) access to information about the process; (3) providing information to the process; (4) access to oral proceedings; and (5) participation in decision-making. Although he identifies some gaps in transparency in the CEC procedure, he concludes that, taken as a whole, it has substantial transparency and is far more transparent than WTO or NAFTA dispute resolution.

Kal Raustiala argues that the CEC submissions procedure is best understood as a "fire alarm" system—that is, it empowers private actors to "pull the alarm," and trigger investigation, when they allege a Party is failing to uphold a legal obligation. He does not claim that fire alarm systems are always preferable to police patrol systems, which rely on efforts by centralized authorities to search for violations, but he says that they have definite advantages in the context of North American environmental cooperation. In particular, he argues that enlisting private citizens in the search for failures to effectively enforce domestic environmental laws is more efficient and effective because it takes advantage of private information about violations and enforcement efforts. He also argues that by enhancing public participation, fire alarms in international treaties can provide greater legitimacy than pure police patrols. He recognizes that the influence it provides private actors "is not large," but he concludes that "for all its weaknesses, the NAAEC is an important step in the democratization of international environmental law. However small the current scope for citizen participation in the NAAEC, the NAAEC is a major advance over most environmental treaties, in which direct public participation nears zero."

Raustiala emphasizes that the empirical impact of the submissions procedure is unclear. Although NGOs have pointed to positive results from the first two factual records issued by the CEC, it is still too early to convincingly gauge effectiveness. "Perhaps the best evidence to date on this question," Raustiala observes, "is the reaction of the NAFTA Parties themselves," which considered curtailing the process in 2000. He argues that "if the NAAEC submissions process were truly toothless, these efforts, which have been the subject of considerable controversy, would not make sense."

David Markell argues that given the nature of the process, which gives important roles to private citizens and the Secretariat but also to the Council, a continuing tug and pull between the former and the latter over the procedure was inevitable. He describes the Council's November 2001 authorization to the Secretariat to prepare five new factual records as the latest chapter in that ongoing battle. He suggests that four of the five resolutions "dramatically change the focus of the factual record that the submitters requested and that the Secretariat recommended by substantially limiting or redefining the scope of the factual records to be developed." The submissions and the Secretariat recommendations had been directed at broad, programmatic failures to effectively enforce specific environmental laws, but the Council directed the Secretariat to develop factual records only on isolated examples of failures to enforce that the submitters had included to illustrate their broader allegations. He argues that it is not clear that the Secretariat would have recommended factual records on such isolated examples, so that the Council may be requiring the Secretariat to develop factual records on matters for which the Secretariat believes a factual record is either not warranted or warranted only as part of a larger inquiry. Markell maintains that the resolutions thus may go beyond the powers granted by the NAAEC to the Council in the submissions procedure. He suggests that this tug and pull—the battle between governments, on the one hand, and submitters, environmental groups, and advisory committees, on the other, over the proper scope of the Council's and the Secretariat's role in the procedure—bears watching for its possible impacts on the credibility and viability of the process.

While the end result of the Article 14–15 procedure is a report on enforcement of environmental law, reports under Article 13 can be on virtually any other environmental issue. Dan Tarlock and John Thorson examine an Article 13 report prepared by the CEC on the San Pedro River in order to assess how effective nonbinding recommendations can be—or, in other words, how authoritative and influential the CEC's voice is. They give the CEC high marks for organizing a process that "narrowed the bounds of discussion for finding sustainable solutions"; for producing a readable, balanced report; for drawing on exceptionally talented experts; and for creating an extensive procedure for obtaining public input. But they also describe the ways that the San Pedro report shows the limits of information disclosure as an instrument of environmental policy, especially when it is applied to small-scale biodiversity conservation of the type at issue along the San Pedro. They emphasize that since there is comparatively little shame in failing to practice biodiversity conservation, pointing out that failure does not necessarily lead to change in behavior. They conclude that, at present, "rule of law" litigation holding agencies to strict environmental standards may continue to be the most effective catalyst for action. But they also note that reports such as the San Pedro report serve as an important reminder that more comprehensive, ecosystem-wide solutions are the best hope in the long run for effective biodiversity conservation.

JOINTLY ADVISING THE GOVERNMENTS

Donald McRae and Kal Raustiala both note that public participation in environmental decision-making can be an important source of legitimacy for international organizations like the CEC. While important, the avenues for public participation under Articles 13, 14, and 15 cannot address the entire range of CEC issues on an ongoing basis. The broadest range for public participation in the CEC is provided by the JPAC, whose mandate under

Article 16(4) of the NAAEC is to "provide advice to the Council on any matter within the scope of this Agreement."

John Wirth, one of the original members of JPAC, recalls that at its very first meeting, in April 1994, JPAC members realized "that it might be an early harbinger of an emerging North American community" and "chose to interact as North Americans rather than see themselves as advocates or defenders of national positions or as representatives of any particular private voluntary organization or interest group." Wirth emphasizes that with only fifteen members, JPAC "could in no way claim to represent all the NGOs, business and professional groups, academics, and state and local governments involved." Instead, "it had to earn its legitimacy and acceptance as a facilitator of open public dialogue." He says that after a rough start, JPAC has become much more adept at running effective public consultations.

Wirth describes several programs that benefited from JPAC participation and discusses its ongoing role in defending another avenue of public participation, the citizen submissions procedure, from efforts by the governments to rein it in. Wirth concludes that "given the broad scope of its mandate, it is clear that in nearly eight years of operation JPAC has risen to the challenge." Wirth argues that "the JPAC model has legs" for other institutions, noting the inclusion of another JPAC in the Canada-Chile Agreement on Environmental Cooperation and lamenting the failure of the FTAA negotiations to recognize the "diverse and useful roles that a strong citizen group like JPAC can play."

Conclusion

We close with some general observations. In light of the fact that the CEC emerged from the ferment over NAFTA, it is ironic that the contributions sharply question the effectiveness of the CEC as a trade and environment institution. The CEC has largely failed to create an environmental voice within the NAFTA institutions. It has sponsored innovative and important studies assessing NAFTA's environmental effects, but to date those studies have not changed the approach to environmental issues within the trade ministries. (They may nevertheless lead to positive results, however, when they are used to draw attention to a particular problem.) Moreover, any effort to forestall pollution havens seems problematic, both because foreign investment does not seem inclined to treat Mexico as a pollution haven and because the CEC does not have sufficient resources by itself to pull up Mexico's level of environmental protection.

More generally, many of the contributors note the limits inherent in the CEC model. The CEC has no great budget to induce others to follow its lead, and in practice it cannot impose environmental standards or economic sanctions upon a recalcitrant government. At best, it can use its limited funds, its ability to facilitate agreement, and its "authoritative voice" to serve as a catalyst. Its success therefore depends directly on the actions of individuals, groups, and governments willing to pursue its goals.

Despite these limits, however, the contributors are generally positive with respect to the CEC's record as a regional environmental organization and as a forum for civil society. The contributions point to concrete achievements in specific substantive areas, such as strengthening Mexico's regulation of toxic chemicals, Mexico's and Canada's PRTR systems, and improving information on continental biodiversity. They highlight the role that the CEC has played in facilitating networking among interested members of the public and in providing financial support (albeit in very limited amounts) for effective local projects. Moreover, the contributors emphasize the importance of the citizen submissions procedure and JPAC, which break new ground in international environmental law.

These observations suggest that attempts to reproduce the CEC model should look beyond the trade context. The idea of a hemispheric CEC attached to the FTAA may be attractive, but the connection to the FTAA seems unnecessary; a freestanding environmental agreement along the lines of the NAAEC would appear likely to provide the same kinds of benefits to other regions that the CEC has provided to North America.

It seems fitting to give a final word to John Wirth, who sums up the record of the CEC as follows: "Still a young organization, the CEC has made extraordinary progress in addressing environmental issues that until recently had little or no resonance across all three countries." By broadening his language about JPAC to include the CEC as a whole, we can also borrow his closing words: "No small achievement."

Contributors

Greg Block is the Distinguished Environmental Scholar at the Natural Resources Institute at Lewis and Clark College of Law in Portland, Oregon. He joined the Commission for Environmental Cooperation (CEC) in 1994 as head of the Legal Division, serving as the first legal officer responsible for managing the citizen submissions process as well as other legal initiatives. From 1995 to 2002, he was Director of Programs at the CEC. Before joining the CEC, he taught comparative and U.S. environmental law in Mexico under the auspices of a Fulbright lecture grant. From 1987 to 1992, he litigated environmental cases with a private law firm in San Francisco.

Edith Brown Weiss is the Francis Cabell Brown Professor of International Law at Georgetown University Law Center. Her numerous professional activities in both international and environmental law have included positions as Associate General Counsel for International Activities at the U.S. Environmental Protection Agency, where she established a new division of international law, 1990–92; President of the American Society of International Law, April 1994–96; chair of the Committee for Research in Global Environmental Change of the Social Science Research Council, 1989–94; U.S. special legal adviser to the CEC, 1998–2002; vice chair of the ABA Committee on International Environmental Law; and elected member of the Council on Foreign Relations, the American Law Institute, and the Commission on Environmental Law of the International Union for Conservation of Nature (IUCN). She is the author of many books and articles in the field and has received numerous awards for her significant contributions.

Sanford Gaines is a professor at the University of Houston Law Center and codirector of the Law Center's Mexican Legal Studies Program in Mexico City. His recent scholarship concerns relationships between trade and environment and international environmental institutions in North

America. From 1996 to 1999, he was Executive Director of the North American Institute (NAMI), a voluntary civic organization with members in Canada, Mexico, and the United States. From 1992 to 1994, he served as Deputy Assistant U.S. Trade Representative for Environment and Natural Resources in the Office of the U.S. Trade Representative, where he had major responsibility for environmental issues in the negotiation of NAFTA, the environmental side agreements to NAFTA, and the Uruguay Round agreements in GATT. He serves on the U.N. Environment Programme Expert Group on International Environmental Agreements and Trade, and he is a past chair of the EPA's National Advisory Committee on the CEC.

Kevin P. Gallagher is a senior research associate at the Global Development and Environment Institute, an economic research institute at the Fletcher School of Law and Diplomacy and Tufts University. He serves as the principal investigator for the institute's work on globalization and sustainable development. Currently, he is researching economic integration and industrial pollution in Mexico to draw out lessons for the Free Trade Area of the Americas. His most recent book is *International Trade and Sustainable Development* (2002, edited jointly with Jacob Werksman).

Robert L. Glicksman is the Robert W. Wagstaff Professor of Law at the University of Kansas. He is a coauthor of the casebook *Environmental Protection: Law and Policy* (3d ed., 1999). He is also the coauthor, with George Coggins, of two books on federal public natural resources law, the three-volume treatise *Public Natural Resources Law* (updated three times annually), and the nutshell *Modern Public Land Law* (2d ed., 2001). He recently wrote a chapter on wildlife and habitat protection for Matthew Bender's *Environmental Law Practice Guide* and a chapter on municipal regulation of hazardous waste in *The Law of Zoning and Planning*. He has written and coauthored numerous other book chapters and articles on public natural resources, environmental, and property law, including articles on the evolution of public land law, national park concessions, pollution on the federal lands, recreational policy on the federal lands, the relationship between environmental agencies and the courts, regulatory reform, and regulatory takings. He has served as a consultant to the CEC.

Mary E. Kelly is a senior attorney and program manager for U.S./Mexico Border Initiatives at Environmental Defense. From 1990 to 2002, she was Executive Director of the Texas Center for Policy Studies, where she worked on border environmental issues, including a primary focus on water resources. She has written and published extensively on the pre- and post-NAFTA environmental challenges and solutions in the border region.

With the Comisión de Solidaridad y Defensa de Derechos Humanos, she completed a study of NAFTA effects on forestry development in the northern Mexico state of Chihuahua. She is also a former chair of the EPA National Advisory Committee on the CEC.

John H. Knox is an associate professor of law at Pennsylvania State University. From 1988 to 1994, he served as an attorney-adviser at the U.S. Department of State, where he participated in the negotiation of the North American Agreement on Environmental Cooperation. He is vice chair of the three North American bar associations' Joint Working Group on the Settlement of International Disputes, and he has served as the chair of the EPA National Advisory Committee on the CEC from 1999 to 2001, and from 2003 to the present. His recent publications include articles on the CEC citizen submissions procedure and on transboundary environmental impact assessment.

David L. Markell is the Steven M. Goldstein Professor at Florida State University College of Law and formerly was a professor at Albany Law School. He served as the first director of the CEC Submissions on Enforcement Matters Unit, the unit of the Secretariat responsible for administering the citizen submissions process. His extensive publication record includes two articles on the CEC, one in the *Georgetown International Environmental Law Review* and the other in the *Environmental Forum*. Two of his publications have received special recognition. A book he coauthored received the 1995 ABA Section of Administrative Law and Regulatory Practice Award for Scholarship and was cited as "the most outstanding work of legal scholarship in the field" published during that year. A 2000 article on domestic environmental enforcement (*Harvard Environmental Law Review*) was selected as one of the best environmental law articles published in 2000. He is a coauthor of an environmental law casebook, *Environmental Protection Law and Policy* (4th ed., 2003), and of *Reinventing Environmental Enforcement and the State/Federal Relationship* (2003).

Donald McRae holds the Hyman Soloway Chair in Business and Trade Law at the University of Ottawa Faculty of Law. He has been an adviser to the Department of External Affairs of the Government of Canada and Counsel for Canada in several international fisheries and boundary arbitrations. He was chair of the first dispute settlement panel set up under Chapter 18 of the Canada-U.S. Free Trade Agreement and has sat on subsequent panels under Chapters 18 and 19 of the Free Trade Agreement and Chapter 20 of NAFTA. He has published widely on international law, the law of the sea, and international trade law, and is editor-in-chief of the

Canadian Yearbook of International Law. He is currently one of the Canadian special legal advisers to the CEC.

Alejandro Nadal is a professor at the Center for Economic Studies, El Colegio de México, where he coordinates the Science and Technology Program. He has a law degree from the Universidad Nacional Autónoma de México and a Ph.D. in economics from the University of Paris, Nanterre. He has published widely on issues of economic integration and environmental protection.

Kal Raustiala is acting professor at the UCLA Law School and Institute of the Environment. He is currently a visiting assistant professor in the Politics Department and fellow in the Law and Public Affairs Program at Princeton. He has published on international law, international relations, and environmental cooperation in such journals as *World Politics*, *Environment*, *Harvard Environmental Law Review*, and *Virginia Journal of International Law*. He is also the editor, with David Victor and Eugene Skolnikoff, of *The Implementation and Effectiveness of International Environmental Commitments* (1998).

Cyrus Reed has worked with the Austin-based Texas Center for Policy Studies (TCPS) since 1994, serving as project director of the Border Trade and Environment Project since 1998. He is coauthor of the *Texas Environmental Almanac* (2000) and has worked at TCPS on a variety of statewide and border environmental issues. He received an M.S. in community and Regional Planning and an M.A. in Latin American Studies from the University of Texas at Austin in 1994 and is currently pursuing a Ph.D. in geography.

Claudia Schatan is chief of the Industrial Development Unit at the U.N. Economic Commission for Latin America and the Caribbean (ECLAC). She was previously a senior researcher and lecturer at Centro de Investigación y Docencia Económica (CIDE) and a visiting researcher at various U.S. universities, including the Harvard Institute for International Development in 1997. Her recent publications include "Free Trade Agreements and the Environment: Implications for Central America" in *Environment for Growth* (2001); "Contaminación Industrial en Países Latinoamericanos pre y post Reformas Económicas," *Serie Medio Ambiente y Desarrollo* 22 (ECLAC, 1999); and "Lessons from the Mexican Environmental Experience: First Results from NAFTA," in *The Environment and International Trade Negotiations: Developing Countries' Stakes* (1999).

A. Dan Tarlock is a distinguished professor of law at Chicago-Kent

Law School. He has published a treatise, *Law of Water Rights and Resources* (1988, with annual updates), and is a coauthor of four casebooks, *Water Resource Management, Environmental Law, Land Use Controls*, and *Environmental Protection: Law and Policy*. He is a frequent consultant to local, state, federal, and international agencies, private groups, and law firms, and is an elected member of the American Law Institute. From 1989 to 1992, he was the chair of a National Academy of Sciences/National Research Council committee to study water management in the western United States. In 1996–97 he was the principal report writer for the Western Water Policy Review Advisory Committee. He is currently one of three U.S. special legal advisers to the CEC.

John E. Thorson is an attorney and water policy consultant residing in Oakland, California. From 1990 to 2000, he served as Special Master for the Arizona General Stream Adjudication. He is Publications Officer for the American Bar Association Section of Environment, Energy and Resources and co-convenor of "Dividing the Waters," an educational project for judges presiding over complex water litigation. He has authored more than forty articles on water resources law and policy, has taught environmental and water law at law schools in Arizona and Montana, and has served as chair of the ABA's Water Resources Committee. His book, *River of Promise, River of Peril: The Politics of Managing the Missouri River*, was published in 1994.

Mark S. Winfield holds a Ph.D. in political science from the University of Toronto. He is Director of the Environmental Governance Program at the Pembina Institute for Appropriate Development. Prior to that he was Director of Research with the Canadian Institute for Environmental Law and Policy. He has published on a wide range of environmental law and policy subjects, including toxic substances and pollution prevention, hazardous waste, environmental governance, biotechnology regulation, and community right-to-know issues. He is a member of the CEC consultative group on its pollutant release and transfer registry (PRTR) program and teaches environmental politics and policy at the University of Toronto and York University.

John D. Wirth received his Ph.D. in Latin American history from Stanford University and joined its faculty in 1966. He was named Gildred Professor of Latin American Studies in 1991. His books include *Smelter Smoke in North America: The Politics of Transborder Pollution* (2000), *Environmental Management on North America's Borders* (1998, edited with Richard Kiy), and *Identities in North America: The Search for Community* (1995, edited with Robert

Lee Earle), as well as many works on Latin American history. He was the cofounder and President of the North American Institute, a trinational public affairs group headquartered in Santa Fe, New Mexico, and a member of the Council on Foreign Relations. In 1994, he was appointed by the White House to serve as one of five U.S. members on the CEC Joint Public Advisory Committee.

Index